Michael N. Marsh is based at Wolfson College, University of Oxford and is a Fellow of the Oxford Centre for Christianity and Culture at Regent's Park College. Following a distinguished career as an academic clinical biomedical research physician, Professor Marsh returned to the University of Oxford to read Theology. He gained a D.Phil for his thesis on neurophysiological and theological approaches to near-death and out-of-body experiential phenomenology.

OXFORD THEOLOGICAL MONOGRAPHS

Editorial Committee

OXFORD THEOLOGICAL MONOGRAPHS

Out-of-Body and Near-Death Experiences

Brain-State Phenomena or
Glimpses of Immortality?

MICHAEL N. MARSH

OXFORD
UNIVERSITY PRESS

OXFORD

UNIVERSITY PRESS

Great Clarendon Street, Oxford OX2 6DP

Oxford University Press is a department of the University of Oxford.
It furthers the University's objective of excellence in research, scholarship,
and education by publishing worldwide in

Oxford New York

Auckland Cape Town Dar es Salaam Hong Kong Karachi
Kuala Lumpur Madrid Melbourne Mexico City Nairobi
New Delhi Shanghai Taipei Toronto

With offices in

Argentina Austria Brazil Chile Czech Republic France Greece
Guatemala Hungary Italy Japan Poland Portugal Singapore
South Korea Switzerland Thailand Turkey Ukraine Vietnam

Oxford is a registered trade mark of Oxford University Press
in the UK and in certain other countries

Published in the United States
by Oxford University Press Inc., New York

© Michael N. Marsh 2010

The moral rights of the author have been asserted
Database right Oxford University Press (maker)

First published 2010

British Library Cataloguing in Publication Data

Data available

Library of Congress Cataloging in Publication Data

Data available

Typeset by SPI Publisher Services, Pondicherry, India
Printed in Great Britain
on acid-free paper by
MPG Books Group, Bodmin and King's Lynn

ISBN 978–0–19–957150–5

1 3 5 7 9 10 8 6 4 2

Contents

Preface

This book originates from a D.Phil. thesis written at Magdalen College, and examined by Professors John Stein (Magdalen, Professor of Neurophysiology) and Paul Badham (Professor of Theology, Lampeter College, University of Wales). I am grateful to both for enthusiastically recommending the thesis for publication. Its necessary revisions, emphasized by the examiners and subsequently by three further anonymous reviewers appointed by the Theology Faculty's Monographs Review Committee, were effected through the patient guidance of its chairman, Professor Diarmaid McCulloch (St. Cross). For all their collective time spent and advice, I am most grateful.

But my primary duty must surely be directed towards Professor John Brooke (lately Andreos Idrios Professor of the History of Science, Harris-Manchester) in thanking him for his supervisory role throughout the preparation of the thesis and its subsequent forging into a book manuscript via the Monographs Review Committee. His gentle guidance, ability to raise incisive questions, and the inevitable quotes from scientific history, provided much encouragement and reassurance during this six-year period. I must also pay tribute to Professor John Barton (Oriel), who, when I was a fourth-year (B. Th.) theology undergraduate here (in the year 2000) following my retirement from academic and clinical medical research, explained to me that contra scientific research, doctorates in the humanities are usually achieved through the application of closely reasoned argument, logically extended. I hope that I might have realized his expectations. Writing this thesis was certainly different from preparing the D.M. and D.Sc. theses which encapsulate my former contributions to biomedical research in the fields of computerized mucosal morphometry and the immunopathology of intestinal host-mediated responses to environmental antigenic challenge.

I am most indebted to other members of the Theology Faculty in Oxford, past and present, who have offered guidance, advice, or a steady hand: (the late) Revd Professor John Macquarrie (Lady Margaret Professor of Divinity Emeritus, ChristChurch), Revd Professor Paul Fiddes (Regent's Park), Revd. Dr Margaret Yee (Nuffield and St Cross), and Mr John Foster (Brasenose). Also Professor Brian Leftow (Oriel) whose suggestions during my Transfer of Status viva provided helpful insights. Furthermore, I owe a debt of gratitude to Dr Christine Mohr (Department of Experimental Psychology, University of Bristol) and to Dr Peter Brugger (University Department of Neurology, University of Zurich) for their time in discussing various aspects of the neurophysiology relevant to their ongoing research and publications into out-of-body experiences, phantoms, and sensed presences.

The work offered is entirely original. Parts of it were presented in public within the University, at the Magdalen SCR/MCR Research Forum; the Oxford Forum for the Medical Humanities (St John's); and the Science and Religion Forum (Harris-Manchester), an Ian Ramsey Seminar; Abingdon School, and a meeting of the Magdalen Chapel Fellowship. I am grateful to all those who attended these meetings, asked questions, or provided incisive comments and suggestions. Finally, other aspects of this work were offered as sermons in the chapels of Nuffield College (Dr Yee) and Lady Margaret Hall (Revd Dr Doig, formerly Fellows' Chaplain, Magdalen), and in the Psychology of Religion Lecture Series (Hilary Term, Dr Yee) in Schools: it was a privilege to have been invited to lecture, and to make contributions at other times during each annual series (2002–8).

Lastly, I should pay tribute to the Dean of Divinity at Magdalen, Revd Dr Michael Piret, to whom fell the unenviable task of monitoring my behaviour whilst I was *in statu pupillari*, necessitating much firm control during my period of collegiate habitation: but he did it with a gentle hand. I recall with some degree of nostalgia the vibrancy of chapel and choral life at Magdalen and the given opportunities of reading and of making intercessions, and not least, the wonderful pre-eucharistic breakfasts in his rooms in St Swithun's (even if the doughnuts were occasionally a little on the firm side).

But life moves on, as I now recollect these images from newer contexts and beckoning horizons within the University.

Wolfson College, and   Michael N. Marsh
Oxford Centre for Christianity & Culture,
Regent's Park College,
University of Oxford
Advent Sunday 2008

List of Figures

List of Abbreviations

AD	Anno Domini
AUB	absolute unitary being
BIS	bispectral analysis
C	cataplexy
CBF	cerebral blood flow (global)
rCBF	cerebral blood flow (regional)
CE	Common Era
CO_2	carbon dioxide
3-D	three-dimensional
ECE	extra-corporeal experience
ECG	electrocardiograph
EEG	electroencephalograph
ER	external religiosity
F	Fahrenheit
G	gravity
IR	internal religiosity
LSD	lysergic acid diethlyamide
LXX	Septuagint
N	narcolepsy
NC	narcolepsy-cataplexy complex
NDE	near-death experience
N_2O	nitrous oxide (laughing gas)
NT	New Testament
O_2	oxygen
OBE	out-of-body experience
OT	Old Testament
Pa	'pressure' of a dissolved gas in arterial (a) blood
pH	hydrogen ion content (1–7 = decreasing acidity; 7–14 = increasing alkalinity)
PH	peduncular hallucinosis
SOP	sleep-onset period

SP	sleep paralysis
SWS	slow wave sleep
T	Testament
TPO	temporo-parietal-occipital
TPJ	temporo-parietal junction
UFO	unidentified flying object
VTA	ventral tegmental area

Introduction: Prospects for Life After Death

I...closed my eyes, so I never saw what happened when the car left the road...the seconds that went by as the car turned over...seemed like an eternity. My body tingled. I had butterflies in my stomach. My mind was worried. Then, suddenly, I became detached from my worldly body...I was seeing my life flash before me...[then] I was in a tunnel-like black space...beyond [which] a light was glowing invitingly. I was encouraged by a strong feeling to enter the light...part of the jigsaw to which I rightfully belonged. I was peaceful, totally content, and I understood I was born on earth and knew the answer to every mystery—I was not told, I just knew the light held all the answers.

Then there was sudden confusion. I had to go back to the tunnel quickly: something was wrong. I was upset and scared [and] thought of my family... and earthly life. I was travelling—I regained my body... and felt tremendous pain, all over my body.

I believe I died for a short time... I know there is some form of life after death and it is a truly wonderful 'Heaven'.[1]

Does this excerpt from a recollected out-of-body and near-death experience offer a veridical glimpse of heaven? Is this, as the lady victim supposes, evidence for the continuity of personhood into an afterlife? These are questions posed by such curious happenings, happenings which have spawned enormous interest into the possibility, if not reality, of life after death.

It is, of course, a unique feature of human self-awareness that life ends in death—a realization which sets us apart from the animal world. There is nothing more certain in life than death: our bodies decay and become dust. *Memento mori*. But is a biological death from earthbound corporeal existence the final frontier, or is it yet a gateway to another world, another existence beyond the known universe?

Traditionally, belief in existence beyond physical parameters has been articulated, for example, by the great monotheistic religions in the metaphysic of God's heavenly realm. Second, a growing appetite for other forms of experiential adventure and which, collectively, could be encompassed by

---

[1] Excerpt abridged from Fenwick Peter and Fenwick Elizabeth, *The Truth in the Light*, New York: Berkley Books 1998, 57.

the term 'New Age Spirituality' has gradually emerged onto the contemporary scene. It offers its varied adherents an alphabetical inventory of practice from Aromatherapy to Zen as means of enlightening their persons, souls or spirituality.

But third, as my introductory excerpt anticipates, there exists the burgeoning field of phenomena known popularly as out-of-body (OB) and near-death experiences (NDE). While certain experiences succeed bereavement, depression or severe loneliness, the majority result from acute medical crises which directly, or indirectly, substantially embarrass cerebral activity. It is the latter phenomenology with which this book is concerned.

My purpose has been to evaluate critically eight key texts[2] which articulate to varying degrees the premise that these phenomenological types bear witness to an afterlife, a non-bodily existence, based on the reported narratives of several hundred experients. It is striking that for most texts, out-of-body and near-death experiences are treated as non-corporeal events. Their physical basis is generally played down in favour of metaphysical claims that these events represent an escape of either mind, soul or free consciousness from corporeality, thus opening up the possibility of some kind of otherworldly, spiritualized departure. That a physical or brain-based neurophysiological explanation is entirely exhausted by the nature of the phenomenology revealed seems, therefore, to have been assumed. In dealing with these issues, I have adopted two approaches, one neurophysiological, the other theological.

From the neurophysiological perspective, the argument developed is that out-of-body and near-death experiences, referred to hereafter with my terminology 'extra-corporeal experiences' or ECE in short, are likely to be generated by metabolically disturbed brains especially during the period when they are regaining functional competence. That position opposes directly the challenge, advanced by one of the authors reviewed, Dr Kenneth Ring, against any neurophysiological explanation for these happenings. That challenge is reproduced as follows:

I would like to advise any neurologically-minded researcher [of] one important constraint. Any adequate neurologic explanation would have to be capable of showing how the *entire complex* of phenomena associated with the core experience (out-of-body; paranormal knowledge; tunnel; light; voices and presence; the appearance of deceased relatives; beautiful vistas, and so forth) would be expected to occur in

---

[2] Raymond Moody, *Life after Life*, 1976: idem, *Reflections on Life after Life*, 1977; Kenneth Ring, *Life at Death*, 1980: idem, *Heading toward Omega*, 1985; Michael Sabom, *Recollections of Death*, 1980; idem, *Light and Death*, 1998; Margot Grey, *Return from Death*, 1985; Peter and Elizabeth Fenwick, *The Truth in the Light*, 1998.

subjectively authentic fashion as a consequence of specific neural events triggered by the approach of death. It is not difficult—in fact it is easy—to propose naturalistic interpretations that could explain some aspect of the core experience. Such explanations, however, sometimes seem merely glib and are usually of the 'this-is-nothing-but-an-instance-of' variety: rarely do they seem to be seriously considered attempts to come to grips with a very puzzling phenomenon. A neurological interpretation, to be acceptable, should be able to provide a *comprehensive* explanation of *all* the various aspects of the core experience. Indeed, I am tempted to argue that the burden of proof has now shifted to those who wish to explain near-death experiences in this way.[3]

One cannot but be surprised, even taken aback, by this imperious statement: it is a challenge providing both the stimulus and rationale for this book. My contention is that a brain-based origin is, indeed, capable of offering a fair-minded account of the events reported. However, such an explanation requires a far greater involvement with neurophysiology and involves a far greater critique of those authors' accounts than attempted to date.

My theological approach comprises three strands. First, I offer a critique of the prevailing view that ECE have to be conceived as quasi-heavenly or religious events. In attempting to undermine that explanatory position, I have drawn on Christian theology[4] as a means of comparing what relationship ECE could have to our understandings of resurrection and the afterlife. Second, I consider the question whether ECE are capable of being ascribed a credible spiritual, or even revelatory, dimension. In pursuing these routes, my hope is that such comparisons will be illuminating not only for persons whose beliefs lie in a New Creation, but also for those who are prepared, at least, to take theological reasoning and argument seriously.

Third, I have exposed a failure on the part of the authors whose texts I evaluate to deal adequately and systematically with the post-experiential subject. That, to my mind, is an important omission, and one I tackle within the context of a theology of personhood. From whatever third-person perspective ECE are regarded or understood, their meanings for subjects cannot be taken away. Yet there is a wealth of meaning that obtains from undergoing an ECE, providing influences on subjects in their subsequent lives that is not seen in other subjects coming near to death, but who do not undergo this additional phenomenology. It is these specific post-ECE influences and changes in personality which I am at pains to open up and explore.

Out-of-body (OB) and near-death (ND) experiences, despite conflation by experients and authors, stand as separate phenomena, as is clearly

---

[3] Ring 1980, 216 (my emphases).
[4] I do this in order to restrict my field of reference since ECE are, largely, western phenomena conceived in terms of its prevailing cultural and religious backgrounds.

demonstrated in Chapter 1. OBE involve the viewing of subjects' bodies from an elevated, extra-corporeal vantage point that is also coincident with the locus of conscious-awareness. The other is deemed to take conscious-awareness into other realms, by means of a 'tunnel' into 'light', and where an assortment of individuals may be encountered. Other subjects may report some kind of life-review or judgemental episode before finding themselves rapidly projected back to earth and into their bodies. In continuing to explore other features of ECE phenomenology, I offer descriptive accounts of hellish experiences, the perceptions of the afterlife perceived by the blind, and a critique of the special case of Pam Reynolds. Ms Reynolds underwent a prolonged brain operation during which she reported having an OBE and NDE. The case has been used as proof that an ECE can occur in the presence of a virtually 'dead' brain (after surgical cooling and local exsanguination).

The extent to which subjects' narratives have been edited and possibly reinterpreted in subsequent publication, is considered in Chapter 2—hence, whether the accounts published are valid descriptions of the events purported to have taken place. Some caution should be exercised in evaluating these reports and the bias to which they may be subject. However, ECE reportage is not only a modern phenomenon, albeit subject to media bias or interference. Many parallels abound: historical and modern, eastern and western, alluding to a worldwide propensity for such phenomenology to be undergone. These testimonies permit the deduction that cultural influences markedly shape the contours of the events reported. That is, there is a substantial input from cerebrally based memory circuits from which the experiential details are, in part, drawn.

In continuing the theme of reliability in reportage, Chapter 3 examines critically the interpretations offered by my key authors of the narrative accounts they received. Here again marked bias is detectable, witnessed in the stylized account of the phenomenology given by Moody. This widely publicized account lamentably fails to acknowledge the idiosyncratic content of each subject's given narrative. It has also spawned the prevalent view that all ECE follow a set pattern: that impression could not be further from the truth. Secondly, some authors have used their books to propose and develop a vast cosmic superstructure, or pseudo-fantasy otherworldly domain, the pursuit of which greatly exceeds the possibilities offered by the kind of subject matter recalled by their interviewed subjects. Despite certain authors' emphasis in encouraging a cosmic perspective, there has been a notable widespread failure to consider seriously the important influence of ECE on subjects' lives. This seems to me to be of a far greater importance than speculative interest focused entirely on 'mystical' or 'cosmic' events.

My overriding task has been to seek another way of interpreting ECE phenomenology apart from the prevailing view that it arises from moribund brains, thus allowing the 'inner person' to escape and sample the delights of the afterlife. The approach I have adopted is radically different (Chapter 4). First, it is clear that all OBE/NDE terminate, as is clearly and consistently recorded in the literature, at the point at which full conscious-awareness once more becomes fully operative. That crucial time-point, at which conscious-awareness is subsequently retrieved, provides a definable third-party reference into the subjective nature of the ECE. That indicates that the experienced phenomenology was undergone in the final moments preceding the abrupt resumption of conscious-awareness.

Second, it can be inferred that ECE in the majority of narratives published are ephemeral events lasting only seconds, or possibly a few minutes. This conclusion obtains from my deploying an arm of dream-state research practice, the use of word counts. The application of word counts to published ECE narratives indicates how short in timescale ECE are. Thus, extrapolating backwards from the salient point of congruence between the end of an ECE and the resumption of conscious-awareness, it is possible to uncover and underscore the transience of the phenomenology. That such dream-like mentation can be conjured during multi-second intervals by a brain rapidly awakening from an antecedent insult is securely upheld by reference to survivors of attempted suicide from the Golden Gate Bridge, and the periods of unconsciousness induced either by forced fainting, or by rotating (military) personnel rapidly in a revolving capsule (centrifugation). Each of these spontaneous, or contrived, events involves *awakenings from states of unconsciousness*. But, as subjects awaken, they experience dreamlets espousing scenes of great beauty, the sighting of deceased relatives, all of which are borne on a highly charged emotional state uniquely relevant to each subject. Finally, such individuals exhibited a great reluctance to relinquish this ecstatic trance-like state during their 'return' to earth, that is, in re-acquiring full conscious-awareness. From that exercise alone, it becomes apparent that ECE are not, nor could be, derivative of moribund brains as is widely supposed.

Third, it therefore follows that ECE are not vague, shapeless journeys towards an imaginary somewhere (or nowhere) but related to the disordered return to functional normality which such massive insults to brain metabolism induce. Furthermore, the mentation characterizing these experiences is the resultant of momentary disinhibition and/or deactivation of key controlling neural influences throughout the brain. It is therefore highly reminiscent of the phenomenological bizarreness and illogicalities characteristic of dream-state modes, a subject to which we will return later.

My overriding premise, therefore, is that OB/ND phenomenology is not about the death of individuals nor about dying, moribund brains. On the contrary it is about a vigorous return to life and hence the reappropriation by brains of their former functional competence, as the organ of conscious-awareness. That is what my radical programme is about and concerned with throughout the book.

I have already suggested that ECE are related to brains awakening from their antecedent insults, and also implied that the content of some ECE reportage is based on pre-existing memories, culturally determined and already laid down in subjects' brains before the event took place. In moving towards my in-depth neurological analysis of ECE phenomenology, Chapter 5 articulates material on the brain and consciousness germane to my argument stressing, in particular, the degree to which our day-to-day environments are created by the brain, and that the content of much conscious-awareness is illusory. I further exemplify that theme by considering 'phantom limb' phenomenology, that is, the ability of the brain to create an illusory limb or organ no longer present. My point is to emphasize that if a normal brain can elaborate a non-existent limb, or a torso in someone with a broken neck, it could also manufacture a non-existent 'body' thereby generating an out-of-body experience. Indeed, there is a large body of experimental neurophysi-ological data clearly showing that disturbances in the neural mechanisms underpinning the creation of 'body-image' give rise not only to illusions of weightlessness and of floating outwith the body, but also to the perception that consciousness likewise inhabits a location outwith the physical confines of corporeality.

A fuller account of the neurophysiological mechanisms concerned with body-image and its perturbations is given in Chapter 6. The several patho-logical variants known and investigated include autoscopic and heautoscopic reduplications of the subject's body, the sensing of invisible presences, and OBE. They arise through mismatched integrations between incoming (afferent) sensory information: visual, proprioceptive (joint position), haptic (tactile), and from the vestibular organs of 'balance' sited within the inner ear and which together contribute to each person's sense of body-image. These afferent sensory systems are integrated in the cortical areas of the temporo-parietal junction[5] (TPJ). Disturbances in personal body-image (egocentric) and its relationship to the subject's near environment (para-centric body-image) may accompany bouts of migraine due to local reduc-tions in cerebral blood flow, temporal lobe epileptic discharges, and vascular

---

[5] A detailed glossary explaining terms and/or functions is given at the end of this book.

insults of brainstem such as arterial thrombosis, embolization or haemorrhage. In addition, physiological perturbations occasioned by tendon vibration, zero gravity conditions, and the use of mirrors in obviating problems
associated with phantom limbs, engender erroneous illusions of subjects'
perceptions of body-in-space. Neurophysiological understandings of body-
image are specifically related to the vestibular system, which underlies the
abnormal perceptions of weightlessness, accelerations, angular gyrations,
and the 180° turn permitting OB experients to view their vacated bodies
face-to-face.

At this point, we should not forget that the 'tunnel phenomenon' is often
accompanied by disturbed vestibular function, as witnessed by the spurious
perception of rapid ascents, angular gyrations, or of accelerations through
darkness and towards the light. There is no doubt that all these aberrant
misperceptions are brain-dependent. To be out-of-body is either a physiological or neuropathological event and firmly anchored in uncoordinated neural
processes: it does not require a psychical, 'mystical', or spiritual component as
an aetiological determinant. On these grounds, I resist attempts to interpret
OBE as otherworldly events, or to be exemplary of mind or consciousness
independent of the neural substrate of their production. Given the perturbed
nature of brains recovering from a period of circulatory arrest, there is no
further reason to suppose that an OBE is other than a manifestation of
mismatched coordination in the temporo-parietal junction (TPJ) among all
the component afferences subserving the construction of body-image, and its
portrayal as internally perceived within each subject's conscious-awareness.

Since the experiential features of extra-corporeal events usually occur when
subjects are seemingly unconscious or semi-conscious, and, importantly, in a
recumbent position, they may be deemed to be analogous to dreaming.
I explore this theme in detail in Chapter 7. In doing so, I resist subjects'
denial that they were dreaming. These people are not conversant with the
numerous forms of dream-state modes now neurophysiologically defined.
Indeed, sleep-onset or hypnagogic, sleep-offset or hypnopompic, and REM
dream-state modes are rich in dream-like ('oneiric') adventures highly reminiscent of ECE narrative accounts. Brain scans of dreaming subjects, in
revealing several critical areas of cortical deactivation, suggest other possible
loci in which the experiential contours of NDE, in particular, could similarly
be affected. Major associative areas of the TPJ are crucial, since damage to this
region impairs or abolishes oneiric competence. I suggest that TPJ lesions
would markedly reduce the propensity to undergo NDE. Should a prospective trial of such patients confirm that inference, vital third-party data
indicating a cerebral location underpinning ECE phenomenology would
thus be acquired. The bizarreness and illogicalities of dreams seem dependent

on the defunctioning of key cortical areas, especially the prefrontal cortex. Analogous functional deficits could condition the content of ECE which, like subconscious dream mentation, is similarly weird, bizarre, intensely anthropomorphic, geo-centred, and personally idiosyncratic.

Chapter 8 centres on the temporal lobe and the rich array of illusory imagery, so reminiscent of ECE reportage, to which it gives way. The next (Chapter 9) deals with sundry topics, including the role of endorphins, hypoxia, carbon dioxide narcosis, which, over time, have been offered as aetiological factors, and the possible paradigmatic role for the anaesthetic agent ketamine. Analysis of all these factors helps to put the neurophysiological argument in perspective. I refer specifically to the temporal lobe and newer outcomes which are signally lacking in the literature a critique of which forms the basis of this book. Explanatory solutions why so few people in life-threatening circumstances undergo ECE have never been advanced: yet emerging work on the temporal lobe may provide approaches to answering this difficulty.

Many authors have adopted a dismissive attitude towards the relevance of the temporal lobe to ECE phenomenology. Modern techniques and surveys have revealed a far wider spectrum of dispositions not previously envisaged. This dispositional spectrum includes personalities inclined towards a *latent* temporal lobe bias, secondly auras that reproduce *in toto* ECE phenomenology without ensuing epileptic seizures, and finally, the classical aura-plus-seizure type of temporal lobe epileptic fit. These advances have accrued from surveys of 'normal' populations, indicating that brain insults during intra-uterine and neonatal periods, childhood and adolescence causally predispose towards latent temporal lobe dysfunction. Non-seizure auras, which encompass psychical and other spiritual encounters, have been eradicated with anti-convulsant drugs. A recent survey of ECE subjects identified ~20% fulfilling the new temporal lobe criteria and manifesting non-ictal, or 'epileptic', spiking EEG wave-patterns. This is new and exciting information. Appropriately designed prospective trials should be undertaken in order to assess the impact of these data to larger cohorts of individuals predisposed to life-threatening emergencies such as cardiac arrests, haemorrhage, and childbirth. Until that work is completed, non-neurological explanations of ECE phenomenology will remain vulnerable to neurophysiologically based criticism and possibility.

I have drawn attention to another facet of the experiential narrative which seems to have eluded the attentions of the authors considered, and which directly impinges on the neurophysiological implications. At the onset of any ECE, subjects display remarkable abilities to traverse with ease all kinds of solid barriers (ceilings, windows and walls) during their 'outward' journeys. Neither do they exhibit any qualms during this *early-phase* component of the ECE, happily leaving behind grieving relatives and families disposed about their vacated bedsides. However, once conscious-awareness begins to exert its progressive influence during the *late-phase* subconscious mentation of ECE, insubstantial obstacles which initially presented no physical impedence to the 'outward' journey, now become insuperable. These I regard as 'cognitive' barriers of the type which we all erect from time to time in our lives. In addition, 'moral' urgencies begin to crowd in, forcing ECE subjects to relinquish their other-worldly abode thus to attend to their earthly responsibilities towards spouse, parents, family, or work. The intrusion of conscious-awareness and the likely re-establishment of frontal lobe activity into the *late-phase* dream-like bizarreness of the ECE is further indicative of cerebrally based mechanisms. Indeed, I assert there are no extra-corporeal journeys and no returns: only hallucinatory events conjured by brains as ordered neurophysiological function rapidly supervenes. These considerations underpin my new classification of the phenomenologies recounted by subjects.

A further corollary of the intersection of subconscious and conscious mentation involves the dual experiencing of physical pain, discomfort, or perceptions of bedside voices and allied clinical activities while subjects are otherworldly. Co-temporal experiencing of conscious and subconscious mentation occurs with lucid dreaming and during heautoscopic body reduplications, and when normal people experience hynopompic awakenings. This is another important neurophysiological argument for my view that ECE phenomenologies are intrinsically brain-based and not perceptions, albeit cerebrally channelled, of independent action realized in some otherworldly realm beyond the body, if not our universe.

Finally, I have explored the manner in which ECE impinge on, and influence, experients' lives. On this aspect of the post-experiential subject, authors' approaches have been poorly researched and evaluated. The greatest impact which ECE have on subjects is to foster steadfast beliefs that the event was veridical. The assertion by some that they ascended to heaven and encountered God or Jesus specifically demand theological responses. The quest is to determine whether these events exhibit an appropriate eschatology of events related to the 'End Time', or are recognizable as spiritual encounters. Problems arise in evaluating the eschatological propriety of ECE narratives, since judgements or life-reviews follow in the wake of subjects' arrival in heaven and their confrontations with supposedly divine persons. Second, other experients find themselves in hell, thence to be rapidly transported into heavenly warmth and light. Third, running through these narratives is the unquestioned assumption of an unbroken continuity of the person through death and into the afterlife. This supposition seems to be in keeping

xxiv   *Introduction: Prospects for Life After Death*

with preconceived ideas about the immortality of mind, soul or consciousness. That assumption is inconsistent with current trends in thinking about
the nature of the person. The idea of a divinely implanted soul that can evade
death and represent the whole person in eternity is foreign to much current
philosophical, psychological and neurophysiological thinking. Death is certainly a far more radical disjunction between earthly existence and what,
ultimately, we shall come to be in the New Creation (Chapter 10). A transference of the person through death and directly into another incorporeal
modality in the afterlife, as evinced by accounts of ECE phenomenology,
lacks the authentic solution to our heart-searching agnosia, and requires
definition of an anthropology and eschatology based on resurrectional theology. And that resurrectional theology must be grounded in the resurrection of
Jesus as conqueror of death, and on the hope that we shall all acquire a new
'spiritual' body when the New Creation dawns, as expressed and anticipated
in the credal tradition.

The intensely vivid, full-blooded geocentric and anthropomorphic accounts of ECE militate against the quietly introversive nature of classical
divine presence or disclosure, as explored in Chapter 11. The widely disparate
descriptions offered by respondents in sampling features and persons characterizing the other-world also make any sensible interpretation of their
views meaningless. Surely if all those people attesting to a specifically heavenly
abode had actually resided there, their reports should be identical. They are
not, and therefore do not provide us with new revelatory information about
the afterlife, and hence with newer moral imperatives that could be
incorporated into devotional practice, or indeed, day-to-day living.

Nevertheless, most subjects are changed by their experience(s), becoming
more tolerant towards society, people and family. This I discuss at length in
Chapter 12, on the grounds that this important facet of ECE phenomenology
has been largely ignored. Here is an issue of far greater import than the
speculative superstructures of spirituality and cosmic brotherhood imposed
by some authors on, but largely irrelevant to, the narrative accounts of
experients and who, in turn, would scarcely recognize such florid departures
from their given testimonies. Here we have the basis of a theology of personhood that exalts post-experiential subjects. Furthermore, although their
glimpses of heaven may be no more than hallucinatory brain perturbations
while recovering, it would not be possible to state that ECE were not occasions
for divine grace. The post-experiential subject has the potential to transcend
this newly gained gift towards other people, like some of those who survived
suicide bids from the Golden Gate Bridge. Here is an issue deserving of
further recognition and to which strategies could possibly be allocated,
designed to harness these emergent personal strengths. Perhaps those societies

formed to promote interest in ECE could undertake more research in this area.

Our immortality may rest on other factors, details of which have still to be revealed to us. It is not my view that the corpus of writings on ECE phenomenology has enlightened us with further specific insights about that afterlife. ECE do not offer paradigms which amplify our understandings of the theology of mankind, of death, or of resurrection since they emanate from hallucinatory events generated by brains recovering from antecedent ischaemic or allied metabolic insults.

1

Getting a Sense of the Other-Worldly Domain

1.1. HAVING THAT KIND OF FEELING: BEING OUT-OF-BODY AND OTHER-WORLDLY

It had been raining, and the woman was rushing to get a bus for a dental appointment across town. Her attention was momentarily drawn towards the man yelling at her as she entered the pedestrian crossing, but the car was already upon her. Its driver, distracted before impact by the needs of a child passenger, failed to notice her as she began dashing across the highway. The victim continues:

I was struck by a black car—that's the last thing I remember, until I was above the whole scene viewing the accident, I was *very detached. I don't remember hearing anything*—it was just like I floated [up to the] *rooftops or a little higher . . . the thing that impressed me most was that I was devoid* of emotion. It was . . . pure intellect. I wasn't frightened . . . it was *very pleasant*. I remember seeing the earring which was smashed . . . my shoe crushed under the wheel . . . my new dress ruined. And *I wasn't thinking about my body* being ruined too . . . I don't think really *that the seriousness of the situation dawned on me* [nor] the realization 'I'm outside my body': . . . the next thing I saw [was] the woman [driver] crying . . . the car [was] dented. And I saw my body—in profile as the attendants lifted me onto the stretcher. I was actually to the front and side of the car, viewing all this. I remember them looking at my eyes . . . checking my pupils. Then they began lifting my body. The way they handled me was something else . . . *this was amusing to me*: they lifted me in an amateurish way . . . underneath my shoulders and knees rather than rolling the stretcher up under me and then lifting me . . . into the ambulance . . . the whole thing was very detached. I remember them putting me—that is, my body—into the ambulance. And the next thing I remember was crying in the emergency room because I couldn't see . . . I awoke blind and couldn't see for about 30min after I fully regained consciousness.[1]

---

[1] Sabom Michael, *Recollections of Death*, San Francisco: Harper & Row 1982, 116ff. Abridged, with my emphases.

One cannot but be impressed by the weirdness of this woman's account of her accident as viewed through an out-of-body experience (OBE). It is only necessary to recall the victim's cold, dispassionate and passive recall of events against our own witnessing of the roadside scenes following a major accident, and the impact of the shocked faces of survivors huddled together giving information to police and other involved parties. She displays no shock, disbelief, concern for possible injury or future disablement: none of these implications are factored into her account. She was '*devoid*' of emotion; she was '*not frightened*'; it was '*pleasant*'; she was '*amused*'. In real life, we would be incredulous and certainly very intrigued by such inappropriate remarks. Her interests were not for her body, but only for her damaged earring, shoe and dress. There is no recall of the associated noises on the street—conversations, passing traffic, the klaxons of police vehicles and ambulance. Yet she 'saw' while supposedly unconscious and temporarily blinded, events which although scant in detail, appeared on recall to be factually correct. However, the few details which she did report were known to her before, and after the accident. In fact, as a result of her OBE, she reported nothing new: that is the important issue here.

This lady suffered transient, mild concussion accompanied by a depressed level of conscious-awareness. We have no corroborative evidence of how long she lay injured on the roadside before arriving at hospital. But we should note that her story, as later remembered and recalled, is of a *continuous narrative*. Yet it should be evident that each of the incidents could have been experienced as isolated events interspersed with deeper levels of unconsciousness during which no memories would have been laid down and available for recall. Moreover, what she does recall are merely a few images and impressions. She does *not* give a sensible eyewitness account of the sequential unfolding of the accident and its progressive management. She could well have been lying on the road for an hour or more while awaiting the arrival of the ambulance. Her verbal report referred, in reality, to a few apparent visual traces that could hardly have occupied but a few seconds of real time as she lay impassively on the road. That is a vital distinction to be borne in mind.

1.1.a. Out-of-Body and Near-Death Experiences

The preceding excerpt gives account of an out-of-body experience, and is a very idiosyncratic recollection of what the victim supposed happened to her after being knocked down and rendered unconscious. OBE, in general, permit the observing of one's entire body and its immediate environment from another vantage point, usually from the ceiling of the bedroom, ward or operating theatre. In such cases, consciousness appears to lie with the floating 'self', the central experience being of separation of body and mind.[2] Usually, the phenomenon is accompanied by heightened auditory perceptions of speech, buzzing, vibrations or ringing tones, and the sensation of weightlessness, floating or other forms of apparent bodily motion. The 'phantom self' is able to pass through physical objects without hindrance.

Additional to OB events are the so-called near-death experiences (NDE).[3] The phenomenology of NDE proper envisions individuals being able to escape the confines of corporeality thus to fly away and enjoy glimpses, so it is alleged, of another, other-worldly realm. Such experiences are often but by no means invariably presaged by movement, often perceived as a rapid acceleration, twisting or ascent through a dark, black 'tunnel' into the glorious light of the hereafter. There, spiritual figures, very occasionally perceived as God or Jesus, or more often deceased friends or relatives, are encountered invariably on a background of intense pastoral beauty and wonderful music. Occasionally a life-review or judgemental episode may be another passing accompaniment of the experience, followed by an abrupt return to the (often painful) body. There may also be sensed a pressing need to resist remaining in this heavenly abode but to return to earth in order to attend to former duties, involving spouses, family or work.

OBE and NDE are neither necessarily associated, nor necessarily sequential, occurrences. For convenience I collectively refer to the two phenomena as 'extracorporeal experiences', or ECE. Neither is a death-threatening occasion an essential prelude to the occurrence of an OBE or NDE. Indeed, the psychological and parapsychological literature is replete with details of numerous people who undergo spontaneous, and often repeated, events of this type throughout life. In one study of Oxford University undergraduates by CE Green,[4] five cases were associated with dreaming; three while going to sleep; and others occasioned by a diverse collection of antecedent phenomena such as impending danger; threatening or embarrassing life-events; imminent drowning; physical exhaustion; occasions of severe tension, anxiety or nervousness; and others precipitated either by the 'grey zone' before a faint; being in a calm religious setting; or even spontaneously without any specific precipitant.[5]

---

[2] Tart C, *J Near Death Stud* 17: 73–99, 1998.

[3] There is a further death-associated phenomenon noted in ill people who, at the point of their departure, experience 'apparitions' of other deceased friends or relatives, often associated with an elevation of mood whilst the individual retains an alert consciousness. I am not concerned here with this type of 'death-bed' phenomenology.

[4] Green C, *J Psychic Res* 44: 111–131, 1967.

[5] deVesme C, *Ann Psychic Sci* 4: 325–331, 1906; Green CE, *J Soc Psychic Res* 43: 357–366, 1966; Tart C, *Int J Parapsychol* 9: 251–258, 1967; idem, *J Am Soc Psychic Res* 62: 3–27, 1968; Osis

In another statistically controlled comparative study of two groups of severely ill patients, 28 were judged clinically by their attending physicians to be life-threatened, while a disease-control group of 30 individuals was considered clinically not to be nearing death. ECE were experienced[6] by a similarly high percentage (~68%) of subjects in each group. The divergent data regarding the prevalence of ECE phenomenology in very sick patients[7] is presumed to depend on patient selection and attempts to do statistical analyses on very small numbers. Other persons, able to bring on ECE at will and extensively investigated with physiological tools (electroencephalogram or EEG, blood pressure recordings or body temperature measurements), have led normal lives over many years without any *apparent* demonstrable intra-cerebral or intra-cranial pathology. From that, it is clear that an ECE is a feature of an apparently 'normal' brain, or in circumstances of determined voluntary control.[8] Evidently, the varied occasions when individuals find themselves out of body is not dependent on an immediately life-threatening cause whether internal (acute cardiac or cerebral event) or external (traumatic; psychologically demanding, or stressful). This is an important contradiction of some authors whom we meet in the next section who appear to assume that ECE imply dying or dead brains.

1.1.b. *A 'Who's Who' of Extra-Corporeal Experiences (ECE)*

Modern origins of this topic lie in the book entitled 'Reflections on Life after Life' published by philosopher-turned-psychiatrist Dr Raymond Moody. Moody himself had never experienced ECE phenomenology, but he was drawn to the subject through his academic background in philosophy and, subsequently, his teaching of the philosophy of medicine to medical students. But the major thrust to his interest in the subject first grew out of hearing a lecture on a previous death-associated event by the psychiatrist Dr George G. Ritchie. Then, secondly, as a later raconteur of the testimonies of other

K and Mitchell J, *J Soc Psychic Res* 49: 525–536, 1977; Morse M, Castillo P, Venecia D, Jerrold M, Tyler D, *Am J Dis Child* 140: 1110–1114, 1986.

[6] Owens J, Cook E, Stevenson I, *Lancet* 336: 1175–1177, 1990; Gabbard G, Twemlow S, Jones F et al, *J Nerv Ment Dis* 169: 374–377, 1981; Stevenson I, Cook E, Clean-Rice N, *Omega* 20: 45–54, 1989–1990.

[7] Sabom M and Kreutziger S, *Theta* 6: 1–6, 1978.

[8] Osis and Mitchell 1977; Tart 1967, 1968; Green E, Green A, Walters E, *J Transpers Psychol* 1: 1–26, 1970.

subjects who, like Ritchie, had experienced what Moody first categorized as 'near-death experiences'.[9]

Dr Ritchie's NDE was exclusively idiosyncratic, arising during what was probably an attack of pneumococcal lobar pneumonia contracted during army training, in the winter of 1943. He found himself flying across a broad river, incapable of conversing with people, yet able to traverse solid objects. He returned to his hospital room and then, undergoing a brief OBE, was empowered to recognize his own body by the $\phi\gamma\delta$ ring on his fourth finger. A progressively bright light began to appear at the foot of his bed, announcing itself to be the 'Son of God'. The light seemed to be aware of all Ritchie's secrets for which he experienced some degree of reproach. There followed another journey during which he was shown a vast library. Finally, on waking up, he was told he had been 'unconscious' for four days, pronounced dead and prepared for the morgue. However, the attendant noticed a slight laryngeal movement, after which intra-cardiac adrenaline was given, resulting in Ritchie's full recovery.

Moody, in subsequently eliciting accounts of similar phenomena from a large group of people, attempted a generalized temporal sequence which supposedly captured the ethos of ECE: movement through a dark tunnel towards a bright light and often preceded by deep, uninterpretable noises; meeting others, including relatives, and then coming into the presence of a 'Being of Light' in whose presence a life-review—instantaneously—took place, perhaps against a background of intense peace, joy, beauty, sounds and even fragrances; then a command to return to earth because varied responsibilities needed to be addressed; finally, a retelling of the event and a changed approach both to the ultimate death process and the subsequent post-experiential life of the subject. It is evident that Ritchie's account offers few affinities with Moody's schema. Unlike many others, Ritchie experienced sights of people in hellish-type circumstances, or moods. Moreover, his vision of 'paradise' was not particularly well-delineated.

Moody's book inspired another academic psychologist from the University of Connecticut, Dr Kenneth Ring. From May 1977, after having seen Moody's book, Dr Ring began assembling a further collection of narratives obtained from over fifty people who were near-death. His departmental study[10] sought to remedy the defects which he perceived to have marred Moody's anecdotal accounts. Ring's objectives were to determine the overall prevalence of ECE

---

[9] Moody Raymond, *Life after Life*, New York: Bantam 1976; *Reflections on Life after Life*, New York: Bantam 1977: Zaleski Carol, *Otherworld Jouneys*, Oxford: Oxford University Press 1988, 101–102; 126 for details of Ritchie's account.

[10] Ring Kenneth, *Life at Death*, New York: Coward, McCann & Geoghegan 1980.

occurring among those facing life-threatening situations, to assess the degree to which each person's ECE corresponded to Moody's 'universal' construct, and to evaluate whether ECE are qualitatively related to the type of death-threatening antecedent, such as attempted suicide, acute cardiac insufficiency or a severe life-threatening accident. From that material he proposed the following experiential criteria: an origin in feelings of peace and well-being, followed by a sense of viewing one's own body—albeit sometimes difficult to recognize—and associated with perceptions of scenes of great beauty, and the dilemma of wanting to stay in that beautiful 'realm' despite the over-whelming coercive need to return to earth's duties and responsibilities. This sequence Ring proposed as the '*core*' experience. Secondly, he coined the '*depth*' criterion which, he asserted, was directly related to the number of phases through which each subject passed and hence a measure of the intensity of the experience.

Interestingly, only ~50% of Ring's subjects had experiences which 'con-formed in an obvious way, at least in part, to Moody's model': of these, about half had 'deep' experiences. But even here difficulties arise with Ring's data, because there were marked differences in the prevalence of reported ECE between self-referring (58%) as against medically referred (39%) cases. This raises considerable doubt as to the clinical circumstances relevant to the self-referrals admitted to his study. Further quantitative analyses showed that 60% of subjects experienced feelings of ineffable peace and contentment; 20% entered the darkness; 17% saw a light. Yet, curiously, only 10% of subjects *entered* the light or found themselves in another world comprising either flowers, lovely music or offering glimpses of deceased relatives. Ring con-cluded that in women, ECE occurred 'far more often with "illness"' whereas for men, ECE were 'more likely to be associated with accidents or attempted suicides'. Religious, and non-religious, people were equally likely to have these experiences.

Ring became firmly convinced that if a transpersonal experience reflects the surpassing of the '*normal*' ego boundaries as 'well as the dimensions of time and place, then there can be little doubt that survivors of ND events have entered such a (transpersonal) state of consciousness'. In a later exposition during a public lecture[11] Ring expressed his newly found idea which saw the corpus of near-death experiences as an 'evolutionary thrust toward [a] higher consciousness for humanity . . . [such] . . . people or others [being] transformed by . . . deep experiences . . . representing . . . a more highly ad-vanced human being'. That these people are 'coming into being' represents

---

[11] Zaleski 1998, 108; and see Ring K, *Heading towards Omega*, New York: Morrow 1985.

'emergence of a new strain of human being' and possibly signalling the 'dawning of a New Age'.

Moody's work was also made known to Dr Michael B Sabom through a psychiatric social worker, Sarah Kreutziger. At that time, Dr Sabom was completing his cardiological training at the University of Florida at Gaines-ville. Sabom was initially most unenthusiastic about the reality, even possibil-ity, of such strange death-associated happenings and regarded Moody's book as 'fiction'. Nevertheless, he agreed to work with Kreutziger (in Gainesville and subsequently during his first tenured positions at Emory Medical School and the Atlanta Veterans Administration Hospital) to investigate patients under his care who suffered acute cardiovascular shutdown. Sabom's intent was to initiate a truly scientific, prospective study of cardiovascular collapses thus to determine the true prevalence of ECE, to compare his findings with Moody's, to evaluate the influence of social factors on the qualitative aspects of each experience and whether those factors influenced the content of ECE, and finally, to decide whether the ECE itself, or the close call to death, influenced later attitudes to dying and to beliefs in the afterlife. Such observa-tions would be made possible by rigorous follow-up of all patients admitted to his prospective study through the acquisition of clinical data amassed during each resuscitation, and then subjected to statistical analysis.[12]

From May 1976 through March 1981, 78 prospectively enrolled patients were reviewed, of whom 33% experienced OBE, 48% had NDE and 19% went through a combined event. The majority (79%) followed acute cardiac complications, 15% were in coma and 6% post-traumatic: not surprisingly, the majority of cases was dealt with in the hospital setting. Thirteen cases (39%) were 'unconscious' for periods greatly exceeding 30 minutes, while 19 (61%) were unconscious for up to 30 minutes: hence the majority of cases received effective resuscitation performed by experienced, hospital-based crews.

Of those experiencing ND events, only 14 described a period of darkness or a void. One subject with three successive cardiac arrests experienced blackness only during the first two, but a sense of movement through the dark during the third, longer arrest: 'like I was lifting up' (*sic*).[13] Seventeen subjects (~22%) saw some kind of light which terminated the initial dark void, the light invariably being small and gradually increasing in size. The transcen-dental environment was invariably described in quasi-geographic terms, as clouds, blue skies, flowers, streams, or a pasture with cattle. Others described gates (golden), the top of a mountain, a road ending at a gate, and a landscape

[12] Sabom M and Kreutziger S, *Death Educ* 1: 195–203, 1977; Sabom 1982; 1998.
[13] Sabom 1982, 42.

full of people of different nationalities each working on their arts and crafts.[14] Only 10 experienced some other 'person' whether sensed as a 'presence' or a 'spiritual being'. Communication was verbal (between 'being' and experiencer), gestural or 'telepathic', and invariably concerned directives to return to earth. Three subjects recognized themselves to be in the presence of God or Jesus; many perceived previously dead forebears within their larger family. Two people experienced a life review, but neither involved contact with the people in, or of, the light.

Dr Sabom became an immediate convert.

Sabom's study is robust, prospective and scientific, indicating that for this series of subjects, ECE (OBE and NDE) were experienced by ~30–50% of subjects. Although Sabom classifies ECE as either autoscopic or transcendental, he follows Moody and Ring in describing each experiential facet. His data showed that demographic factors or previous acquaintance with ECE phenomenology were not determinative, and that the narrative content of ECE was independent of all factors investigated, save that some females and non-skilled subjects tended to encounter other, deceased people during their experiences. A reduced fear of dying and an increased belief in an afterlife was reckoned by the majority of subjects to have been caused by the ECE rather than the threat of death itself.

So far, I have briefly alluded to six books written by three North American physicians. My case study also involves two other books by UK authors, Margot Grey and the man-and-wife team, Dr Peter and Elizabeth Fenwick.[15] Grey describes herself as a humanistic psychologist, and practises as a London-based psychotherapist. Grey's book, written as a means of investigating the cross-cultural attributes of ECE phenomenology, follows very much the approach and sentiments of Kenneth Ring and, in my opinion, adds little to the field of study. There is an attempt to classify hellish experiences, but with so few relevant narratives on offer, the exercise contributes little of value.

On the other hand, Peter Fenwick, a London-based physician and neuro-psychiatrist, is extremely well known for his many writings and contributions to meetings, press and media coverage of the subject of ECE. For most of his professional life, Dr Fenwick has devoted his time to these phenomenologies and promoted them through the media. His book, written jointly with his journalist wife, Elizabeth, refers to the collected narratives of more than 300 subjects qualitatively assessed with regard to every nuanced aspect of the experiential detail offered by subjects in their recollections. These details are given in eleven chapters, following two essays which introduce the subject.

---

[14] Sabom 1982, 209: table 12.
[15] Grey 1985; Fenwick and Fenwick 1998.

Despite so much qualitative detail, there are no systematic figures given, so that it is difficult to determine what percentage of their total sample underwent each specific item of the 'core' experience. There is much speculative material in the closing four chapters concerned with possible mechanisms, including scientific considerations, and possible outcomes and meanings. I am not totally reassured that the Fenwicks' position is convincing because it lacks firm assertions as to what ECE are caused by, or actually represent. I refer to the various aspects of their study in the following pages. Two chapters, devoted to hellish experiences and the experiences of children, are particularly welcome, providing a basis for further critical insights and developments.

The foundations for my book are thus based on the assessment of eight previous books on ECE phenomenology written by five authors, and incorporating a total series of freely offered accounts by more than 700 subjects. In making that statement, I should also make clear that I have not, personally, engaged with any ECE subject. The case which I present in this book is dependent entirely on the material and authors' opinions (based on that material) presented in these standard works which are widely considered to embody the canonical definition and contours of ECE phenomenology. There is one further, but important point. Much of this published material refers to adult patients, only the Fenwicks taking the opportunity to deal with children's recalled ECE phenomenology. There are reasons why a more detailed approach to infantile and childhood ECE is necessary and important, and I deal with that topic and its implications for understanding ECE phenomenology in a later chapter. At this stage, I wish to refer to work carried out by the American paediatrician Dr Melvin Morse. His deep clinical, as well as spiritual, interest in these events caused him to suffer great difficulty and even aggression in his professional life. It is a tribute to his personal courage and beliefs that he continued pursuing this subject matter against much criticism and disparagement inflicted by professional colleagues and managers with whom (in an academic medical setting) he was working.

Morse's retrospective study involved children who had attended University Hospital Medical Center, Seattle, WA. The prevalence of ECE was approximately 10% (12 ECE) controlled against a sample of 121 severely ill children who did not have any relevant experiential recall.[16] Eight of 12 described OBE (~70%). The figure of 10%, despite the critical condition of the children reviewed, is considerably lower than either Ring's prevalence of 39% (physician selected) and that of Sabom (1982), of whose later sample of 116 near-death survivors, 62% underwent ECE, among whom the majority (50%) only

[16] Morse et al 1986; Morse Melvin and Perry Paul, *Closer to the Light*, New York: Villard Books 1990.

experienced OB events.[17] This may be due to the much higher preponderance of cardiac cases in the adult groups which, in Sabom's study, accounted for 60% of all life-threatening incidents. Some children gave accounts of dark tunnels and stairways to the light, encounters with people in white often conceived in terms of God or Jesus, but fewer visions of an organized 'paradise' beyond. Typically, the recollection was of light, rainbows or flashing scintillations. Only one child saw his grandfather, and only one had the extremely rare event (among children) of a life-review. In several instances the child had to make a decision to return: none, in this series, was ever told or coerced to return to home or parents. Therefore, it is quite clear that in comparison with the typical stories given by adults, the paediatric experiences were far less developed, detailed in their phenomenology, or stereotyped. I refer to this topic later in Chapter 4.

Having introduced the broad outlines of OBE and NDE phenomenology, and the authors and their books descriptive of this phenomenology, I now proceed to pay particular attention in the following section to specific features of these events.

1.2. SPECIFIC CASE-STUDIES

1.2.a. Hell's Angels?

While there is a high preponderance in NDE reports ($\sim$50–60%) of a perceived heavenly venue, albeit invariably described in geomorphic language for those experients who reach this 'realm', far fewer subjects relate unpleasant or terrifying excursions. In their reviews of ECE, Peter and Elizabeth Fenwick[18] usefully devote a small chapter to hellish experiences in their publication *The Truth in the Light*. These experiences add perspective to their account in quoting the 1982 Gallup Poll of 1500 American adults, of whom approximately two-thirds professed to be religious and to believe in the afterlife. Belief in an afterlife equated with the prospect, and good chances, of attaining heaven, presumably a belief and expectation connoting the Judaeo-Christian tradition. When questions about the possibility of hell were asked, only $\sim$50% of the sample expressed such a belief, while entertaining only the remotest possibility of finding themselves there.

---

[17] Sabom 1982, 81ff. Sabom calls OBE 'autoscopic' experiences—an incorrect usage of the term.

[18] Fenwick and Fenwick 1998, 187ff.

The question arises whether the scarcity of hellish NDE relates to cultural factors and declining religious belief, especially in such a concept as hell, or whether there are neurophysiological factors also at play which determine this skewed outcome. Certainly the vagueness of the descriptions of hell most probably reflect a lack of current interest in the place, and because there is no prevailing cultural consensus as to what hell might physically entail. We no longer labour with the visual imagery of horned demons dressed in scarlet, unquenchable fires or bottomless pits. The Dives and Lazarus paradigm is no longer seen in such vivid physical dimensions and pain. The eschatological precepts of Antiquity and the Mediaevalists fail to hold either our imaginations or sensibilities captive any longer.

Dr Maurice Rawlings, an American cardiologist, gives the following account from an individual awaiting surgery after a severe assault:

I felt the presence of something or some power. Next blackness . . . I was drawn into total darkness. It felt like a big hollow room—a very large space and totally dark. I asked the power who I, and who he or it, were. He answered (by a flow of energy): 'The Angel of Death'. I believed him. The Angel said my life was not as it should be, that he could take me on but that I would be given a second chance, and that I was going back. The next thing I remember I was in the recovery room, back in my body. But the encounter was real to me, and I still believe I was with The Angel of Death.[19]

This ND account of a weird encounter with a so-called 'Angel of Death' is almost unique: few others appear to have experienced this sinister character. I note that the command to return coincides precisely with the subject's abrupt resumption of conscious-awareness. His immediate preceding experiences, therefore, correspond to the period when he was coming round from the anaesthetic, a period that would have lasted only a few moments. In another study of ECE in the NW Pacific states of America,[20] only one respondent experienced 'hellfire and damnation'. This man appeared to have descended in a downwards direction by mistake and was firmly told to go back. While below stairs, however, he was confronted by 'millions of hateful, miserable people presided over by a "presence": [or] the devil himself . . . [who] had his little horns on'. Another man[21] perceived himself to be wrapped in tinfoil, 'being roasted and turned by devils with tongs . . . and using their very long syringes to inject red-hot fat into [his] flesh'. Other recorded experiences in this genre[22] point to a sense of despair; of seeing other wretched people in seemingly hopeless conditions, or hostile individuals

[19] Rawlings Maurice, *Beyond Death's Door*, New York: Nelson 1978, 116–117 (abridged).
[20] Lindley J, Bryan S, Conley B, *J Near-Death Stud* 1: 104–124, 1981.
[21] Fenwick and Fenwick 1998, 189.
[22] Grey 1985, 56ff; Fenwick and Fenwick 1998, 187ff.

and spirits attempting to pull or even inflict harm on the experient (an event which never physically materializes); or the sensing of an evil force or power. Since many of these recorded encounters are excerpted from an obviously longer, given narrative, it is not always possible to evaluate them within the context of the entire ECE.

Perhaps the most outstanding account, and one exemplary of many of the previously mentioned narratives and sentiments, is that recalled by Ian Wilson of the American, Professor Howard Storm. At the time, Storm was chairman of the Department of Art at North Kentucky University, Cincinnati.[23] While on an artistic tour of Europe, Storm developed severe abdominal pain and was taken to a local Parisian hospital. Having been apparently left in this subacute state overnight, he experienced an OBE during which he floated out of his body. Then he heard voices calling his name (although in *English*) from the corridor outside his room. Storm continues his record of the ensuing events:

I went to the doorway [and in the dimness] the people were 20, 30, 40 feet away—tall and small . . . males and females [as evident from their profiles]. But every time that I would approach somebody they would back off into the mist . . . they wouldn't answer anything directly . . . I couldn't get a straight answer and that bothered me a lot. [He followed these people at their behest]: it felt like we walked for days and weeks but they would chorus me on. And then I started to feel very, very tired and weary, and my stomach was burning [note the intrusion of this-worldly body-sensed (= somaes-thetic) pain and discomfort into the other-worldly event]. The fog was getting thicker and thicker and darker and darker and we ended up like I couldn't see anything not even see my hand in front of my face. The people around me kept moving in closer and closer and closer, so that now they were just beyond my reach. I could feel from their voices where they were and I said 'I'm not going any further, I don't like this at all, I don't like you. I don't want any part of this and I want to go back'. I was swearing at them . . . and they at me . . . and we started yelling and screaming . . . and pushing and shoving . . . and they started hitting me. And I would swing around and try and hit somebody . . . I was kicking and slugging and clobbering, and everything I did they laughed at! I'd make real contact, hitting so hard that I'd really hurt my hand, and the person would laugh hysterically. And meanwhile they were tearing at me . . . and it was incredibly painful. I realize[d] that the point of the whole game was simply to put pain on me, and that my pain gave them pleasure.

[Then] I heard myself coming from inside me, saying to my consciousness: 'Pray!' . . . and so I used little bits and pieces of things that I could remember . . . a few snatches of the 23rd Psalm and a little bit of the Lord's Prayer, all the formal stuff I could think of. The [people around me] didn't like it at all . . . they were yelling and

[23] Wilson I, *Life after Death*, London: Pan Books 1997, 137ff (abridged, with my parentheses).

screaming at me to stop [and not to be a fool]. Nobody could hear me. What did I think I was doing? If I mentioned God they said there was no such thing ... why was I relying on all that superstition and nonsense? I liked the effect it was having on them ... and I became more and more forceful ... swearing, mixing swears with prayers ... and they got angrier and angrier ... but they also got more and more distant until they were all gone.

In the darkness I became aware of a star or small light ... and it started getting very big very fast, and I realized that it was coming straight at me ... and it came right on me and as it did I came back off the floor and all of me came back together ... and I was aware that the light was a Being. And we went out of that place, and there was a strong sense of moving upwards very rapidly ... we travelled together and I was in ecstasy ... having orgasms of every sense and of your intellect ... it was wonderful. I thought 'I'm afraid': then my friend said to me: 'Oh, that's OK. We'll stop here ... We don't want you to be afraid'. (Abridged.)

Wilson continues:

Storm now found himself surrounded by several other Beings of Light, or as he called them, 'centres of radiance', each with slightly different characteristics and slightly different hues of 'a lot more colours than we can see'. Storm was thoroughly humbled by the 'incredible love and perfection and beauty' with which he was surrounded, and felt extremely unworthy. The Beings showed him a holographic-type [*sic*] review of his life. Eventually, having been told by them that he should return [to earth], he argued that he couldn't bear to leave them. As he made the painful decision not to stay, he woke up and found himself being taken to theatre. Importantly, the experience so profoundly affected him that he became converted from staunch atheism, being subsequently ordained in the Zion Church of Christ in Norwood, OH.

In reading these various reports of 'hellish' ECE, it is particularly noticeable that where the information is given, the experient either wakes immediately from the darkness, or then proceeds towards an ever-enlarging light or finds the light coming towards him or her, so that 'hell' now immediately reverts to 'heaven'. The logical, and indeed theological, propriety of such an acute 'U-turn' seems bizarre and, as far as the Judaeo-Christian tradition is concerned, must be unique in the rapidity of the exchange. Yet such a monumental reversal seems never to have been considered odd by the ECE fraternity. From a neurophysiological perspective, other conclusions can be drawn: but first, I consider two further cases discussed by Wilson.

The first, of an Australian woman (with a Gram-negative septicaemia), who sensed she was falling into an abyss ... hell ... which was moist, dark, malodorous and contained nasty shapes. As she fell further downwards she was 'in absolute terror and despair', but as she cried out (for help) she found herself in the arms of someone in heaven. The second, of a cardiac case borrowed from Rawlings.[24] Rawlings was battling with a postman whose heart repeatedly stopped during a cardiac catheterization procedure. Each time circulation was restored the man screamed out that he was in hell, imploring Rawlings not to give up on his efforts to sustain a normal cardiac rhythm. It was also noted that the man was trembling, sweating and expressing an appearance of someone in great inner fear and terror. Finally the man called out: 'Don't you understand? I am in hell...every time you quit I go back to hell...don't let me go back to hell!'. Unfortunately, the subject could not recall what his experiences had been, but before resuming normal consciousness and heart rhythm, he experienced a second other-worldly dimension, but in a heavenly realm.[25]

From these accounts I conclude that the phenomenology narrated by subjects during their sequential episodes while in a subconscious state reflects, not the beginning of an outward journey, but the neurophysiological manifestations of a brain commencing its re-entrant course towards full conscious-awareness. That view is in keeping with the central argument of this book. The obvious variety in the narratives given during the return of these subjects to full conscious-awareness would depend on many factors including the rate of return either from a subconscious twilight zone or a deeper level of unconsciousness, the state of the cardiovascular system including the degree of atherosclerosis, the extent of lowering of blood pressure, and subjects' ages.

Storm, during his NDE, was in such a twilight zone because he was simultaneously and consciously aware of his abdominal pain and the exhaustion due his deteriorating clinical condition. Furthermore, the length of his account reflects a fairly prolonged experience lasting many minutes. The Australian woman's experience was similar to a delirium, and as frightening as those experienced by patients with high fevers, or with acute alcoholic delirium, or so-called 'delirium tremens'. To these latter cases, after withdrawal from alcohol, there may appear apparitions, usually of spiders or mice of the most frightening size, colour, shape and quality.

Clearly, a hellish experience is not the exclusive preserve of ND experients: neither does one necessarily have to be ascribed to a visit to 'hell'. That descriptive label could be applied figuratively to any other allied clinically dependent state, as with the chronic alcoholic or others with prolonged febrile episodes or uncontrolled septicaemia. In the case of Rawlings' postman, we are not told how long the successive periods of cardiac arrest persisted: however, he would have been receiving cardiac and circulatory stimulants which may have influenced the speed at which his brain was re-perfused with

---

[24] Rawlings 1978, 17ff.
[25] Wilson 1997, 150.

blood and thus how long the intervening periods of the subconscious state (when he was in 'hell') lasted. He, like the woman and Storm, all eventually experienced the light and a sense of warmth or even, as with Storm, a moment of supreme ecstasy, the neurophysiology of which states will be discussed in a subsequent chapter. Finally, we note that Storm's fictive rising upwards occurred while he was engulfed in the light and accompanied by a celestial Being. Therefore, a sense of movement does not necessarily have to be tied to the dark 'tunnel' illusion.

1.2.b. Do the Blind See in Heaven?

The issue whether during ECE, the congenitally blind experience visual panoramas identical to those of the normally sighted is an important question. This has been pursued by Kenneth Ring.[26] One point bearing crucially on this matter turns on the interviewing technique employed. It is very difficult to cross-examine blind patients so as to determine precisely what they are attempting to describe from within a non-visual world, relative to the highly visualized world of a twenty-first-century interrogator. It is not evident, therefore, precisely, what is to be understood when a blind person refers to seeing 'grass, flowers, trees and birds'. In their paper, Ring and Cooper make no attempt to verify how all the objects referred to were, or could have been, visually identified.

From excerpts of interim transcripts of interviews, two impressions are immediately apparent: (i) the (mis)use of leading questions by the interviewers and (ii) the full and uncritical acceptance by these interrogators of superficial statements and vague responses given by those interviewed. In stating (idem, p. 119) 'that coming close to death appears to restore [their] sight to normal, and perhaps in a *superior acuity*' (my emphasis), these authors have obviously confused visual sight with hallucinatory 'sight' actually experienced during ECE. Moreover, their attempt to provide third-party corroborative support for objects observed in the real world was extraordinarily weak.

Of all 31 cases cited, only 14 subjects were congenitally blind, of whom 10 experienced NDE, and 4 OBE. In the reporting of selected cases, the authors clearly came up against the difficulty of interpreting precisely what each blind subject is attempting to express. The cognitively perceived meaning given to words by normally sighted persons is quite different from that

---

[26] Ring K and Cooper S, *J Near-Death Stud* 16: 101–147, 1997.

intended by the blind. What do congenitally blind subjects understand by a tree, and what would be drawn if they were given pencil and paper?

Ring and Cooper cite the testimonies of two congenitally blind subjects, 'Vicki' and 'Brad'. Following a collision and having been thrown from her car, Vicki sensed her non-physical body to be like 'light': then she caught a 'glimpse' of the mangled car. Later, she 'observed' her resuscitation, heard the doctors 'talking', but failed to 'communicate' with them. Her OBE converted to an NDE as she floated out of the hospital roof and, while feeling herself ascend upwards, she experienced a great exhilaration. Having then been sucked through a darkened tube, she emerged onto grass in the presence of flowers and trees, being encompassed in 'light' which could be 'felt'. Love emanated from all objects 'seen'. Then her grandmother and two other dead schoolmates 'appeared' before her, the latter now in their (later) prime. She 'gained' total knowledge and understanding, and 'saw' a brightly illuminated figure whom she 'recognized' as Jesus. He 'coerced' her into returning to her heavy, painful body.

Brad, recalling an incident 25 years earlier, developed respiratory arrest during a severe bout of pneumonia. During his OBE he 'saw' his body on the bed and his blind bedmate leave the room to get assistance. One doubts whether that could be a true, calmly observed eyewitness account of a life-threatening emergency involving oneself. Brad then ascended through the ceiling, 'saw' snow outside and the banks created by snowploughs, 'recognized' a children's playground and a hill which he used to climb. 'I remember being able to see quite clearly' (p. 113).

Profoundly serious difficulties in the interpretation of these reports arise. Ring and Cooper initially suggest that blind subjects report 'the same kinds of visual impressions as sighted persons do when describing their OBE and NDE' (p. 115). Unfortunately these reports are not transcribed verbatim, but as edited accounts: thus the interpretation rests on the cognitive percepts of two, normally sighted authors. It requires great care to ensure that what has been written is a completely true reflection of what was stated, and thus intended, by each of the blind subjects interviewed. Vicki is said to have 'observed' her resuscitation, and could 'see' the light. Yet previously she had declared forthrightly that she had never seen light nor understood the concept (of light) (p. 109). If she had never experienced light, then she would neither be able to conceive of, nor be able to verbalize her experiences in terms of a concept (light), of which she had no previous cognitive knowledge or understanding. Furthermore, she apparently 'observed' doctors, 'heard' their voices yet failed to 'communicate' with them (pp. 110–112). I am not sure I can make sense of that: can one supposedly 'see' and 'hear' people yet not be able to communicate with them? Her report, therefore, is no different from other examples given on preceding pages in this chapter and which are not true eyewitness accounts of either the temporal progress, or the evolution, of real events and activities.

Now, on further enquiry by the authors of this paper, both Vicki and Brad modified their original statements. On subsequent interview, they both made it clear that the 'visual' experiences initially conveyed to the interviewer were more like *feelings*, rather than actual *viewings* of objects or scenes. Thus Vicki (p. 117): 'I had a real difficult time. Its really hard to describe because it wasn't visual' (p. 134). And Brad: 'I was aware of the things physically mentioned. However, whether it was seen through the eyes I could not say—it was something like a tactile sense—I could not really say that they were visual per se because I had never known anything like that before' (pp. 134–135). These people were trying to articulate perceptions based on tactile sensing. It is very difficult for normal people to be able to clearly understand what experiences these subjects were attempting to encapsulate through words.

This difficulty is further exemplified in the case of partially sighted Marsha. This is a case study which upholds my earlier criticisms of an exceptionally poor interviewing technique. The result was to secure neither convincing evidence of what Marsha was describing, nor good rapport between Marsha and her interviewer:

Interviewer: Could you describe it? Could you see it in detail? [her body]

    Marsha: Yeah, it just looked like me. I was, like, asleep.

       Int: And how was your vision, if I could put it that way, when you were looking down on yourself?

       M: It was fine . . . It was normal.

       Int: When you say normal, you mean clear?

       M: Yeah, everything. There was no problem with it.

       Int: Were you able to see better than you could in the physical world?

       M: Oh, yeah.

       Int: What was your perception like in this room [in the other-worldly portion of *her* OBE]?

       M: Everything. I could see everything . . . all the people, all the way back. Everything.

       Int: In what way? Could you be a little more specific?

       M: It was perfect. It was not like your eyes to see. I don't know what normal vision would feel like. It couldn't be my eyes because my eyes were back over here. I could see gold . . . on the walls . . . white birds and angels. . . .

       Int: When you saw birds and the people and the room, were you seeing it in detail or just like you see now?

       M: No, no. It was detail. It was white light . . . and gold on the walls.

Apart from the way in which Marsha was led by so many questions, there is, in my view, a complete failure to draw out from her precisely what is meant by the words (a) of attribution—'perfect', 'normal', 'fine', 'white' and (b) those relating to real objects but never visualized like normal people—'gold', 'birds', 'angels'. There was no thoughtful attempt to compare Martha's use of group (a) and (b) words with respect to *our* visual world, *her* experiences during her NDE, or thirdly *her* usual, non-visual internal world which would still have been full of brain-derived conceptual imagery. Of course, in her internal world, she would conceive images of herself and of worldly objects, in addition to her own internalized concepts of the meaning, for example, of the words 'gold' or 'bird'. That is the inevitable result of conversing verbally with normally sighted adult persons. Therefore, it is not at all surprising that Marsha's internal visual world would seem normal to *her*, and hence that 'everything was the way it was supposed to be'. So an ECE is not necessarily the means 'in which "sight" can be restored—even to a superior acuity'. That inference could hardly be correct and, indeed, is most unlikely to be so.

Next, Ring and Cooper turn to corroborative evidence obtained from 31 respondents to support their claim that the blind see in heaven. But unfortunately, neither of the two cases offered in respect of this further critical evidential claim had, in fact, been blind from birth. Let us firstly consider Frank's case. Frank's 'witness' failed to confirm his ability, during a spontaneous OBE, to define the colour and pattern of a tie given to him previously. The female donor in question was alleged to have purchased and delivered the tie. When later contacted, she unfortunately was completely unable to recall the incident, and hence, crucially, could not uphold Frank's claims.

Secondly, for Nancy, allegedly 'seeing' her partner sitting in the hospital corridor during her OBE is hardly novel or convincing. Given that she was having her thorax opened for a *'cancerous chest tumour'*, we are hardly surprised that her friend, Leon, had been expectantly waiting in the corridor outside the operating theatre. In fact, he had awaited news of the surgical outcome for at least 10 hours. In giving his version of events, Leon said he called Nancy by name as she was suddenly rushed out of theatre towards the Intensive Care Unit. The reason for this emergency dash was the result of a gross surgical error (her superior vena cava was completely severed, and then mistakenly re-sutured, resulting in an acute caval obstruction with immediate massive oedema of the face and upper torso and, as would become apparent post-operatively, *blindness*). But Nancy did not respond, either because she was unconscious, or, if still conscious, incapable of doing anything, including catching sight of Leon. And that, unfortunately, was the point at which Nancy's OBE came to an end.

And that, also, is the extent of the 'corroborative evidence' offered by Ring and Cooper. We could hardly be the wiser.

It seems to me that all these accounts have been taken literally by Ring and Cooper as proof that OBE/NDE provide objective evidence for a spiritual world outwith the physical body, and for the existence of an other-worldly realm into which blind ECE respondents have been offered a privileged *visually based* glimpse. With the data presented in this particular paper, I firmly conclude that such alleged proof is unwarranted, and second that the proposed '*spiritualized*' form of sight, denied to these blind subjects in the physical world, is entirely misconceived.

1.2.c. The Exemplary Case of Pam Reynolds

Pam Reynolds was a 35-year-old woman who came to Dr Sabom's attention twenty years after an operation performed for a basilar artery aneurysm (a swelling due to a weakness in the arterial wall and likely to rupture, often with catastrophic results). We are not told what symptoms and over what timescale it had been troublesome. The basilar artery arises from the junction of the two vertebral arteries ascending within the cervical (neck) vertebrae, then continues its upward course on the under-surface of the lower brainstem (into the posterior cranial fossa) to supply the brainstem and posterior parts of the cerebral cortices. Surgical removal of this very large aneurysm was performed in Phoenix, Arizona, by an operative technique termed 'hypothermic [= below normal body temperature] cardiac arrest'.[27]

The procedure requires severe cooling of the patient to 60 °F (normal ~98.4 °F) during which procedure the electroencephalogram and electrocardiogram become flat. While surgery to remove the aneurysm takes place, the cardio-pulmonary bypass machine is turned off so that all blood circulation to the body ceases, while the blood remaining within the brain is drained under gravity by putting the patient into a sitting-up position. From the operative surgeon's notes, this critical phase in the surgical procedure was commenced at 11.25am. By 12 noon cardio-pulmonary bypass was being re-established, although the spontaneous return of the pulse was complicated by episodes of abnormal cardiac rhythm (ventricular fibrillation). A proper heart beat was eventually secured after application of two shocks from the cardiac defibrillator. At 12.32pm, cardio-pulmonary bypass was terminated, at which

[27] Spetzler R, Hadley M, Rigamonti D, Carter P, Raudzens P, Shedd S et al, *J Neurosurg* 68: 868–879, 1988; Williams M, Rainer G, Fieger H, Murray I, Sanchez M, *Ann Thoracic Surg* 52: 1069–1075, 1991.

point her body temperature, although having risen to 89.6 °F, was still significantly hypothermic.

The entire exercise was prolonged. It began at 7.15am when Pam was wheeled into the anaesthetic room, after which the surgeon began cutting out a right-sided posterior bone flap in her skull (around 9am). After 45 minutes he had assessed the aneurysm and decided to proceed with the standstill operation. At around 10.50am he gave the order for cardio-pulmonary bypass, and body cooling, to be commenced. Not until 2.10pm was the patient moved to the recovery room, still with an endotracheal tube in situ, although whether a ventilator was still being used to assist respiration is not given. If that had been the more likely case, then sedation would have been necessary to overcome the continued discomfort of the tube and the interference of the pump with her own respiratory efforts. The use of sedatives would have influenced her ultimate recall of events. At least she was conscious, speaking, and not demonstrating any obvious neurological deficit as a result of the procedure, a position confirmed twenty years later when recounting her story to Sabom. After that long interval, there was no evidence of any persistent brain damage caused either by the severe body cooling or the period of complete circulatory arrest during the operation. The operative details are those abridged by Sabom,[28] who obtained the surgical notes from Phoenix.

Pam's case has become an icon for ECE phenomenologists. That is because she experienced OB/NDE during her operation, supposedly during the period when the EEG and ECG tracings were flat. It is considered remarkable that although her brain and heart monitoring records were those which normally would be ascribed to 'dead' persons, she was able to undergo such experiences, as she later recalled. Let us first observe Pam's own verbal narrative which stands as the complete, unedited account of her experiences. We then consider how Sabom reacted to her story on hearing it several years later: his transcript starts at Pam's first remembered recollection:

Pam's near-death experience began to unfold. She recalls her story in remarkable detail:

The next thing I recall was the sound: it was a natural D. As I listened to the sound, I felt it was pulling me out of the top of my head. The further out of my body I got, the more clear the tone became. I remember seeing several things in the operating theatre when I was looking down. It was the most aware that I think that I have ever been [*sic*] in my entire life. I was metaphorically sitting on [the surgeon's] shoulder. It was not like normal vision. It was brighter and more focussed and clearer than normal vision.

---

[28] Sabom 1998, 37–51, 184–191.

There was so much in the operating theatre that I didn't recognize, and so many people.

I thought the way they had shaved my head was very peculiar. I expected them to take all of the hair, but they did not. The saw thing that I hated the sound of looked like an electric toothbrush and it had a dent in it, a groove at the top where the saw appeared to go into the handle, but it didn't. And the saw had interchangeable blades, too, but these blades were in what looked like a socket wrench case. I heard the saw crank up. I didn't see them use it on my head, but I think I heard it being used on something. It was humming at a relatively high pitch and then all of a sudden it went Brrrrrrrrrr! like that.

Someone said something about my veins and arteries being very small. I believe it was a female voice and that it was Dr [ ], but I'm not sure. She was the cardiologist [*sic*]. I remember thinking that I should have told her about that. I remember the heart–lung machine. I didn't like the respirator. I remember a lot of tools and instruments that I did not readily recognize.

There was a sensation like being pulled, but not against your will. I was going on my own accord because I wanted to go. I have different metaphors to try to explain this. It was like the Wizard of Oz—being taken up into a tornado vortex, only you're not spinning around like you've got vertigo. The feeling was like going up in an elevator real fast. And there was a sensation, but it wasn't a bodily, physical sensation. It was like a tunnel but it wasn't a tunnel.

At some point very early in the tunnel vortex I became aware of my grandmother calling me. But I didn't hear her call me with my ears. It was clearer hearing than with my ears. I trust that sense more than I trust my own ears. The feeling was that she wanted me to come to her, so I continued with no fear down the shaft. It's a dark shaft that I went through, and at the very end there was this very little tiny pinpoint of light that kept getting bigger and bigger and bigger.

The light was incredibly bright, like sitting in the middle of a light bulb. It was so bright that I put my hands in front of my face fully expecting to see them and I could not . . . I noticed that as I began to discern different figures in the light—and they were all covered with light, they were light, and had light permeating all around them—they began to form shapes that I could recognize and understand. I could see that one of them was my grandmother. I don't know if it was reality or projection, but I would know my grandmother, the sound of her, anywhere.

I recognized a lot of people . . . [various relatives] . . . they were specifically looking after me. They would not permit me to go further . . . it was communicated to me—that's the best way I know how to say it, because they didn't speak like I'm speaking—that if I went all the way into the light something would happen to me physically. They would be unable to put me back into the body, like I had gone too far and they couldn't reconnect. I wanted to go into the light, but I also wanted to come back—I had children to be reared.

Then they [deceased relatives] were feeding me . . . [but] not through my mouth . . . something sparkly. I definitely recall the sensation of being nurtured and being fed and being made strong. I know it sounds funny, because obviously it wasn't a physical thing, but inside the experience I felt physically strong, ready for whatever.

My grandmother didn't take me back through the tunnel, or even send me back or ask me to go . . . I expected to go with her but it was communicated to me that she just didn't think she should do that. My uncle said he would do it . . . back through the tunnel. I did want to go. But then I got to the end of it and saw the thing, my body. I didn't want to get into it—it looked terrible, like a train wreck. It looked like what it was: dead. I believe it was covered. It scared me and I didn't want to look at it. It was communicated to me that it was like jumping into a swimming pool. No problem, just jump right into [it]. I didn't want to [but my uncle] pushed me. I felt a definite repelling and at the same time a pulling from the body. The body was pulling and the tunnel was pushing . . . it was like diving into a pool of ice water . . . it hurt!

When I came back, they were playing 'Hotel California' . . . When I regained consciousness, I was still on the respirator.

Pam's OBE occurred at points within the two-hours and ten-minutes interval (8.40–10.50am) during which the surgeon raised the rear, right-sided temporo-occipital bone-flap in order to inspect the aneurysm and assess the feasibility of removing it. Before continuing, we should note that Pam's eyes were lubricated and the eyelids taped together, while special earplugs were inserted into her outer ears in order to transmit tones necessary for monitoring brainstem function. We are not told whether these plugs rendered Pam completely oblivious of all external adventitious sounds. The OBE concerns two aspects of the procedures undertaken during this two-hour period—the use of the saw in raising the bone flap, and the difficulties encountered in achieving satisfactory vascular access to her groins in order to establish cardio-pulmonary bypass.

With regard to the bone flap, I shall consider what Pam alleged she saw and heard: clearly, she was unable to use her eyes. She thought she was sitting on the surgeon's shoulder and looking over him. Yet despite occupying this grandstand position, she provides no account of the cutting procedure, only surprise at the small area of hair that was shaved from her scalp: 'I expected them to take all of the hair, but they did not'. That information, of course, was available to her after the operation and could have been subconsciously woven into her narrative at some later stage. Her description of the bone saw used was inaccurate and did not fit the model actually used in her operation. She heard the bone saw '*crank up*' yet, despite being positioned by the surgeon's shoulder, she (incredibly!) never observed it in use: 'I didn't see them use it on my head but I *think* I heard it being used *somewhere*' (my emphases). That statement indicates, beyond any doubt whatsoever, that she saw nothing of the saw in the theatre on that day, but was only aware of its sound.

The problem arises as to whether she actually did, or could, hear the saw, despite having her ears plugged. Against the possibility that she was unable to hear any externally produced sounds by air conduction, there is no doubt that she actually heard the saw internally, by means of bone conduction. Most of us are familiar with the analogous situation of the dentist's drill whose sound is substantially transmitted through bone, in addition to external air conduction. Similarly, the internalized 'body-image' of the sound of our own voices is predominantly dependent on bone rather than air conduction, explaining why hearing a recording of our own voice seems so different from our inbuilt mental preconceptions of its varying timbres. We should also be aware that the bone flap was cut immediately around the site of her right ear, so that there was direct contact between the scalp bone being severed and her internal ear mechanism (for audition) within the adjacent (petrous temporal) bone on that side.

Sabom alleges during his interview with Pam that she did not perceive anything before hearing the bone saw. He also states that the craniotomy was begun *at the same time* as the groin incisions were being made in preparation for the bypass procedure. Thus Pam's OBE does correspond with the timing of the saw and the alleged conversation about the smallness of her femoral (groin) vessels. However, her account is sequential: Pam clearly derived no information during the operation that the events were contemporaneous. 'I *believe* it was Dr [~][speaking] but *I'm not sure*' (my emphases). We note the complete uncertainty here regarding her testimony. It is as vague as her remarks about the use of the bone saw '*somewhere*' although she was supposedly looking over the surgeon's shoulder and directly into the field of surgery '*with heightened visual acuity*' at the time. The likelihood is that her impression about the conversation could have been inferred post-operatively, relayed to her directly through nursing or medical staff. She would naturally have enquired why *both* groins had been opened when perhaps she only expected one to have been used. Reynolds may have picked up conversations by the same female doctor when she and other members of the surgical team handed over responsibility to the personnel in the recovery suite, while their patient was still sedated, drowsy and possibly cool (her last stated temperature still being in the moderately severe hypothermic range). My own conclusion is that Pam could not have heard the conversation in theatre with earplugs in her ears: her information must have come from another source and those which I have indicated seem to be the most likely.

Finally, some comments on time and timings. We can relate Pam's OBE account to the initial operative procedures when her head and groins were opened: her experiences, however much she was conscious or unconscious, correspond. Yet we should be aware that Pam's account of this phase in her ECE is contained within 325 words for a period exceeding two hours in real time, as documented in the surgical notes. Her account is extremely minimalist and signally fails to provide a proper commentary on the events as they evolved—only fleeting and inaccurate perceptions of two alleged, and importantly, non-sequential happenings, as reported. I conclude that Pam did have an OBE, but it is by no means as impressive as the many others recorded in the literature, and that it clearly occurred well before body cooling was initiated. Pam notes that she did not like the respirator, suggesting that her levels of anaesthesia and sedation were shallow and that she may therefore have consciously been aware of some sounds during the early stages of the operation. Her visual record is unimpressive. She neither saw her head being opened, nor did she competently report the most crucial detail of the operative technique employed: that is, her head was turned *sharply to her left and held there rigidly by a robust, mechanical three-point pin head-holder,* in order to allow the surgeon to proceed. That militates impressively against claims that veridical experiences of external reality occur during OBE (I make more general observations on this point in Chapter 6). All we can be sure about is that during these initial stages of the operative inspection, Pam reported having evanescent glimpses of herself 'looking' over the surgeon's shoulder, giving a puzzling description of the saw which she 'heard' but clearly did not actually 'see' or 'know' where it was being used, and of 'recalling' fragmentary items of conversation about her groin vessels which could have been incorporated into her memory *after she had come out of theatre.* The operation was planned to get her through a technically very difficult piece of neurosurgery, not designed to answer questions about ECE. As a result, the issues become very unclear and indecisive when employed critically as proof of extra-corporeal existence.

Sabom continues his account of Pam's operation and ECE. He arrives at the stage when her body core temperature had been lowered by almost 40 °F. During this stage, bypass having been terminated, there was no measurable blood pressure, pulse, cardiac activity, electrical brain activity or brainstem activity, as assessed through the special earplug monitoring devices. Pam was now in a state popularly known as 'suspended animation'. Yet at this critical juncture in his text, and presumably without intended deception, Sabom offers the following unbelievable comment: 'sometime during *this* period Pam's near-death experience *progressed*' (emphases mine). Sabom therefore implies that Pam experienced the next (NDE) stage in her recorded narrative comprising ascending vortex, expanding light and sight of many deceased relatives, when all bodily function had ceased. That is, when cardio-pulmonary bypass was stopped, her brain had been drained of blood, and her core body temperature had been markedly depressed to 60 °F. That, of course, is impossible, viewed from any physiological perspective. Because her brain (as the 'flat' EEG was taken to indicate) was dormant, it obviously lacked the ability to activate the cerebral processes associated with sensory perception and, importantly, with memory, an essentially necessary function if Pam was ever to recall any of these perceived events at a later time. Thus, to indicate that Pam's NDE commenced during that particular stage of the operation is absurd, as it is likewise for others to believe and transmit, as true fact, what Sabom, without any warrant, is alleging here. Yet Sabom persists: 'During "standstill" Pam's brain was found to be "dead" by all three clinical tests— her EEG was silent, her brainstem responses were absent, and no blood flowed through her brain. Interestingly, *while in this state*, she encountered the "deepest" near-death experience of all [his previously reported] Atlanta Study participants' (my emphases). 'Had the surgeons brought her back from the dead?', he asks. The answer is clearly no, for the additional reason not included by Sabom is that Pam was markedly hypothermic as intended by the procedure, thus protecting her from the prolonged metabolic sequelae of having no functional circulation during that critical period of the operation.

After the aneurysm was clipped, Pam's body was rewarmed through the re-establishment of cardio-pulmonary bypass (between 11.25 am and 12 noon). Here Sabom adds: 'Pam's body appeared to be waking up, perhaps at a time during her near-death experience when she was being strengthened'. The reference marks the occasion when Pam's relatives fed her with '*sparkly stuff*'. At 12 noon, ventricular fibrillation occurred which needed the help of the defibrillator. This occurred at least one, or possibly two, hours before Pam began to regain consciousness. Sabom supposes that this was her ' "return" from her near-death experience', indicative of the moment when Pam's grandmother refused to take her back through the tunnel. That cannot be correct either, as I explain below.

It is very difficult to be certain when Pam first regained conscious-awareness, because she was still on the respirator with her trachea intubated. She thus required sedation in order to allow the machine to have priority in ventilating her lungs. It is unfortunate that we cannot pinpoint Pam's first conscious awakening, since that is the critical key to unravelling her experiences retrogradely. The time of her achieving conscious-awareness is of immense importance, because this moment coincides with the end of her NDE, as clearly defined by her expression: 'it was like diving into ice-cold water... it hurt!' However, I suggest that it most likely occurred between 1 and 2 pm. Pam's account of her 'return' comprises only about 300 words. Extrapolating backwards, it becomes plain that her most recent mental experiences, recalled and formalized in a few hundred words, would have lasted for only one, or at most two minutes immediately preceding, and terminating with, the dive back into her painful carcass. We should observe another very significant facet of Pam's experience. It was, in comparison with many other reported incidents, a rather more prolonged event, and came about not because her brain function was impaired by an acute loss of blood pressure, pulse and cerebral circulation, but because her brain was still warming up (not forgetting that bypass was stopped while her body temperature was still significantly 10 °F *below* normal).

I conclude that Pam's 'NDE' account, from the perceiving of the vortex until jumping into the water, occurred rapidly as a series of interconnected remembered vignettes arising in her mind as the brain was re-perfused and rewarmed and thus able to recommence some semblance of function. At any time point *before* that interval (certainly before 1pm) her brain would have been too cold to have engendered the events experienced and, more importantly, to have set down the necessary memory traces for later recall. Without such properly laid down memories, there could have been no narrative to offer. Sabom's postulated claim that these events occurred considerably earlier, before or around the time when they began rewarming her body from 60 °F, that is, when she was nominally 'dead', even if considered in terms of memory function alone, is therefore completely untenable. We should also observe that the reported OBE was quite distinct from the NDE: these processes, as exemplified here, are separate phenomena.

In summary, the celebrated case of Pam Reynolds is, when critically dissected, most unimpressive and distinctly uninformative. It fails to offer any new insights or novel data pertinent to the field of ECE phenomenology.

In this chapter, I have reviewed the phenomenology of OB and ND experiences, dispassionately evaluated specific examples, and introduced the perspectives taken on their several narratives by five selected key authors. Having established the substantive background to the experiential phenomena, my task in the next chapter concerns a thorough evaluation of the probity of many published accounts and ascertaining whether ECE phenomenology, in general, can sensibly be viewed as endowing its subjects with pre-cognitive and other psychical powers. Following that, there ensues a cross-cultural account of ECE phenomenology, examined from both historical and contemporary geographical accounts. The simplistic naivety seen in some of the historical material casts severe doubt on the authenticity of the events recalled and on the 'celestial places' alleged to have been visited as being located externally to the subject, rather than images most likely to have been constructed by subjects' brains under acute metabolic stress.

2

Surveying Past Horizons

2.1. MAKING SENSE OF THE COLLECTIVE
ECE NARRATIVE

[Sarah] had something else to show that amazed her, and the rest of the surgeons and nurses during her cardiac arrest—the [operating theatre] layout, the scribbles on the surgery schedule board in the hall outside, the colour of the sheets covering the operating table, the hairstyle of the head scrub[bed] nurse...even the trivial fact that her anaesthesiologist that day was wearing unmatched socks. All this she knew even though she had been fully anaesthetized and unconscious during the surgery [for her gallstones and subsequent] cardiac arrest.

But what made Sarah's vision even more momentous was the fact that, since birth, she had been blind. (My parentheses added.)

At face value, this excerpt taken from the book by an American physician, Dr Larry Dossey,[1] appears to be the apotheosis of any exemplary ECE offered by a blind subject. Indeed, it would buttress the assertions of Ring and Cooper that a transcendent form of vision immediately becomes available to congenitally sightless people undergoing ECE.[2] Third, it is also the kind of report certain to be welcomed and employed in encouraging belief (like Pam Reynolds' case) in the validity of OB/ND experiences and their other-worldly significance. However, when challenged by Kenneth Ring[3] to identify the woman responsible for this narrative, Dossey shamefacedly admitted to a cleverly crafted hoax.[4] Given such blatant deception in a text purportedly offered as '*scientific*', we might begin to feel a certain loss of confidence, if not a sneaking sense of disbelief about the entire enterprise.

But is it conceivable that the entire ECE corpus both in its recent contemporary record, and its historical and geographical contours, should be entirely

---

[1] Dossey Larry, *Recovering the Soul: A Scientific and Spiritual Search*, New York: Bantam Books 1989, 17–18 (abridged).
[2] Ring and Cooper 1997.
[3] Ring and Cooper 1997, 102–103.
[4] Wilson 1997, 101.

dismissed as a complete fabrication? Clearly, the impossibility of gaining third-party intelligence on every account offered will always raise the question of veridicality and credibility. A further difficulty is occasioned by the burgeoning literature on ECE phenomenology so that one should always be wary as to whether the testimonials given are always true accounts of experiences actually undergone, rather than subject to the added influence of uncritical reportings by the media and popular press.

In this chapter, my emphasis and concerns will shift to greater in-depth criticism of ECE phenomenology related to its interpretation and meaning and, more generally, to its cultural relativity—historically and geographically. Subjects[5] undergoing an NDE believe themselves to have been rewarded with glimpses of the afterlife and indisputable convictions that an other-worldly domain does exist. Such convictions are private, unassailable and independent of previously held religious belief.

Conversely, the view generally taken by the authors we met in the preceding chapter, as well as many others, that such 'journeys' actually do take place outwith the body, if not the known universe, may be erroneous. It is a view certainly open to other scientifically, and theologically, based interpretations. Such a critique underpins the foundational tenets of the present book. ECE, in my view, are not extra-corporeal events dependent on a dead or dying brain, or the escape of soul, mind or consciousness into a newly discovered paradisean other-world, but illusory phenomena likely to be brought about during restitution of cerebral function as full conscious-awareness is being regained by the subject. That is the difference, a difference which will be asserted and more fully developed below.

2.1.a. Is ECE Testimony Truthful and Believable?

The archetypal protagonist demanding the strictest evidential basis for all statements and propositions of fact, Professor Alfred J. Ayer who held the chair of Logic in the University of Oxford, was found wanting in his published account, 'What I saw when I was dead'. In it, Ayer alleged that a carelessly swallowed sliver of smoked salmon, resulting in asphyxia and a cardio-respiratory arrest, precipitated his NDE. While unconscious, he was 'pulled towards a red light . . . exceedingly bright and painful'. That is a most atypical occurrence. Ayer also experienced encounters with ministers of the universe and was frustrated at his inability to cross the (presumed) River Styx.

---

[5] Ring 1980, 168; Sabom 1982, 186; Grey 1985, 105; Sabom 1998, 196.

Although at first confessing[6] that this experience had 'weakened' his pre-existing stance for the finality of death, Ayer later recanted, on the explanatory ground that his brain had 'not' died during the episode.

In a later interview with Ayer's attending doctor, previously a medical undergraduate at Ayer's own foundation, New College, Oxford, it was established from the case notes that no bits of fish were recovered from Ayer's trachea intubated and inspected during his resuscitation. And on a further occasion when the doctor was curious to learn how a positivist philosopher[7] envisaged the credibility of NDE phenomenology, Ayer surprised him by confessing: 'I saw a Divine Being. I'm afraid I'm going to have to revise all my various books and opinions.'

This case highlights the dilemma of accepting, on trust, reported first-person testimony without independent third-party corroboration. Here is a man who throughout his life purportedly sought 'truth' and its cogent evidential base. Yet, from those aware of the verbal deviations frequently employed to occlude certain of his private indiscretions, Ayer was clearly never averse to bending the data to suit local requirements. His case points up the difficulty about ECE narratives when either personal reputations are at stake, or because of the colossal impact of the experience on subjects' subsequent lives. These narratives also bear heavily on the metaphysical issues of eternity and the possibilities of a spiritual realm beyond the grave, as well as on the eschatological expectations of those within the Judaeo-Christian persuasion.

Of course, there is always the ever-present risk, if not inevitability, that every account will become stylized, stereotyped, and edited in its subsequent tellings and re-tellings.

This becomes less a question of overt deception rather than ironing out irregularities or imperfections in the remembered event thus to render it internally rational, and externally presentable in public. Blanks in the apparent sequence of events, given the extent to which they are remembered and later recalled, are always liable to 'filling in': this is a phenomenon most relevant to the visual system in the cognitive conscious and subconscious modes of day-to-day living, and hence very germane to the issue of ECE reporting. The reporting of events is always subject to observer error and false recall of multiple memory fragments, as evident from witness reports to any

---

[6] Ayer AJ, 'What I saw when I was dead', *Sunday Telegraph*, 28 August 1988, reproduced in Miethe T and Flew A, *Does God Exist?* New York: Harper Collins 1991, 222–228; and in Edwards P (ed), *Immortality*, New York: Prometheus Books, 1997, 275.

[7] Cash W, *National Post*, 3 March 2001; Rogers B, *A.J.Ayer—A Life*, London: Chatto & Windus 1999, 349.

police investigation. Memory is fallible and openly subject to suggestion and deviant perceptions. Indeed, the stereotype ECE is so widely known today that there already exists the danger that it is being consciously implanted into the collective public mind, thus serving as a potential framework driving the content of future constructs of a purported ECE. Another quest of mine is to dispel such mythology.

For example, a 'nowhere' NDE[8] was reported of a woman developing hysterical paralysis and apparent loss of consciousness following an X-ray contrast examination of her spinal column. When the 'crash' team arrived at the bedside, her vital signs were normal. An attempt at tracheal intubation occasioned her prompt return to 'consciousness' and robust refusals of further resuscitative manipulation. In recalling her experience, however, the woman declared that 'she had journeyed across a river, seen her father's face, heard beautiful music and was surrounded by angels. On hearing her husband's voice, she recrossed the river to find herself waking up in his loving arms'. This was a fabricated ND experience throughout, but clearly based on descriptions familiarized through the popular press and journals, and agency of television.

2.1.b. Are ECE Veridical Accounts of Real Events?

This is a crucial outcome: in other words, are the reported events always truthful, or even beyond reproach, when we are considering the validity and ultimate meaning of ECE. For example, as evident from earlier examples concerning the woman knocked down by the black car, blind Marsha, and Pam Reynolds with covered eyes and earplug inserts, their alleged visual experiences could never have been experienced via the normal sensory channels. Each woman lacked normal sight, the one having been temporarily blinded after her collision with the black car, the next—Marsha—being severely partially blind, or Pam Reynolds, whose eyes were taped together as routine protocol for any operative procedure. The sensory data reported could have been inferred from information known prior to the event or culled afterwards, although reported as if directly pertinent to the event itself. The accident victim heard nothing although she was lying in the road where a cacophony of related sounds and noises should have been present. Her auditory world was as silent as a grave while her visual reports were non-sequential, contrary to that expected from a sensible, visually competent eyewitness. Other data, as with Pam's account of the cranial bone saw, were

---

[8] Walker Francis, *J Am Med Assoc* 261: 3245–3246, 1989.

inaccurate. She heard sounds which, given that her ears were blocked (the extent of imposed external 'deafness' cannot be assessed), are likely to have been effected through bone conduction, as explained above. That Pam Reynolds lacked direct insight into her experience is demonstrated by her verbatim reporting of a seamless, unbroken progression of events. That, clearly, was not so.

Auditory awareness persists during anaesthesia,[9] while a heightened sensitivity to conversations of immediate concern to the patient, details of which are remembered, is by no means unusual in surgical practice. For Pam, the noise of the saw and the conversation relating to the smallness of her femoral vessels were both emotionally significant for her. Like the woman knocked down, Pam's account was narrated as a sequential train of supposedly occurrent events, although the evidence from her surgical case notes provided clear, objective evidence to the contrary. Obviously, Pam Reynolds had scant awareness or insight into her surroundings, or of their temporal unfolding, in the operating theatre on that eventful morning. That is another difficulty in accepting her given account.

In addition to the apparent relocation of conscious-awareness to the new and distant perspective or vantage point, commentators have been signally impressed by the apparent heightened sensory awareness accompanying ECE. I note that Ring and Greyson incorporate OB phenomenology into their respective weighted scoring systems in order to determine their apparent 'depth'. That may be inappropriate. Greyson's 'NDE score' regards OBE as a psychical component of a full ND experience.[10] I shall dispute that understanding when considering the neurophysiological basis of body-image in a later chapter. Nevertheless, the outcome has led to the placing of memorable artefacts (objects, or bits of paper with written numbers or words on them), unbeknown to medical staff, around hospital or laboratory areas, hoping that experients during their flights will see these items and report their content to the investigators. In my opinion, based on the case data given, the pursuit of such procedures would be entirely futile. I do not regard NDE and OBE to be entirely veridical experiences of events allegedly undergone: they are not true eyewitness accounts. That is the important outcome of my critique of these experiences.

---

[9] Cherkin A and Harroun P, *Anesthesiol* 34: 469–474, 1971; Wilson S, Vaughan R, Stephen C *Anesthes Analges* 54: 609–617, 1975; Howard J, *Med J Austral* 146: 44–46, 1987; Moerman N, Bonke B, Oostling J, *Anesthesiol* 79: 454–464, 1993.

[10] Greyson 1983, 369.

2.1.c. The Idealized and Somewhat Misleading
Paradigm of Moody

Finally, with reference to the credibility of ECE reportage, I now wish to return to the account given originally by Raymond Moody in 1976, and to expose its imagined idealization of what each experience should be. It is very misleading to read this account in the belief that it portrays an invariant, archetypal sequence to which all experients are subject. This is Moody's account:

A man is dying and, as he reaches the point of greatest physical distress, he hears himself pronounced dead by his doctor. He begins to hear an uncomfortable noise, a loud ringing or buzzing, and at the same time feels himself moving very rapidly through a long dark tunnel. After this, he suddenly finds himself outside of his physical body, but still in the immediate physical environment, and he sees his own body from a distance, as though he is a spectator. He watches the resuscitation attempts from this unusual vantage point and is in a state of emotional upheaval.

After a while, he collects himself and becomes more accustomed to his odd condition. He notices that he still has a 'body', but one of a very different nature and with very different powers from the physical body he has left behind. Soon other things begin to happen. Others come to meet and to help him. He glimpses the spirits of relatives and friends who have died already, and a loving, warm spirit of a kind he has never encountered before—a being of light—appears before him. This being asks him a question, non-verbally, to make him evaluate his life and helps him along by showing him a panoramic, instantaneous playback of the major events of his life. At some point he finds himself approaching some sort of barrier or border, apparently representing the limit between earthly life and the next life. Yet, he finds that he must go back to earth, that the time for his death has not yet come. At this point he resists, for by now he is taken up with his experiences in the afterlife and does not want to return. He is overwhelmed by intense feelings of joy, love and peace. Despite his attitude, though, he somehow reunites with his physical body and lives.

Later he tries to tell others, but he has trouble doing so. In the first place, he can find no human words adequate to describe these unearthly episodes. He also finds that others scoff, so he stops telling other people. Still, the experience affects his life profoundly, especially his views about death and its relationship to life.

It might be argued that Moody's synthesis was cleverly executed, in that while he merely related particular aspects of each of his received testimonies, these were *preceded* by, and incorporated into, his own 'ideal' or 'complete' experience which embodied all the common elements 'in the order in which it is typical for them to occur'.[11]

---

[11] Moody 1976, 21ff.

But beware! This nicely rounded account of an idealized ND experience is deceptively ambiguous for several reasons. First, in being strategically placed at the beginning of his book, such a dramatic account conditions readers before being able to independently examine Moody's evidential testimonies and draw their own unbiased conclusions. Second, Moody declined to give any statistical analysis of the number of respondents experiencing each of the sequential phases of their evolving NDE. This account masquerades as an ideal model. But it is not based on sifted data, but is just representative of opinion conditioned and driven by what Moody imagined *ought* to be the case. There was sufficient information and opportunity from which to construct a provisional hypothesis, but that was not undertaken. Third, Moody had no grounds to speculate that the testimonies which most closely and completely conformed to his model occurred in patients who were 'dead' for the longest periods thus allowing them opportunity to experience a 'deeper form of ND event'. Because of the retrospective nature of the material he was working with, he could not have possessed that necessary kind of information. Fourth, Moody conflates OBE and NDE as *sequential phases of the one experience.* That is a further error on his part. For example, that is not how Ritchie's experience developed. Neither was it the case with Pam Reynolds, whose OBE occurred several hours before her emergent NDE began taking shape.

2.2. CULTURAL RELATIVITY: ECE IN HISTORICAL AND GEOGRAPHICAL CONTEXT

Earlier, I made reference to Ritchie's ECE narrative on account of its failure to conform to Moody's idealized synthesis. But Ritchie's testimony also bears a close relationship to some other historically based accounts of 'other-world' journeys, a literature of which Moody and Ring were initially unaware. Indeed, when publishing their books, they thought they were describing an entirely new phenomenon. Perusal of the historical and geographical ECE literature affirms that there is no universalized typology for this phenomenology: we must take note of the incisive cultural impact.

In the historical literature, the shaman is the prototypical other-world traveller whether venturing into deep, dark caves to the ocean floor, or towards the seventh level of the heavens, occasioned by means of an ecstatic frenzy engineered ritualistically or through some other 'psychophysical charade'. Indeed, Weston La Barre[12] takes the shamanic argument to the extreme in proposing that knowledge of the supernatural derives '*de facto*' from prophets and shamans influenced by hallucinogenic drugs. Thus the supernatural is entirely subjective: the '*mysterium tremendum et fascinans*'[13] simply comes from within. It is the ecstatic trance, dream or fugue about the inner spiritual spark, the yearning for fertility, and the ineffable feeling of escape from the inner anxieties of death creating the need for an immortal, everlasting soul. In states of sensory deprivation or dream-states, the subjective self emerges to reveal its autobiographical signature. Today's priests are merely administrators of the church. Jesus was the great shaman-seer, an impresario of the eternal Spirit and helper God.

2.2.a. Historical Other-World Journeys—Western Approaches

So much for the romantic view! It might do well for some of the world's most esoteric forms of pantheism, but there is scant evidence that Judaeo-Christian monotheism owed it origins to hallucinogenic ritual. Yet the journeys or fugues of shamanic origin are reflected and elaborated in Babylonian, Sumerian, Egyptian, Hebrew and Hellenistic mythical literature. Its remnants are still evident in the Merkabah traditions of Jewish mysticism, the Sufi movement of Islam, Gnosticism and Zoroastrianism, and Christianity in Christ's harrowing of hell. And even, perhaps, in baptism with the idea of being immersed into the 'death' of Christ and rising purified, with him and in him. St Paul's brief (self-)reference (2 Cor 12: 1–4) of a '*curious ascent to the third heaven*' was later elaborated in the third-century MS known as the Vision (or Apocalypse). In this Paul, viewed on a par with Elijah and Enoch, is seen to ascend to heaven and descend into hell to recover souls in dire distress. The detailed description of two observed souls being subject to some rough handling on their way to eternal damnation would be sufficient to strike a note of terror into any medieval malefactor with regard to his own ultimate judgement and threat of eternal fire. Hell's pains are detailed to the utmost.

The dialogue of sixth-century Gregory contains a real account of a near-death experience of a Roman soldier struck down in a plague epidemic. On subsequently regaining consciousness, he gave account of his near-death odyssey. He was confronted by a bridge, below which flowed a dense, foul-smelling river. Beyond it were green fields and beautifully coloured flowers

---

[12] La Barre W, in: Furst Peter (ed), *Flesh of the Gods*, London: Allen & Unwin 1972, 261–278.
[13] Otto R, *The Idea of the Holy*, Oxford: Oxford University Press 1936.

where people in white, their houses, and a sweet-smelling odour, were envisaged. Those burdened with sin fell as they crossed the bridge, while those
unladen by guilt made their way easily to the other side. In that hellish place,
the soldier recognized one person now weighed down in foul slime by a
massive chain—his punishment for over-zealous cruelty on earth. Another
poor individual having slipped over the edge of the bridge was being hauled
upwards by white-garmented spirits while simultaneously restrained by hid-
eous-looking men on the river. As this contest evolved, the soldier was sent
back to his body, so he was never able to recount what ultimately happened to
the unfortunate victim.

Bede's history (1968) of the English people and church, written in AD 731,
contains an account of an eighth-century Northumbrian nobleman called
Drycthelm, who was a devout man.[14] He fell ill and deteriorated until one
night when the 'crisis' came he appeared to have died (this is also likely to
have been acute pneumococcal lobar pneumonia, as in Ritchie's case). By
daybreak however he returned to life and sat up, much to the horror of those
weeping and keeping vigil at his bedside. After they had fled only his wife
remained, to whom he declared: '*Do not be afraid . . . for I have truly risen from
the grasp of death . . . and I must not live as I used to*'. Indeed, he joined a
monastery forthwith, was tonsured and allocated a room within the monastic
house, spending the rest of his life in prayer and taking frequent baths in ice-
cold water.

As Bede continues his account of the journey, Drycthelm is being guided by
a man clothed in shining white:

we walked in a north-easterly direction until we came to a very broad and deep valley
of infinite length. The side to our left was dreadful with burning flames, while the
opposite side was equally horrible with raging hail and bitter snow blowing and
driving in all directions. Both sides were filled with men's souls, which seemed to be
hurled from one side to the other by the fury of the tempest. For when the wretches
could no longer endure the blast of the terrible heat, they leaped into the heart of the
terrible cold: finding no refuge there, they leaped back again to be burned in the
middle of the unquenchable flames. A countless host of deformed spirits was tormented far and wide in this wretched condition without any interval of respite as far
as the eye could see, and I began to think that this was Hell, of whose intolerable
torments I had often heard tell. But the guide said: 'Do not think this; for this is not
Hell as you imagine'. When he had led me to the further end, much alarmed by the
terrible scene, I saw the place suddenly begin to grow dim, and darkness concealed
everything.

---

[14] Bede, *A History of the English Church and People*, London: Penguin Classics 1968, 289ff.

And as we went on through the nocturnal solitary gloom, frequent masses of dusky flames suddenly appeared before us, rising as though from a great pit and falling back into it again. These masses of flame continued ceaselessly leaping up and falling back again into the depths of the chasm, and I saw that, as the tongues of flame rose, they were filled with the souls of men which, like sparks flying up with the smoke, were sometimes flung high in the air, and at others dropped back into the depths as the vapours of the fire died down. Furthermore, an indescribable stench welled up with these vapours, and filled the whole of this gloomy place. When I had stood there for a long terrified time, I suddenly heard behind me the sound of the most hideous and desperate lamentation, accompanied by harsh laughter, as though a rough mob were mocking captured enemies. As the noise increased and drew nearer, I saw a throng of wicked spirits dragging with them five human souls howling and lamenting into the depths of the darkness while the devils laughed and exulted. I saw among them one man tonsured like a clerk, a layman, and a woman. The wicked spirits dragged them down into the centre of the burning chasm, and as they descended deeper, I could no longer distinguish the weeping of the men from the laughter of the devils, but heard only a confused noise in my ears. Meanwhile, some of the dark spirits emerged from the fiery depths and rushed to surround me, harassing me with their glowing eyes and foul flames issuing from their mouths and nostrils. They threatened to seize me with the glowing tongs that they brandished in their hands, but although they frightened me, they did not dare to touch me. [Then] there appeared behind me a bright shining star which grew in size as it approached me. As it approached, all the evil spirits took flight.

The newcomer whose approach put them to flight was my former guide. He soon brought me out of the darkness into an atmosphere of clear light, and as he led me forwards in bright light, I saw before us a tremendous wall which seemed to be of infinite length and height in all directions. As I could see no gate, window, or entrance in it, I began to wonder why we went up to the wall. But when we reached it, all at once—I know not how—we were on top of it. Within lay a very broad and pleasant meadow, so filled with the scent of spring flowers that its wonderful fragrance quickly dispelled all the stench of the furnace that had overcome me. The light flooding all this place seemed greater than the sun's rays at noon. In this meadow were innumerable companies of men in white robes, and many parties of happy people were sitting together. I began to wonder whether this was the Kingdom of Heaven, but my guide said: 'No, this is not the Kingdom of Heaven as you imagine'. When we had passed through these abodes, I saw ahead much more lovely light, and heard in it a sweet sound of people singing, while a scent of such surpassing fragrance emanated from the place that the earlier scent now seemed quite trifling. And even the wonderful light flooding the flowery meadow seemed thin and dim compared with that now visible. Hoping that we should enter this delightful place, my guide suddenly halted and, without stopping, retraced his steps and led me back along the road by which we had come.

'Do you know what all these things are that you have seen?' 'No', I replied. Then he said: 'The valley with burning flames and icy cold is where souls are tried and punished who delayed confessing and had recourse to penitence at the hour of death. Because they confessed only at death, they will be admitted to the Kingdom on the Day of Judgement. But many are helped by the prayers, alms and fasting of the living, and especially by the offering of the Masses. The fiery noisome pit is the mouth of Hell, and whosoever falls into it will never be delivered throughout eternity. The flowery place is where souls are received who die having done good, but are not so perfect as to merit immediate entry into the Kingdom. But at the Day of Judgement they shall all see Christ and enter upon the joys of His heavenly Kingdom. And whoever are perfect in word, deed, and thought, enter the Kingdom as soon as they leave the body. You must now return to your body . . . but if you will weigh your actions with greater care and study to keep your words and ways virtuous and simple, then when you die you will win a home among these happy spirits'. Meanwhile, I know not how, I suddenly found myself alive among men once more.

A final glimpse at this literature comes from the Second Vision of Adomnan, written about the eleventh century in Ireland. Its origin was based on the presupposition that the Feast of John the Baptist in 1096 would bring apocalyptic horrors of the Day of Judgement: certain signs indicated this forthcoming catastrophe. It was based on the fable that an Irish monk, Mog Roth, had played a role in the Baptist's beheading such that the Irish people had been singled out for special treatment. This mythology was endorsed by the Vision, which described the Heavenly City on a hill and guarded by gates and gatekeepers. In front were two bridges, one which broadened nearer the city and was for the righteous; the other, which became progressively and impossibly narrow, was for all sinners who, on crossing, could only view the City in the distance, thence being destined to fall off into the pit below. There they would be tormented by fire that wrapped around them and came down in showers. There were specific torments designed for bad kings, morally lax people and irresponsible schoolteachers who, in addition to suffering additional rings of fire about their necks, were coerced into eating rotten dog flesh given to them by those children whom they had ill-informed in the classroom.[15]

2.2.b. Cross-Currents—Hints of Eastern Promise

Examples have already been presented of the cultural influences which clearly inform the narrative content of ECE. Drycthelm's recounted imagery is impressively descriptive of the rich, imaginative, metaphorical world of the medieval

---

[15] Hudson Benjamin, Time is Short, in: Bynum C and Freedman P (eds), *Last Things: Death and the Apocalypse*, Philadelphia (PA): University of Pennsylvania Press 1999, 101.

mind, notably with its somewhat naive depictions of heaven and hell. In contrast, the modern allusions to hell speak of dark, incommensurable voids, with people seen as wretched individuals devoid of hope, sometimes fighting each other or the experient who, importantly, never bears the residual marks of such assaults on the physical body, as Storm's account reveals. Thirdly, we witness in some accounts a sudden progression from experiences of hell followed by an experience of heaven, occasionally with a rescue by a heavenly being or angel. Such an abrupt switch, in what in real time could only occupy a few minutes, is inconsistent with the Christian tradition's sequence of the Last Things.

Our attention now turns to comparisons between typical western forms of ECE and those reported from other parts of the world. My reasons for this are that there are comparative reports, both historical and geographical, which contrast with the western-based material perused so far. For example, there are reports from fifth–sixth-century China providing dramatic contrasts with those recorded by Bede. Next, we have contemporary reports from the Pacific Rim and from India providing further stark contrasts with the current reportage typical of America and England. We travel to regions where Christian monotheism is not the predominant religious persuasion and, where the full influence of westernized cultural ideology has yet to pervade and colour the many communities inhabiting the more extreme parts of the globe.

Dr Allan Kellehear, the Australian sociologist,[16] makes the important point, however, that as 'westernization' creeps ever eastwards, the opportunities for examining pure cultures and societies not yet tainted by such influences will become progressively reduced. So, although reports from such areas are not vast in terms of numbers interviewed or ECE cited, they are of crucial value in providing the evidential basis that culture influences the experiential phenomenology reported by individuals inhabiting non-western civilizations. Indeed, the contextual background to NDE, worldwide, provides the necessary material from which the brain utilizes and conjures the relevant phenomenologies alluded to above and explored further below.

One approach in the attempt to universalize ECE, thereby proposing that they do represent an other-worldly realm, has been to identify key features specific to all reported ECE. I think there is a difficulty in applying that attempt as a working principle. Even in our samplings of the western literature, we have seen that recalled narratives do not follow an invariant blueprint. That is the manifest problem with the approaches of Moody, Ring and others. Yet, it has been urged that the 'tunnel' phenomenon and 'life review', for example, represent such unifying criteria. For example, an approach in establishing the

---

[16] Kellehear A, *J Nerv Ment Dis* 181: 148–156, 1993.

tunnel percept as a fundamental canon of ECE phenomenology was attempted by Dr Susan Blackmore.[17] Of 19 responses to an advertisement placed in *The Times* newspaper of India, six cases fulfilled NDE, but based solely on criteria derived from studies conducted in the West (i.e. Moody, Ring etc.). Of these six cases, one subject alleged he 'floated in a dark space'; two sensed upwards movement, one of whom also saw non-motile coloured spots; while a fourth subject, whose head was spinning round at an unimaginable speed, 'travelled a few million miles . . . towards a bright light'. The sixth subject felt herself 'going through complete blackness [accompanied by] a tinkling sound of tiny bells in [her] ears'. In passing, we should take note of the marked auditory inputs together with perturbations of body-image in space (vestibular components of acceleration and rotational spinning) giving rise to the illusion of fictive motion (see Chapter 6) accompanying these experiences.

Based on these self-reported, uncorroborated accounts, she concludes that 38% (3/8 cases) is a representative estimate of 'either tunnels, specifically, or . . . dark places' within the Indian population, and thus is 'in line with western data'. This is a most extraordinary and extremely brave statistical conclusion to arrive at, given the paucity of Blackmore's three contributory data points. Such a weak conclusion was rightly criticized by Pasricha[18] and colleagues, whose investigations involved detailed systematic analyses of ECE in several northern and southern Indian provinces (see below). Notably, there are very significant cultural divides between north and south India with regard to education, ability to speak English, adoption of western ways of life, religious persuasions, social customs and even dietary staples. The gross bias, therefore, in soliciting views from an English-speaking, northern (Indian) newspaper is immediately apparent. Kellehear,[19] in an extensive comparison between western and non-western ECE, concluded that each is culturally bound and to some extent influenced by historic religious traditions (Christianity and Hinduism). He is obviously impressed by the absence of 'tunnel' phenomena, and the apparent sparseness of OBE and western-type 'life reviews' among non-western (American and European) peoples. The type of non-western 'review' usually takes the form of a book presumed to reveal all the details of the subject's previous life. Dr Kellehear sees tunnels, literally, as modes of actual passage from one place to another, or symbolic of

[17] Blackmore S, *J Near-Death Stud* 11: 205–217, 1993b.
[18] Pasricha S, Stevenson I, *J Nerv Ment Dis* 174: 165–170, 1986; Pasricha S, *Nat Inst Ment Health Neurosci J* 10: 111–118, 1992; Pasricha S, *J Sci Explor* 7: 161–171, 1993; Kellehear A, Stevenson I, Pasricha S, Cook E, *J Near-Death Stud* 13: 109–113, 1994.
[19] Kellehear 1993.

rites of passage or transfer, from one physical or spiritual domain to another. The life review is inculturated in western society as a mirror of personal probity, self-esteem and confidence. In more 'primitive' cultures or societies, such attributes may reside in the co-active consciousness of community as symbolized in the natural artefacts of plants, trees, stones and rocks, or weather. Kelehear's argument may find additional support elsewhere in the relationship between experients' phenomenology and its causative agent.

My own view here is that it may be a conclusion based on too narrow an interpretation related solely to social custom and mores while not considering, for example, the underlying neurophysiological possibilities. Again, it is important to point out that some investigators have not evaluated personal ECE phenomenology, but looked rather at generalizations about cultural trends, beliefs and traditions, without the accompanying certainty that the terms used by these subjects, such as OBE, NDE, soul, spirit, were understood in the same way in which those investigators intended, given the wide linguistic distances and nuances in understanding. Others,[20] for example, have looked for demographic attitudes towards psychical and paranormal phenomena which do not provide detailed information about personal experiences of OBE/NDE.

2.2.c. Strange Goings-On around the South-East Pacific Rim

Next, I turn to reports from the south-east Pacific region: first from the Elema, Gulf Kamea and Rigo peoples of Papua New Guinea. This is more a review of beliefs and experiences among these peoples than a collected anthology of specific events recalled by particular individuals. Only the Kamea and Rigo have beliefs in OBE and an afterlife. Much of the folklore is based on magic and the role of sorcerers whose identity is unknown or a closely guarded secret. It is doubtful whether the Kamea know what an OBE is like (as defined on western criteria): their response to being questioned was that during sleep, or at death, the spirit often leaves the body, while sorcerers can induce an OBE themselves. How that is accomplished is far less certain, because of the secrecy and hence lack of public knowledge surrounding these activities. The Rigo have similar beliefs that the spirit may leave the body at night, known as the natural OBE. Magic OBEs, on the other hand, are self-induced by (female) sorceresses under the influence of drugs obtained from

---

[20] Haraldsson E, Gudmundsdottir A, Ragnarsson A, Loftsson J, Jonsson S, in: Roll W, Morris R, Morris J (eds), *Research in Parapsychology*, New York: Harper Collins 1977, 182–186.

plants: these sorceresses can help other people make long nocturnal journeys while their bodies remain in the bed.

While interesting, these accounts do not provide evidence that ordinary people leave their bodies or ever have transcendental journeys to the spirit world as a result of the medical conditions identified in the west as triggers. In these remote regions, death comes early in life, medical facilities are poor and not well developed, so that resuscitative techniques, such as the west is accustomed to, occur rarely. Thus, there is little opportunity for a corpus of subject-originating accounts of ECE phenomenology to accrue which informs us and hence permits comparisons with that of western culture. Nevertheless, the accounts obtained[21] reflect a marked cultural influence on what is believed about the body, death and the afterlife.

Another allied study comes from the Kaliai people of West New Britain, Papua New Guinea.[22] These people have been continuously missionized by the Roman Church since 1949, so cultural aspects of their society have been tainted by western religious concepts for at least one generation. Despite that, Counts averred that the traditional Melanesian socio-cultural ethic, together with its former cosmology, still remain intact. Thus, the concept of a unitary cohesion of spirit (or 'soul', this latter being a westernized religious accretion to their vocabulary) is alien: the spiritual aspect comprises either an 'essence' or 'image' (=shadow). Illness results in an escape of the spirit from the physical body, thence being unable to reunite with it until the illness is cured: if not, death ensues. In those circumstances the subject's essence, or image, might be seen several miles away. At death, the spirit component hovers around the deceased's grave until decomposition of the corpse begins. Only in latter times has the idea of a 'soul' rising directly to God arisen, an event dependent on a mass being said, and only if the relatives can afford it. A second concept (pronounced 'mate', analogous to the Hebrew participle מת meaning dead) refers to the sick, the old and infirm as well as the dead, and thus defines a state that may persist for many years. Death is a prolonged event, beginning with unconsciousness, staring eyes, restlessness and sphincter relaxation and finally an absence of pulse, heart beat and respiration. The corpse is viewed publicly until bloating sets in, when it is buried.

One man, a headmaster, became very ill with difficulty in walking (possibly an acute septic knee joint, but the details preclude firm diagnosis), generalized bodily aches or pains and loss of appetite. He became aware of ancestors taking him along a road that led to a white, bearded man shrouded in long white garments, and appearing as if illuminated. There was a reversal and he

---

[21] McIntosh A, *J Soc Psychic Res* 50: 460–478, 1980.
[22] Counts D, *J Near-Death Stud* 3: 115–135, 1983.

was told to go home, having first had ginger rubbed into his leg (a folk remedy for overcoming sorcerer-induced wound infection).

A second young man had appeared to his family to be dead, so preparations for the funeral rites and the digging of his grave were put into effect by family and villagers. When he died, 'everything went dark, but I went through a field of flowers . . . I walked along a road and met two men at a fork. I had to decide which way to go and followed one into a village'. He was taken up the outside stairs into a house (a customary stilted dwelling) where he heard a voice say that it was not time and he must go back. The house then began to revolve as if suspended in space, another neurological manifestation of a disturbed body-image mechanism. Rather than attempt to get out, the man began describing the interior contents of the dwelling-house, which now, bizarrely, contained men with steel, while others were engaged in building ships and cars. 'I was to come back, but there was no road . . . so [I] followed a beam of light and walked along it.' That somehow got him down the steps of the house. On glancing back he saw that there was no longer any house but only a forest and a narrow path. He returned by way of the path to his family house and re-entered his body. He said he was unconscious for six hours. He had a desire to return to the scene of his experience because it was a 'happy place'.

A third account came from a man who was a plantation labourer. He 'fainted', was taken to his house and put to bed. He was 'unconscious' for over two days and was pronounced dead on arrival at a medical aid post. Then he was met by a friend and uncle whom he followed along a path. The two men went up into a house, but from which the man was barred from entering by a fence. He therefore continued his journey alone and came across more houses, his arrival being announced by a loudspeaker. People on the balconies of the raised houses pointed at him and told him to sit on a series of magnets. Having not been retained by them, he was presumed to be innocent and invited upstairs into one of the houses. Another man was not so lucky: his body was carved up and his bones ground up in a machine, boiled, placed on a plate and eaten by a dog and pig. This long story (herein abridged) ends with encounters with his daughter, she having brought him into his house after the original fainting episode, and then with another woman with bloodshot eyes and tongue hanging down to her chin.

This account is extremely bizarre, and dreamlike, and the hallucinations could have been related to his illness of which we have no clinical details. He goes on a journey, is 'tried' by the magnet test and acquitted, has further visionary experiences including a light, and then wakes up. His experience thus occurs in the terminal phases of his period of unconsciousness and would have lasted a few minutes compared with the two-day period when he had no apparent conscious-awareness. The visionary part of his encounters is highly culturally dependent. It is based on his own secluded way of life and lacks the contours of a 'heaven' typically pervading the narratives offered by English or American subjects. The two earlier accounts do have some resemblance to 'western-type' ECE. Case 1 saw an illuminated figure that interestingly, given this man's western education, was white and clad in white robes, being encountered after he had journeyed along a path. There was a visionary experience of men dancing and singing followed by the application of ginger to his leg immediately before he regained consciousness. The second young man experienced a period of darkness, then a field of flowers followed by a visionary experience of people and a beam of light along which he travelled in order to reach home. His period of unconsciousness seemed to be accurately timed at six hours, yet the experience narrated could only have lasted a few minutes, ending with his return to full consciousness.

All the stories exhibit bizarreness, illogicalities and disjointedness, just as in subconscious dream-states. Yet all the experiences contained elements of a journey, some semblance of a trial or intended review, except in the case of the second man, and a 'light' in the form of a westernized individual in white robes or other visionary scenes experienced in the light, or involving a beam. The visionary scenes were highly culturally biased, through either indigenous or westernized influences. In summary, all these experiences were transitory events of differing length, as reckoned both from their respective word counts, and through extrapolating backwards from the time-point at which the experiences came to an end; that is, when they *coincided* with the re-establishment of full conscious-awareness.

2.2.d. The Indian Experience

I now return to India to consider more fully Pasricha's systematic studies around Bangalore, south India. These studies were preceded by a smaller survey in north India.[23] Its results revealed a general pattern in which each subject was taken by messengers to appear before a person or committee with a book, followed by the realization that each of the persons summoned either was not ready for death or had been mistaken for others of the same name. There were reprimands for those who had brought these subjects to the committee, after which every victim returned home. There are reflections of Hinduism here, since the messengers are Yamadoots belonging to Yama, or Yam-raj, the Hindu god of death and his bookkeeper, Chitragupta. These encounters were not pleasant, ecstatic or heavenly in the manner of western

---

[23] Pasricha and Stevenson 1986.

NDE. There was also bizarreness, as with a man who had his legs amputated so preventing his return. Once the mistaken call was realized, he was shown a collection of severed legs from which he was able to identify those belonging to himself and which, somehow, were then re-attached. Another man reported that the individual who pushed him back (to earth) had a very hot hand: the man narrating this incident was febrile because on regaining consciousness, he developed an abscess on his arm necessitating treatment by a local physician. Presumably his experience was a delirium-induced hallucination caused by the developing infected focus.

Like Storm, whose abdominal pain and weakness were apparent to him during his ECE, this man's incipient abscess likewise intruded into the content of the experience. In other words, a conscious sensory (or somaesthetic) sensation can be experienced *simultaneously* within the context of an ECE. That surely indicates a functioning aspect of the brain occurrent in the physical world and yet coexisting with a hallucinatory, other-worldly experiential event in another part of the same brain. Other commentators might still insist that the story was a spiritual or other-worldly event, but would not agree. Indeed, it is directly analogous to conscious/dream-state coincidences that have been well documented during lucid dreaming, narcolepsy and other abnormalities of sleep-based experiences, and for which no connotation of an extra-physical dimension or spiritual realm would realistically be thought, or even considered, to be their likely underlying mechanism(s).

Pasricha's other studies involved villages around Bangalore.[24] Thirteen ECE were recorded, the overall rate per population being 1–2%. The small numbers render a realistic comparison with northern India impossible. Taken together, all her studies revealed that subjects were taken to other realms (the Kingdom of the Dead, or Yamapatna) by Yama's messengers (Yamadoots) or someone else; were sent back because of mistaken identity or because they were not ready to die; or who returned volitionally. The cultural–religious influence of Hinduism is nevertheless obvious. No tunnels were observed, contrary to Blackmore.[25] Another specific feature was that subjects alleged that they were either injured or branded during their ordeal. Marks were offered in proof, but there was no independent corroboration that the disfigurements existed *before* the occurrence of the events recalled. There was only one coexisting OBE. The majority of subjects (70%) did not revise their attitudes to death and there was no reporting of life reviews or judgements. Despite the systematic approach employed in these studies, we should remember that the incidence of ECE was extremely low (<2%) and also note

---

[24] Pasricha 1992, 111–118: idem 1993, 161–171.
[25] Blackmore 1993b; and see Kellehear et al 1994.

the precariousness of Pasricha's subject database in relation to the overall population (~800 million) of India.

These are nevertheless interesting studies revealing a clear bias towards Hinduistic figures associated with death. The entire series is so small that other definitive conclusions about Indian-type ECE cannot be made with certainty. For example, there is no warrant for claiming that 'tunnels', or even 'movements towards a light' are either prevalent or not, within this society at large. Only considerably larger studies countrywide could ever hope to resolve such issues. Nevertheless, Blackmore did elicit some experiences of darkness and tunnel-like experiences from northern Indian, *Times*-reading subjects presumably subject to western influences. Nevertheless, it must be borne in mind that even for western ECE, the prevalence of tunnels is only about 30%, and of the [L]ight and its associated phenomenology, ~50–60% of experients sampled.

2.2.e. Tales from Medieval China

In another interesting approach to the analysis of cultural influences on ECE, Karl Becker[26] informs us about the origins of 'Pure Land' (Ching T'u School) Buddhism in China. The evolutionary history of Buddhism in China was moulded by a strong, pre-existing respect for the dead and even ancestor worship. This social ethos depended on belief in a soul which hovered around the body until disposed of, thence to haunt the house or go to some other paradisal locus. The fate of souls could be influenced by family prayers offered during the forty-nine days elapsing from death. Mourning rituals by the deceased's immediate family were widely practised including fasting, praying, making penances and wearing sackcloth. The unitary sense of body and soul in the history of Chinese thought came into conflict with the concept of Buddhistic *anatta*, that of the illusoriness of material existence. Such concepts were sidelined in Ching T'u. Instead, use was made of little-used sutras which provided some legitimacy for pre-existing views concerning body, soul, death, cosmology and the afterlife. In this emergent system, heaven was portrayed as a bejewelled realm full of beautiful flowers and fountains attainable by all through faith and piety. Continuity of the soul took precedence over the Buddhist idea of continual rebirths in the achievement of nirvana. There also derived a hierarchical notion of heaven and hell, presided over by a type of chief minister, Yen-lo, analogous to and derivative of the Hindu God of Death, Yama(raj). Of the several Bodhisattvas (those about to achieve nirvana

[26] Becker K, *J Near-Death Stud* 1: 154–171, 1981.

associated with these developments), Amida (first–second centuries) presided over the western Pure Land.

Becker[27] was at pains to trace the early origins of Ching T'u in China, by inspecting the accounts and experiences of its 'patriarchs' during the first five centuries of its development, but mainly from the fourth century onwards. By that time the bodhisattva Amida had come to be revered as a supernatural, deific figure through whom a pathway to salvation could be secured. The first of these Pure Land masters was Tao-an. In AD 385 when he died, it was recorded that 'a strange priest appeared [to him] and pointed to the north-west where the clouds opened and a beautiful heaven became visible to his dying eyes'.

Tao-an's pupil, Hai-yuan, encouraged the burgeoning devotion to Amida. He founded the White Lotus Society because it is in the lotus, at the middle of a clear lake, that people are finally reborn into a realm without craving or suffering. Hai-yuan is recorded to have had many visions of the Bodhisattva of Infinite Light, often associated with bouts of fever throughout his later years. A later disciple was Seng-chi, about whose dying moments the following account is recorded:

He was afflicted by a grave disease, and then he devoutly wanted the Western Country . . . he asked the monks to gather at night and recite for his sake. During the fifth watch, Chi handed the candle to his fellow-students and requested them to go around with it among the monks. Then he lay down for a moment, and in his dream, he saw himself proceed through the void, still holding the candle, and he beheld the Buddha Amitabha who took him up and placed him on the palm of his hand: in this position he went through the whole universe in all directions. Suddenly he awoke and told everything about his dream to those who nursed him, who were grieved at this sign of approaching death and yet consoled at his vision. When he examined his own body, there were no longer any signs of disease and suffering whatsoever.

The following night, he suddenly sought for his sandals and stood up, his eyes looking into the void with anticipation, as if he was seeing something. A moment later he lay down again, with a joyful expression on his face. Then he said to those who stood at the side of the bed: 'I must go', and when he had turned over on his right side, his life breath and his words became simultaneously extinguished.

Another similar experience later befell a fifty-year-old northern Chinese Taoist, T'an-luan:

On one occasion he recovered from a serious illness when he suddenly saw a golden gate open before him. With this experience, he decided to search for an elixir that would bring about everlasting life . . . On his way back to the north he met the

[27] Becker K, *J Near-Death Stud* 4: 51–68, 1984.

Buddhist monk Bodhiruci, who told him that in Buddhism there was a formula for attaining everlasting life that was superior to that of the Taoist. Upon being asked to reveal the formula, Bodhiruci taught him the texts of the Pure Land school, whereupon T'an-luan became so convinced that he discarded the Taoist texts which he had obtained, and concentrated on the attainment of the western (Amida) Paradise. This conversion took place about 530 (AD) and for the remainder of his life he devoted all his time to the propagation of the Pure Land tenets.

Here Becker notes that a northern Chinese Taoist, having been told of the Amida school, travelled to south China to seek out this new means of attaining eternal life and, secondly, in doing so renounced his indigenous Chinese Taoism for an imported Buddhism now adopted and developed by the Ching T'u school. Bodhiruci must have perceived the parallel between T'an-luan's visionary experience and the concept of the heavenly realm which underpinned Amidaist piety. Conversely, that same parallel obviously convinced T'an-luan to give up fifty years of one practice in favour of the one that had made sense of his vision as its earthly manifestation, as witnessed in the discipline of Amidaism. The monumental effect of that vision on the future lifestyle of a fifty-year-old man, steeped in another tradition until that moment of conversion, should not be underestimated.

There is a thread of identity traceable in these historic accounts. Each individual was subject to some kind of illness, fever or bodily frailty resulting in an experience akin to NDE while they still lived. Subsequently there was renewed earthly vigour in the physical body. Following that, there occurred a conversion experience involving a considerable change in philosophy or beliefs. The change in outlook represented a major, radical change after almost a lifetime's study of the indigenous Tao or Yogi disciplines to that of the (imported) Amida school. Such conversions were accompanied by a fervour to set up new monasteries, expand the community of faithful monks and preach widely to the common folk. These events are highly cultural, the visions being of the deified and revered Buddha Amida: he is therefore a 'Christlike' figure who, as an extremely holy man on earth (Bodhisattva), preached and did good works before returning to heaven in his final rebirth as a Buddha.

These accounts provide important parallels to those historic western narratives concerned with other-world, spiritual journeys. It is evident that the latter (eastern) narratives were hostage to prevailing cultural paradigms extant at their time of writing. They resonate particularly with Drycthelm's visions of the heavenly city, and of the excruciating torments of hell depicted, and his unity of purpose in shaping the remainder of his life. That, as we have seen, involved a subsequent term of extreme piety and personal hardship thus to ensure certainty of attaining those delights of which his visionary journey had revealed such tantalizing insights.

2.3. THE ARGUMENT SO FAR

2.3.a. Some Pertinent Critical Observations

I have considered in this chapter whether the written corpus of ECE phenomenology is credible, can always be trusted as representative of the experiences alleged to have befallen its subjects, and is not merely a stylized, or even imaginary acount of some previous dream-like state that may have taken place. Despite some notable exceptions, one must conclude that the experiences reported are, in general, regarded as real by those undergoing them. Nevertheless, one should beware: I have drawn attention to certain authors and experients whose accounts have not always been entirely consistent with the facts. Furthermore, there is always the risk that events recalled by subjects, because of the ever-present fallibility of memory, will be modified to render the story intelligible and presentable to a probably sceptical audience. In addition, we must always be alert to the influence of the media in conditioning reports and even bringing predetermined biases to the narratives offered. This is the problem of trying to get a handle on first-person subjective experiences: I shall be offering novel ways of breaking that impasse in a later chapter.

Given that we can accept the reported phenomenology of ECE, the need arises to offer explanatory hypotheses, from third-party perspectives, why it occurs. For all the authors introduced in Chapter 1, there is a common belief that OBE and NDE are, or could be, manifestations of life outwith the physical confines of body or brain. In their view the attainment of that transitory life is envisioned as an escape of soul or of mind or free consciousness into the other-worldly realm. That soul or mind is able to make a journey and have a glimpse of that realm, is a natural consequence of such a position. But we must note important caveats to that published viewpoint.

First, contra Moody and Ring in particular, there is no canonical sequence definitive of the evolving phenomenology which any one subject could expect to undergo. Several verbatim examples have been quoted which contradict that kind of idealized construct. Second, if there were a canonical sequence, then those fewer subjects who have experienced several ECE should undergo the same sequence. Furthermore, their experiences should be identical. That, however, is not the case,[28] thus casting doubt not only on Moody's synthesis, but also on the supposition that these individuals are actually travelling and returning to some specific other-worldly 'place'. Third, we must note the

---

[28] Sabom 1982, 116.

consequence, as the ECE evolves, of the concurrence of this-worldly sense manifestations such as pain in the case of Howard Storm above, or the inflammatory hotness of an Indian developing an abscess, with the experiences of the afterworld. That duality of conscious awareness occurs with other known internal brain-states, such as lucid dreaming, during the 'twilight zone' when subjects are coming round from a general anaesthetic, or with loss of consciousness following a fainting attack, and during heautoscopic[29] excursions between the person's body and a hallucinated phantom of it.

Fourth, we must accept that during OBE, the reported viewing of the subject's body and of events occurring within that immediate vicinity are not true records of those supposed events. That is, they lack the veridicality which we would expect of an average eyewitness account as a reasonably true reflection of the recent historic events being reported. Several examples given above firmly refute that hypothesis, such as the lady knocked down by the black car, and Pam Reynolds' account of the use of the bone saw and her doctors' approaches in establishing cardio-respiratory bypass. Clearly, during an OBE, subjects are not using their visual apparatus in a normal physiological manner. Neither do congenitally blind subjects suddenly acquire the facility for 'transcendental' sight, only to lose it again on recovering from their ECE.

Compared with OBE, NDE purportedly take experients into a spiritual realm beyond body and brain, thus offering them a privileged view of heaven, or even of God or Jesus. I have discounted Moody's romanticized account of ECE phenomenology. Also, we should note how, in published narratives, the perception of [L]ight and [P]ersons has attained a unique metaphysic with the use of capitalized terms, implying a relationship to 'real' people to whom some importance, or even religious reverence, is due. While the majority of NDE embody some sense of peace, joy and even ecstasy, others, less frequently, are frightening, unpleasant and disturbing. Explanations must embrace both affective extremes. On the one hand, there could be a neurophysiological explanation, on grounds of metabolic perturbations, electrical or neurochemical, or reductions in regional cerebral blood flow. Alternatively it could be insisted that a truly supernatural realm, analogous to heaven and hell of conventional western monotheism, exists and was glimpsed—and even visit-

---

[29] During a heautoscopic event (Damas Mora J et al, *Br J Med Psychol* 53: 75–83, 1980), subjects' consciousness oscillates between their bodies and a perceived, extra-corporeal phantom of themselves. The experience may be accompanied by a sense of motion, and even affect towards the double. Internal heautoscopy involves hallucinating body organs in extra-personal space (Brugger P and Regard M, *Cogn Neuropsychiatr* 2: 19–38, 1997). One woman, undergoing cardiac surgery, 'saw' her heart bumping away beside her with ribbons coming out of it (Fenwick and Fenwick 1998, 193): the nature of the hallucinatory ribbons, in this case, is far from clear.

ed. Given the latter supposition, an explanation as to why those few subjects after experiencing 'hell' were instantaneously transported to the peaceful environs of a 'heaven', and during a few seconds of real time, would be required. Could such rapid reversals be consistent with Christian notions about death, resurrection and eternity?

The underpinning fact about these events is that, for the majority including those subjects whose narratives are recorded by the authors chosen for this study, their experiences have been the consequence of a severe, life-threatening clinical emergency during which cerebral function had been profoundly interfered with. It is my view that much of the recorded phenomenology undergone occurs not while the brain is at its weakest state (despite consistent authorial claims that this is the case), but as it is recovering function and returning to full conscious-awareness. We should note that all these subjects recover and, more importantly, that they remember their experiences: if they had not, then there would be no story to tell and ECE phenomenology would be an undiscovered realm of neuro(patho)physiology.

2.3.b. What do History and Geography Tell Us about ECE?

It should be recalled that Bede's narrative about Drycthelm evolved in sequential fashion: Satanic and heavenly realms were revealed to him in geomorphic continuity. His depiction of tormented souls alternately battered by frozen wastes or scorched by sulphurous furnaces stands in sharp contrast to the heavenly realms inhabited by happy people, and is surely a construct determined by his medieval background. To the modern mind those descriptions seem rather amusing, resembling equally disturbing pictures on similar themes made available to the illiterate masses by Gothic glaziers through stained-glass windows. They also effect striking comparisons with the testimonies derived from more 'primitive' societies, contemporary or historic (eastern), and representative of their particular, and often inward-looking, cultural practices and religious sensibilities. These observations suggest that the content of ECE originates from brain-associated, neurophysiological constructs cognitively determined and, in part, largely derivative of memories already encapsulated in neuronal circuitry. I state *in part*, because there is evidence that the brain manufactures spurious 'memories' *de novo*,[30] as is also the case with dreaming during which upper cortical [frontal lobe] controls are known to be deactivated.

---

[30] For example, see case reports in Daly D, *Arch Neurol* 11: 59–60, 1975.

If my proposal has any virtue, no surprise should be registered about the differences between Drycthelm's medieval portrayal of a juxtaposed heaven and hell, the vision of paradise for the Papua New Guinea Kaliain people as a world of 'factories, automobiles, highways, airplanes, European houses ... and manufactured goods',[31] or the contemporary British and North American celestial paradigm embodying a somewhat anonymous, anodyne place of soft breezes and wafting strains of angelic music amidst a display of beautifully coloured flowers, blue skies and radiant sunlight.

The frequent occurrence of ECE in normal people throughout the world[32] in whose lives a near death-related incident or crisis has never arisen, underscores the premise that there is nothing particularly 'mystical', 'psychical' or even 'other-worldly' about them. Moreover, OBE can be reproduced by electrical stimulation of the brain, or through the pharmacologic effects of various drugs. Thus, in the particular case of 'crisis' OB experiences, I conclude that they result from neurophysiological disturbances of egocentric space perception. My inference is that subjects' 'consciousness' never leaves their physical bodies, and that their brains, therefore, generate the means through which those illusions are perceived.

In the preceding accounts, I have offered some criticisms of authors' handling of certain topics. In the next chapter, my intention is to carry out a systematic evaluation of authors' interpretations of the narrative material which each received. I detect two worrying trends. First, the extent to which the material is used to support a view that undergoing an ECE gives rise to, or strengthens a pre-existing capacity for pre-cognitive and psychical competence. Second, I raise concerns over the type of cosmic visions which certain authors draw in their books. These are constructions which, in my view, vastly exceed the humble basic material from which less exuberant conclusions should have been drawn.

---

[31] Counts 1983, 130.
[32] Sheils D, *J Soc Psychic Res* 49: 697–741, 1978.

3

Authors' Interpretations of ECE Phenomenology

So far, we have reviewed the gross phemomenologies of OBE and NDE as constitutive of ECE, examined special exemplary cases, and effected a comparative culturally oriented appraisal historically and geographically. The intimate relationship between cultural influence and the resultant typologies of the experiential phenomenologies undergone by the various subjects has been illustrated. Important conclusions need to be consolidated.

I have emphasized the inconsistencies between OBE narratives compared with what would normally be assumed and expected from true eyewitness reportage of the experiences undergone. That is quite evident from the stories elicited from the lady knocked down by the black car, or from Pam Reynolds, whose supposed recall of what actually took place on that day in the operating theatre was inaccurate. She was completely oblivious of the anomalies: first, in offering an entirely seamless, continuous narrative, albeit her OBE and NDE occurred separately over a known interval of at least two hours; second, in alleging that the two major components of her OBE were consecutive when, in fact, they were simultaneous.

From a perusal of the historical and geographic accounts available, it is evident that the subconscious experiences which subjects report, in being firmly tied to cultural determinants, are indicative of their cognitively determined provenance. That is most vividly exemplified in Drycthelm's account of typical medieval perspectives on hell and heaven, perspectives no longer congruent with current western narratives given by Britons or Americans within the last twenty-five years. Unless my conclusions are invalid, we might expect all reports to be reasonably uniform for any particular time and location. That memory plays an important role in permitting these experiences to be recalled provides further strong evidence favouring a cerebrally based origin, a basis difficult to conceive if the events, as is widely claimed, originate outwith the physicality of body, and especially of brains that are moribund, and hence non-functional.

These considerations, in my view, firmly begin to adumbrate a likely cerebrally engineered theory of ECE, as opposed to brains being influenced by
extra-cerebral, and in this context, extra-worldly events. I now move on in this
chapter to consider the manner in which authors have, themselves, elucidated
these phenomena. This is most important in providing the backdrop upon
which my own thoughts and conclusions in regard to these phenomenological
issues can be further developed in succeeding chapters. The outcome hinges on
two major factors: authors' conceptions of the afterlife, and the problem of the
acquisition or enhancement of psychical powers.

3.1. AUTHORS' PERSPECTIVES ON SUBJECTS'
NARRATIVES: THE BIG COSMIC PICTURE

Analysis of authors' accounts of ECE initially requires a critical appraisal of
the presumptive 'core', as well as the propositional notion of 'depth', that have
been allocated to these phenomena. My primary objection to the idea of a
'core experience' derives directly from Moody's idealized synthesis,[1] that is, of
a fabulous account presumed to encompass the temporal and sequential
phenomenology universal to the underpinning all ECE. That construct was
apparently upheld through the later studies of Ring[2] and Grey,[3] despite the
differing percentages of subjects experiencing each progressive phase of the
emergent core phenomena in each author's samples.[4] What is also curious
and hence, to my mind, self-defeating of the core hypothesis, is that only a
progressively dwindling cohort of subjects is permitted to sample the later,
and clearly the more delectable, stages of the unfolding celestial event. One
wonders, therefore, whether the opportunity to experience the fullest ame-
nities of the afterlife is so capricious and uneven as to resemble one's chances
of achievement, or success, on earth.

A second objection is directed against the necessity of 'depth' as fundamen-
tally descriptive of ECE. Ring, to my mind, confuses the issue in relating the
alleged depth of the experiential encounter with the afterlife to the number
of items sampled. Ring's weighted index[5] reflects that relationship, scores

---

[1] Moody 1976, 21ff.
[2] Ring 1980, 32, 39ff.
[3] Grey 1985, 30ff.
[4] Ring 1980, 40, fig. 1; Grey 1985, 31 table 1.
[5] Ring 1980, 32–33, table 4.

exceeding 10 (accounting only for 26% of his entire cohort) being adjudged consistent with a deep experience. However, I am not aware that subjects, on reflection, have ever classified their ECE in terms of 'core' or 'depth'. Neither do ECE subjects, to my knowledge, describe their experiences antithetically as 'shallow'. These constructs are artefacts in the minds of authors and, by imposing an interpretation beyond anything implied in the original narrative, cannot be taken as truly realistic representations of the phenomenology reported. A more realistic interpretation of the 'depth' of an ECE could simply relate to its duration: the longer the evolutionary unwinding, the more bits and pieces of phenomenology would be undergone and remembered. In adhering to an invariant 'core' sequence and postulating a 'depth' criterion, authors allow themselves to be painted into a corner for the obvious reason, evident from the hundreds of narratives published, that there is no canonically stereotyped experience, either during its early-phase, or late-phase, components. Several pieces of evidence support this assertion.

The first piece of evidence is that OBE and NDE are separate phenomena: they stand alone, as already noted, and probably have differing neurophysiological aetiologies. Therefore, they should not be conflated into any hypothetical model. In passing, we should recall that Greyson[6] regards OBE as psychical phenomena, employing them in his scoring system as means of differentiating ECE from non-ECE. Moreover, it should be noted that many experients return to their bodies immediately after an OBE, such as Anne following surgery, or Eleanor with toxic delirium due to pneumonia and pleurisy.[7] Other subjects, in performing striking phenomenological 'U-turns', regained their bodies by re-entering the tunnel, subsequent to a neurosurgical procedure, road traffic accident, and a dissociative experience possibly due to nitrous oxide intoxication. Such obtuse reversals are clearly inconsistent with and fail to corroborate the *prototypic, forward-projected sequence* variously imposed by Moody (1976), Ring (1980) and Grey (1985).

Secondly, account should be taken of the disparity between successive ECE undergone by the same experients but at different periods of their lives. If ECE were real, veridical journeys to the realm of afterlife, however that is conceived, and irrespective of the subject involved, we might expect them to be identical. Many curious examples and disparities have been noted by Sabom, Fenwick and Fenwick, and Serdahely.[8] Serdahely concludes 'that each ECE is tailored specifically to fit the needs of [each] person'. Yes—but that is hardly

---

[6] Greyson B, *J Nerv Ment Dis* 171: 369–375, 1983a.

[7] Fenwick and Fenwick 1998, 27, 76.

[8] Sabom 1982, 116–123; Fenwick and Fenwick 1998, 36–39; Serdahely W, *J Near-Death Stud* 13: 185–196, 1995.

convincing since it fails to answer the most obvious question arising—that is, by [W]hom, or by what these events were individually tailored. And, in response to the overriding difficulty why ~70–80% of individuals never undergo ECE, the answer is that they do not need one. That aside, it is clear that ECE rarely follow a prescribed, invariant form, but are far more dependent on the circumstances of the moment and the age and disposition of the subject. My next task is to evaluate further the interpretative perspectives drawn from the narratives elicited by each of the authors in terms of possible biomedical aetiologies.

3.1.a. Have ECE Outstripped Science's Power of Explanation?

Despite his statistical comparisons and referential scientific background, Sabom's chapter devoted to physical causes is somewhat long and patchy: he rejects all major aetiological contenders. So, like the Fenwicks, he is left to ponder the mind–brain question and the possibility during ECE of a splitting of mind and soul away from corporeality. What convinces him to lean in that direction is that subjects apparently gain knowledge of their environment, achieved as they observe its unwinding from a privileged position beneath the ceiling. The difficulty in going down that explanatory pathway is that the visual and sensory perceptions reported may, or may not, be veridical. This points out the need for use of a technique able to determine the extent to which a subject during any part of an ECE is either 'unconscious', that is, completely unresponsive to the environment, or in some other type of subconscious existence, or, indeed, conscious. Therefore, the possibility that new knowledge may be gained during OBE by no means provides convincing evidence for either a mind–brain split, or a mind–body separation. It would, indeed, be a most profound observation to demonstrate such a separation. But it would necessarily demand exceptionally tight data on which to be founded. At present, one can accept the distinction between the cerebral engine and its phenomenological outcomes, but to have the latter without the former is most difficult to envisage, despite the many unproven or speculative assertions to the contrary. Each ECE, despite certain general similarities, appears to be a unique experiential event for each individual, and related to the unique personal history from which it arises.

That is the problem confronting the Fenwicks.[9] Referring to four accounts (respondents Davies, Smith, Whitmarsh and Mill) which are obviously idiosyncratic, these authors conclude that 'the . . . "realm" . . . to which people

---

[9] Fenwick and Fenwick 1998, 151ff.

travel is something created by their own minds, and will be different for everyone'. Here, at least, we have the first glimmer of an idea that ECE could be generated from the brain, rather than by some other events exterior to subjects' moribund brains: 'mechanisms must underlie the experiences: they are not out of anywhere'.

Moody, the originator of the current, growing interest in ECE phenomenology, offered a very reserved approach, refusing to be drawn to any particular explanatory model. Despite that refusal,[10] he felt strongly that the narratives he received were 'very significant' and 'very persuasive', becoming 'real events to [him]'. There seems little doubt, despite a rather non-committal afterview, that he was drawn to the view that these experiences did add up to something that neither modern science nor philosophy adequately explain. They exceed our present understandings of death and, in particular, what might lie beyond. He was dismissive of conventional explanations, whether based on pharmacological, physiological or neurological premises. Neither did he warm to psychological explanations, such as dreams, hallucinations or delusions. For all such proposals 'questionable doubts arise requiring a newer type of evaluative paradigm'.

We have already encountered Ring's objection to neuroscientific explanations of ECE and particularly to young, upstart scientists employing a 'this' or 'that' mechanism to explain each successive facet of the evolving experience. Like Moody's requirement for a new kind of paradigmatic account, Ring dismissed all possible scientific approaches in ten pages. As a result 'we find ourselves at the threshold of the scientific study of "impossible" events— parapsychology', contrary to the well-known public unease and scepticism regarding precognition, psychokinesis, telepathy, clairvoyance and allied goings-on. Having determined the failure of ordinary science to account for every facet of the 'core' experience while, at the same time, ignoring an extensive corpus of relevant neurophysiological data available to him (even in 1980), he devoted over three times more discussion to the emergence of free consciousness and its ascent into the fourth dimension of holographic enlightenment and understanding.[11] Ring, notwithstanding, then finds that parapsychology, likewise, is insufficient to frame the entire phenomenology of the 'core' experience. Parapsychology needs buttressing with a ' "states-of-consciousness" component, known in neuroscience as the holographic theory or paradigm'.

Similar criticisms apply to Grey's (1985) study. Like Ring, she rapidly dismisses conventional scientific explanations in less than six text pages,

---

[10] Moody 1976, 156–182.
[11] Ring 1980, 207–252.

while her own interpretations occupy a further 25 pages. Grey[12] firmly believes that death is not the end of existence, that free consciousness can exist outwith the corporeal body, and that mystical idealization offers the best explanatory means of confronting ECE and their '*psychical*' outcomes. Access to this mystical or spiritual state can only be accomplished once '*consciousness*' is free of corporeal dependency. She dismisses the possibility that future neurophysiological research will prize open the depths of ECE. Extraordinarily, she then continues to assert that her findings are 'in no way intended to represent evidence of a life hereafter, as clearly not one of the respondents went further than surviving the initial stages of death'. Based on the material presented, readers are left to develop their own opinions. Nevertheless, Grey is convinced that having an ECE is one way through which we can taste other realities, even though her view is not intended as an endorsement of that assertion. The obvious response to that reversal is why she thought it necessary to go to press and make such utterances public.

Having briefly surveyed key authors' approaches to ECE and their dismissal of scientific explanation (with perhaps the exception of Fenwick and Fenwick), my final duty is to elucidate further the types of non-physicalist interpretation which these authors, severally, have placed upon their respondents' narratives.

3.1.b. ECE and Authors' Interpretations: Reaching for the Cosmos

Sabom's approach to the meaning of ECE is staightforward. While unable to explain why transcendental experiences (= NDE) afford glimpses of the afterlife, he is persuaded, in their manifesting an escape of soul, that NDE represent the work of the Spirit or the power of God: 'it is a spiritual encounter that is both "real", "otherworldly" as the soul is in the process of leaving the body'. Four criteria underpin his assertion: an occurrence within the spiritual realm, a pertinence to religion and hence to the transcendent, unavailability for scientific quantification, and, finally, that they are real events and hence neither hallucinatory, imaginary nor dream-illusory. In Sabom's view,[13] ECE are spiritual adventures and divine revelations. Inclusive of visions of Jesus, ECE provide inspirational models for the future life-direction of subjects they involve.

The interpretations of the Fenwicks are uncertain: they query whether ECE are internally generated cerebral events, psychophysical phenomena, or

---

[12] Grey 1985, 41, 186–187.
[13] Sabom 1982, 185–186.

outwith the physical domain of body or brain—that is—spiritual. They are unable to muster any substantive evidence that mind exists without its under-lying brain or, more importantly, that memories could be manufactured and stored in some place outwith the cerebral cortex.[14] They recognize meaning in the world and in the life of the universe, as expressed through varied cultural-religious perspectives on the afterlife and disembodied survival. If there is no meaning in the universe as severe reductionists insist, then life for billions of people—past, present and surely in the future, becomes entirely pointless, cold, limited, and unfulfilled. But how could meaning be secured, either on earth or in the future, and do ECE shed any light on, or give substance to, that longed-for meaning? My feeling is that these authors, in reviewing their narrative-testimonies, are unable to articulate any real theory that ECE do, in reality, point to an afterlife or existence of mind outwith corporeality.[15]

The least conventional interpretation is envisaged by Ring and, following closely on his coat-tails, Grey.[16] Both firmly believe that consciousness escapes the brain. For Ring,[17] OBE act as springboards for the disembodiment of consciousness, a splitting-off process at death releasing the centre of self-awareness from the constraints of physicality, thus to rise to the *'fourth dimension'*. At this point their views begin to diverge.[18] Grey holds that in leaving the dualistic world of mind–body, consciousness dissociates into the *sushami nadi* or pathway of energy (*prana*) located in the spinal cord, giving rise to the luminosity (or 'light') experienced by 'many'.[19] Corporeally free,

---

[14] Fenwick & Fenwick 1998, 256.

[15] In later work, Peter Fenwick has more persistently advocated the view that as the brain dies, consciousness does escape, thus raising (for him) new issues regarding the nature of mind and brain and their independent existence.

[16] Ring 1980, 220ff; Grey 1985, 41.

[17] The problem here for Ring is that not all ECE are preceded by OBE. The numerical data are 37% (Ring 1980, 40, fig. 1), 52% (Sabom 1982, 52) and 21–32% (Grey 1985, 31, table 1), indicating that ∼50–60% of subjects never report this occurrrence. That other ECE terminate with an OBE undermines considerably Ring's position, as well as his concept of a universal, sequential 'core' experience.

   Ring argues that not all subjects may have known they were having an OBE (idem 1980, 220), a curious statement indeed if separation from the body (as Ring insists) markedly heightens subjects' perceptiveness (idem, 229; 232).

[18] For Grey, any technique (eastern) permitting consciousness to acquire independent function of the body (kundalini, yoga, pranayama meditation, and 'third eye' (Shira Yoga)) facilitates this ascent. The third eye is evolutionarily connected to the pineal gland, which is not redundant, but 'still evolving'. With accelerated growth, it permits subjects to see events on a larger panoramic canvas. Pineal development also collapses temporal progressions and se-quences, thereby engendering a newer sense of oneness and eternity (Grey 1985, 189ff).

[19] The probity of that statement is undermined by observing that of ∼700 collective subjects, only about 50%, as a crude average, admit to seeing a light (16% (Ring), 39% (Grey), 28% (Sabom), 43% (Greyson 1990), 56% (Lindley et al 1981), 72% (Fenwick and Fenwick)).

consciousness is enabled to function independently beyond the world of sensibilities thus becoming immediately aware of the fourth dimension. Ego-death is an intense emotional experience, embodying a 'tremendous sense of encompassing oneness' and awareness of a 'higher transcendent order'. This is invariably followed by a 'sense of rebirth' (reincarnation) and the certainty that consciousness enjoys physical independence. Fine words, indeed, but scarcely supported by firm, empirical data.

Hellish experiences arise when subjects have unresolved psychological aggravations in life. Thus the NDE appears to represent, in an *'ever increasing frequency'*, an evolution towards the attaining of enlightenment, and that in attaining that heightened form of consciousness, such individuals become united in a universality of brotherhood, love and compassion.[20] Individualism is mutating into a wider collective cooperative, based on increased self-responsibility. Therefore, we do not necessarily have to die so as to experience these newer levels of higher consciousness. The afterlife is but an illusory chimera: there is no heaven or hell. We need enlightenment to lift our own lives from the mundane of the here-and-now into one of those exalted planes via the agency of the collective consciousness of the universal cosmic mind.

Ring, on the other hand, sees free consciousness (or 'entity', 'replica', 'second body', even 'soul') entering the tunnel towards the light.[21] Here the experiencing of a presence, voices, judgement, or encountering former deceased people, and the decision to return home, represent a shift of consciousness into the 'fourth dimension'. The perception of movement and weightlessness[22] is literally that of unembodied mind-awareness in transit to this higher plane of existence. Indeed, the light is a vision of one's 'higher self'. One's inherent divine nature which, embodying all knowledge, is now capable of initiating its own life-review. This, according to Ring, is what subjects often interpret as being in the presence of God. These latter experiences are to be understood through holographic theory whose 'origins lie in neurophysiology and physics'.[23] As a laser can reconstruct an object from a representation of itself through interference patterns so the brain, in interpreting the world by analysing received frequency domains, portrays them as the environmental objects with which subjects are familiar. ECE, mysticism, and eastern philosophy all provide means of appreciating these orders of (holographic) reality that lie behind our day-to-day world of sensible appearances. Nevertheless,

---

[20] Grey 1985, 193–195 (and see Ring 1980, 255).

[21] Ring 1980, 220ff.

[22] As we shall see later, these changed perceptions of bodily characteristics have an alternative explanation in terms of vestibular function as disturbed brains recover from their previous insults.

[23] Ring 1980, 234–5, 240ff.

Ring backtracks on the mechanisms of separation on grounds that any answer would take us into 'the wilds of esoteric speculation' (222–233). But why?— even if we knew precisely what those words mean.

There are other difficulties. Ring supposes that those who '*stick*' in the tunnel experience hell, although we are not told through which agency the adhesion is manifested. Unfortunately for Ring, the published literature fails to identify a single subject who remained caught in this predicament: and, furthermore, had that been the case, clearly we on earth could never have been informed of such a catastrophic outcome. Of the very few hellish experiences recorded in the literature, subjects are always finally rescued by spiritual beings and taken to heaven. Next, despite the alleged power intrinsic to holographic theory, a proper and definitive judgement on its appropriateness as an explanatory framework 'cannot reasonably be undertaken' because we, as earthbound humans, do not exist holographically.

Ring's threshold for the scientific study of the 'impossible' seems to have collapsed without affording us any further substantive innovatory or revelational insights. In other words, this is neither an all-embracing analysis nor a complete explanation by Ring of all facets of ECE phenomenology. This is a strange whimpering finale to what was earlier heralded as (his) freedom to 'explore other experimental categories, as against those failed approaches stemming from conventional neuroscience'. Here we see a grandiose approach whose speculative superstructure vastly outstrips the data upon which it should have been based, and which ultimately fails miserably to account for the narrative phenomena relayed to him. Doubtless few subjects would immediately recognize the implications of their experiences as viewed either through Ring's eyes, or those of Grey. This assertion could hardly be bettered than by a remark of one of the Fenwicks' correspondents. Having watched a television broadcast on ECE, she declared a total inability to recognize the content of the experiences as advanced on the programme!

In conclusion, it seems to me that these collective approaches to explanatory scientific hypotheses, and their 'other-worldly' interpretational outcomes of the phenomenology narrated by respondents, are weak, superficial and, in parts, dismissive. Of the authors reviewed, only Sabom provides any reasonable documentation of pertinent research papers. For the remainder, their referencing, relative to the breadth of material surveyed, is somewhat selective, while the omission of important details about other workers' publications cited in the text does not make follow-up for the reader particularly easy. One might have expected from each authorship, possibly, more engagement with existing scientific material and a more considered assessment of the outcomes considered. For Ring and Grey, their cosmic interpretational constructs far exceed the data received through their respective narratives.

Throughout each book published by all these authors, the text is continuously disturbed by frequent anecdotes as though offered to prop up weakly developed argument, although sufficient narrative material included in earlier chapters was adequate in providing a more measured, competent, descriptive overview of ECE phenomenology,[24] its possible basis, and ultimate meaning.

3.2. THE PROBLEM OF PRE-COGNITION AND ACQUIRED PSYCHICAL POWERS

In this section, I am concerned with the specific approach made by authors to the alleged acquisition of precognition and other psychical powers by subjects as a result of their undergoing an ECE. Furthermore, such evidence is aggressively deployed as affirmative evidence for the veridicality of ECE. Two major arguments favouring psychical explanations (as against neurological constructs) are advanced. First, on subjects' propensity during OBE to observe their bodies and resuscitations, this being regarded as exemplary of the supposed existence of mind (or soul or free conscious-awareness) beyond its neural substrate.[25] For example, in his scoring system, Greyson (we should recall) holds the curious opinion that an OBE is a manifest psychical phenomenon.[26] Second, on subjects' supposed acquisition of precognitive information about contemporaneous or future eventualities. It is this latter contentious issue which I critically evaluate in detail below.

3.2.a. A Preliminary Critique on Acquiring So-Called Precognition

The alleged acquisition of psychical powers is a favoured ploy in counteracting reductionist or psycho-physical explanations of ECE. Yet that ploy founders on two counts: first, because of the very small number of cases used in evidence (in comparison with the thousands of ECE testimonies published overall), and second, because of the very lack of strict, independent third-party corroborations of the special information alleged to have been acquired. I emphasize that I am only concerned with the claims of the authors

---

[24] Sabom 1982, 1–150; 1998, 11–73; Fenwick and Fenwick 1998, 5–196; Ring 1980, 39–103; Grey 1985, 30–91.
[25] Moody 1977, 108ff; Ring 1980, 213–214; Grey 1985, 115–133.
[26] Greyson 1983, 369.

who constitute my investigation. Grey,[27] for example, offers three cases of supposed post-experience clairvoyance for which no solid evidence is at all given. The simultaneity of two telephone calls could hardly be taken as convincing evidence: that conclusively underpins her case. And it hardly seems a likely explanation that a loss of time/space is a precondition of future prophecy. As Grey herself states (178) in avoiding the obvious consequence: 'there is no obligation to accept these apocalyptic pronouncements as being of any significance for future world conditions'. Following Ring, she quotes: 'interpretations of prophetic visions need to be made with utmost caution because of their capacity if taken seriously to generate a . . . range . . . of . . . reactions based on fear, hysteria or simply passivity'.

But unfortunately, Ring's basis upon which Grey so heavily relies is, itself, most uncertain. Let us critically examine Ring's evidential base. His Case 25 suffered a hypotensive episode during childbirth, simultaneously foreseeing a child who would have a heart problem and be gifted. At first, Ring[28] 'did not have time to investigate this [him]self', so the event lacked any immediate, objective corroboration. Yet later in the same book (75) we are invited 'to recall Case 25 which presents more striking data *consistent with the assumption that ND experiences can sometimes disclose pre-cognitive information*' (my emphases here and below). Finally (126), the same case hardens into 'a woman who, on nearly dying, *received pre-cognition information* about her newly delivered baby and felt she had to come back'. Other unconfirmed cases involved foresight of a future husband and children five years hence, which 'only suggests pre-cognition knowledge [but] no convincing evidence of it'; of a young man possibly having a daughter with the girl to whom he had just become engaged, and of a man who, during his NDE, sensed his wife telling him of his brother's death.

Much of this circumstantial, and poorly documented, material is akin to the celebrated OBE case of Maria who reported seeing, on a third-floor window sill at the other end of the hospital, a shoe having a worn patch over the little toe and a lace stuck under the heel. The Fenwicks[29] (thankfully) are right in dismissing this testimony 'as hearsay rather than hard fact'. These same authors cite other supposed cases of prophetic foresight, but without convincing corroborative back-up. Clearly, the material offered by all authors is poorly researched and documented. Many cases could be due simply to chance or circumstance. What is needed is a stringent, prospective study between age/sex-matched controls and ECE subjects, in order to determine

---

[27] Grey 1985, 115–116.
[28] Ring 1980, 35–36.
[29] Fenwick and Fenwick 1998, 257.

the true basis of these alleged powers, thus to reveal if ECE of themselves are able to confer, or uncover, a latent predisposition for precognition or even prophecy, or not.

Because we are being given solicited, retrospective reports, they suffer, as with all other previous writers' offerings, from a lack of critically acceptable and corroborative third-party evidence. That is particularly crucial to certain 'key' case reports of the Fenwicks regarding knowledge gained in the absence of presumed loss of sensory afference. It is beyond credibility that Mary[30] physically '*saw*' the nurse while simultaneously being unable to '*feel*' the physical effects of her ministrations. Regarding the precognition of her head bandages (following neurosurgery), could she not have seen other similar patients in the ward during the pre-operative period? Furthermore, from their weight, extent and 'feel' (presumably she could move her arms during that three-day post-operative period, given that the operation was on her head), she could have deduced much information about how her dressings would have appeared. That is, the information gained by her is by no means watertight evidence for extra-sensory perception, as offered by the Fenwicks. Is this, we may ask, the type of information necessary to critically convince a sceptical public that precognition really occurs? For Jean it is unclear whether she was anaesthetized in preparation for a re-exploration of her abdominal incision, or whether the pack was simply reintroduced intra-vaginally. Scull would have seen his wife's red suit and formed memories of it on many past occasions before his admission to hospital. Despite having sojourned in a 'side ward with high windows' for 48 hours, he still had to be taken to it in the first place. He would therefore have vicariously noted and memorized during the period of his admission some details about the ward, its layout and reception area, and, moreover, stored memories of it because of the gravity and urgency, as well as the novelty, of the occasion. It is not too difficult then to envisage a quasi-hynopompic dream-like reconstruction of events that just happened to coincide with real events.

In view of the absence of the much-required third-party independent corroboration, we are never told nor given tabulated data by any author how many OBE *never* coincide with reality. Non-coincidental events are, of course, far less newsworthy anecdotes. Conversely, striking coincidences in-variably acquire a significance that far outweighs their actual importance, but are more likely to be eclectically published, despite the triviality of events offered as evidence of precognition. Similar sentiments apply to the congeni-tally blind woman reported by the Fenwicks.[31] The blind learn to use and

[30] Fenwick and Fenwick 1998, 30–31.
[31] Fenwick and Fenwick 1998, 85–86.

share the visually laden vocabulary of normally sighted people. This hearsay report, as it stood in the Fenwicks' reporting, reveals no further insights about the issue of non-sensory acquisition of external data. Such reportings require incisive questioning in order to establish precisely what blind people are saying, and their meanings intended by the words employed in ordinary conversation. That stringent criterion has never seemingly been met in the ECE literature. The same criticism applies with some considerable force to the paper of Ring and Collins considered in Chapter 2, which failed completely, in my view, to establish that the blind 'see' during an ECE.

It is also necessary to be aware of the intrusive, and ever present, difficulties which frustrated Charles Tart in his attempts to provide accurate documentation of telepathic and other extra-sensory perceptions under stringent laboratory conditions. Despite his use of selected subjects able to render themselves out-of-body, their performances under laboratory test conditions for the tasks set up by him were by no means impressive.[32] The odd 'hit' is by no means convincing, and could always be due to chance. There has been, to my mind, an extraordinarily long-continued absence of persuasive, systematic evidence for the alleged occurrence of 'psychical' phenomena. We might also be concerned that for over one hundred years, there have been no major developments or insights deriving from this field of endeavour, despite our increasing technological resources. We need more data, derivative of a far larger corpus of credible events studied prospectively under even stricter, updated laboratory disciplines than attempted by Tart. Until those data are forthcoming, my inclination is to ignore the batch of exemplary 'cases' offered in the ECE literature by this handful of authors as of boringly trivial significance. The responsibility for providing that strict evidential base lies with those who continue to promote psychical competence as a true, demonstrably reliable, and acceptable outcome of ECE in particular, or of 'mind' in general.

As a corollary to the psychical outcomes of ECE, Sabom (1980) records no examples among his sample of 116 subjects. Yet, curiously, in his later book (1998) he states that visions and precognition were common in comparison with non-ECE cardiac controls. However, there was no difference in frequency of these phenomena pre- and post-experience. The possibility of a predisposing cerebral origin for these alleged powers thus arises and requires further investigation by the appropriate, and strictly controlled, prospective studies.

---

[32] Tart 1998.

3.2.b. Further Problems Arising from Ring's Psychical Account

Much is made of the alleged occurrence of psychic phenomena in the wake of NDE, in Ring's later book, *Heading Towards Omega*. According to Ring the 'empirical evidence supporting the claim that NDE . . . trigger psychic activities is very impressive indeed'.[33] Ring has actually come to believe that NDE facilitate the spiritual awakening and transformation of many subjects, thus 'resembl[ing] a full-blown mystical experience—and [that] is the key—the effects of [NDE] also resembl[ing] those that stem from a mystical experience'. I am unable to clarify the grounds upon which Ring, himself, is able to make this overwhelming claim. Moreover, I shall be giving reasons below why I think NDE are not 'mystical' experiences. Yet despite that conclusion, there is the possibility that ECE could be a source of divine grace capable of enhancing subjects' inner perceptions regarding their future existence and behaviour here on earth. I expand on these matters when considering the post-experiential subject in Chapter 12. Nevertheless, I am not convinced that there is much to suggest that, in the mainline monotheistic traditions, 'mystical' experiences lead to any widespread enhancement and outward manifestation of psychic ability.

Ring's Psychic Experience Inventory aims to elicit changes wrought in subjects' psychical powers (clairvoyance, telepathy, precognition, déjà vu, OBE, and so on) and secondly, to measure alterations in belief(s) concerning the spiritual, psychic and occult worlds. He found that 80% of his subjects became more 'intuitive', 96% claimed 'to be more in touch with an inner source of knowledge or wisdom', while ~50% became 'more clairvoyant and experienced more pre-cognitive flashes, déjà vu phenomena, and contact with spiritual guides' (1985, 172–173). These conclusions are not given in a regular, tabulated form, but just stated. In assessing pre- and post-ND beliefs (with the use of an arbitrary scale: -2, -1, 0, $+1$, $+2$), 64% came to believe in ESP, 84% in spiritual and psychic healing and 68% in spirit guides (1985, 317, table 4). These findings seem to parallel other similar studies.[34]

However, there are considerable methodological problems with these studies. Ring's numeric data are scanty and difficult to interpret. Table 4 (1985, 317) is particularly opaque, and I am totally unable to understand what his figures are supposed to tell us. Greyson's study was based on advertised recruits who were members of the International Association for Near-Death Studies (IANDS), while Kohr obtained his sample from a research base of the

---

[33] Ring 1985, 166ff.
[34] Greyson B, *Theta* 11: 26–29, 1983b; Kohr R, *J Am Soc Psychic Res* 74: 395–411, 1980; Kohr R, *Theta* 10: 50–53, 1982.

Association for Religion and Enlightenment (ARE). Kohr, at least, used a control cohort that exceeded his NDE group by the correct ratio of 4:1.[35] Nevertheless, all studies were in part retrospective, uncontrolled for the circumstances or nature of the NDE, unblinded, and heavily biased towards female respondents. Without those caveats being strictly addressed and the societal (IANDS and ARE) biases totally removed, the data cannot be taken as definitive.

These data also need to be evaluated in the light of other studies of the paranormal in the general population, and concerning which the NDE was not the central issue. Ross and Joshi[36] studied 502 subjects from a larger cohort of residents in Winnipeg, Canada. Their male:female ratio was more balanced than in Ring's and Greyson's studies, which both suffered from a predominance of (IANDS-associated) females. Overall, ~66% of Canadians reported having one paranormal experience, and 10% more than four. Importantly, subjects traumatically or sexually abused as children revealed a clearly increased susceptibility to paranormal experiences than non-abused subjects (p<0.001). The prevalence of déjà vu phenomena was so common (~55%) that the investigators hardly thought it worth considering them as true psychic events. The occurrence of pre-cognitive dreams (18%) and mental telepathy (16%) was high, although Gallup and Newport (1991) observed 25% of their US poll admitting to telepathic events. Non-dream precognition showed a prevalence of 6%. It is not easy to compare item for item in this and the other studies referred to above. Nevertheless, the point must be emphasized that psychical phenomena are extremely common throughout the (North American) general population, occur more frequently in younger persons, and not only are associated with childhood traumas, but may also be the sequelae of preceding brain damage, such as infections, closed head trauma, or other types of intrinsic cerebral neuropathology. This clearly is in line with discussions given in Chapter 8 pertinent to latent temporal lobe disease.

Sabom's[37] investigations revealed no difference pre- and post-NDE for 'visionary' and 'pre-cognitive' activities, although in comparison with non-NDE cardiac controls, both events were significantly more common. Neither was there any difference in OBE frequencies between NDE subjects and controls. These latter data are at variance with those of Ring and of Greyson.[38]

---

[35] Kohr 1982.

[36] Ross C and Joshi S, *J Nerv Ment Dis* 180: 357–361, 1992.

[37] Sabom 1998: visions 40% vs 15%, p<0.0001 (p. 157); pre-cognition 56% vs 21%, p<0.001 (p. 162).

[38] Ring 1985, 317, table 4; Greyson 1983b, 28, table 1.

Thus, Sabom's data highlight the possibility that the NDE is not the principal predisposing cause of increased psychical activity, but that other factors such as brain trauma or infections in earlier life, as especially pertinent to latent temporal lobe dysfunction, are more than likely to be antecedently operative. To have clarified that issue would necessarily depict Ring's and many other studies on this subject in a completely different light.

3.3. THE FUTURE TASK

In respect of all that has been surveyed in this chapter, certain conclusions become evident.

First, I have shown that the use of the terms 'core' and 'deep' as commensurate descriptors of ECE phenomenology are specious, and thus inappropriate. There is no canonical sequence: that is clearly apparent from any careful reading of the many published narratives. Each account is idiosyncratic and directly related to the personal history and location from which each arises.

Second, my complaint is that the possibility of scientific explanations has all too rapidly been dismissed without sufficient appraisal of the relevant literature. That has resulted in a very skewed account of the phenomenology, and one that seems to have arisen purely from pre-existing notions of what should be the case. It is again quite obvious that the conclusions of Ring and Grey fall within this category. It is simply not possible that such exuberantly speculative outcomes about ascents to the fourth dimension, universal spirituality, or cosmic brotherhood could be underpinned by the data provided by subjects' experiential narratives. It is no surprise that the subjects who provided these narratives in good faith would hardly recognize the meaning of a 'core' or 'deep' experience, nor the emergent superstructures advanced by these two authors.

Third, I find it necessary to counter the excessive emphasis put on the psychical outcomes that ECE are reputed to engender in subjects. The conclusions reached are based on poorly documented, circumstantial evidence, and lacking essential, independent third-party corroborations. Here, then, we need the help of incisive scientific methodology. In order to determine precisely what the true relationship may be between ECE and the acquisition of psychic and allied powers, prospectively controlled trials are required. Subjects need to be compared pre- and post-experience, and with sufficiently large, geographical control groups. The latter are vital because of the widespread claims within various societies of a disposition towards psychic competence.

ECE phenomenology has done nothing to enhance the existing poor record of supposedly demonstrable happenings outwith the known physical confines of body, or universe. Moreover, in general, the field of parapsychology and other psychical goings-on, despite its long history, has failed to substantiate its claims or postulated capabilities.

Critical requirements would demand the gathering of pre-NDE statements of beliefs and psychic events/powers through administration of the appropriate questionnaires, brain-scanning and allied investigations, the prevalence of earlier traumatic influences on personality, viewed in parallel with adequate, representative appropriate (geographic-/age-/sex-matched) control groups. Far greater effort is required to independently corroborate the psychic powers allegedly acquired by NDE subjects. I note that this was difficult to achieve in the study of Groth-Marnat and Summers,[39] through use of informed close family members, such as spouses, who completed relevant questionnaires. Earlier on, I referred to Charles Tart's difficulties, under fairly tight laboratory conditions, to monitor paranormal phenomena, despite the occasional success.[40] If these events continue to evade capture through use of conventional scientific technologies, then the need for more stringent documentation becomes absolutely necessary. Since psychic phenomena vary with age, the numbers of recruited subjects should be large enough to permit intelligent, comparative statistical analyses of 10–15-year cohorts throughout the adult age span.

Prospectively organized studies of the varied phenomenologies hold the key to the way forward, and would permit recruitment of additional ECE subjects independent of the bias created vicariously through retrospective studies. More care should be exercised in the selection of patients, perhaps avoiding the inclusion of those who belong to organizations whose primary aim is to foster interest in ECE or other forms of parapsychological activity. A comparative European study would be a useful counter to the bias that is detectable in some current US work. Psychic phenomena are now happily coming into the province of psychiatric practice. It would be useful to itemize and define each type of psychic experience in order to introduce uniformity and comparability into the field. Another crucial need is ensuring that all questionnaires are designed by those competent in this discipline. Questionnaires should include control questions (so-called 'red herrings') to provide the necessary internal consistency for validating respondents' answers given.

In studies as complex as these, it is essential that statisticians are co-opted so that adequate numbers of subjects, controls in the correct proportion, and

[39] Groth-Marnat G and Summers R, *J Hum Psychol* 38: 110–125, 1998.
[40] Tart 1998.

appropriate methodologies are employed in order to answer the questions posed by the research. A renewed scientific rigour and candour is called for, which should replace the hitherto anecdotal reportage and interpretation of much NDE and allied phenomenology to date. Until all these issues are clarified, elucidated and adopted, some of us might still be a little reticent in supposing that an NDE is a key gateway leading to the possibility of increased psychical awareness, or to the attaining of a higher cosmic consciousness, or unity.

This is but a brief, yet necessarily incomplete, outline. But it is clearly evident from the foregoing that ECE research, rather than progressing still further into the realms of the psychical or other esoteric philosophies, needs to be firmly reoriented towards the brain. From that perspective, the possibility of addressing the many unanswered questions concerning phenomenological ontology arises which, in view of recent advances in neurophysiological research, now await urgent clarification. The critical issue here is that data should be accumulated from as many subjects, 'victims' or controls as possible, and, where appropriate, from as many subjects as possible, pre- and post- event, in order to eradicate retrospective and other forms of bias that render existing studies valueless or questionable. The most efficacious method of procuring useful (computerized) data would involve multi-regional, or multi-national, cooperative trials, statistically validated. This kind of study is vital in order to bring small, disparate groups together under one controlling administrative influence. That would avoid the many methodological mishaps which have plagued previous studies, and contribute to overcoming the woefully small (and often biased) numbers of experients, unevenly matched male-to-female ratios, and statistical errors arising through use of small-group analyses. Small-group work is never likely to offer the prospect of providing robust answers to these critical questions. On those grounds, local studies that continue to exhibit these recurrent defects, or provide additional anecdotal coverage, would neither be worth pursuing—nor reading.

Important new insights, addressing the questions which I have raised, and meeting the challenging impact of the latest neurophysiological advances, can only be generated and effected through this form of disciplined, generalized approach to the phenomenology of ECE.

Having reviewed authors' interpretative shortcomings in their attempts to provide realistic interpretations of ECE phenomenology, I now turn to my own approach, and to the varied possibilities amenable and employable, in furthering our understandings of this subject.

4

Objective Analyses into ECE Subjectivity

In the preceding chapters, I offered brief sketches illustrative of ECE phenomenology as seen through the eyes of five selected authors and their eight publications. There followed a critical analysis of how these five authors, themselves, had viewed the testimonies offered by their respective clientele. In that critique, not only did I emphasize the diverse interpretations put upon these revelations but how the conclusions—both cosmic and psychical of Ring and Grey in particular—had vastly outstripped the limited potential of the narratives offered by their subjects. In reviewing ECE phenomenology in its geographical and historical context, I drew attention to the extent to which subjects' cultural backgrounds coloured, and thus informed, the experiential phenomenology reported. That implies a necessary contributory input from the brain in deploying relevant stored background material and in portraying past memories pertinent to each individual's habitat and unique life-history. Clearly, on those grounds alone, one would never anticipate, nor indeed expect a canonical, irreducible sequence that could underwrite the idiosyncratic content of any individual's OB or ND experience. We need neither 'core' nor 'deep' ECE.

My overriding complaint, however, was of a poorly developed approach towards more thorough and thoughtful scientific explanations of ECE, taking into account the clinical and laboratory information already available to all authors at their respective times of writing. Hence the reasonable call for further well-planned, prospective studies to undercut the intrusive biases which have plagued and tainted so much previous research into this area. Indeed, I venture to assert that much of what has been written in these books has resulted in a generally unsatisfactory outcome. Unsatisfactory, first, with regard to the many available neurophysiological avenues through which ECE phenomenology could have been approached objectively, albeit analogically, and from which new insights might have been drawn. In subsequent chapters, I shall consider various brain-state modes from which such useful insights could have been recruited.

Second, because these non-scientific approaches have fostered the collective view that ECE phenomenology points to an experiential afterlife when, in fact, that may not necessarily be the case. And third, because of the particular stance assumed by these authors at the outset of their projects. Ring's book[1] was effected 'in a scientific spirit of enquiry and conducted using scientific proce-dures'. Sabom[2] declared himself to be writing a 'scientific study', while Peter Fenwick[3] referred to himself as a 'scientist'. These and other texts written by these persons continue to be upheld as balanced accounts of ECE phenomenology: they are widely quoted and accepted as canonical expositions on the subject.

If that is the case prevailing, then I feel obliged to defer from that position.

4.1. INITIAL APPROACHES TO A MORE OBJECTIVE ACCOUNT OF ECE PHENOMENOLOGY

From the seven hundred or more accounts recorded in the canonical texts referred to, one striking yet simple observation stands out. ECE phenomenolo-gy ceases abruptly as conscious-awareness is regained (Figure 1). I know of no

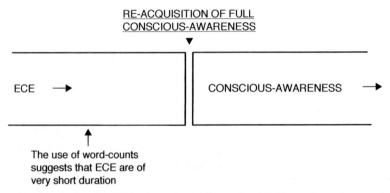

Figure 1. Hundreds of published reports indicate that NDE terminate as conscious-awareness is resumed. Second, the number of words employed in these narrative reportings suggest that NDE are ephemeral events, occurring within a very short interval (seconds or minutes) within the period during which the brain is not moribund, but regaining full conscious-awareness. That these events are remembered throughout, although possibly incompletely, nevertheless demands a functional, rather than dying, brain.

---

[1] Ring 1980, 15.
[2] Sabom 1982, 5.
[3] Fenwick and Fenwick 1998, 197.

published account to the contrary, while the importance of this observation lies in its objectivity. That crucial time-point at which the experience ends now renders ECE phenomenology open to third-party analysis and reflection. Second, we can extrapolate backwards from that time-point to determine the approximate temporal duration of ECE. That has been realized by my borrowing a technique employed by dream-research workers. Their deployment of word-counts to subjects' accounts of dream-associated (= oneiric) activity permits assessment of the duration and number of ideational units comprising dream mentation.[4] Analytical approaches of this kind, for example, have realized important comparative differences between rapid eye-movement (REM) and non-REM (NREM) dream-sleep modes.

Some of the longest recollective material of ECE has been offered by Drycthelm and Howard Storm. Both subjects were in prolonged, but fairly 'light' subconscious states of mind due to episodes of toxic-delirium. More relevant to our quest is the account given by Pam Reynolds, who experienced separate OBE and NDE during her long (four-hour) neurosurgical operation. Counts of a few hundred words from her verbatim testimony indicate that each experience lasted no more than a few minutes or less, as is also the case with dreaming. If this line of argument is correct, then we can combine this approach with the other referent, the point at which the subject awakens in real time as the ECE terminates. Extrapolating backwards from the moment of awakening, we are led to the inevitable conclusion that ECE in general are short-duration events, occuring during the last few moments heralding the re-establishment of full conscious-awareness. So, although a cardiac arrest resuscitation could last from 30 minutes to an hour or more,[5] the accompanying ECE would only occupy the terminal phases of the precipitating crisis—minutes or, for some subjects perhaps, seconds only.

From that chain of objective reasoning, a third most important insight arises, and one which wholly alters pre-existing perspectives about the nature of ECE. They become not vague, shapeless journeys towards an imaginary somewhere (or nowhere), arising from a morbid or agonal brain from which mind, consciousness or soul has escaped. Rather, they are manifest outputs derivative, in part, of the somewhat disordered contortions of brains that, in those last frenzied moments of the event, are rapidly recovering and awakening from their antecedent insults, and which, by inference, remain functionally unharmed. There has been a common failure among the authors analysed here to pay due regard to subjects' return to life and what that could imply functionally, that is, neurophysiologically. Indeed, too little emphasis has been

---

[4] Antrobus J, *Psychophysiol* 20: 562–568, 1983.
[5] Sabom 1982, 202, table 6.

given to the fact that ECE subjects have to wake up and regain full conscious-awareness.

But am I correct in using word counts: first, as indirect measures of the duration of near-death experiences? Second, in inferring that those final moments leading up to the resumption of conscious-awareness last only for seconds or a minute or two? And third, that brains, while recovering from fairly major insults to their functioning, can conjure up the kinds of phenomenological experiences widely reported in the literature during such extraordinarily short time-intervals? I maintain that I am correct, there being good warrant for these assertions. Three sets of objective data buttress this claim.

4.1.a. Attempted Suicide from the Golden Gate Bridge

Since the opening of the bridge in 1937, approximately 500–600 bodies[6] have been recovered by the local authorities from the waters of San Francisco Bay. Of those collective suicide attempts, only ten subjects are known to have survived, of whom eight have been interviewed. The vertical drop from the bridge at low water mark is 260 feet, the period between leaving the walkway and hitting the water below is about 4 seconds, and the terminal speed on impact is ~75–80 mph.[7] Six out of those eight interviewed survivors did not remember the impact: therefore they were probably unconscious before hitting the water. During their suicide bids, survivors experienced feelings of space, of self, and of loss of time. In addition, there were sensations of great peace, beauty, and transcendent oneness and unity with the universe or with humanity. One subject described the sequence as he regained consciousness: 'dark, grey brown and the light'. Obviously, this was the phenomenological outcome of the neurological process during which his conscious-awareness was regained very shortly after that four-second period.

4.1.b. Self-Induced Loss of Consciousness

Second, there are data on syncope (fainting) brought on by young students during a period of hyperventilation (rapid, deep, regular overbreathing)

---

[6] Rosen D, *West J Med* 122: 289–294, 1975; Seiden R, *Suicide Life-Threat Behav* 8: 203–216, 1968. (Cumulative total now exceeds 1,200 deaths: *San Francisco Chronicle*—'Lethal Beauty', 2005.)

[7] Snyder R and Snow C, *Aerospace Med* 38: 779–783, 1967.

followed by a forced Weber-Valsalva manoeuvre (attempted forced expiration against a closed larynx). Syncope, induced in 42 subjects, lasted 12 ± 4 seconds.[8] Of those occurrences, visual and auditory experiences were noted by 25 (60%). Interestingly, the majority assigned their experiences to the period of unconsciousness, the remainder thinking they occurred during the process of recovering conscious-awareness. The visual imagery revealed a spectrum from greyness, coloured patches or light to perceptions of formed scenes, situations or persons. Likewise, auditory hallucinations ranged from noises, rushing sounds or screams, to human speech. Most felt detached from reality, peaceful and an unwillingness to return and come back to life.[9] Of the subjects 47% thought they were in another world, 20% were confronted by 'preternatural' beings, 16% underwent OBE, and 8% experienced 'tunnels'. Many felt their experience was akin to previous drug adventures. This phenomenology, as the authors pointedly recognize and remark on, is virtually identical to that reported for ECE.

This method of achieving syncopal loss of conscious-awareness through hyperventilation, causes hypocarbia (low partial pressure in the blood of the gas carbon dioxide, CO_2), cerebral vasoconstriction (arterial narrowing) and hypoxia, while the reductions in venous return and cardiac output (forced Weber-Valsalva manoeuvre) result in high amplitude, slow wave activity in the EEG, or even a 'flat' tracing.[10] During the short period of unconsciousness, there is presumed disconnection of higher cortical centres from the thalamus and upper brainstem, thereby allowing these bizarre phenomenological experiences to occupy subconscious mentation as recovery ensues. In these studies, the period of unconsciousness was not as prolonged as those normally arising from clinical crisis-events. Nevertheless, the capacity of the brain to synthesize such subconscious imagery and for it to be remembered, during such a small interval as reawakening comes about, is of critical import and therefore must be taken note of. The obvious importance of these studies emphasizes the objective, but measurably short, timescales during which the resultant phenomenologies evolved.

[8] Lempert T, Bauer M, Schmidt D, *Ann Neurol* 36: 233–237, 1994.
[9] Lempert T, Bauer M, Schmidt D, *Lancet* 344: 829–830, 1994.
[10] Howard P, Leathart G, Dornhorst A, Sharpey-Schafer E, *Br Med J* 3: 382–384, 1951; Klein L, Heyman H, Sieker H, *Am J Med* 37: 263–268, 1964; Gotoh F, Meyer J, Takagi Y, *Arch Neurol* 12: 410–423, 1965; Duvoisin R, *Arch Neurol* 7: 219–226, 1962.

4.1.c. Data from Aircrew Centrifuged to Unconsciousness

Thirdly, in using data from military aviation sources,[11] I refer to experiments and observations on induced loss of consciousness effected through centrifugation of selected aircrew, resulting in head-to-foot cerebral hypoxia and ischaemia through rapid G_z-force acceleration. The 'z' subscript refers to a force acting in the vertical body plane (head-to-feet), as opposed to a frontal ('x', back-front) or lateral ('y', through-shoulders) plane of applied force. Such acceleration-hypoxic forms of induced unconsciousness persist for up to 20 seconds, or about 40 seconds if the subsequent period of confusion is included. Importantly, a fairly invariant pattern of sequenced psychophysiologic events obtains. The experiential outcomes were related to the degree of centrifugal G force applied and sustained, and hence to those parts of the brain remaining functional, compromised and/or de-inhibited from higher centre control. 'Dreaming'[12] occurred with the most strongly applied G_z force, that is, with the greatest degree of enforced cerebral ischaemia, and was located to a precise 12-second window during these carefully timed experiments.

The dreams evoked by this experimental mode of inducing cerebral ischaemia were of high emotional content, associated with detailed visual imagery, vestibular components of floating or other fictive movement, and illogical experiential sequences. Relatives or friends figured predominantly in these dreams, while memories and thoughts were specifically relevant to the individual's personal history, precisely as is witnessed with ECE. I quote:

I was floating in a blue ocean, on my back . . . asleep but not asleep. I knew the sun was up . . . like someone trying to wake me up. I woke up and was on the centrifuge. I did not want to wake up—I could see myself on the water, and also look at the sun: the sky was blue and the sun very yellow.

Or:

I was being propelled by something like a magic carpet.[13]

[11] Whinnery J and Jones D, *Aviat Space Environ Med* 58: 943–947, 1987; Forster E and Whinnery J, *Aviat Space Environ Med* 59: 517–522, 1988; Whinnery J and Whinnery A, *Arch Neurol* 47: 764–776, 1990; Powell T, *Aviat Med* 8: 301–316, 1956; Burton R, *Aviat Space Environ Med* 59: 2–5, 1988.

[12] Forster and Winnery, 1988.

[13] Forster and Whinnery 1988, 520; Whinnery J, *J Near-Death Stud* 15: 231–258, 1997, specifically 245–246.

Here there are strong vestibular influences giving rise to powerful illusions of fictive movement accompanied by visual vividness, a profound sense of ecstasy, and a sensation of light before consciousness supervened.

It was also quite apparent that mnemonic function was one of the first cognitive functions to return, thereby permitting the subsequent phenomena to be remembered. Also, like ECE experiences and the Golden Gate survivors, the memories remained crystal clear and of high intensity for many subsequent years. Clearly, the persistence of memory for ECE subjects has no special relevance to their encounter with death. The sequence of experiential recall embodied 'tunnel' and vestibular phenomena, visual hallucinations, emotive feelings, audition, and finally motor competences. Moreover, the confusion attending the post-recovery period is clearly not a barrier to later detailed recall of the experiences undergone. Importantly, some of these pilots refused to accept that they had been unconscious until they viewed their video-recorded episodes of centrifugation. Moreover, some of their experiential accounts from ~50% of subjects contained confabulatory elements, possibly associated with the desire to conceal the observed lapses in conscious-awareness as an attempt to maintain professional dignity and continue flying.

Here, we see a clear, reproducible cycle in brain reactivation as consciousness was re-established analogous to that accompanying ECE recovery. Indeed, G_z-enforced dreams seem to be microcosms of the ECE event. It is very noteworthy that the experiences remembered by centrifuged aircrew led the experimenters to conclude: 'it is interesting that a coherent visual illusion can be generated within such a short period of time'.[14] Most interesting, indeed. And even more interesting that none of the authors I consider here made use of these striking evidential contributions towards a more balanced scientific understanding of ECE phenomenology.

There is, however, one subtle difference worthy of attention. Subjects recovering from induced syncope or centrifugation were clearly aware that they were not approaching death and therefore were not going to die, unlike the majority of ND subjects. Thus, despite the obvious neurophysiological similarities in the patterns of narrative recall, the former accounts lacked specific descriptive reference to 'heaven' or 'heavenly bodies' (i.e. God or Jesus Christ). The implication of this signal difference is further evaluated below in section 4.3.a.

---

[14] Forster and Whinnery 1988.

And finally, in relation to ECE narratives, I should point out once more that for these experiences to be remembered and thus recalled, sufficient brain function has to be in place for the relevant new memory to be laid down. That strict requirement, noted by Whinnery and colleagues in the G_z studies outlined above, must always apply, even if it were insisted that the subject was experiencing extra-corporeal 'free' consciousness or spirituality. An ECE cannot occur when the brain is 'dead', 'down', or at its most hypoxic or ischaemic. If that were the case, then there could be no establishing of memories for the events that are later recalled. In fact, there would be no story to tell at all. Conversely, it is important to note, whether for dream-state modes or ECE, that while the illusion of having acquired vast knowledge and insights is remembered, the content of that new information is not.

I think the flaw with Dr Fenwick[15] is his assertion that 'consciousness' escapes and exists independently of the brain when the latter is 'dead'. On the contrary, using the timed data from the three examples cited above (Golden Gate bridge attempted suicides, loss of consciousness from hyperventilation/ forced Valsalva manoeuvres, and G_z-enforced centrifugal brain ischaemia), it is patently obvious that a great deal of subconscious mentation and imagery can be synthesized in a few seconds of cerebral real-time but only, as experimentally demonstrated, in those last few moments during which the brain is reawaking, contingent with restoration of a competent circulation. We need neither 'dead' brains nor the forced deus-ex-machina-necessity of 'free consciousness' to account for the illusions undergone and reported: that only adds confusion to circumstances amenable to a more convincing, neurophysiologically based explanation.

I also think Dr Fenwick is wrong in supposing that the confusion exhibited by people on awaking after a cardiac arrest precludes vivid recall of brain-associated perception, as opposed to his notion of free-floating conscious perception. Subjects are confused after acute vascular occlusion to the brain, yet are perfectly able to describe vivid events which occurred while being unconscious. We can also be very drowsy after a dream, yet recall it with perfect memory once the post-awakening period of drowsiness has passed. Moreover, those memories persist, not only for ECE—and as if something 'mystically' exclusive therefore pertained to them alone—but with G_z-enforced experiments and for the Golden Gate bridge survivors, as well. These memories could be put down either in the prelude to the establishing of unconsciousness, as is more probable for OBE, or during an NDE experience which is more the outcome of a brain rapidly regaining its former state of full conscious-awareness.

---

[15] Fenwick P 2004a, b.

To be fair, Fenwick is talking only about cardiac arrest-induced ECE.[16] However, his view again falters because subjects who do not lose their blood pressure or suffer acute circulatory shutdown experience identical forms of imagery. Fenwick's proposal, based on such a shaky metaphysical foundation about free-floating 'consciousness' and 'dying brains', seems highly improbable. His proposals are also capable of other interpretations, and it is those other interpretations which I am in the business of exploring and articulating.

4.2. GRAMMATICAL CRITIQUE OF ECE NARRATIVE: SEMANTICS AND SYNTAX

Having introduced the key element of my argument—that much of ECE phenomenology is a rapidly evolving accompaniment of waking brains abruptly ceasing as consciousness is regained—I now turn to consider the grammatical material of ECE narratives: this comprises another objectively based critical approach concerned with their semantic content and syntactic structure. In these approaches, I borrow and apply additional technical methods employed within the world of dream-state research. The inference will reinforce my claim that we are dealing with intra-cerebral, rather than extra-corporeal, circumstance. That is, ECE originate through direct synthesis from, or out of, the brain rather than being pointers to events occurring external to the brain as might be engendered by a sojourn in some type of other-worldly realm.

4.2.a. Semantics—Anthropomorphic and Geomorphic Reference in ECE Narrative

The semantic properties of recalled ECE narratives, like dreams,[17] may be characterized by particular words: illogicality, incongruity, bizarreness and banality. Here are some initial exemplary vignettes:

'then I became aware that Jesus, or perhaps an angel, was standing by the bed. He led me gently through the window and across the hospital lawn, which had been transformed into a heavenly scene'.

---

[16] Parnia S, Waller D, Yeates R, Fenwick P, *Resuscitation* 48: 149–156, 2001; Parnia S and Fenwick P, *Resuscitation* 52: 5–11, 2002.
[17] Hobson JA, Stickgold R, Pace-Schott E, *NeuroReport* 9: R1–R14, 1998.

It requires little expertise in literary criticism to detect the incongruity and illogicality offered by this fragment[18]—of an individual being taken with the help of Jesus or of an angel through a glass window, likely to be double-glazed in a hospital ward, followed by a descent onto a hospital lawn now suddenly turned into a makeshift heaven. That, I suggest, is pure dream-world fantasy.

Or another, involving this extraordinarily silly conversation (my emphases added):

a voice said, 'Gill, you know who *I* am', and I thought, '. . . this is God and He knows me by name'. Then the voice chuckled and said, '. . . there is someone here you *do* know'. It was her grandfather who died two years peviously. On this occasion, God seems not to have noticed that Gill recognized Him as well as her grandfather whom He then introduces to her. Despite the error, God seemed to be very amused with himself when introducing the older man.

This rather silly bizarre conversation continues:

'Grandfather,' I said, 'I'm not staying here. Hamish [her husband] can't cope, and I've left a pile of shirts to be ironed and he doesn't know how to do them.[19]

In another account[20] from Papua, New Guinea, similar elements of bizarreness, illogicality and incongruity are clearly evident. A man enters one of the typical stilted dwelling-houses characterizing Melanesian society. On opening the front door, he is immediately confronted by a vast engineering plant where steel is being forged into the manufacture of motor cars and ships, although there is no water or dockyard in the geographical vicinity. Subsequently, he leaves the house by following a beam of light, and looking back, finds that the house has now been replaced by a forest and a path. He takes the pathway homewards and re-enters his body. That sequence is extremely bizarre and sequentially illogical—just as in dream-states.

Even more incredible is the meeting of an experient with his father:

dressed just like he used to be in grey trousers and a cardigan. He hadn't changed a bit. We chatted quite naturally and he joked . . .[21]

Really? One wants to ask the author in providing this illustrative portrayal of the afterlife, whether of a 'secular' or 'religiously conditioned' provenance, why it is so uninteresting, but also, so resolutely anthropomorphic. There is nothing at all original here: only a picture boringly identical to life on earth, and an emphasis on the apparent humdrum celestial existence of its elderly citizenry.

---

[18] Fenwick and Fenwick 1998, 79.
[19] Fenwick and Fenwick 1998, 80 and 100–101.
[20] Counts 1983, 120.
[21] Grey 1985, 79.

Next, given all the varied accounts and narratives we should be impressed, too, by their banality and non-uniformity. Eternity, in its realized narrative recall, becomes a 'place' individualized by as many experients who are willing to testify, and, overlain by overwhelming anthropomorphic and geo-centred imagery. Here is another excerpt[22] which collectively is illustrative of the thrust of my claim:

I found myself in front of a nice [prefabricated dwelling] . . . the front door was open and I could see my mother inside. I went up to the door and said: 'I've brought you a present, Mum'. It was some lovely blue silk, enough to make a dress. She took the material and put it on the table and then got out a pair of scissors. I said: 'Mum, what are you doing? You know you don't know how to do dress-making'. She said: 'It's alright, they've been teaching me since I got here' . . . 'Can I come in?' . . . It looked so nice and welcoming, but my mother said: 'No, you can't, it's not your time to stay'. I said: 'Please Mum, it's so lovely here, I don't want to go back'. But she was very firm and would not allow me to cross the threshold.

If a truly spiritual realm had been sampled, we might have expected that something radically new, unexpected, original—even revelatory, perhaps!— might have been opened up to us, invoking insights coincident with its supposed reality and other-worldly provenance. Despite all that has been confessed and widely published, no data have been provided capable of further expanding our current, darkly illumined perceptions of the afterlife. Neither does the eternity so depicted correspond to any construal based on the scriptural and eschatological formulations of the Judaeo-Christian tradition, despite the fact that within so many of these sylvan depictions figures allegedly purported to be, or actually to represent God, Jesus or, in terms of Indian (Hinduistic) experiences, Chaptagutra and his accomplices. The utter banality of the afterlife so described needs to be fully realized, and emphasized.

In support of the transcendental significance of ECE, it is invariably argued that the uniformity of reportings obtained from so many subjects provides firm evidence for their veridicality in portraying a 'spiritual' or 'other-worldly supernatural' domain to which these subjects were privy. If that assertion were true, then given the many hundreds of anecdotes published, we ought surely now to be able to construct an extraordinarily accurate description of the contours of heaven, the heavenly life, together with convincing images of what God or Jesus really look like. However, a closer, critical reading of the accounts offered reveals considerable variance between them: there is scant certainty that an identical place, or even the Godhead, have ever been exclusively sampled by any ECE subject. For

[22] Grey 1985, 54.

example, consider the following excerpts taken at random from prominent writers on this theme:

Of heaven:

a field of beautiful corn;
a garden filled with beautiful flowers: animals, pictures . . . colours of pink, yellow, blue etc;[23]
when you get to the other side there's a river—just like in the Bible—just like a glass;[24]

    I was in a most beautiful landscape, the flowers, the trees, the colours . . . I heard the most wonderful music and there was an organ playing as well: The surroundings were or appeared to be marble, in structure pillars. There seemed to be something in front of me that looked like a crypt: . . . but I can only describe it as heaven . . . of intense light, of intense activity, like a bustling city . . . nothing like floating on clouds or harps[25]

Of heavenly (otherworldly) persons:

Just as clear and plain the Lord came and stood and held his hands out for me. Well, he stood there and looked down at me and it was all bright then . . . He was tall with hands out and he had all white on, like he had a white robe on . . . It [the face] was more beautiful than anything you've ever seen. His face was beautiful, really and truly beautiful. His skin was almost like it was glowing and it was flawless, absolutely flawless;[26]

when I suddenly found myself in this gentle glowing light . . . below the three beings above me . . . dressed alike in high-necked silver-coloured tunics . . . with silver turbans on their heads. And from a jewel in the centre of each forehead or turban three 'laser' beams emitted, meeting in the centre;
at end [of tunnel] . . . three old Chinese men [with] long white beards [wearing] white robes;[27]

I saw Jesus Christ. I was aware of him by the print of the nails in his hands and his feet and I remember I was very amused.[28]

It is evident that these excerpts most obviously resemble the contours of the happenings, memories, conceptualizations and ups-and-downs that pertain to everyday life on earth. A pervading sense of weirdness and bizarreness firmly engenders these accounts which typify dream-states and daytime reveries. In their cultural modalities—historic or contemporary, western

[23] Fenwick and Fenwick 1998, 75–77.
[24] Moody 1977, 17–18.
[25] Grey 1985, 50–51.
[26] Sabom 1982, 49.
[27] Fenwick and Fenwick 1998, 81–82.
[28] Grey 1985, 52.

or eastern, Christianized or not—the narrative panoramas evoked are firmly geomorphically and anthropomorphically this-worldly. We not only have reference to flowers, grass, trees, country lanes, lakes, breezes, but also committees, clerks, books, administrative errors in personal identification, trials by magnet, and commands sometimes given by God, Jesus or even parents or grandparents, ordering newly arrived experients to get back to earth, and so refusing outright their continued residency as spiritual citizens.

The overall impression given by these accounts of the so-called other-worldly realm, thinking specifically of western accounts, is entirely reminiscent of impressions gained collectively through each experient's personal life from stained-glass windows and other forms of ecclesial iconography, the typical Sunday school illustrations of Jesus, films and media, the worlds of fine art and literature, other sources of more mediocre artwork, and, of course, the imagination. Indeed, the stories 'brought back' seem to be an amalgam of all varied metaphorical attempts by living people to express the inexpressible. Interestingly, since God is so rarely illustrated in facial or personal terms, we should take note that very few portrayals of him are offered in these narratives. On the other hand, it is noticeable how frequently grandparents figure in these accounts, and play a role—presumably reflecting the strong psycho-social bonds that exist between the aged and young in many extended families. That children very rarely appear in these reports seems not to have occasioned any dismay from our key writers: these two anomalies are therefore all the more remarkable.

4.2.b. Syntax—'And Then I . . .': Narrative Reference to Time and Person

At the beginning of this chapter, I referred to the use of word counts in establishing the short-term, ephemeral nature of ECE. Next, I considered semantic examples of the earthbound banality, illogicalities and incongruity of the recollected narratives offered by experients. Note was also taken particularly of the major inconsistencies in the collective descriptions of heaven and of the heavenly figures supposedly encountered. Now, in terms of narrative syntax, I draw attention to the presence of conjunctive prepositions and to their widespread use in later, rationalized public accounts given.

Typical constructions include the following, and are indicative of a patch-work of remembered vignettes strung together, rather than of a temporally sequenced flow of experiential happenings: 'Then, there appeared . . .'; 'Next, I found myself . . .'; After that . . .'; 'Following that . . .'. These grammatical constructs are precisely those associated with recalled dream-states, in that they relate to passive events. There is an absence of intent, agential control, or hint of personally directed action ('So . . .'; 'in order to . . .'; 'my purpose was to . . .'); nor is there reverse causality ('because so-and-so . . .'; 'as a result of x, then y . . .'; 'since that, I did/decided to . . .'). Like dreams, a substantial part of ECE imagery seems to characterize purposeless activity. On those grounds, the interpretations by authors that this represents a realistic view of a 'mysti-cal' other-worldly realm lacks conviction.

Another feature of ECE narratives is that the experient always seems to be a detached subjective observer of the supposed celestial locus which he or she comes to inhabit:

the doctors had all given up . . . they said *I* was dying [and] *I* was feeling the life going out of *my* body . . . *I* could still hear what everyone [the medical personnel attending her] was saying . . . [then] . . . *I* heard God's voice talking to *me*. He had the most gentle, loving voice. He told *me* that if *I* wanted to live *I* was going to have to breathe.[29] (My emphases in this and succeeding passages.)

During these events there seems to remain a continued sense of personhood: all reports are in the first person:

I remember that *I* could see *myself* walking away. *I* was . . . 20 feet away . . . *I* could see *me* walking away. *I* was wearing[30] this grey suit that *I* bought last year and *I* was walking away from *myself* hanging there.[31] (Report by an attempted suicide victim.)

Others imagine possession of another kind of body, although sensed in terms of physicality:

I had a piece of clothing on . . . very loose . . . and *I* remember having *bare feet* . . . it was very different [from my physical body] . . . very thin, very delicate . . . very light. *My face and hands* were the same. Because *I* remember trying to touch *my face* to make sure everything was okay . . . [and] . . . *I* could feel it.[32]

---

[29] Moody 1977, 27.

[30] He was *NOT* wearing a grey suit. In fact, he wore something completely different. This is another typical instance of the inaccuracies which accompany ECE reportings, indicating quite clearly that they are not necessarily veridical eyewitness accounts of what is alleged to have been observed or undergone by any of these subjects.

[31] Ring 1980, 46.

[32] Ring 1980, 52.

The pronominal 'my' here implies continuity of 'self' which could, presumably, also obtain with someone now without a physical body. Yet there are strong referential concerns not only about corporeal attributes, that is, a fleshly human body, in these narrative accounts of ECE, but with earthly clothing. It is, however, difficult to interpret, within the presumed context of afterlife, the continuing sense of 'self' because there has never been reference in the relevant literature to any ECE subject claiming to have possessed a 'resurrected body', nor what form or even degree of corporeality such a resurrected body might possess. That criticism applies to the majority of recalled experiences whether or not the predisposing circumstances threatened cerebral blood supply. Neither, one might suppose, should the different types of 'people' observed during these extra-terrestrial events so unmistakably resemble the configuration of human beings. Here is one respondent's anthropomorphic description of a '[B]eing of light' that is highly suggestive of Jesus:

It was this vivid gold, yellow... then *I* saw a form there [note reference to physical location] ... *I* can see that form now ... it had blond-gold hair and it had a beard, a very light beard and a moustache. It had a white garment on ... [and] ... there was a red spot here [pointing to a Sacred Heart on the chest on his gown] ... and a chalice in his hand.[33]

The visual clues about corporeal imagery apply not only to *'people of [L]ight'* seen during an NDE, but also to long-dead family relatives invariably reported to be wearing the same suits or dresses when last seen alive on earth. This innate sense of structural and bodily corporateness, whether concerning the experients themselves or other so-called people observed during an ECE, demands further exploration. It is highly probable that such internal images and perceptions of body shape are, as indicated by these many examples, derivative of internally generated cerebral mechanisms[34] in brains that could hardly be hypoxic. Truly spiritual 'persons' or even incorporeal or disembodied 'consciousness', as the authored excerpts given above variously indicate, should neither rely on so-maesthetic competence nor allude to or require functioning body parts for supportive activity. Indeed, by the very definitions and implications imposed by the collective authorship under review, any persisting body part and its allied function would no longer be present, available or necessary in the other-worldly domain proposed by these writers.

---

[33] Ring 1980, 60.
[34] Melzack R, *Canad Psychol* 30: 1–16, 1989.

4.3. THE INTRUSION OF COGNITIVE ACTIVITY INTO THE SUBJECTIVE WORLD OF ECE

4.3.a. Physically Based Influences on ECE Phenomenology

Above I gave my arguments for the assertion that much ECE phenomenology occurs as the brain recovers its functional capacities from its preceding ischaemic insult (note that this situation is different from that physiologically pertaining to normal dream awakenings). But the model initially proposed, in suggesting that ECE terminate precisely as conscious-awareness supervenes, requires updating. That this updated modification is required emerges from further critical readings of the narrative reports published, readings which have obviously escaped the minds of the authorship publishing them.

In particular, I draw attention to the conscious perception of somaesthetic afferent inputs (Figure 2) in parallel with the unfolding subconscious mentation of the ECE. While undergoing ECE, subjects do hear local voices of clinical staff or feel the pain of a needle jab, the searing burn from cardiac defibrillator electrodes, or a sense of suffocation as an oxygen mask is applied to the mouth and nose and strapped in position. There is, in fact, a duality of perception, an awareness both of the immediacy of the physical milieu with voices, scenes or other this-worldly events (e.g. pain) appropriate to the circumstances surrounding the event, yet accompanied by simultaneous

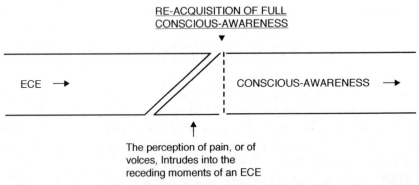

Figure 2. The model of the termination of an NDE indicated in Figure 1 is not strictly accurate. For example, it is clearly evident that for many subjects stimuli within their immediate worlds, such as pain or voices, impinge upon their minds and are subsequently remembered. This observation provides a further insight that there is an intermingling between the subconscious (NDE) mode, and emerging conscious-awareness as the brain recovers from its preceding insult.

perceptions of a spiritual realm or other-world that offers scenes of great beauty and colour, together with feelings of awe, love and ecstasy. The juxtapositional perception of the conscious and subconscious during the course of some ECE, of the this-worldly with the other-worldly, points to neurophysiological processes. Such duality of perception underlies the mechanism of lucid dreaming, and to a lesser extent that of hypnagogic dream-onset and hypnopompic dream-awakenings, and certain brain pathologies (see below).

These influences were particularly noticeable in the case of Howard Storm's peritonitis and an Indian subject with an abscess brewing in one of his arms. David Whitmarsh, a naval seaman with a respiratory arrest following electro-cution aboard, became aware of 'pressure' caused by assisted respiration applied through the old-fashioned approach known as the Holger-Nielsen technique.[35] His conscious perception of the force of the movements applied by the resuscitator around his shoulder joints appeared to be pushing him downwards while he, subconsciously, was simultaneously attempting to rise upwards. Another less common, yet significant effect, is that of body distor-tions. One woman[36] during childbirth felt that her body was diminishing in size. Such abnormal perceptions of body are a common feature in migraine attacks[37] or, more rarely, of epileptic aura,[38] and are presumably due to disordered functioning of the posterior parietal cortex (which constitutes our cognitive perceptions of ego- and paracentric body-imagery and spatial awareness).[39] In Whitmarsh's case,[40] his tunnel was 'angulated downwards'. James was 'falling down' his tunnel as he experienced 'a kaleidoscopic burst of changing colours' (56) suggesting widespread disordered cortical functioning due to arterial hypoperfusion.[41] A kaleidoscopic burst of colour implies impaired activity within the primary occipital striate cortex. From all this, one has to conclude that the conscious perception/misperception of bodily sensations, shape or position could not occur if that consciousness resided outwith the body and, more importantly, outside its disordered brain. No author seems to have recognized the impossibilities of that state of affairs.

---

[35] Fenwick and Fenwick 1998, 154–155.
[36] Fenwick and Fenwick 1998, 119.
[37] Lippman C, *J Nerv Ment Dis* 117: 345–350, 1953; Todd J, *Canad Med Assoc J* 73: 701–704, 1955.
[38] Leker R, Karni A, River Y, *Acta Neurol Scand* 94: 383–385, 1996.
[39] Stein J, *Neuroscience: An Introduction*, Chichester: Wiley 2006, 241ff.
[40] Fenwick and Fenwick 1998, 51.
[41] Price J, Whitlock F, Hall R, *Psychiatrica Clinica* 16: 26–44, 1983.

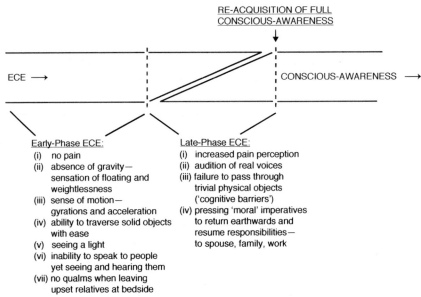

Figure 3. A more definitive, considered analysis of NDE (than those presented in Figures 1 and 2) reveals the concept of early-phase, and late-phase, phenomenology. The latter, indicated by the paired vertical dotted lines, indicates the period of time during which this-worldly stimuli interrupt the subconscious mentation of the terminating experience. Features describing early-phase events contrast markedly with those occurring during the late-phase. Emphatic of the changed demeanour of subjects during the late-phase NDE is the burgeoning influence of the pre-frontal cortex, as suggested by the reluctance of subjects to traverse 'physical' barriers and the increasing 'moral' pressure for them to reappropriate previous earthly responsibilities or cares.

4.3.b. Reality Regained: Returning Consciousness Modulates the Late-Phase Experiential Contours of ECE

For another piece of evidence exemplary of a coexisting duality of perception, I turn to another subtle, yet signally important distinction, which has evaded significant comment or any attempt at explanation in the books I am evaluating. It concerns the sharp antithesis between the complete absence of concern for work, family or children during the initial *early-phase* ECE, and subjects' remarkably changed perspectives during *late-phase* ECE. Then, their much-felt urgency or even sense of overwhelming guilt becomes very apparent, when the necessity to return to earth and resume former responsibilities is either forced on or chosen by them, rather than to stay otherworldly (Figure 3).

Several examples arise.[42] Richard, with complications following an appendicectomy, had far more interest in the 'light' than concern for his grieving parents. Ella, during a prolonged recovery from her anaesthetic, willed herself to go towards the 'light' without any thought for her husband and children. Alf, while floating above his bed during an episode of pneumonia, had no emotional concern for his weeping mother kneeling at his bedside. That attitude contrasts strikingly with the later urgent compulsion to return to earth and take up again former personal ties, responsibilities and jobs. That antithetic and emphatically late-phase difference, I suggest, is due to reawakening of the frontal cortex from its immediately previous dormant phase at the nadir of the crisis. It is in this part of the brain where moral decision-making occurs.

It is my view that these terminal aspects of ECE occur just as conscious reawakening occurs, being conceivable in terms of reactivation and recoupling of the lateral-orbital frontal cortex, and dorso-lateral pre-frontal cortex[43] (Figure 4). Other parts of the brain, having generated their own subconscious mentation which, like dream-states, is somewhat bizarre, illogical and incongruous, are now being told by the pre-frontal cortex, as it fully recovers its own controlling influences and critical faculties, 'stop all this fantasy; wake up—its time to get going'. The overwhelming moral coercion to return to earth and attend to one's responsibilities is consistent with the re-establishment of critical pathways from the frontal lobes to other parts of the cortex, thalamus and related structures. Moreover, the abrupt termination of the event, coincident with the reappearance of conscious volition, would then be consistent with the full reconstitution of frontal lobe activity.

There is also an inconsistency in the manner of return. Some experients make the decision for themselves,[44] such as Linda and James. Others say the return just happens, while for others, including Avon, Ella and Anne, they were commanded to return. The so-called 'barrier' is none other than a manifestation of the return of cognitive function, thus helping to establish

[42] Fenwick and Fenwick 1998, 58–59, 70–71, 169.

[43] Joseph R, The Frontal Lobes, in: *Neuropsychology, Neuropsychiatry, and Behavioral Neurology,* New York: Plenum 1990, 157ff; Bradshaw J, The Frontal Cortex and the Control of Behaviour, in: *Developmental Disorders of the Frontostriatal System,* Hove: Psychology Press 2001, 19ff; Bechara A, Damasio A, Damasio H, Anderson S, *Cogn* 50: 7–15, 1994; Decety J and Sommerville J, *Trends Cogn Sci* 7: 527–533, 2003; Markowitsch HJ and Kessler J, *Exp Brain Res* 133: 94–102, 2000.

[44] Fenwick and Fenwick 1998, 98, 102–103.

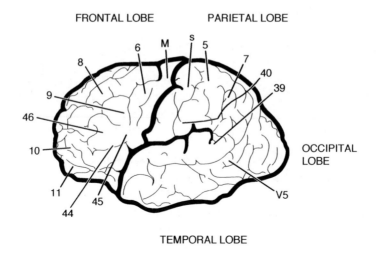

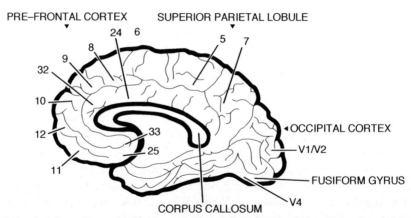

Figure 4. Schematic representations of the lateral (upper) and inner (lower) aspects of the cerebral cortex. The motor cortex (M; area 4), pre-motor (6) and sensory (S) cortices lie adjacent to the Sylvian fissure separating frontal from (anterior) parietal lobes. The posterior parietal lobe comprises superior parietal lobule (5, 7) and inferior parietal lobule (39, 40) with roles in generating body-image. The occipital cortex is largely given over to vision, comprising primary visual areas (V1/V2) and areas concerned with motion (V5) and colour (V4), the latter located predominantly in the fusiform gyrus on the lower, inner aspects of each hemisphere. The hemispheres are connected by a dense band of nerve fibres, termed the corpus callosum. The non-motor areas of the frontal lobe, or pre-frontal cortex, PFC, comprise the dorso-lateral PFC (areas 9, 10, 44, 45, 46), orbito-frontal (11, 13, 25, 32, 47), and medial areas (32, 33, 25, 24). Its overall function is to shape personality and demeanour, attention, motivation, moral sensibility and ethical concerns, and strategic planning.

and rationalize the incipient ending of the excursion as conscious-awareness resurfaces.

Barriers, of various sizes and shapes, decisions made as a prelude to returning to earth, and the urgency to resist the pleasure of going onwards rather than resuming earthbound responsibilities, are signs indicative of the progressive intrusion of a waxing of conscious-awareness into the waning subconscious mentation of the ECE. It is noteworthy that during the *late-phase* return to consciousness, experients are impeded by trivial, earthly barriers, revealing that they are mental constructs, or metaphors, betokening the increasing influence of awakening cognitive processes on the end-stage phases of these events. That is, they are 'cognitive barriers' that signal commencement of the '*inward*' trajectory back into the conscious world. No author seems to have noticed that subjects, in their *earlier* subconscious state as the NDE begins, experience no difficulty whatsoever in traversing far more difficult physical obstructions, such as walls, double-glazed windows in wards, ceilings and roofs, as they commence their '*outward*' flights towards the tunnel or light. The two phenomena, to my mind, are all of a piece. The initial *early-phase* experiential disregard for family and the ease with which solid objects are transversed stand in striking contrast to the *late-phase* terminal inability of subjects to cross insubstantial barriers, and the manner with which their true, worldly responsibilities assume an increasingly moral urgency coercing them to return. That vivid antithesis emphasizes the divide between a dream-like fantasy world and its progressive replacement by the incipient dawning of conscious reality. It should not be forgotten that in the course of normal living, we tend to construct similar 'cognitive' avoidance-barriers when the going gets particularly hard and unpleasant, challenging or frightening.

I think these considerations more than adequately answer one of the Fenwick's queries[45] as to 'how it is that people manage to think so coherently at a time when one would have expected logical thought to be impossible'. The key is to look in the right place, and at the right time—not at supposedly dead brains, but at ones that are rapidly and vigorously reawakening themselves—and to recognize that such coherent cognitive functioning does occur (and could *only* occur) during that terminal revitalizing process. Once that is understood, the problem dissolves.

[45] Fenwick and Fenwick 1998, 2.

4.4. EVIDENCE THAT PRE-EXISTING COGNITIVE PARADIGMS INFLUENCE THE EXPERIENTIAL CONTOURS OF ECE

The previous section drew attention to the principle that the resumption of conscious-awareness progressively engrafts onto the terminal declining phases of ECE phenomenology. That defines what I have termed the *late-phase* components, as opposed to the *early-phase* components which may comprise elements of OBE together with the floating into space that so often characterizes the onset of an NDE, including the 'tunnel'.

There is, yet, a further mechanism through which the subconscious mental activities of ECE are presumptively anticipated through pre-existent cognitive paradigms. Moreover, this further dimension to the likely neurophysiological structuring of ECE provides added weight in compelling acceptance of brain-generated (conscious) inputs to this type of phenomenology. These aspects I now proceed to draw together. None of the authors I am reviewing has made specific note of these cortically induced influences on the phenomenology experienced. Several instances have arisen throughout the ECE narrative accounts in which conscious-awareness, and hence culturally conditioned 'cognitive' influences, have, in some way or other, directly modulated the experiential contours of the 'other-worldly journey'—and see brief allusions to this in other case material in Chapter 2. It is important to my quest that I now address this last particular cultural influence.

4.4.a. Pre-Existing Brain-Based Perceptions of Death and of Dying Define Other-Worldly Typologies

In proceeding, the problem needs addressing by first tackling the prevailing assumption among the authors cited herein that the uniformly qualitative phenomenology of ECE is indicative of the existence and reality of a spiritual realm. With that assumption I most strongly disagree: the possibility of a spiritual realm cannot be based on their conclusions since, as I have insisted, each narrative report is idiosyncratic and fails to corroborate the 'core' or 'thanato-mimetic' sequence. On the contrary, another question arises: that is, why, within what I regard as idiosyncratic individualized experiences, the predominant typologies do result in the perception of some kind of other-worldly realm, or even 'heaven', and encounters with known spiritual figures. Moreover, it is in facing an acute crisis even though it may not be inevitably lethal that many subjects grossly overestimate the threat to their continuing mortal existence.[46] ECE result only from an acute antecedent event. I am not aware that ECE involve subjects who have lain unconscious for months or even years before recovering some measure of conscious-awareness. Neither, as noted above, do these types of other-worldly spiritualized imagery invade the experiences of subjects who know they are *not* about to die, or who know they are *not* in a death-threatening circumstance as when awaking from faints or a period of laboratory-induced centrifugation.

It is my contention, therefore, that the impact of sensing themselves to be dying, or of just having died, induces every subject to recall their previous, and somewhat conventionally uniform, cognitively bound models of what it is like to die and 'to be on the other side'. Such model apprehensions of the hereafter will already have been synthesized from subjects' imaginations, past experiences, impressions based on vicarious religious and other secular influences, thoughts and constructions arising out of personal and local deaths and attendances at funeral services, and their overarching constructions about the future afterlife. As the ECE gets underway, these model apprehensions will now be subconsciously unfolded, being directly recalled from memories already implanted in the brain.

I give some cogent examples to drive home this important point: pre-existing and prevailing cognitive activities do shape the contours of later subconscious mentation. There are several pertinent case-reports providing exemplary evidence which underpins this viewpoint. The first is of a 29-year-old English woman[47] subject to repeated temporal lobe seizures since the age of 8. At the time of clinical presentation, she had recently received from The Netherlands an official photograph of her brother's tombstone in a British Second World War military cemetery. Following receipt of this photograph, her pre-ictal auras henceforward always comprised rows of tulips, serried lines of gravestones and linear arrays of lamb carcasses. Clearly, the impact of this highly emotionally charged experience had major repercussions on the character of her later seizural auras. Importantly, a transferral of her cognitive and affective dispositions had now become realized in another part of the brain concerned with the elaboration and spreading of her pre-epileptic auras. Moreover, the witnessing of the lambs was perhaps a metaphorical representation of her innermost feelings although we know neither the circumstances of her brother's death, nor her

---

[46] Owens et al 1990; Gabbard et al. 1981.
[47] Karagulla S and Robertson E, *Br Med J* 1: 748–752, 1955 (Case3B, p. 751).

depth of grief, nor the duration of her loss and what it meant to her. We might surmise it was fairly significant: recall the disastrous horrors of Arnhem in order to feel the poignant impact of the phrased imagery 'like lambs to the slaughter'.

The second example[48] involves a girl who, aged 7, encountered a man who threatened to put her in a sack filled with snakes. This threat was later re-enacted in her subconscious dreams (at age 11), subsequently to become a daytime aura (at age 14), accompanied thereafter with occasional tonic seizures. Investigations revealed right-sided temporo-occipital cortical atrophy. A third case centres on an American veteran. His armed service in Vietnam became transferred to his subconscious as very frightening dreams. EEG showed bilateral temporal spikes. He subsequently responded to the anti-epileptic drug, carbamazepine.[49] It is significant that in all three cases, underlying temporal lobe damage presumably facilitated the transfer of the original cognitive stimulus to the ensuing pre- and inter-ictal auras.

In like manner it is understandable, as the prospect of death or thoughts of having died are faced, how the ensuing ECE phenomenology would directly reflect the memories, perceptions and apprehensions which all subjects might imagine or believe ensue at the moment of death, and beyond. The variety of retrospective narratives offered, all intensely geomorphic and even anthropomorphic for those supposing themselves to have been in the presence of God or Jesus, or a reviewing committee, are clearly evident from an appraisal of each subject's personalized account. The imagined descriptive contours of the afterlife are represented in subconscious mentation as vivid, but often somewhat bizarre, quasi-dream-like sequences and encounters, many examples of which have been given in the preceding pages. There are no pearly gates: confronting death during an actual life-threatening crisis certainly concentrates the mind. It is a serious business and not the occasion for recall of music hall jokes or newspaper cartoons. Indeed, these images are representative of the deepest concerns and inarticulate instincts which we all secretly, and to variable degrees, harbour in the recesses of our hearts about the finality of death. This repressed imagery is played out on the neurophysiological matrix of a somewhat confused brain, as each cortical area gradually recovers its functional role towards the re-expression of full conscious-awareness.

---

[48] Epstein A, *Biol Psychiatr* 17: 1207–1215, 1982 (see pp. 1211 and 1213).
[49] Stewart J and Bartucci R, *Am J Psychiatr* 143: 113–114, 1986.

4.5. A RE-CLASSIFICATION OF OB AND ND
EXPERIENTIAL PHENOMENOLOGY

To summarize, my argument is that the foundation for much out-of-body and near-death phenomenology is the *recovering* brain, which provides the neuronal basis for whatever bits of those phenomenologies are experienced. However, the experiences undergone are coloured and rendered non-uniform by two critical insights. First, because the stored perceptual model idealizations of what might be entailed in dying and accessing the afterlife are personally and psychologically idiosyncratic. Second, because the circumstances of and recovery from each ECE depend on several important biological and environmental factors[50] which are personally and clinically idiosyncratic. These, to my mind, are crucial factors which demand careful analysis. They alter considerably prevailing concepts and expectations of what ECE are really about.

In introducing and articulating my own interpretations of ECE, I have pursued a critical approach towards the actual testimonies offered by subjects. From these, I have attempted to draw out, at this stage more by logic than by scientific analysis, what clues these accounts yield in expanding our understandings of the extraordinary events to which the latter bear witness. With that approach, I have already begun to shift perceptions away from overriding 'mystical' interpretative constructs to one which, now, inevitably leans towards a more straightforward, but neurophysiologically grounded, aetiology. These conclusions, now brought to light, make it difficult to avoid the likely relevance of a biomedically based aetiology. It is with these newer implications, tilting towards a more informed approach to scientific outcome, that my text now engages.

It is on these grounds that I propose an entirely new reclassification of ECE phenomenology. The OBE is envisioned as a perturbation of the complex neurophysiological mechanisms that construct body-image and its relationship to peri-personal space, as I shall discuss in further detail below in Chapter 6. Allied perturbations of egocentric body space include autoscopy, heautoscopy and the sensing of invisible presences. The NDE, on the other hand, can more usefully be understood as two entities—*early-phase* and *late-phase* components (Figure 3) rather than the proposals already discussed and rejected: I want nothing to do with 'core' and 'depth' experiences. The early phase component, like OBE, may involve aberrant functioning of the vestibular system together with a visual component, due possibly to the incipient

---

[50] These include the subject's age, degree of atheromatous arterial degeneration, previous 'stroke' events, congenital malformations of the cerebral arterial tree, the period of time without a circulation or an effective blood pressure, history of smoking, and so on...

revascularization of the visual cortex and relevant association areas which result in the subject's retrospective perception of 'moving' through an illusory tunnel and 'onwards' into a light. Early-phase phenomenology is predicated on, and conditioned by, premorbid cognitive constructs in subjects' minds of what dying and the afterlife would be like. Another most striking feature of this incipient dawning of the return to full conscious-awareness is the absence of pain, the ability to traverse at ease solid objects such as walls or ceilings, and the unconcerned indifference of floating off a bed around which may be sitting weeping relatives.

Thus, early-phase phenomenology contrasts sharply with late-phase characteristics which herald the progressive, and final, reassertion of full conscious-awareness. Here, during the short, ephemeral evolution of ECE, consciously perceived somaesthetic activities, together with other 'higher' mental functions, interdigitate with, and progressively overtake, the preceding subconscious dream-like fantasy of early-phase mentation. Furthermore, late phase behaviour is now coloured by 'moral' intrusions in respect of earthly people and responsibilities, in parallel with the lack of desire, or ability, to overcome physical barriers.

Already, I have hinted at certain scientific approaches which underpin many of my conclusions, thus providing incisive counter-arguments to the material, and emergent views, expressed in the canonical texts. Much ECE phenomenology can be logically traced to a waking, rather than an agonally dying, brain. From all that, strong evidential claims arise, indicative of neurophysiological, rather than spiritualized, other-worldly explanations for these events. Moreover, neurophysiologically based explanations should, in future, begin to enjoy a far greater role in accounting for the varied facets of these phenomena. Indeed, in making such claims, I am immediately freed from the straitjacket of brokering dead brains, but instead, offered the means of engaging with considerably more fruitful neurophysiological opportunity and possibility. These will be explored in the succeeding chapters.

The reclassification offered here notably avoids the fabulous reconstruction of Moody, and the spurious proposals of Ring of the artificial notions of either 'core' or 'deep' experiences. The phenomenology is emphatically idio-syncratic, as each testimony clearly demonstrates, comprising preconceived ideas about the afterlife which are replayed in memory as the event unwinds. No event can be forced into an imaginary core or depth sequence: each ECE in its personalized idiosyncrasy is, in part, dependent on the manner by which the brain is revascularized. This novel classification has nothing to do with dying or dead brains, Ring's absurd *'thanatomimetic' sequences*, nor with the escape of soul or consciousness into another other-worldly realm whose descriptive features are banal, bizarre, illogical and intensely geo-/anthropomorphic. On the contrary, my theory is firmly based on neuroscience, and thus fully capable of offering explanations which are rationally conditioned and logically constructed. Phenomenologically, at base is a personal, idiosyncratic event that is revealed in personal, idiosyncratic language.

In taking recourse to a thoroughly scientifically based account of ECE phenomenology, I am not suggesting that one specific aspect of neurophysiology provides a definitive answer to the unravelling of the whole problem. Rather, I think that any solution rests on analogical comparisons, by drawing attention to various brain-states or aspects of cortical function, normal or aberrant, which illustrate how pieces of the entire phenomenological jigsaw could, conceivably, come together. In the following five chapters, we shall be examining several areas which have that direct relevance to ECE phenomenology.

From what has already been written above, it will come as no surprise to the reader that these neurophysiological explorations relate not only to the realm of waking-consciousness, but also to 'unconsciousness', and other 'subconscious' states of existence. While these words of themselves have little precise meaning, and hence are difficult to define from a strict neurophysiological perspective, they nevertheless point to a spectrum of existential states between either being fully consciously aware or being entirely unconscious and therefore unresponsive to any environmental stimuli.

Consciousness is also important to our theme, however, since a large proportion of 'everyday' conscious-awareness is partly subconscious, and partly illusory (see Chapter 5). Since ECE phenomenology is, in my view, an illusory dream-like event engendered by the brain while in the process of awaking, it is important to understand the parameters of 'normal' wakeful illusion, in order to effect comparisons with the reduced conscious states during which illusory ECE phenomenologies arise and evolve. In thinking about this illusory world, our attention is immediately drawn to the vast extent to which our brains operate outside the realms of wakeful conscious perception throughout our lives.

In developing the theme of 'consciousness' in the next chapter, emphasis will be oriented towards the so-called 'phantom limb' phenomenon, not only because it is a reasonably well-known circumstance, but because it draws attention to the ability of the brain to create mental constructs of body parts no longer physically extant. Such explorations provide the grounds for demonstrating how the body may appear to its owner to be outwith the physical domain, as witnessed during OBE. In the succeeding chapter, I shall then develop my case that OBE can be conceived entirely as brain-based illusory phenomena, as opposed to declarations that mind can exist outwith the brain (and body), thereby providing: first, veridical documentation of events opaque to normal sensory inputs; and second, explanations for so-called psychical competence.

5

Conscious-Awareness:
Life's Illusory Legacy

5.1. THE ILLUSORY FOUNDATIONS
OF CONSCIOUS-AWARENESS

The preceding chapter encapsulates my argument that ECE are probably best accounted for in terms of funtional perturbations of brains in their recovery from severe preceding metabolic insults. From such a view two corollaries follow. First, that it runs counter to other speculative opinions suggesting or, indeed, asserting that ECE phenomenology anticipates the reality of life in the afterworld and offers focus for the enhancement of psychical powers and competence. Second, it is a view that demands a fuller descent into the neurophysiological processes likely to be associated with the emergence of ECE phenomenology. In articulating this second corollary, we encounter the problem that while ECE are presumptive neurological artefacts and therefore either illusory or hallucinatory products, much of normal conscious-awareness is also, to a large extent, illusory. Thus we need to know precisely, as far as current knowledge permits, where we stand in deliberations about the nature of consciousness, the meaning of conscious-awareness, and the illusory typologies which characterize so much of wakeful existence. The following chapter, therefore, is of vital importance as well as crucially germane to my continuing argument espousing a neural basis for ECE.

A definition of consciousness or conscious-awareness is difficult because the concept is obstinately abstract, although much is known of the mechanisms underpinning the experiences of consciousness (particularly of sight and audition). Nevertheless, there is no explanation as to how, or why, consciousness should necessarily arise out of the rather more basic neural activities comprising brain metabolism. An alternative expression—'being conscious'—conveys another experiential facet to its meaning, since we are all aware of what it is like to be conscious or consciously aware and how that differs from being unconscious (during recovery from a faint or having an anaesthetic), or inhabiting the nocturnal subconscious world of dreams. While that sense of being conscious reminds us what it feels like to be consciously aware, it offers scant help in advancing our elucidatory investigations.

5.1.a. Conscious-Awareness

The notion of 'being conscious' is critically emphatic of the importance of the first-person perspective which should not be lost sight of when the causal effects of consciousness are under consideration. Within that private, first-person subjective sphere of being conscious, different states-of-awareness are recognized including self-consciousness, thought, imagination and emotion. Yet throughout much of life, many processes are effected without any input from, or entry into, conscious-awareness such as dressing oneself, walking along a road, or driving a vehicle in dense traffic. Attention only becomes focused when an irregularity intrudes—a missing shirt button, or a confrontation with flashing blue lights on the carriageway. Most metabolic activities are also outwith the sphere of conscious-awareness, like respiration, or the control of pulse or blood pressure although, in part, neurally based. Some intestinal motility experts refer to the 'brain in the intestine' on account of its extensively rich neural complexes necessary for controlling digestion, absorption and propulsion. Yet despite having that enormous neural component, the intestine does not exhibit consciousness. Sensations such as cramp, fullness or urgency are referred to the brain and integrated into the mind which subserves one's sense of unitary being.

Yet we do not think life is analogous to watching a long film show, or dreaming. Conscious-awareness is a reality: that is the crucial issue. From that reality illusion arises, despite our current inability to understand fully the relationships between neural process, emergent consciousness, and the creation of the illusory state-of-mind. A slice of liver maintained in warm culture medium will secrete bile: a slice of brain under identical conditions exhibits neural firing and the release of neurochemical transmitters but does not extrude or elaborate 'consciousness'. At least, one would be most surprised if a group of cultured neurones in a Petri dish 'felt' comfortably warm, collectively was able to 'note' the passing of the day, or even became 'resentful' when being disturbed by a laboratory assistant. We would be even more taken aback if it were suggested that cultured neurones experienced the occasional illusion. Are we, humankind, nothing more than 'a pack of neurons' as Crick has suggested?[1]

---

[1] Crick Francis, *The Astonishing Hypothesis: The Scientific Search for the Soul,* London: Simon & Schuster 1994, iii.

The above exemplifies the problem of determining how the brain gives rise to those qualia-like percepts like colours, the smell of freshly baked bread or mown grass, or the plaintive call of an oboe, which erupt into our continuing life of conscious-awareness. That is what David Chalmers has famously termed the '*hard problem*' in our attempts to grapple with the nature of conscious-awareness.[2] Hence the difficulty in deciding whether near-death or out-of-body experiences are any more true, or illusory, than the routine experiences of daily living. Indeed, to the experient, ECE are regarded as real and thus full of meaning. But that is like dreams: they also seem entirely real—until we awaken. Therefore, why should there be any difference between waking from a dream or waking from an ECE? It is for that reason that I consider dream physiology in depth in a subsequent chapter, since we know much of what happens to the brain during dreaming. From that information, it is possible to relate dream content to the parts of the brain which remain active, and those which are deactivated, and thus make some inferences about what might be happening during an NDE.

5.1.b. Exploring Likely Possibilities: The Fast and Slow Lanes of Conscious Perception

There is a further important neurophysiological fact that impinges on our portrayal of conscious processing. And that is that conscious-perceptions are 'late': this means that the average time interval between a stimulus and its registration in conscious-awareness is approximately 250–300 milliseconds. Comparatively, that is much slower than the average latency of subconscious processing, whose speed is of the order of tens of milliseconds.

For example, a tennis player in the Men's Singles Final at Wimbledon will have moved towards the net and returned serve *before* he is actually consciously aware of seeing the ball leave the server's racket. The reason for this has now been well established. There are two major visual systems both stimulated by light falling on the retina.[3] Once the light stimulus from the retina has reached the primary (occipital) visual cortex, the systems diverge. The dorsal action 'stream' is fast and results in motor responses which are unconscious, while the ventral 'stream' is slow and leads to a conscious cerebrally processed percept of the original retinal stimulus. The decision of the player to run to the net and return serve is effected by the dorsal stream responsible for activating the appropriate musculature. Much later, the

[2] Chalmers D, *The Conscious Mind*, Oxford: Oxford University Press 1997, xiii.
[3] Mishkin M, Ungerleider L, Macko K, *Trends in Neuroscience*, October 1983, 414–417.

ventral stream 'replays' to the player not only what he thought had actually taken place but what he considered to be his executive responsibility for those actions. Through other experimental means, a subject may come to think that he was responsible for an action when no such responsibility, in fact, was involved.[4]

From another perspective,[5] relative to the continuously rapid scanning (saccadic) sweeps of our eyes, it is estimated that ~20% of our visual life is 'blind'. The perceived 'stream of consciousness' is replayed by the brain as though offering a faithfully video-recorded edition of events already (by 200–300 milliseconds) gone. Again, we should note that the steady, smoothed and apparently continuous act of 'seeing' is a cerebrally, and not retinally, engineered event. The constant, rapid bobbing about of our eyeballs has little relationship to what we think we saw, or are seeing. Yet the 'filling in' which our brains effect is based on a considerable degree of past experience and therefore statistical knowledge of what the world is like: hence the success of the (unseen) return serve. Probably the same with penalties: I doubt whether a goalkeeper actually sees the ball when kicked from such close range. It may be pure luck whether he moves, falls or stretches out his arms into a saving position.

The other side to visual illusion is characterized by experiences or drawings which emphasize the tricks that our eyes play on us: many are well known. For example, distant railway lines appear to converge at the horizon. There are also the well-known paradoxes of the duck/rabbit phenomenon, or the opposition of facial profiles that can be read, alternatively, as a beautifully sculpted vase. Most of us will be less aware of the illusory states brought about by the neurophysiological mechanisms subserving body-image, and which additionally generate the perceptual construct of egocentric and paracentric body space which are discussed in the following chapter. These perturbations in body-image lie at the root of abnormal experiences such as: first, seeing an autoscopic mirror image of oneself; second, feeling that one's consciousness is alternating between oneself and one's double (heautoscopy); third, the sensing of external 'presences'; or fourth, having an OBE.

In exploring the relationships between apparent conscious reality and illusion in relation to ECE phenomenology, I turn to the intriguing, so-called 'phantom-limb' phenomenon, and how subjects are deluded into believing that a body part continues to exist. This phenomenology, I think, will give readers unaccustomed to thinking about consciousness a chance to understand how easily the brain constructs illusion. Specifically, these examples

---

[4] Wegner DM and Wheatley T, *Am Psychol* 54: 480–492, 1999.
[5] Martinez-Conde S, *Progr Brain Res* 154: 151–176, 2006.

have a bearing on how a subject may experience being out-of-body, or even undergoing a near-death event. Indeed, from the outset, it is highly probable that these phenomena are generated entirely by internal cerebral mechanisms in brains that could hardly be considered to be hypoxic, and certainly not in any sense agonal.[6]

5.2. 'PHANTOM LIMB' PHENOMENOLOGY: THE NEUROPHYSIOLOGY OF ABSENCE

The popularized term for the 'phantom limb' phenomenon, was originally coined in 1872 in describing the symptomatology of ninety American Civil War amputees.[7] This, in its basal form, refers to the continued memory of a body part previously removed through trauma or a planned surgical procedure. The phenomenon[8] applies to, and is most commonly thought of in terms of a lost limb, but it is also relevant to the severing of an arm, hand or finger; and the resection of a breast, tooth or eyeball. It can also result from removal of an internal organ to which conscious somatic representation applies, such as a diseased uterus for painful fibroids. In the case of a removed bladder or rectum, persistent sensations of crampy abdominal pain, fullness, bursting, evacuation or urgency may extend for considerable intervals post-operatively.

5.2.a. Variations on a Theme

Now consider another variant: traumatic avulsion or cleavage of the leash of nerves (brachial plexus) caused by a severe wrench to the arm, thereby severing all neural connectivity to the cervical cord. In this circumstance, the cerebral phantom arises despite the presence of what is otherwise a normal arm with intact blood supply.[9] However, if the limb is moved without visual control, the subject lacks insight into its real position: once the real arm has been re-visualized, the subject cognitively fuses the phantom to it.

---

[6] Melzack 1989.

[7] Carlen P, Wall P, Nadvorna H, Steinbach T, *Neurology* 28: 211–217, 1978.

[8] Weinstein S, Vetter R, Sersen E, *Neuropsychologia* 8: 185–197, 1970; Cohn R, *Arch Neurol* 25: 468–471, 1971; Cogan D, *Albrecht v Graefes Arch Klin Exp Ophthalmol* 188: 139–150, 1973; Schultz G and Melzack R, *Perception* 20: 809–825, 1991; Dorpat T, *Comprehens Psychiatr* 12: 27–35, 1971.

[9] Wynn-Parry C, *Pain* 9: 41–53, 1980.

This phenomenon has been verified with experimental anaesthesia applied locally to the brachial plexus.[10] If, during blindfold, the limb is moved elsewhere, its real position can be ascertained again only through visual contact, after which the imagined phantom is 'thought' back into its rightful position. These data clearly indicate that in the absence of peripheral somaesthetic information, the subject defaults to his innate cerebral image, conceiving the limb to be elsewhere other than its prevailing anatomical position. That is, body shape is largely dependent on central (cerebral), rather than purely peripheral, nervous signals: under normal physiological conditions, the two images are always fused. From this, let us consider additional aspects of phantom body-imagery, resulting from accidental transection of the spinal cord.

5.2.b. Phantom Body-Images in Para-/Quadriplegia

Paraplegia and quadriplegia, due to complete transections of the spinal cord, result in a phantom body which, in parallel with brachial plexus avulsion or local anaesthetic block, seems to fill the existing body parts. When the eyes are open, phantom and reality are fused and perfectly coordinated: dissociation occurs if the body or limbs are moved by nurses without the victim being first made aware. The perceived imagery is much sharper for distal structures like large toe and heel, knee or hip, an outcome emphatic of their large cortical representations. On being asked to move a paretic, or paralysed, limb,[11] subjects' behaviour and facial expressions resemble those of normal individuals attempting to recall a fact, to deliberate or concentrate on some problem. The gaze is distant and non-focused, suggesting a volitional initiation pattern which takes origin in the conscious-awareness of the cerebral cortex.

5.2.c. Phantom Limb Imagery in Congenital Limb Absence (Aphakia)

In the earlier clinical literature the conceivability of phantoms occurring in children with congenital aplasia (aphakia) of upper or lower limbs was dismissed, on grounds that there would not have been any sensory impressions recorded in the cerebral cortex from which later, and persisting, memory

---

[10] Melzack R and Bromage P, *Exp Neurol* 39: 261–269, 1973.
[11] Bors E, *Arch Neurol Psychiatr* 66: 610–631, 1951 (especially 624–625).

phantoms could be generated.[12] Melzack and Loeser[13] reviewed thirty such patients (age range 5–8 years), finding a prevalence of phantom limb experiences in five subjects (17%). Case 4 was a 10-year-old female with left upper limb dysmelia. Although lacking the distal two-thirds of this arm, her phantom, now shorter than that of the actual limb, comprised thumb, fingers and a faint image of a palm. Another 11-year-old female[14] was bilaterally peromelic (lacking forearms and hands). Yet in her earlier years, she happily employed her phantom fingers for solving simple arithmetic sums.

These cases clearly indicate that, despite absence of incoming sensory afferents, the brain contains some kind of inherited inbuilt engram which, in representing parts either completely or in part, informs the subject's conscious-awareness.[15] This view is strengthened by the nature of the given reports which, although derived from young people, were as bizarre as those tendered by adults. Had those children been imagining or even confabulating their phantoms, they are more likely to have portrayed complete limbs rather than the actual accounts offered, being referential to one or two fingers, or a thumb, or the possibility of a palm. The phantoms usually configure distal parts, in parallel with the normal somatic representations of the body in the parietal lobe. The parts usually involved in important functions are afforded far greater cortical territoral representation. However, the cerebral 'location' of these phantoms[16] does not reside in the primary sensory cortex, but in the premotor and parietal cortex (Figure 4), as confirmed by appropriate technology (fMRI and transcranial magnetic stimulation), in the same way that pain-qualia representing intensity or quality, are expressed in other cortical locations than in primary sensory areas. The latter provide the location at which the pain stimulus is perceived.

Phantom limb phenomenology (like conscious-awareness) expresses the overwhelming belief that this is 'me', this is what 'I' am actually experiencing and perceiving, despite the imaginary phantom being brain-engineered. This idea of corporateness expresses the essence of body-image. The experience of body-image is unitary and of an integrated quality welded to the powerful percept of self: uniquely, entirely and totally non-shared with, and unrelated to, any other individual. It is also the one outstanding feature of ECE narratives which captures the firm sense of personal subjectivity which embodies them. Each ECE narrative is always expressed in the first person,

[12] Weinstein S and Sersen E, *Neurology* 11: 905–911, 1961; Weinstein et al 1964.

[13] Melzack R and Loeser J, *Pain* 4: 195–210, 1978.

[14] Poeck K, *Cortex* 1: 269–275, 1964.

[15] Ramachandran VS and Hirstein W, *Brain* 121: 1603–1630, 1998.

[16] Weinstein et al 1964; Brugger P, Kollias S, Muri R, Crelier G, Hepp-Reymond M-C, Regard M, Regard M, *Proc Nat Acad Sci [USA]* 97: 6167–6172, 2000.

or with the pronominal possessive, and hence similar to another illusory brain state—that of the subconscious dream mode.

This excursus has introduced us to the widespread illusory nature of waking conscious-awareness. I have also illustrated the means through which the brain can emulate a body part which no longer physically exists. If the brain can recreate a lost part, or even the torso and limbs in a paraplegic subject, it takes little more imagination to conceive of a brain recreating the entire person in a distant locus, together with its 'consciousness', and distinct therefore from the actual reality of corporeality. Indeed, we have already met some aspects of this phenomenology when considering the mirror image illusion (autoscopy) and its near parallel, heautoscopy. The latter phenomenon is of particular interest because of the manner in which conscious-awareness oscillates between the true self and the visualized phantom, together with sensations of movement or even affect towards the other. These latter types of illusion, together with that engendered by the brain in the so-called 'phantom limb' experience, demonstrate how much 'other body' deception occurs in normal life. This may just be what near-death and out-of-body experiences entail: we will determine more of the likely neurophysiological origins of ECE in the succeeding chapters.

In the next chapter, I deal with the mechanisms which underlie our sense of body-image, out of which arise consideration of the concepts of ego- and paracentric body space. These are important topics to pursue because they inform the extent to which much of our personal geography is subject to those mechanisms, but importantly, how easily our minds can be misled by perturbations to, and within, this complex neurological system.

6

The Temporo-Parietal Cortex: The Configuring of Ego-/Paracentric Body Space

In the previous chapters, foundational arguments for the assertion that ECE are brain-based phenomena were established. In the preceding chapter, I began our formal entry into the world of neurophysiology by considering the illusory nature of conscious-awareness, referring specifically to the so-called 'phantom limb' phenomenon. This provides a basis for understanding the manner in which a normal brain can engineer body parts which are no longer anatomically present. We can distinguish most examples of these normal, consciously perceived illusions from other examples, such as the subconscious realm of sleeping, or the hallucinatory experiences brought about by drugs or other pharmacological manoeuvres. In addition, I think it is possible to assert that ECE phenomenology is illusory because of the manner in which it arises from a brain rapidly recovering from a severe, temporary interruption to its functioning.

I now proceed to develop these claims further by discussing aspects of the neurology and pathology of body-image, how the brain represents body-in-space, and the many illusory phenomena that may obtain therefrom. These considerations have important repercussions for improved understandings of ECE phenomenology, especially in relation to being out-of-body and to the many ways in which the brain can conjure up such illusions. The subject matter of this chapter continues with an evaluation of the posterior parietal cortex and its role in subserving the construction of body-image.

As I embark on this, and the succeeding three chapters, a more general point needs to be stressed. That is, I do not advance the view that any of the neurophysiological or neuropathological examples I shall be discussing necessarily underlie the origin of every ECE. However, I emphasize that other authors' failures to have entertained such scientific approaches have strengthened the need for a more enlightened appraisal and therefore a more fully understood outcome relating to ECE. I hope the ensuing contributions will help to make that clear, and to show, precisely, where those many and newer insights can exert their influences and impact on this field of study.

Neurophysiological explanations, in my view, more than adequately account for ECE phenomenology. In this chapter, a thorough analysis of OBE phenomenology is undertaken, in relation to our current neurophysiological understandings of self-in-space. Not to have engaged with these neurophysiological themes has, in my view, left the resultant field poorer. It is my case, backed up by a sturdy scientific database, that OBEs are overwhelmingly brain-associated events. 'Mystical' experiences, metaphysical or other mystery explanations of these experiences become increasingly redundant as postulated causal aetiologies, while the persisting requirement for such explanation grows ever smaller, as the progress of scientific knowledge expands these areas of brain functioning.

6.1. THE POSTERIOR PARIETAL CORTEX AND BODY-IMAGE

The innate sense of body-image which humans, higher primates and probably other animals possess is by no means a statically organized neuro-anatomic construct. Percepts of intra-personal or egocentric, and of extra-personal or paracentric body space require constant updating and reorganization, based on visual, proprioceptive, haptic and vestibular influences[1] in response to continued changes in the external world (Figure 5). Perturbations of the sense of spatial bodily mentation can be demonstrated physiologically, and exemplified through pathological conditions.

6.1.a. Physiological Considerations

Egocentric space perceptions rely on vestibular inputs from the semicircular canals and adjacent otolithic components of saccule and utricle comprising the inner ear. These afferent inputs reach the brain via the VIIIth cranial nerve. Proprioceptive information from stretch receptors in muscle tendons and joint capsules enter the brain via ascending afferent nerve bundles. Paracentric space perception is largely subserved jointly by visual and proprioceptive afferences.

---

[1] Farrell M and Robertson I, *Neuropsychologia* 38: 585–595, 2000.

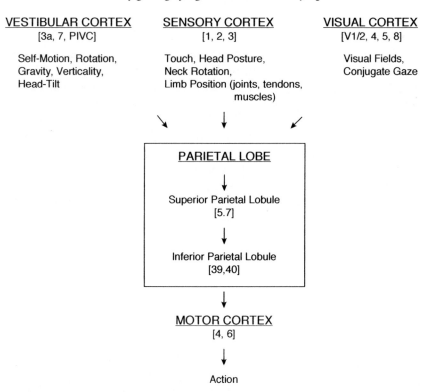

Figure 5. This simple block diagram illustrates the main players contributing to ego- and paracentric space, or body-image. The incoming information from these three afferent sources impinges on the inferior parietal lobule (Brodmann 39, 40) in creating this percept. The vestibular system, arising from the inner ear, comprises semicircular canals, saccule and utricle which detect motion relative to gravity and give rise to perceptions of the vertical, direction, rotation and accelerations. For simplicity, the diagram excludes other important contributors to body-image such as the cerebellum, limbic system, hippocampus and memory.

The neurophysiological coordination of these afferences is effected by the posterior parietal cortex (Figure 5). This comprises Brodmann areas 5, 7 of the superior parietal lobule and Brodmann areas 39, 40 for the inferior parietal lobule. These two regions weld together sensory, proprioceptive, vestibular and visual inputs into a 'body-image'.[2] Through additional

[2] Stein JF, *Behav Brain Sci* 15: 691–700, 1992; idem, The Posterior Parietal Cortex, in idem and Stoodley C, *Neuroscience: An Introduction*, Chichester: Wiley 2006, 235–244; Anderson R, *Phil Trans R Soc Lond B* 352: 1421–1428, 1997; Anderson R, Shenoy K, Snyder L, Bradley D,

intra-cerebral connections a detailed conscious perception is assembled whereby subjects become aware of the shape of their own bodies, how their bodies are aligned with respect to space, and how objects within the field of view are located relative to the body. These relationships permit appropriate motor responses to events within the immediate, or more distant, environment, responses that are also dependent on memory and attentional alertness to its ever-changing contours and events.

Although in normal waking existence the eyes, limbs and head are rapidly changing position, neither our perceptions of space nor our visual fields of view are interpreted as though life was always being lived on a helter-skelter or 'bouncy castle'. The varying afferent inputs are functionally coordinated into smoothed, stable, abstract internal frames of reference pertinent to body-in-space and space-to-body: these afferents are continuously being updated through time. The maintenance of the egocentric or internal body-image and body-in-space framework is thus independent of actual ocular, head, neck, body, or limb and joint movements. Likewise the sense of space-to-body is represented by reference to external coordinates. These are based on the gravitational sensation of going upwards and downwards, or the geographic sense of moving forwards, backwards or to left and right. Memory plays a further important role in permitting subjects to know and remember their own body shapes and contours, and their environmental relationships.

It is clearly obvious that perturbations of the functioning of these coordinating brain centres can severely disrupt body-imagery. Lesional pathology of varied kinds, especially involving the right parietal lobe, can give rise to the inability to recognize coins in the pocket, or to employ the left hand constructively. In severer cases, the left side of the environment is entirely neglected while the corresponding side of the body may be interpreted as non-self, foreign, or the property of another person.

6.1.b. Tweaking the Body-Image: Physiologic Examples

The apparent shape and orientation of the body can be rapidly altered through various experimental manoeuvres, resulting in disordered, illogical sensations of illusory motion or of impossible limb positions. These neurophysiological insights are important indicators of how *normal* persons with *normal* brains are easily deluded by absurd perceptions of their bodily disposition, pertinent to location or movement. In one such test, subjects

Crowell J, *Ann NY Acad Sci* 871: 282–292, 1999; Colby C and Goldberg M, *Ann Rev Neurosci* 22: 319–349, 1999.

Figure 6. When vibrations of a certain frequency are applied to the biceps tendon the brain erroneously thinks the arm is extending away from the body. In addition, the brain creates the added illusion that the nose is elongating, since the fingers remain in contact with it. This is known as the 'Pinocchio effect'. (Taken from JF Stein and CJ Stoodley, *Neuroscience*, Chichester: Wiley 2006, fig. 17.2. Reproduced with permission.)

touched their noses with their right hand as the biceps tendon of the fixed right arm was subjected to a specific vibrational stimulus. The resultant illusion was that their noses seemed to elongate—by as much as 300cm (1 foot) for some subjects. This is known as the so-called 'Pinocchio effect'. Conversely, vibration applied to the triceps tendon gave rise to the belief that the nose was now being pushed backwards into the head. In considering the Pinocchio effect, the biceps tendon vibration is centrally interpreted by the brain as a forward 'movement' of the arm (Figure 6). Since the head and hand-to-nose positions remain fixed, the nose is simultaneously interpreted to have elongated thus to maintain contact with the illusory recession of the hand.[3]

In further experiments with subjects lying supine on a floor with forearms flexed vertically upwards and held by restraints, biceps tendon vibration gave rise to the illusory belief that the trunk was now moving backwards, and downward, through an angle of tilt of up to 25° below the horizontal. This is due to decreased functioning of the otolith organs in the middle ear when the head is horizontally, rather than vertically, disposed. These observations are of signal relevance to OBE, which almost universally occur in a supine, rather

---

[3] Goodwin G, McCloskey D, Matthews P, *Science* 175: 1382–1384, 1972; Lackner J, *Brain* 111: 281–297, 1988.

than a sitting or erect position.[4] From these brief reports, it is evident that disruptions to the normally existing balance between collaborative multiple afferent and efferent neural signals rapidly lead to illusory egocentric mis-perceptions of body position, orientation or weight.[5] Apart from the invari-able need of a supine position, OBE are also more likely to occur when other sensory afferences are reduced. Such reductions are facilitated by a quiet environment, dim lighting conditions, darkness, concentrated meditative practices, sleep onset, or a subconscious state of existence.

Beyond the physiological, there are pathological examples whether due to space-occupying lesions or reductions in cortical blood flow. All illuminate the illusory cerebral contexts through which misperceptions of body-image arise.

6.2. ABNORMAL DISTURBANCES OF BODY-IMAGE

It has been noted that OB phenomenology refers to occasions when perci-pients state that their '*consciousness*', having vacated the physical body, '*travels*' without corporeal assistance, and '*sees*' things which were not apparently directly visible from the original perspective. The major question here is whether OBE are true examples of extra-corporeal existence, sentience or consciousness offering cast-iron demonstrations of a 'mental' life indepen-dent of brain, or whether they are a product entirely of induced illusory/ hallucinatory brain-states. Another explanation for those few subjects who appear to report allegedly real events in their vicinity during an OBE is that, like lucid dreamers, they may be simultaneously conscious and in a subcon-scious mode of existence. In that regard, we must always remain alert to the impossibility, at the present time, of knowing whether any subject is completely unconscious or not.

6.2.a. Migrainous Auras and Altered Body-Image

There is much evidence indicating that OBE are caused by internal brain-states. For example, among some of the psychological auras of migraine, those due to a marked temporary cortical ischaemia[6] are: striking instances of

---

[4] Blanke O, Landis Th, Spinelli L, Seeck M, *Brain* 127: 243–258, 2004.
[5] Pavani F, Spence C, Driver J, *Psychol Sci* 11: 353–359, 2000.
[6] Gorji A, *Brain Res Rev* 38: 33–60, 2001; Goadsby P, *Trends Molec Med* 13: 39–44, 2007.

autoscopic perceptions of a passive mirror-image of oneself, OBE, sensed 'presences', vestibular activation, and distortions in perceptions of body-image. These phenomena occur in ~15% cases of maigraineurs, are frequently depicted in migraine art,[7] and may involve the presence of a double or of having two bodies. During this sense of 'doubling', additional features arise such as the attribution, to the double, of additional and fictive cognitive and affective properties.[8] During one migraine-associated OBE (Lippman, Case 1), a 37-year-old housewife was able to observe herself dealing with her husband and family: 'it was as if I was in another dimension... There was "I" and there was "me"'.

The phantom body of another 48-year-old regular migraine sufferer seemed to be more real, while her true physical body was viewed as the more illusory. This seems to be an example of heautoscopy, in that her hallucinatory 'other' was capable of mental volition, thought and independent visual activity. Another subject, an accountant, regularly experienced a double who, simultaneously adding up a second set of identical figures arrived at a correct total just as he, himself, completed the real set.

Other patients of Lippman had sensations of being very tall or very small, or of parts of their bodies changing in shape and 'feel', or of the body apparently splitting vertically into left and right halves, or as if the body was swinging like a pendulum into and out of the adjacent phantom, together with vivid, coloured dreams or horror nightmares.[9] These phenomena even occur in migranoids—those not always experiencing headaches. A woman (Lippman 1953, Case 6) became accustomed to finding herself in two places at once, the hallucinatory phantom in an elevated position observing what she was doing, and, during which, '*time seemed to be suspended*'. The conclusion is clear: certain people with a paroxysmal vascular abnormality of their brains are able to undergo OBE much in keeping with those OBE associated with near-death events. The occurrence of horror dreams, dependent on migrainous vascular dysfunction, likewise, recalls the similar hellish types of NDE.

[7] Moersch F, *Am J Psychiatr* 3: 697–716, 1924; Podoll K and Robinson D, *Cephalgia* 19: 886–896, 1999; a reviewer of this MS suggested publishing comparative pictures from migraine and ECE subjects. However, I am unaware of any artworks published by the latter.

[8] Lippman 1953; idem, *Am J Psychiatr* 107: 856–858, 1951.

[9] Lippman C, *J Nerv Ment Dis* 116: 346–351, 1952; idem, *J Nerv Ment Dis* 120: 273–276, 1954.

6.2.b. Temporal Lobe Epileptic Auras and Being Out-of-Body

I now draw attention to the types of auras (for 'aura' see Glossary) of temporal lobe epilepsy with relevance to OBE. This relationship is important in regard to the quality of the paroxysmal auras occurring in complex partial seizures. These auras precede a full epileptic fit and its attendant loss of consciousness. Pre-convulsive auras derive from the temporo-parietal lobe, and their content reflects heavily on its role in body-image construction. Disorders of body-image[10] typically involve corporeal transformations or displacement, either absence illusions of a phantom limb, the presence of additional supernumerary phantoms, or heautoscopic experiences. Experientially, these auras comprise integrated visual, sensory, auditory, vestibular and somaesthetic components which variously derive from the initial spread of electrical discharges passing through the temporo-parietal and occipital junctional zones of the cerebral cortex. Their phenomenological identity to ECE is very hard to dismiss.

Epileptic auras of this type have an important psychological impact. They are extremely real and veridical, compelling in their effects, and firmly tied to the personal life history and memories of each subject. The affective component, presumably deriving in part from deep mesial structures (hippocampus and amygdala), is a further dramatic accompaniment. The entire episode becomes a unified, subjective experience. Nevertheless, like dreams and many ECE, 'time' is invariably distorted, so that there is no real evolution in the narrative event recalled, since the experience 'goes nowhere'.[11] Some cases[12] describe vestibular components to their auras—of twisting or turning, being pulled or pushed to one side, while during intra-operative electro-cortical stimulation, patients sense they are rolling off the table or experiencing other spatial displacements of torso or limb. The following quoted excerpts illustrate well the generalizations given above:[13]

First, a young lady with a right posterior temporal lobe focus who sustained concussion and mild brain injury following a road traffic accident. Following the original impact, she was unconscious for two hours and amnesic for the preceding 24 hours:

[10] Lunn V, *Acta Psychiatr (Scand)* 46 (Suppl 219): 118–125, 1970; Devinsky O, Feldmann E, Burrowes K, Bromfield E, *Arch Neurol* 46: 1080–1088, 1989; Epstein A, *Arch Neurol* 16: 613–619, 1967; Halligan P, *Cogn Neuropsychiatr* 7: 251–268, 2002; Halligan P, Marshall J, Wade D, *J Neurol Neurosurg Psychiatr* 56: 159–166, 1993; Ionasescu J, *Acta Psychiatr Neurol (Scand)* 35: 171–181, 1960.
[11] Halligan P, Marshall J, Ramachandran V, *Cogn Neuropsychol* 11: 459–477, 1994; Gloor P, *Brain* 113: 1673–1694, 1990.
[12] Salanova V, Andermann F, Rasmussen T, Olivier A, Quesney L, *Brain* 118: 607–627, 1995; Blanke O, Perrig S, Thut G, Landis Th, Seeck M, *J Neurol Neurosurg Psychiatr* 69: 553–556, 2000.
[13] Devinsky et al 1989.

[I] left my body and saw it from above that it was lying in a pool of blood in the car. Then I got up, walked around the car, and began banging on the driver's window. [I saw] a man who instructed me to get back into the car. [Then] the voice of an older [unrecognized] man [said]: 'Don't go. Come back and have a child.'

An eye-witness could not corroborate any of this hallucinatory confabulation. One month later she had another aura in which the same man's voice told her that he wanted to take her away from her body. Subsequent auras involved her seeing her own body, dressed in similar clothes, but appearing motionless.

Second, a 29-year-old man with seizures since the age of twelve felt as though he was ascending to the corner of the room, from where he could look down on his body. Although clothed identically, his hair was always combed, even if he knew that was not the case, while the aura continued. With his body motionless below, his '*mind above*' was free to move around the house and view family members in other rooms. Third, a 35-year-old woman with a long history of absences and tonic-clonic convulsions, was alone in a hotel room. During a seizure she fell between two adjacent beds and became entangled with the bedclothes as her limb thrashing movements continued. Then:

[I] saw a light move from my body on the floor. It lit up the room, and rested up in the corner. Somehow I became the light source up above. [I] looked down and saw [my] body, jerking in all four extremities, tangled up in the sheets. A man's voice then said to me: 'Relax, relax, you're gonna smother if you don't': I watched the whole episode as if I were at the movies. Then [my] body on the floor woke up, the voice stopped and I felt [myself] slip back into my body.

Finally, a 41-year-old woman developed complex partial seizures in her twenties. She experienced being out-of-body as though her consciousness was hovering in the upper corner of the room. An associated sense of religious ecstasy involved her talking to God and feeling she was in His presence. Other patients with various pathologies, including temporal lobe epilepsy, reported feelings of sensing another (invisible) presence.[14] One example[15] is of a male computer operative with a six-year history of déjà vu experiences due to a cerebral tumour (right temporal lobe astrocytoma). After its removal, he reported sensations either of carrying an unidentified object, or of another person standing behind him. These episodes occurred several times a day, but further follow-up details were not given.

[14] Brugger and Regard 1997; Brugger P, Regard M, Landis Th, *Neuropsychiatr Neuropsychol Behav Neurol* 9: 114–122, 1996.
[15] Ardilo A and Gomez J, *Epilepsia* 29: 188–189, 1988.

It is quite evident, in perusing these striking accounts of patients with temporal lobe pathology, that, if these narratives were subjected to analysis by a 'blinded' judge, there might be difficulty in critically distinguishing them from the narratives recalled by people undergoing an OBE or NDE, whether due to causes physiological, or pathological such as cardiac arrest. Both the experiential phenomenology, and its neurophysiological basis as understood to date, indicate a complex series of differing illusory or hallucinatory, extra-corporeal events. I therefore reiterate the point made above: complaints by writers on the subject of ECE declaring that crisis OBE are experientially different from OBE experienced in other circumstances or through other pathologies, are weak, unconvincing, and carry little weight.

Additional critical insights into this kind of phenomenology have been highlighted recently.[16] In this short experimental study, investigative findings are described on a 43-year-old woman who for eleven years had suffered from complex partial seizures emanating from a focus somewhere in her right temporal cortex. As part of her pre-operative assessment, sixty-four subdural electrodes were implanted into her skull and then focally stimulated. The outcomes of these stimulations under such conditions evoked reports that she was 'sinking into the bed'; 'falling from a height' or 'floating' about 2m above the bed subjacent to the ceiling. Higher stimulatory currents caused her to 'see myself in bed [from above] ... but ... [she] only saw her legs and lower torso' and felt that 'they were changing in shape and size'. On another occasion when she thought that her arms were rapidly coming towards her, she took evasive action—that is, her hallucination was perceived as real, despite being conscious and having her eyes open at that time. This is an example of the simultaneous perception of illusory mentation in a conscious subject. Other illusions of body parts moving relative to her trunk were experienced even when her eyes were closed. The authors note the differences between this lady's ability to see her lower half and arms from those total perceptions elicited by Penfield[17] when electrically stimulating the temporo-parietal regions of patients' brains. The responses obtained for the laboratory of Olaf Blanke[18] were derived from electrodes overlying the aural/balance/spatial awareness 'centres' towards the posterior, superior aspects of the right temporal lobe, but possibly involving the inferior parietal lobules.

---

[16] Blanke O, Ortigue S, Landis Th, Seeck M, *Nature* 419: 269–270, 2002.
[17] Penfield W and Perot P, *Brain* 86: 595–696, 1963.
[18] Blanke et al 2002; Blanke O and Arzy S, *The Neuroscientist* 11: 16–24, 2005.

6.2.c. Additional Neuropathological Insights

A more systematic, in-depth approach came from the same laboratory,[19] involving four individuals with complex partial seizures due to two right-sided, and two left-sided temporal foci; one patient with a vascular lesion of uncertain nosology, and a sixth with a mild, left-sided hemiplegia resulting from a right-sided temporo-parietal cortex lesion and history of migraine. In OBE subjects, the experiences comprised extremely vivid, life-like visions of people and objects of direct personal relevance. They also involved spontaneous 180° rotations of the entire body allowing percipients to view their vacated bodies from a detached position, and to experience other vestibular components of elevation and floating, and graviceptive perceptions of body lightness or weightlessness. Self-recognition of the vacated body was immediate, even if the vacated body now appeared to be younger, differently attired, or offering an altered hairstyle.

These latter observations imply a role for central cognitive recognition of body contour, and the utilization of self-memory. The pathological locations, although in these six cases showing no left—right lateral preponderance within the temporal cortex, were closely distributed around its postero-lateral aspects. Common to the majority of these analysed case-histories and experiences, importantly, were focal disturbances arising within the vicinity of the temporo-parietal zone.

Four of these patients underwent autoscopic events: notably, one underwent both OB and autoscopic experiences. She had partial complex seizures arising from the left temporal cortex from identified foci in the superior temporal gyrus, angular gyrus and left pre-central gyrus. Her pre-convulsive OB auras comprised a loud humming noise suggesting recruitment of the primary auditory cortex and sensed behind her, elevations of her legs, and of rising to the ceiling and viewing herself in bed from that position. Her autoscopic disturbance was characterized by seeing herself from behind, although she felt herself to be concurrently in both positions—a form of heautoscopy.

Another patient with right-sided cortical ischaemic damage and a history of migraine felt himself rising up in his chair thus to witness his seated double moving away from him while he remained elevated, during which he experienced graviceptive illusions of weightlessness and floating. In rapid, alternating succession, he was able to view his wife who was actually sitting in a chair opposite him as the aura progressed, both from his elevated, and from his original floor-based position. This form of heautoscopy may provide another

---

[19] Blanke et al 2004.

explanation of the concurrence of illusory phenomena in an otherwise fully conscious individual. In this man's case, there were associated affective components of elation and great happiness.

A third male case with left fronto-temporal-insular and temporo-parietal foci was sitting in a chair when he slowly rotated backwards in the horizontal position, thus coming to think that he was now behind the nurse attending to an intravenous infusion in his arm. He thought his body looked about ten years younger and differently attired. In both instances, the visual scenes were highly coloured, vivid and, importantly, veridical of events pertinent to the immediate physical locations. There were vestibular sensations of rising or turning; of reduced otolithic activity engendering a sense of weightlessness or lightness, together with the immediate 180° rotation of the body in order to permit viewing of the vacated body.

6.3. THE UPS-AND-DOWNS AND INS-AND-OUTS OF EGO-/PARACENTRIC BODY SPACE

From a neurophysiological perspective, it is evident that the conceptual aspects of self (viewed specifically as person-in-space) are inbuilt cortical phenomena. That was demonstrated by the burgeoning field of recent studies into phantom limb phenomenology, as outlined in the preceding chapter. Phenomenologically, this is the neurophysiology not only of *absence*, whether of limb, finger, breast, bladder or uterus, but also of body-image *illusion*, whether in relief of spasm of a phantom hand[20] by means of a mirror-image of the remaining hand, nose elongation and other illusions resulting from tendon vibration,[21] or a sense of being upside-down when in a spacecraft under G_0 (zero gravity) conditions.[22] In these settings the brain constructs illusory images that are clearly inappropriate to prevailing physical conditions.

It might be insisted that much of the evidence for the concept of a body-schema for ego-/paracentric spacial representations is based entirely upon data culled from pathological examples, such as temporal lobe epilepsy, strokes or migraine. However, Reed and Farah,[23] in an insightful paper,

---

[20] Ramachandran VS and Rogers-Ramachandran D, *Proc R Soc Lond B* 263: 372–386, 1996.
[21] Goodwin et al 1972; Lackner 1988.
[22] Lackner J, *Ann NY Acad Sci* 656: 329–339, 1992.
[23] Reed C and Farah M, *J Exp Psychol Hum Percept Perform* 21: 334–343, 1995.

demonstrated that the body-schema concept holds for control, non-brain-damaged subjects as, of course, we might have expected. In the given sets of tasks performed by their subjects, the data revealed that the physiological mechanism for body-schema is supramodal. By that is meant that the experience emanated from cortical association areas coordinating visual and proprioceptive information. This experiment reaffirms the central role played by the multimodal association areas of the parietal lobules and temporo-parietal junction. These latter areas additionally encode body parts for self as well as for other people's bodies, being modal for arm and leg representations. Finally,[24] in exhibiting processes devoted solely to body space, position and parts, the concept of body-schema has been demonstrated to be functionally separable from other mechanisms which subserve identification of parts, or components, of non-living objects.

These neurophysiological principles have been further explored and extended in recent studies where self-consciousness was apparently transferred to an illusory phantom body elaborated by means of head-mounted, 3-D video-goggles.[25] In apparently normal young volunteers, self-awareness could be displaced to a location in front of, or behind, the subject. Additional 'tests' employed by either the stroking of a hand or feigned injurious blows to the chest demonstrated their transferral to the 'virtual body' created via the video headgear. These are important studies because they demonstrate that self-reference is manipulable by experimental techniques in addition to direct electrical or transcranial magnetic stimulation (TMS) of the brain. However, some subjects felt that they were not out-of-body: thus these novel approaches need to be much further refined in order to reveal more about the occurrence, and possible mechanisms, of these experiences.

We have seen, from various physiological and pathological perspectives, that the elaboration and representation of an internal ego-/paracentric body-image[26] require neural mechanisms based on inputs derived from visual, haptic (sensory), proprioceptive (joint position) and vestibular inputs. The vestibular organs within the inner ear enjoy a central contributory role in creating this internal, abstract egocentric 'space'. They specifically provide information on linear accelerations, head tilt and graviception via the otolith hair functions in saccule and utricle, and rotations and angular accelerations

[24] Anderson R, Snyder L, Bradley D, Xing J, *Ann Rev Neurosci* 20: 303–330, 1997; Calvert G, Campbell R, Brammer M, *Curr Biol* 10: 649–657, 2000; Matsuhashi M, Ikeda A, Ohara S et al, *Clin Neurophysiol* 115: 1145–1160, 2004.

[25] Ehrsson HH, *Science* 317: 1048, 2007; Lenggenhager B, Tadi T, Metzinger T, Blanke O, *Science* 317: 1096–1099, 2007.

[26] Stein 1992; Zacks J, Rypma B, Gabrieli J, Tvesky B, Glover G, *Neuropsychologia* 37: 1029–1040, 1999; Farrell and Robertson 2000; Grush R, *Brain and Mind* 1: 59–92, 2000.

effected through the semicircular canals.[27] In terms of OB phenomenology, I am concerned here not with peripheral disorders of these organs within the inner ear, but with disturbances in their central connections as a result of various types of brain pathology, and their resultant symptomatology.

Perceptual (cognitive) disturbances in ego-/paracentric body/spatial relationships depend, in part, on mechanisms known as the subjective visual vertical (SVV) and room tilt illusions (RTI). The former defines differences between the visual and gravity (G)-dependent sense of being upright, the latter is descriptive of the relationship between subjective position and the orientation of the horizon (or subjective proprioceptive vertical: SPV). A weightless astronaut might think himself and his craft to be upside-down due to his zero gravity (G_0) environment, resulting from otolithic graviceptors (SPV) being inoperative in G_0, while SVV (inner ear saccule, and visual) data continue to function during weightlessness. Other subjects can be made to undergo either 90° or 180° illusory changes in their visual field panoramas by slow rotation about the z (head-to-foot) axis: this is equivalent to a pilot's view of the horizon at the nadir of a barrel-roll, with sky below and land above.[28]

The relevance of these considerations relates to the phenomenon, rarely if ever commented on or even appreciated in the ECE literature, that during OBE, experients are immediately rotated about their z-axis by 180°, yet without any sense of body motion as the inversion occurs. The likely possibility is that it is entirely internal and neural, resulting from ischaemic malfunctions disturbing the self-representational circuitry within the brainstem and cerebral cortex. On the other hand, it is evident that for less acutely precipitated OBE, necessary requirements of a supine position, quiet surroundings with low or absent illumination resulting in reduced visual and proprioceptive afferences to the brain, together with a slowing of pulse rate and lowering of blood pressure would provide the cumulative antecedents necessary to precipitate the occurrence of floating out of the body with a 180° reversal in body attitude.

Beyond the physiological, there is a great deal of information[29] culled from patients with vascular insults to the brainstem, brain injuries, tumours, epilepsy, and lesions of the parietal cortex which, among other body-schema

---

[27] Gresty M, Bronstein A, Brandt T, Dieterich M, *Brain* 115: 647–673, 1992; Brandt T, Dieterich M, *Ann NY Acad Sci* 871: 293–312, 1999; Tiliket C, Ventre-Dominey J, Vighetto A, Grochowicki M, *Arch Neurol* 53: 1259–1264, 1996: Mittelstaedt H, *Zool Jhrb Physiol* 95: 419–425, 1991.

[28] Lackner 1992; Mittelstaedt H and Glasauer S, *Clin Invest* 71: 732–739, 1993.

[29] Dieterich M and Brandt T, *Neurology* 43: 1732–1740, 1993; Brandt T, Dieterich M Danek A, *Ann Neurol* 35: 403–412, 1994; Charles N, Froment C, Rode G et al, *J Neurol Neurosurg*

defects, cause body-to-horizon and horizon-to-body inversions. These perceptual illusions[30] are deemed to arise from central otolith-ocular disconnections or disturbances in the brainstem or cortex—and experientially from within the posterior temporal and inferior parietal cortex. It is noticeable that many of the reports referred to above involve vascular insults, such as stroke or migraine, and mass lesions like tumours or abscess formation, each seriously interfering with blood supply to these vital centres. This area is also the watershed between the two vascular supplies to the brain,[31] namely the middle cerebral artery arising from the internal carotid artery, and posterior cerebral artery being the terminal branch of the vertebro-basilar system. Therefore, it is not improbable that a similar 180° reversal of the cortically perceived visual horizon experienced during an OBE could relate to a concurrent disturbance in this critical vascular region of the cerebral cortex.

It is very difficult, therefore, to concur confidently with van Lommel,[32] for example, that temporal lobe epilepsy or other models of ECE phenomenology are 'not identical to NDE': nor would I wish on the evidence we have, or be brave enough, to postulate that 'NDE pushes at the limits of medical ideas about the range of human consciousness and the mind–brain relation'. It is not possible for third-party opinions to be aligned with the first-person experiential perspective concerning these varied phenomenological events. How can an OBE (or NDE) induced by temporal lobe disease be differentiated from an OBE (NDE) induced by cardiac arrest? And if so, on what grounds? And by what other postulated mechanism(s)? And how can there be such certainty without direct corroborative data? And how would we adjudicate?

On the other hand, by engaging with these forms of brain pathology and their resultant experiences, I maintain that new and important insights can be derived and applied to ECE phenomenology, as I have attempted herein. Neither do I claim that such models are fully explanatory, but what I do claim is that in dismissing such disorders and their contributory neurophysiology, many authors have deprived themselves of a means of exploring further

Psyciatr 55: 188–189, 1992; Mehler M, J Neurol Neurosurg Psychiatr 51: 1236–1237, 1988; Slavin M and LoPinto R, J Clin Neuro-Ophthalmol 7: 729–733, 1987.

[30] Bottini G, Sterzi R, Paulesu E, Vallar G, Cappo S, Erminio F et al, Exp Brain Res 99: 164–169, 1994; Friberg L, Olsen T, Roland P, Paulson O, Lassen N, Brain 108: 609–623, 1985; Slavin and LoPinto 1987; Steiner I, Shahin R, Melamed E, Neurology 37: 1685–1686, 1987; Stracciari A, Guarino M, Ciuicci G, Pazzaglia P, J Neurol Neurosurg Psychiatr 56: 423–429, 1993; Teuber H and Mishkin M, J Psychol 38: 161–175, 1954; Solms M, Kaplan-Solms K, Saling M, Miller P, Cortex 24: 499–509, 1988; Smith B, Neurology 10: 465–469, 1960.

[31] Price et al 1983.

[32] van Lommel P, van Wees R, Meyers V, Elfferich I, Lancet 358: 2039–2045, 2001 (esp 2044); van Lommel P, Adv Exp Med Biol 550: 115–132, 2004.

the underlying neural basis of ECE phenomenology. I shall also show (chap 7) what can be achieved with neurophysiological comparisons between ECE and various dream-states. The new insights thereby realized should, by now, be obvious.

6.4. OUT-OF-BODY PHENOMENOLOGIES: THE EXPERIENTIAL REPERTOIRE

During autoscopy,[33] subjects experience a vision of themselves as if in a mirror, that is, with a 180° y-axis (through-shoulder) reversal. The observed phantom is undoubtedly the subject, is extremely vivid and three-dimensional, while consciousness resides with the subject. The experience is only visual. A 33-year-old teacher with left-sided seizures was admitted and a tumour (a rapidly growing malignant glioblastoma multiforme) was excised from the right fronto-temporal region of the brain. Two days post-operatively, she turned one evening in bed to be confronted by her double sitting beside her. She thought a mirror had been left on the bedclothes, but on reaching out, realized it was a phantom of herself. 'She' was very quiet, staring steadily, without blinking.[34] As with all autoscopic phenomena, the subject's consciousness was firmly rooted in the subject, and not in the doppelganger.

Secondly, heautoscopy, in addition to the visual autoscopic illusion, combines some degree of detachment from the self as seat of full conscious-awareness. Indeed, consciousness *oscillates* between person and illusory phantom: this is a most important insight. Vestibular accompaniments of floating, or of bodily lightness, are usually present, while the 'ghost' is less vivid or even transparent, yet still three-dimensional in quality. Moreover, the appearance of the double may be smaller, larger, younger or older, and sometimes of the other sex. Nevertheless, the identity is firmly that of the subject:

I would sit at the table and have beside me or in front of me another 'me' sitting and talking to me. That's my double. I do hear him . . . has the same voice as me, maybe a bit younger . . . indeed, he seems to be a little bit younger than me.[35]

Thirdly, a variant of heautoscopy is the sense or feeling of another presence (FOP): no visual sensations are involved. If the FOP is due to pathology, the

---

[33] Lunn 1970; Brugger and Regard 1997; Brugger P, *Cogn Psychiatr* 7: 179–194, 2002.
[34] Brugger and Regard 1997.
[35] Brugger and Regard 1997.

sensed presence is ipsi-lesional, with associated affective affinities expressed by the subject towards the phantasm.

And fourthly, we come to the OBE proper, that of one's mind or consciousness viewing the body from another extra-corporeal vantage point either at ground level or, more usually, from an elevated perspective. This chapter has been primarily concerned with OBE, of which several typical examples have been given in the preceding text. The question remaining to be discussed is whether OB phenomenology is purely psychological or even 'psychical' in origin, or is directed by determinable and explicable neurophysiological facts and observations.

Blanke and Mohr[36] in carrying out an extensive review of 113 subjects, found 41 cases amenable to analysis from modern neurophysiological perspectives. Of these, 20 were autoscopic, 10 heautoscopic, and 11 OBE. In brief, autoscopic phenomena appear to arise from the occipito-parietal cortex, are often unilateral due to pathological involvement of the visual tracts, and are entirely passive encounters with another 'self' within paracentric space. Of far greater interest are the neurophysiological interrelationships between heautoscopy and OBE, the former occurring more often from a seated or standing position, but OBE invariably from a recumbent posture. This bodily position nullifies graviceptive otolithic stimulation and therefore more readily predisposes to the commonly experienced sense of non-gravitational weightlessness and floating in space.[37]

These authors concluded that OBE predominantly ($\sim$70%) derive from the *right* parietal/upper temporal region. Furthermore, disturbing this area with an extraneously applied electromagnetic field (TMS) causes body schema disorganization in normal subjects. Clearly,[38] these externally induced effects presumably disrupt the continual updating of the body schema from its four primary external inputs. Temporal lobe epilepsy was by far (80–90%) the predominant aetiology. Importantly, during OBE, experients view their bodies as detached and inert from their elevated vantage point. Conversely, heautoscopic subjects have a considerably more 'dynamic' relationship with their doubles. Here, consciousness appears to be divided or split between either perspective, while other subjects are able to perceive simultaneous existences in two places.[39]

---

[36] Blanke O and Mohr C, *Brain Res Rev* 50: 184–199, 2005.

[37] Blanke and Mohr 2005.

[38] Blanke O, Mohr C, Christoph M, Pascual-Leone A, Brugger P, Seeck M et al, *J Neurosci* 25: 550–557, 2005.

[39] Blanke et al 2004; Blanke and Mohr 2005; Lunn 1970.

It is therefore not difficult to perceive that an acute vascular disturbance followed by recovery could temporarily dismantle these highly coordinated and interdependent systems leading to momentary aberrations in body position (disembodiment), a sense of motion or spinning (vestibular mismatching), and disturbances in person-oriented agency. Our sense of conscious corporateness (egocentric body schema) and its relation to the immediate environment (paracentric body schema) is a mentally contrived 'virtual reality', in continuity with other forms of subconscious mentation, which is extremely vulnerable to a variety of cerebral insults.[40] Further ongoing research[41] is uncovering additional defects associated with OBE and a dysfunctional temporo-parietal junction giving rise to psychotic and schizotypic personalities, a propensity towards anxiety, panic and depression, and acquisition of a dysmorphic sense concerned with bodily proportions.

The issue, therefore, could not be clearer. A normal brain can knock up a non-existent 'phantom' limb or organ, a cerebrally engineered engram of a bodily torso in tetraplegic subjects with a broken neck, a mirror image of one's body during an autoscopic event, the spontaneous sensing of an invisible 'presence', and the apparent projection of conscious-awareness to a locus far beyond the confines of the physical body during heautoscopy (partially), or the occurrence of an OBE (fully). Importantly, these events do occur in normal people: they do not need 'mystical', metaphysical or psychical explanations. Neither do they have anything to contribute about mind or conscious-awareness existing in absence of cerebral support.

6.4.a. Are OBE Acceptable Accounts of Real Events?

However, I return to OBE viewed specifically from the perspective of the alleged representation of 'mind' or 'consciousness' independent of physical support. Having extensively covered the modern conceptual neurophysiology of OBE, I have no recourse but to emphasize their cerebral origins. Yet there is a continuing unease about that kind of explanation, since the phenomenology suggests that mind or consciousness can exist, and continue functioning, outwith the body. Sabom, for example, refers to six cases[42] who, during their OB experiences, were able to report on specific focused details exclusive

---

[40] Kahan T, LaBerge S, Levitan L, Zimbardo P, *Consc Cogn* 6: 132–147, 1997.
[41] Murray C and Fox J, *J Nerv Ment Dis* 193: 70–72, 2005; Murray C, *Metaphys Epistemol Tech* 19: 2000, 149–173; Mohr C and Blanke O, *Curr Psychiatr Rep* 7: 189–195, 2005.
[42] Sabom 1982, 83–115.

to their individual resuscitations. These cases are certainly worthy of attention and of serious thought.

But my first objection to the notion of these experiences representing mind operative outwith brain is, notably, their triviality. Subjects' narratives comprise isolated recollections of this, or that, little detail—the insertion of a needle, the shape of the defibrillator electrodes, the use of contact lubricant. None of these patients has ever given a fluent, sequential eyewitness account of the entire procedure: neither did Pam Reynolds, nor did the lady knocked down by the black car, described above in Chapter 1. There is also a very alarming disparity among all these subjects between the apparent cognitive activity displayed, and the absence of pain, or for some subjects audition, the inability to converse with people or doctors, and the complete lack of affective connection with the seriousness of the event and the threatened extinction of life. That casts considerable doubt on whether a complete, competent mind was actually operative during these or other resuscitations. Whatever the conscious state of these subjects, it is evident that some data necessarily had to enter their brains, otherwise they would not have been able to recall, from later memory in their real bodies and minds, what apparently did happen. Clearly, there were no dead brains. In passing, we should be reminded of more recent experiments in cognitive psychology pertinent to the ability of subjects to perceive without consciously being aware that they had done so.[43]

To date, the degree to which these subjects were either unconscious or in a subliminal mode of existence has not been ascertained. That an individual in a momentary quasi-moribund state happens to give a few recalled details about the dials and knobs on a machine, or a nurse's hair-do, is hardly an overwhelmingly convincing demonstration that 'mind' or 'consciousness' have, on these occasions cited, existed and functioned independently of body or the brain. That, clearly, will not do. What we do need is some robust indication that mind was capable of exhibiting entirely different, coherent mental accomplishments *away from the body*. That kind of information we still await—expectantly.

My second objection is the incisive issue whether the total personality of any subject could capably enjoy the corporeal independence claimed without the neurological underpinning of the brain. That, signally, has not been demonstrated in any report. We are led to believe that ongoing experiments[44] with cards or markers being placed on high light fittings in intensive care facilities will hopefully lead to someone revealing the hidden code. Badham

[43] Merikle P, Smilek D, Eastwood J, *Cogn* 79: 115–134, 2001.
[44] Sabom 1982, 190; Fenwick 2004c.

and Badham[45] called for such an experiment over twenty-five years ago. Yet, according to Dr Fenwick's statements published on the internet, his pupil Penny Sartori after five years' work did not find any OBE patient (of eight) able to report on her cards. We are therefore required to believe that the patients were 'not in the right place' or were 'more interested (obviously—as one is *now* required to believe) in observing the course of their resuscitations'. These investigators would be far better employed making carefully timed BIS (see p 131–2) observations (or using some other analogous technique) throughout subjects' resuscitations, noting the precise time when conscious-awareness returned and correlating those data with the conscious or subconscious experiences each surviving individual was able to remember. On the contrary, what we have are thousands of OBE reports throughout the literature, but still no piece of convincing data on what can only be described as a most dismal and unpromising front. That, in itself, is massive and sufficiently potent proof. But further, I claim Sartori's data (if Fenwick's internet reports are correct) to further my view that OB subjects are not 'out' of their bodies and cannot 'see' their immediate physical environment.

My third objection is centred on a much greater problem. That arises from unwarranted attempts to read off data from a resuscitative procedure, designed to restore a life hanging precariously in the balance and rightfully belonging to an entirely different sphere of activity. We should not require of personnel involved in heroic life-saving procedures to make additional, reliable and clear-headed observations irrelevant to the acute problem in hand, and only to be used to permit another set of retrospective 'investigators' to claim that mind exists outside the body. Without independent, dispassionate observations on whether patients' eyes were open, how long they remained conscious in their place of resuscitation before being moved elsewhere, how their levels of consciousness fluctuated during the entire event, what their BIS score might have been, and thus whether glimpses of the procedure, staff members, and general disposition of the apparatus could be taken in, even while subjects were not necessarily too aware of their surroundings, we will never be certain or convinced.

Finally, it should be quite evident that the foregoing explorations hardly get to the root of the problem. The issue of real existence outwith the brain and its experimental demonstration raises enormous, if not insuperable, neurophysiological and philosophical challenges. Attempts to overcome such challenges with the use of concealed marker cards are, to my mind, facile in the

---

[45] Badham P and Badham L, *Immortality or Extinction?* London: Macmillan 1982, 76.

extreme. Given the weight of neurophysiological data underpinning OBE and allied phenomena, I can hardly believe that intelligent people can so obstinately continue to pursue such hopelessly insubstantial ends. The solution to the existence of mind outwith its brain is far less simplistic. For all these reasons, I do not consider the viewing of one's body, or of resuscitatory procedures being applied to it, as an appropriate veridical 'proof' that any subject's mind, soul or free consciousness has actually existed and functioned *coherently* in space. Nor do I believe that such experiences have to be construed as 'mystical', supernatural or even religious, either in content or in context. If only somebody—'out there'—and 'out-of-body'—could have an original idea . . . !

6.4.b. OBE are Neurological Disturbances of Body-Image

In the light of these advances and revelations, the problems and challenges facing those who persist in attempting to argue that these aberrations are not brain-determined neurophysiological constructs, but phenomena originating outwith the natural, conscious world of everyday function and sensibilities, are rapidly increasing. I have shown that in pathological terms, a great deal of this phenomenology is determined by temporal or parietal lobe disease, and particularly with epileptic foci, migraine, or stroke lesions. The study of these conditions has therefore offered a most fruitful exposure of the illusory/ hallucinatory disturbances engendered, in particular, by neurophysiological and neuropathological disturbances in the region of the temporo-parietal junction. Epilepsy provides a focus for an abnormal discharge which imposes hypoxic influences on those regions affected and progressively recruited into the spreading and accelerating discharge. In other physiological examples, the causative aetiology is related to reduced visual, haptic and proprioceptive inputs, the influence of overbreathing, a quiet and subdued atmosphere with low or absent illumination, the role of pain and N_2O narcosis in obstetric cases, and the major impact of arterial atheroma in impairing regional cerebro-vascular blood flow.

These findings are of critical importance to OBE considered more generally under the umbrella of ECE phenomenology. Of all cases reported, by far the greatest number are due to pathological causes as the text at various places above illustrates. It might be insisted that too much attention has been afforded to pathological conditions, but it should not be forgotten the majority of ECE phenomenology occurs more under the influence of pathological than physiological conditions. Nevertheless, the reality of the body-image has been clearly demonstrated in young, healthy control subjects not known to have any underlying cerebral pathology.[46] Its functional basis is manifest through multimodal activity, is referential both to the self and to others, and is hierarchically disposed in that head, shoulders and upper torso are far more predominantly perceived than legs and feet. That, in fact, is true of one's own daily experience—the upper body and face assume far more importance in personal self-awareness—and of the image preferred for presenting to the outside world, as also of the impression gained from viewing and assessing the demeanour, compositeness and 'personality' of others, especially when encountered for the first time.

From all this, I assert that an OBE does not have to be ascribed to purely psychological or postulated 'psychic' causes. There is a vast quantity of neurophysiological data indicating that the brain can replicate all of the experiential facets of OB phenomenology. Furthermore, additional clarifications and greater understandings will accrue. Despite those authors who are reluctant to engage with, or be convinced by, neurophysiological explanations,[47] my own view is that it is becoming very difficult to continue insisting that 'crisis OBE' are experientially different from OB events whatever their varied neurophysiological or neuropathological aetiologies (such as temporal lobe epilepsy, migraine, vascular disorders, or electrical brain stimulations). Indeed, it would not be unreasonable to expect, given what I have claimed, that the onus of proof requires those same workers to explain precisely why they think such experiential differences exist, to bring forward arguments that permit valid differentiation of the one form of experience from the other, and to enunciate precisely where neurophysiological process diverges from their proposed causative 'psychic' or other-worldly-domain mechanisms deemed responsible for those events.

OBE phenomenology occurs not only when subjects are invariably in a horizontal position, but when they are either unconscious or in a subconscious mode of existence. Another circumstance when aberrant subconscious mentation may occur is during the sleep-dream mode. In the following chapter, I consider the neurophysiology and neuropathology of sleep, because I think that certain aspects of dreaming can bring further important contributions to our understandings of the mechanisms whereby ECE, and in particular NDE, might be generated.

---

[46] Reed and Farah 1995.
[47] Ring 1980, 216; van Lommel et al 2001 (esp p. 2004); Greyson B, *Gen Hosp Psychiatr* 25: 269–274, 2003.

7

Falling Asleep, Perchance to
Dream—Thence to Reawaken

In this chapter, I continue my neurological theme relating to the realms of
conscious-awareness and its disturbances, and their relevance to ECE phenomenology. Here, it is my intention to make a comparison between dream-
state modes and NDE phenomenology. The first, and most obvious reason for
doing so is because NDE occur when subjects are either unconscious or, at
least, in some kind of subconscious state.

My second reason stems from various brain-scanning techniques which
identify those areas of the brain which are shut down or functionally disconnected at certain stages throughout the dream-sleep cycle. Thus, if the subconscious production of dreams, or what is technically termed 'dream-state
mentation', is effected when key areas of the brain are disconnected, there
seems no reason to believe that similar subconscious mentation could not
occur in people whose brains, temporarily, are functionally compromised
while recovering from the event responsible for that dysfunction.

Third, I pursue this course because the experiences associated with entering
(hypnagogic) or departing from (hypnopompic) sleep are closely reminiscent
of the NDE narrative report. Thus, similar parts of the brain could be
contributing to either type of experience. My fourth approach arises from
analytical techniques applied to dream recollections, itemized by dream
researchers as ideational units and particularly word counts, the latter having
a direct bearing on the objective dissection of NDE reportage. Fifth, other
types of abnormal dreaming including sleep paralysis, narcolepsy/cataplexy,
and lucid dreaming, bring additional insights to my case, thereby promoting a
more informed neurophysiological understanding of ECE (NDE) phenomenology. Such insights offer an alternative stance against prevailing explanatory parapsychological and psychical paradigms widely offered in the pertinent
literature.

These many reasons, to my mind, strengthen the case for considering
dream-state neurophysiology, while not advancing any necessary identity
between a dream and NDE. In the anthologies that I have been evaluating,

authors emphasize the fact that to experients, ECE are *not* dreams but 'real' events. It may therefore seem surprising, if not perverse, to have attempted forging some kind of interconnecting link. But such a conclusion would, in my view, vitally miss the point. Indeed, my response is that because ECE, like dream-state modes, occupy subconscious states, some neurophysiological parallels between them can very reasonably be drawn out. That is because dream-state physiology has uncovered much about the mechanisms and relationships between sleep, degrees of 'unconsciousness' and its associated forms of perceptual awareness or subconscious mentation.

In addition, statements of the kind that ECE are not dreams cannot be taken literally as reliable indicators of any comparative neurophysiological lack of associations or connections. Ordinary folk are not in a position to offer that kind of assurance. They lack detailed knowledge of the various dream states now identified over the last fifty years by neurophysiological research. To have taken subjects' statements at face value, and hence to have ignored completely dream-state neurophysiology, risked missing crucial relationships or principles which could have shaped the opinions of the authors that I make specific reference to. Indeed, I mantain that conclusion is upheld, as is clearly exemplified from a perusal of authors' collected published narratives.

From an entirely different perspective, the reported subconscious mentation of ECE is open to interpretations pregnant with spiritual overtones or biblical reference. These interpretations frequently afford supposed insights into life beyond the grave if not glimpses of what, in the Christian tradition, are termed heaven or eternity. Furthermore, recorded narratives embrace figures perceived to be God or Jesus. The difficulty here is whether such memories, for that is how NDE are *now* recalled and thence reported, portray a credible reality beyond the universe. Alternatively, they could merely represent sundry recollections of varied sorts which the brain delivers during these hallucinatory episodes. If that is so, the scenes and people visualized necessarily articulate the subject's idiosyncratic perceptions of spirituality, God and eternity, reflective of subjects' personal dispositions. That is, cultural influence significantly informs and shapes the contours of the narrative, as I explained in Chapter 2.

It is my view, however, that NDE narratives lack corresponding resonances with those dreams, trances or visions recorded in the scriptural annals of the Judaeo-Christian traditions. Those biblical typologies attest to numerous encounters of prophets or other holy men and women with God, as exemplified in the great theophanies of Isaiah's vision in the Temple (Isa 6: 1–4), of Daniel's phantasmic percept of the Ancient of Days (Dan 7: 9) or, in later times whilst *en route* to Damascus (Acts 9: 5), of Paul's dramatic confrontation with the Risen Christ. Note that scriptural dreams also find employment as literary devices through which particular individuals are singled out by divine agency for the prosecution of defined tasks, the receipt of interpretative understandings, or disclosure of revelatory insight. Peter's experience in his dream of unclean beasts is interesting not only for the divine contravention of Jewish food laws but especially noteworthy for the manner of its literary expression, as of 'another' standing alongside Peter as the *subject* of that trance (ἐγένετο ἐπ᾽ αὐτὸν ἔκστασις: Acts 10:10). Another very appropriate example is the somewhat curious Pauline reference (2 Cor 12: 2–4) to 'a man who ascended up to the "third heaven" (ἕως τρίτου οὐρανοῦ) whether in the body or not . . . into paradise'. Even if Paul was obliquely referring, in third-person speech, to an event which he himself had experienced fourteen years previously,[1] it seems quite clear that it was to have a later and profound significance for him (2 Cor 12: 7) in his newly inspired task of promulgating the gospel throughout the Diaspora.

Despite the differential emphases and comparisons in construing biblical experiences of the divine and spiritual world, and ECE, we now turn back to the main focus of this section. The subconscious visualization of formed images, with or without the somatosensory accompaniments of touch, sound or olfaction, characterizes dream phenomenology. Thus NDE, like dreams, could be envisioned as states of subconscious mentation and awareness, despite an externally perceived state of apparent unconsciousness, and sometimes death. These parallels, therefore, demand analysis of the neurophysiology of sleep and its attendant phenomenology of dreaming. More importantly, they suggest possible experimental approaches aimed at uncovering further the neurophysiological basis of NDE phenomenology. For in stating this, we must constantly bear in mind that numerous victims recover full consciousness without evident neurological defects, indicating that their brains were not, nor could have been, dangerously anoxic or even severely hypoxic at the outset of their adventure.

I proceed by examining the process of falling asleep, and then assessing the neurophysiological aspects of rapid eye movement (REM) and of non-rapid eye movement (NREM) sleep-modes. This is followed by an account of hypnagogic and hypnopompic sleep modes, considered in relation to the parallels existing between them and the phenomenology of ECE. A third offering concludes with a discussion of the pathologies which either inhibit or intensify dream-state mentation, and how these functional aberrations

---

[1] Murphy-O'Connor J, *Paul: A Critical Life*, Oxford: Oxford University Press 1997, 320.

relate specifically to the NDE viewed, from this book's perspective, as an analogous brain-state.

7.1. SLEEPING AND DREAMING

7.1.a. On Falling Asleep

Although there is a clear distinction between alert wakefulness and deep sleep, the process of falling asleep is far less definable. There is still a gulf between the objective laboratory signs of sleep, and the subjective impression of going to sleep. Similar sentiments apply to OBE in that we have already seen how difficult it is to know whether subjects are awake or unconscious in relation to their reportage of alleged external happenings. However, quantitative approaches to the measurement of levels of unconsciousness, as for example during anaesthesia,[2] could very easily be employed in future ECE studies.

The basis of this emerging technology arises from quantitative analysis of conventional EEG (electroencephalographic) traces by means of fast Fourier computation.[3] One such outcome is termed *bispectral analysis*, a computational analysis of the differences between wave activity ('sinusoids') at differing frequencies, from which the bispectral index, BIS, is derived (Figure 7). This calculation provides a dimensionless numeric scale (100–0), which decreases continuously as levels of consciousness fall, during which subjects become progressively more unresponsive.[4] There is also good correlation between BIS and cerebral metabolism, as determined by positron emission tomography.[5] It is evident that this technique could easily be deployed during resuscitative attempts, at which times specific visual and auditory signals could be given. Any subsequent relationships between memory of such stimuli, BIS, and OB/ND events should they occur, would help in resolving the problem whether subjects were deeply unconscious (BIS<60) at the time and therefore experiencing hallucinations, or whether they were capable of responding to specific environmental cues and hence accurately reporting what they experienced, albeit seemingly 'unconscious' to outside observation.

[2] Myles P, Leslie K, McNeil A, Chan M et al, *Lancet* 363: 1757–1763, 2004.
[3] Wallace B, Wagner A, Wagner E, McDeavitt J, *J Head Trauma Rehab* 16: 165–190, 2001.
[4] Rampil I, *Anesthesiol* 89: 980–1002, 1998; Sigl J and Chamoun N, *J Clin Monit* 10: 392–404, 1994.
[5] Alkire M, *Anesthesiol* 89: 323–333, 1998; Rosow C and Manberg P, *Anesth Clin N Am* 19: 947–966, 2001.

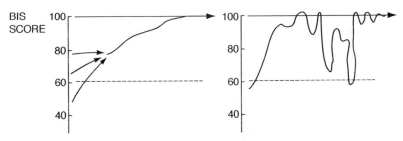

Figure 7. The BIS score is a numerical index of consciousness, indicated by the horizontal solid line with 100 representing a state of full conscious-awareness. In comparison, the horizontal dotted line at 60 represents an acceptable level of surgical anaesthesia. It is unknown from what preceding subconscious level ECE phenomenologies ultimately derive. The acquisition of full conscious-awareness could be direct, albeit from variable bases, and dependent on each subject's causal aetiology, as illustrated in the left-hand panel. Alternatively, the return to normality, as indicated in the right-hand panel, could involve several alternations between conscious or near-conscious states of awareness and deeper levels of unconsciousness during which neither mentation nor memory would ensue. In such cases, the experience might comprise several remembered vignettes, but be recalled as one seamless event.

Important studies have taken place since it was first discovered[6] that the brain during certain phases of the sleep cycle is more active and awake than in its daytime mode of wakeful attentiveness. Neurophysiologic studies have now identified several distinct phases representative of the passage from wakefulness, through drowsiness, to true and deep sleep, a sequence termed the sleep-onset period (SOP). The most detailed compendium relating to SOP describes nine phases (Hori),[7] although for most purposes SOP is more easily regarded as comprising four consecutive stages, as detailed below.[8] Just to add to the investigational difficulties, during Hori sleep-onset phase 1, 82% of subjects declared themselves awake as opposed to 7% who thought they were asleep, while in Hori phase 9, 26% declared themselves to be still awake while 44% deemed themselves to have been fully asleep. The borderland between consciousness and subconscious states is not easy to investigate.

    [6] Aserinsky E and Kleitman N, *Science* 118: 273–274, 1953: Dement W and Kleitman N, *J Exp Psychol* 3: 339–346, 1957.
    [7] Hori, Hayasahi, Morikawa 1994.
    [8] Ogilvie R, *Physiol Rev* 5: 247–270, 2001.

Stage I SOP, popularly known as 'nodding off', engenders an overwhelming sense of drowsiness when the eyelids seem very heavy, muscles relax, and the eyes roll slowly from side to side. Subjects may not necessarily be aware that they were transiently asleep, and if upright, their heads roll gradually forwards, thus invariably jerking them back to their senses. In comparison with the full waking state, the EEG reveals ~50% a-wave activity comprising low-amplitude, high-frequency waveform. Stage II is characterized by sleep and complete muscle relaxation. EEG a-wave activity is reduced and replaced by sharp spindle and K-complex configurations. In Stage III, the subject is deeply asleep and rapidly enters Stage IV accompanied by raised thresholds for external sensory stimulation and difficulty in arousal. The EEG typically reveals high amplitude, very low frequency δ-wave activity. Stages III and IV, collectively known as slow-wave-sleep (SWS), occupy ~30 minutes of the entire SOP cycle, the latter lasting ~60–90 minutes. Dreaming occurs during SOP: in SWS (III–IV) it is termed non-rapid eye movement (NREM) sleep, while in SOP I, a more vivid REM-like form of dreaming occurs, termed hypnagogic dream-mentation.

When SWS terminates, some striking physiological changes supervene. The EEG suggests that the subject is awake, the predominant δ-wave activity being now replaced by the reappearance of non-synchronized low-amplitude, high-frequency α-β-waves. The eyes make intermittent, phasic rapid side-to-side movements or 'saccades', yet apart from that, the remaining anti-gravity body musculature, excepting the muscles of respiration, is paralysed. Pulse, blood pressure, body metabolism, and temperature increase. The subject has now entered the first period of so-called rapid eye movement (REM) sleep, lasting ~30 minutes, during which vivid dreaming occurs: subjects roused from REM sleep usually report they were dreaming. Having passed this phase, the cycle repeats through Stages I–IV. During an average 8-hour period[9] about 5–6 cycles recur, although the time spent in REM sleep progressively rises while that of NREM sleep sharply decreases.[10]

7.1.b. Wakefulness, and NREM and REM Dream-State Modes

Current understandings of the interrelationships between waking and the dreams characterizing NREM/REM sleep derive from analysis of EEG tracings,

[9] Horne J, *Experientia* 48: 941–953, 1992.
[10] Simple diagrams of EEG changes throughout the cycle may be found in Horne J, *Sleepfaring*, Oxford: Oxford University Press 2006, 130; Hobson JA, *Dreaming*, Oxford: Oxford University Press 2003, 41; Bear M, Connors B, Paradiso M, *Neuroscience*, Baltimore: Lippincott Williams & Wilkins 2001, 616, fig. 19.10.

interrogation of dream-subjects awoken at specific times during the sleep cycle, and culling of data,[11] especially relevant to humans, from brain scanning technologies applied during the sleep–wake cycle. Brain scanning data, despite many technical and interpretative difficulties, identify areas of brain remaining active, thus suggesting the distinguishing neurophysiological parameters of various sleep-dream modes. In the established phase of SWS, cerebral blood flow (CBF) is reduced overall by ∼30%,[12] and cerebral glucose metabolism by 40%;[13] these are very significant changes in comparison with waking state. In respect of ECE, it is useful to compare these reduced levels of blood flow and oxygen supply with those attending a cardiac arrest and its subsequent treatment. When the arrest occurs, oxygenated blood is still present within the intra-cerebral circulation, although the rate of oxygen extraction now rises in order to sustain oxidative metabolism within the neuronal and peri-neuronal (glial) tissues. Given the institution of some effective cardiac resuscitation, a reduced CBF, ∼30–50% below normal, could still then be compatible with an undamaged brain as, indeed, the outcome of such procedures amply demonstrates. That outcome is usually dependent on a concurrent source of applied oxygen.

During SWS, scanning technology reveals loci where changes in the uptake of oxygen, computed through the distribution of ($H_2{}^{15}O$) indicative of regional (r) CBF, or the uptake of glucose (^{18}fluoro-deoxyglucose) as measures of tissue metabolism, occur. (Note that the superscripts in this sentence refer to isotopes of oxygen and fluorine, respectively, and not journal or other footnote references.) Since rCBF and glucose metabolism are tightly linked, either methodology provides data related to local alterations in brain physiology. During SWS, marked reductions in rCBF involve the brainstem, cortico-junctional areas, and much of the frontal cortex, including the important pre-frontal higher executive association areas of lateral orbital and dorso-lateral cortices. In parallel with the deactivated pre-frontal curvature, rCBF is reduced in other major secondary polymodal association areas within the temporal and parietal lobes. The significant falls in rCBF during stages III–IV SWS are indicative of large-scale reductions in metabolic support for synaptic transmission, and basal neuronal and glial cell metabolism.

We enter more secure terrain when considering REM sleep and dreaming. When the REM sleep-mode follows NREM, certain marked alterations occur in brain physiology, in addition to the EEG wave forms discussed above.

---

[11] Maquet P, Peters J, Aerts J et al, *Nature* 383: 163–166, 1996; Maquet P, Degueldre C, Delfiore G et al, *J Neurosci* 17: 2807–2812, 1997; Maquet P, *J Sleep Res* 9: 207–231, 2000; Braun A, Balkin T, Wesensten et al, *Brain* 120: 1173–1197, 1997; Nofzinger E, Mintun M, Wiseman M et al, *Brain Res* 770: 192–201, 1997.

[12] Braun et al 1997.

[13] Maquet P, *Behav Brain Res* 69: 75–83, 1995.

Global CBF overall rises by 17% over SWS, but there are also important increases in rCBF across brainstem and cortices including the limbic and paralimbic systems, and reactivation of the medial forebrain areas. Importantly, the centres for executive control and self-monitoring in pre-frontal cortex, as in NREM, remain deactivated: that is of direct relevance to the bizarreness and illogicalities attending REM dream-state mentation.

In addition, it is likely that vestibular afferent nerves (via the VIIIth cranial nerve which takes origin from the inner ear structures that are concerned with balance and body-in-space mechanisms) are activated. They transmit data through the brainstem to areas of cortical activity, thus playing a contributory role in the universally dream-associated sensations of moving, flying and rushing, or of being pulled, dragged, rotated or hurled through 'space'. Such motor accompaniments are typical of REM-associated dreaming in comparison with NREM-associated dreaming.[14] These data collectively are obviously of high importance[15] for explaining the hallucinatory experience of fictive movement during the early phase of NDE, particularly in relation to the so-called 'tunnel' phenomenon. Such motion is clearly vestibular in origin, and not visual, a significant point repeatedly overlooked, ignored and certainly not elaborated upon in depth by any previous investigators commenting on this intriguing aspect of ECE phenomenology.

7.1.c. State Boundary Control is Effected by Reciprocal Aminergic Mechanisms

The discovery of REM sleep, originally from nocturnal EEG studies,[16] was a key advance in sleep-dream research. This discovery was further consolidated when it was demonstrated that REM sleep in the cat could be abolished by brainstem transection at the level of the pontine mesencephalon, while remaining unaltered if the transection was made at a slightly lower level. The intervening area of brainstem is now known to contain neurones central to the generation of the side-to-side eye saccades, or rapid eye movement (REM) characterizing this type of sleep. The neural impulses, easily identified in the cat brain, have become known as PGO waves, because the relays originating from these neurones in the brainstem, or *P*ons, further involve the visual circuitry of the lateral *G*eniculate body and *O*ccipital (visual)

---

[14] Braun et al 1997.
[15] Hobson et al 1998.
[16] Aserinsky and Kleitman 1953.

cortex. The relevance of these findings to the human are somewhat less certain.[17]

The foundational studies outlined above have envisioned a predominant sleep-dream model founded upon the view that REM sleep-states are the physiological correlate of dreaming. According to the Harvard dream laboratory of Dr AJ Hobson, REM sleep is triggered by pontine or mid-brainstem neurones known as Meynert's Nucleus and the pediculo-pontine complex which secrete acetylcholine as their fundamental neurotransmitter, and thus known as 'cholinergic REM-on' cells. Their influence is inhibited by 'aminergic REM-off' cells. These inhibitory nuclei, localized at an adjacent part of the brainstem, comprise *loci coeruleus* or nor-epinephrine secreting cells and the *dorsal raphe* involved in serotonin production (Figure 8). Furthermore, reciprocal interplay[18] between the two systems determines the state boundary controls of the sleep–wake cycle, dream content, and even daytime sensori-motor conscious-awareness. Nevertheless, Hobson and colleagues acknowledge that they are not comprehensively explaining David Chalmer's 'difficult bit'—that is, how the attributes of conscious-awareness and abstract cognitive ideation create a unique, experiential realm, including qualia, beyond the essential physically based neurophysiological process.[19]

The corollary to that model is that the central region of the mesencephalic pontine brainstem masterminds dreams and dream phenomenology. The cerebral cortex, being relegated to secondary player status since it is driven from below, attempts to make sense out of the impulses it receives. For the Harvard research group, dreaming is merely an epiphenomenon of the mechanisms responsible for REM sleep. Hobson and colleagues insist that dream imagery represents the response of the cortical forebrain to 'chaotic impulses arising through the ascending brainstem nuclei'.[20] On the one hand, that speculative model is compatible with brain-scanning data on human subjects, demonstrating that REM sleep-mode is accompanied by activated forebrain structures predominantly including the medial limbic affective centres and fronto-medial cortex, while the dorso-lateral pre-frontal cortex, associated with full wakeful vigilance, diminished self-reflectiveness and attention, remains deactivated.[21]

[17] Datta S, *Cell Molec Neurobiol* 17: 341–365, 1997; Salzarulo P, Lairy G, Bancaud J, Munari C, *Electroencephalogr Clin Neurophysiol* 38: 199–202, 1975.

[18] Hobson J and McCarley R, *Am J Psychiatr* 134: 1335–1348, 1997; Hobson et al 1998; Hobson JA, Pace-Schott E, Stickgold R, *Behav Brain Sci* 23: 793–842, 2000; Datta S, *Neurosci Biobehav Rev* 19: 67–84, 1995; Aston-Jones G, Bloom F, *J Neurosci* 1: 876–886, 1981.

[19] Chalmers 1997.

[20] Hobson et al 1997; 2000; Hobson and McCarley 1997.

[21] Braun et al 1997; Nofzinger et al 1997; Maquet 2000.

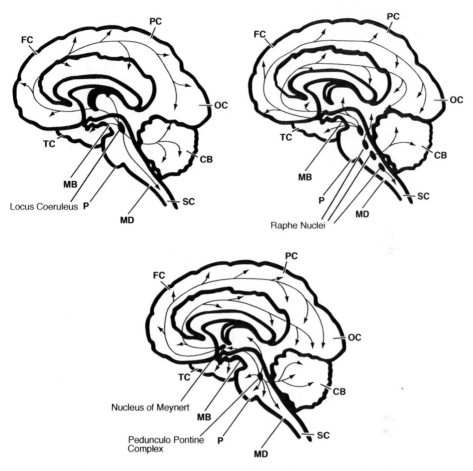

Figure 8. These are schematic representations of the major components of the 'cerebral amine fountain', which release nor-epinephrine (upper panel), serotonin (5-hydroxytryptamine, 5HT) (central panel), and acetylcholine (ACh) (lower panel) into various centres within the cerebral cortices (FC, frontal cortex; PC, parietal lobe; OC, occipital cortex; TC, temporal lobe), cerebellum, CB; brainstem (MB, midbrain; P, pons; MD, medulla oblongata), and spinal column, SC. These amines are elaborated by loose conglomerations of nerve cells (= nuclei, some of which carry eponymous or other more romantic names) within the upper and middle brainstem (Locus coeruleus for nor-epinephrine; Raphe nuclei for 5HT, while two major centres, the Nucleus of Meynert and the pediculo-pontine complex, elaborate acetyl-choline). The 'oozing' of these effector molecules into the cerebral cortex is responsible, in part, for wakefulness (5HT and nor-epinephrine), or somnolence and sleep ('cholinergic' effects of ACh).

However, the neurophysiological mechanisms resulting in REM sleep do not necessarily always give rise to dreaming. In humans, there is evidence of some degreee of dissociation: REM sleep-modes and dreaming are not necessary congruent phenomena. Almost 30% of awakenings from REM sleep-mode fail to elicit dream reports, while ~10% of NREM dream reports are indistinguishable from REM dream reports. Thus dreaming, perhaps accounting for ~25% of total dream time per nocturnal cycle, may be of NREM type. Furthermore,[22] as the cycle terminates during the early morning, NREM dream reports more closely resemble REM reports, even though the brain is now exposed to an increasingly aminergic neurochemical milieu favouring wakefulness. We shall be returning to this theme when considering the neuropathology of sleep and dreaming.

7.1.d. Hypnagogic Hallucinations Occurring during Sleep Onset

Hypnagogic hallucinations are visions or dream-like images appearing during stage I SOP, that is, between full wakefulness and light sleep.[23] With reference to SOP, it is during Hori stage 5 ('H5') when hypnagogic events most likely occur. As Hori's study showed, it is difficult to be sure whether subjects are still awake and aware at this particular stage. Proposed criteria of true sleep are the replacement of occipital α-wave by slower 4–7Hz θ-wave activity,[24] or, the establishment[25] of 12–14Hz spindles in the EEG. Hypnagogic activity appears to precede either set of criteria.

The dream-like mentation at or around sleep onset[26] has been analysed. The hallucinatory content of hypnagogic sleep episodes differs little from REM-associated dreaming. Comparatively there are some detectable subtleties, in that REM-associated dreams appear, on average, to be much more 'dreamlike' and more highly dramatic or bizarre. It is not always easy within the setting of an experimental sleep laboratory to foster the conditions necessary for experiencing the hypnagogic state. The latter demands a reduced level of sensory, that is environmental, input while simultaneously retaining a sufficient degree of arousal to permit continued awareness, the

---

[22] Solms M, *Brain Behav Sci* 23: 843–850, 2000.

[23] Vihvelin H, *Acta Psychiatr Neurol* 23: 359–389, 1948; Manford M and Andermann F, *Brain* 121: 1819–1840, 1998.

[24] Liberson W and Liberson C, *Rec Adv Biol Psychiatr* 8: 295–302, 1965.

[25] Dement and Kleitman 1957.

[26] Ogilvie 2001; Foulkes D and Vogel G, *J Abn Psychol* 70: 231–243, 1965; Foulkes D, Spear P, Symonds J, *J Abn Psychol* 71: 280–286, 1966.

absence of movement, and adoption of a restfully passive demeanour before the commencement of the experimental period. Useful experimental subjects are capable of being trained through the use of specific biofeedback procedures serving to prolong the hypnagogic state.[27]

A specific feature of hypnagogic dreaming is the sudden aquisition of 'knowledge' about an object, state of affairs or person's face, even though neither are scrutinized with the detail which, in waking life, would be necessary for complete recognition or perception. We should carefully note that the sudden eruption of 'complete knowledge' is directly pertinent to the 'all-knowing states' characterizing NDE. The latter subjects become seemingly aware of all there is to be known in the contents of vast libraries of books, or what other persons were thinking about them during extra-corporeal journeys. It is also evident that the images, visual and auditory, are located external to and not within the subject's awareness. In general, visual followed by auditory and then somaesthetic modalities, is the order of sensations experienced during hypnagogic hallucinations, as with REM dreams and NDE. The imagery of the hypnagogic state is itself complex,[28] varying from the experiencing of lights to panoramic landscapes or other extensive, well-formed scenes: the latter may be exceptionally vivid and characterized by much movement and activity. Subjects describe these resemblances in terms of the rapidity with which the hypnagogic imagery changes, its vividness and chromatic brilliance thus being distantly reminiscent of the 'forms' such as honeycombs,[29] webs, tunnels and spirals described by Kluver in reference to experimentally administered LSD. As one laboratory subject remarked— 'having an hypnagogic hallucination is the best way of hallucinating without actual recourse to taking LSD'.[30]

Auditory sensations during the hypnagogic period cause subjects to hear their own names being called[31] or to be directly addressed by persons visualized during the experience. Other cognitively determined auditory auras such as music or chime-like bells occur, these being commonly reported also by NDE subjects. A third feature, presumably related to the recruitment of the vestibular apparatus and to the vestibu-

[27] Green et al 1970.

[28] Schacter D, *Psychol Bull* 83: 452–481, 1976; Leaning FE, *Proc Soc Psychic Res* 35: 289–409, 1926.

[29] Ardis J and McKellar P, *J Ment Sci* 102: 22–29, 1956; Dybowski-Poznan M, *Kwart Psychol* 11: 68–94, 1939.

[30] Schacter 1976. It is not my view that LSD-type aberrations of brain function are sufficiently like ECE to warrant detailed further comparative analysis, and are therefore excluded from this book.

[31] Liberson W and Liberson C 1965.

lar connections through midbrain, thalamus and cerebral cortices, are sensations of movement such as floating upwards or falling, and of weightlessness. Commoner than these passively sensed events are other vigorously experienced episodes of flying, of rapid acceleration, or of being 'wrenched out of one's body'. These may further be elaborated in terms of spinning, swirling, of being hurled through a tunnel or of being moved rapidly forwards. That these events are remembered and thus available for later recall indicates that they have to be processed by the cerebral cortex by way of the neural networks already alluded to, and further rationalized by the subject in his recall of the events.

With either hypnagogic illusions or NDE, there is a paradoxical conflict between lying passively on a bed and simultaneously being moved around in 'space' in the manner reported. This is indicative of a dissociation between the phenomenal self, 'consciously' perceived as ego-/paracentric body-space by the cortex during either type of experience. Such events have also been associated with feelings of calm, peace, or joy, thus indicative of a presumptive input from neurophysiological systems involved in affect and emotion.[32]

There seems to be a marked element of suggestibility relevant to hypnagogic dream-content, as revealed by the proneness of subjects to report influences arising from their immediate environment during this twilight zone of the SOP. Indeed, external stimuli have been noted to be readily incorporated into the hypnagogic experience and hence act as major contributors to the dream-like imagery of the occasion.[33] This further pointer arises in relation to the ability of OB/ND subjects to recount accurately many phases in the resuscitatory process while still apparently 'unconscious' and, yet, still exquisitely aware of the immediate environmental surroundings.

This is not to say that the early events during OB/ND experiences are necessarily hypnagogic. But what I do suggest is the importance of observing their striking resemblances and hence of noting the opportunity for allied brain-states to be operative as consciousness, in either of these two experiences, fluctuates between wakefulness and either sleep or another subconscious mode. We also note that OBEs may simultaneously be experienced during either event. The neurological basis of hypnagogic dream-hallucinations is, at best, presumptive compared with the data on REM sleep. Nevertheless, it is impor-

---

[32] Twemlow S, Gabbard G, Jones F, *Am J Psychiatr* 139: 450–455, 1982; Cheyne J, Newby-Clark I, Rueffer S, *J Sleep Res* 8: 313–317, 1999a.

[33] Stickgold R, Malia A, Maguire D, Roddenbury D, O'Connor M, *Science* 290: 350–353, 2000.

tant to draw attention to the closeness of the phenomenologies experienced, whether in the physiological stage I (SOP), or in the abnormal circumstance during which a patient with cardiac arrest, undergoing external cardiac massage, also experiences an ECE. The mechanism(s) undergirding that phenomenology would surely demand the coordinated operation of major neural pathways between brainstem and cerebral cortex, thus bringing into question whether the brain of ECE subjects could realistically be regarded as dying, or even dead.

7.1.e. Insights from the Sleep-Paralysis Phenomenon Referable to OBE

It is known that the hypnagogic delusional condition is a manifestation of another syndrome, the sleep paralysis (SP) phenomenon. SP may be qualitatively defined as a transient quasi-conscious state of involuntary immobility recurring either during SOP—that is, hypnagogic, or when awakening occurs—hypnopompic. In either circumstance, subjects are paralysed yet able to open their eyes and report their experiences. So, like ECE, dream-like experiences are able to intrude into waking consciousness. Dependent on cultural background, ~25–40% of individuals are subject to some form of SP. SP, itself, is part of another triadic symptom-complex that includes narcolepsy and cataplexy. In a recent open survey[34] of 264 participants with SP, 28 (11%) reported having an OBE, some of whom additionally experienced auditory and visual hallucinations, and 'sensed presences'. I stress that some of the OBE subjects tried to identify objects previously placed on wardrobes or cupboards in order to show, while paralysed, whether they were awake or unconscious. All such attempts failed.

For example: 'I think I'm awake, so I look at my alarm clock to check, and if the bright green LED is not there, then I immediately know that it is a sleep disorder experience.' And another: 'So far, I haven't been able to identify anything, so I guess what you can see is just stored in the memory of your surroundings.' Or: 'I looked at "me" sleeping peacefully in bed as I wandered about. Trouble is the 'me' in the bed was wearing long johns . . . I have never worn such a thing.'

These examples reinforce the statements made above concerning the lady knocked down by the black car, blind Marsha, and Pam Reynolds. There is no

---

[34] Buzzi G and Cirignotta F, *Sleep Res Online* 3: 61–66, 2000: Buzzi G, *Lancet* 359: 2116–2117, 2002.

normal sight, nor sightings, during an OBE. Conversely, any veridical observations made and remembered must be due to ordinary conscious perception, even if the subject is apparently 'unconscious' to outside observation. There is another telling, paediatric example reported by Morse and Perry.[35] As she floated above the bed during her OBE, Cindi casually reminisced about the doctors she 'saw' who were apparently 'pushing on [her] chest... [although she] ... couldn't really see any details'. She certainly could not! The resuscitation lasted several hours during which internal cardiac massage by a cardio-thoracic surgeon was necessary, requiring an incision through her chest wall to enable him to massage her heart. Being fully unconscious means being opaque to the truth, whatever subjects think (and confess) what they saw, heard or felt.

It is most notable in regard to the occurrence of SP in circumstances associated with neither dying nor near-death, that the phenomenology of being out-of-body has never been conceived in terms of 'other-worldly' dimensions. Indeed, it is quite clear that the inability to 'see' objects planted by subjects around their bedrooms led these ordinary folk to conclude, quite sensibly, that the event was *in the mind* and, most certainly, not *out-of-body*. The data afforded by Buzzi and Cirignotti, therefore, have a signal relevance to the manner in which crisis OBE have been, and continue to be, interpreted.

Accompanying SP are a number of anomalous sensory phenomena intrinsic to hypnagogic (sleep-onset) and hypnopompic (sleep-offset) experiences. The burgeoning of this worldwide cultural mythology distinctly mirrors the historical and transcultural fabulous accretions which characterize ECE phenomenology. Cheyne and Girard[36] classify SP as *intrusive*, that is perceived menacing presence accompanied by auditory and visual hallucinations, the *incubus experience* comprising pressure on chest, suffocation, choking, and *vestibulo-motor* ('VM') involving floating, flying, and having an OBE. The incubus experience, culturally and historically, has contributed to a rich folklore referential to lethal demons, vampires, old hags, or spirits which during their nocturnal visitations sit on their victims' chests, and make to suffocate them to death[37] or attempt sexual intercourse with females. Such supernatural misinterpretations of neurologically determined events associated with hypnagogic sleep phenomena, and also ECE, are of considerable interest, culturally and scientifically. The parallelisms are thus of great relevance to this study, but need not be pursued any further.

The phenomenology of SP reveals a gradient of experiential and emotional content ranging from the average hypnagogic (or hypnopompic) event to

---

[35] Morse and Perry 1990, 37 (Case 8): my editing.
[36] Cheyne JA and Girard TA, *Cogn Psychiatr* 9: 281–300, 2004.
[37] Cheyne JA, Rueffer S, Newby-Clark I, *Cons Cogn* 8: 319–337, 1999b.

terrifying nightmares. Cheyne and Girard relate the VM spectrum to differential degrees of neural stimulation thus influencing the 'distance' seemingly travelled by subjects and the 'intensity' of their beyond-the-body experiences. They note how with low-amplitude electrical stimuli applied to the 'vestibular cortex' of the brain, Blanke and colleagues[38] evoked sensations of sinking or falling, while with higher currents, autoscopy and OBE were elicited. Interestingly, ECE phenomenology, if due to a waking brain and the possibility of increasing neural stimulation from a preceding state of 'unconsciousness', and increases in regional cerebral blood flow consequent upon a period of reduced or prolonged lack of blood pressure, could result in bizarre experiences and a belief that a vast journey had been accomplished beyond the confines of corporeality. Such phenomenologies are likely to arise from within the temporo-parietal-occipital junction. Furthermore, in the next section I suggest that lesions of this brain region are very likely to impair the capacity for ECE, as is also the case for dreaming.[39]

7.1.f. Narcolepsy/Cataplexy Complex: REM Intrusion into Conscious-Awareness

Sleep paralysis, occurring in ~6% of the population,[40] is a feature of a much less common abnormality of sleep termed narcolepsy (N). N has a European prevalence rate of ~0.05%[41] and is characterized by excessive daytime sleepiness, episodes of nocturnal waking and, in 70% of subjects, cataplexy (C)—a sudden loss of muscle tone evoked by emotion or laughter. Additional features of NC,[42] and typical of REM sleep-mode, are hynagogic hallucinations (in ~30% of subjects) and sleep paralysis (in ~25%). The REM-type hypnagogic hallucinations come with the first few minutes of the sleep-onset period, are felt to be real and their content often of a frightening nature. In order, prominent afferent modalities experienced are visual, then auditory, followed by tactile sensations. OBE are further accompaniments of the syndrome.[43]

[38] Blanke et al 2002.
[39] Solms M, *The Neuropsychology of Dreams*, Mahwah (NJ): Erlbaum 1997.
[40] Ohayon M, Zulley J, Guilleminault C, Smirne S, *Neurology* 52: 1194–1200, 1999.
[41] Ohayon M, Priest R, Zulley J, Smirne S, Paiva T, *Neurology* 58: 1826–1833, 2002.
[42] Aldrich M, *Neurology* 46: 393–401, 1996; Overeem S, Mignot E, van Dijk J, Lammers G, *J Clin Neurol* 18: 78–105, 2001; Chetrit M, Besset A, Danci D, Delarge C, Billiard M, *J Sleep Res* 3: 43, 1994.
[43] LaBerge S, Levitan L, Brylowski A, Dement W, *Sleep Res* 17: 115, 1988; Nelson K, Mattingly M, Acmitt F, *Neurology* 68: 794–795, 2007.

A loss of state boundary control (see above) is a possible explanation of the NC syndrome complex.[44] Normal REM sleep-mode, as we have seen above, is characterized by rapid eye movement dreaming, postural (anti-gravity) muscle paralysis, and a high-frequency, low-amplitude α/β wave-form EEG. The additional features of the NC complex may be viewed as the intrusion of the REM dream-state into the waking consciousness of these subjects, due to nocturnal phase shifts in REM state controls and hence the occurrence of precipitate muscular paralysis into their daytime activities.[45]

Narcolepsy is a genetically determined condition,[46] its underlying neuro-pathological basis still being uncertain. Most recent investigations reveal a deficiency, possibly due to auto-destructive processes involving hypothalamic cells, in the production of hypocretin. Hypocretins are critical to arousal and target the locus coeruleus (Figure 8), which elaborates nor-epinephrine in the upper brainstem. The disturbances in the sleep–wake cycle in N are thus possibly explicable on this basis.[47] Through mechanisms as yet undiscovered, the deficiency of hypocretin may be responsible for the cholinergic/aminergic imbalance, and thus loss of state boundary control, which underlies the symptomatology of NC. Thus, mutually inhibitory interactions between cerebral REM-on and REM-off areas that control state boundaries may be subject to unwanted influences in the sleep-wake cycle, or intrusions of the one into the other.[48]

Features of REM intrusion are not solely confined to NC subjects. Elements of each, such as sleep paralysis, hypnagogic hallucinations, autoscopy, are found commonly in surveys of presumed normal people,[49] and secondly in those with associated pathologies such as Parkinson's disease, alcoholic delerium tremens, and peduncular hallucinosis (see Chapter 9 below). Third, a recent survey of NDE subjects revealed that they experienced more hypnagogic visual and auditory events, sleep paralysis and attacks of cataplexy[50] in comparison with age-/sex-matched controls. These authors suggest that sub-

---

[44] Broughton R, Valley V, Aguirre M, Roberts J, Suwalski W, Dunham W, *Sleep* 9: 205–215, 1986.

[45] Montplaisir J, Godbout R, *Sleep* 9: 159–161, 1986; Montplaisir J, Godbout R, *Sleep* 9: 280–284, 1986; Lammers G, Arends J, Declerck A, Ferrari M, Schouwink G, Troost J, *Sleep* 16: 216–220, 1993.

[46] Rogers A, Meehan J, Guilleminault C, Grumet F, Mignot E, *Neurology* 48: 1550–1556, 1997.

[47] Overeem et al 2001.

[48] Manford and Andermann 1998; Lu J, Sherman D, Devor M, Saper C, *Nature* 441: 589–594, 2006.

[49] Ohayon et al 1999, 2001; Aldrich 1996.

[50] Nelson K, Mattingly M, Sherman A, Schmitt F, *Neurology* 66: 1003–1009, 2006.

jects predisposed to NDE have an arousal system open to REM intrusion events. Central to arousal is the locus coeruleus, which elaborates nor-epinephrine and which in concert with serotonin (Figure 8) promotes wake-fulness during the wake–sleep cycle. It is therefore not immediately clear from the report of Nelson and colleagues why this system, which facilitates wake-fulness, should be associated with sleep-onset hallucinations, sleep paralysis, cataplexy, or indeed, ECE phenomenology. The locus coeruleus is, however, stimulated by haemodynamic[51] and hypoxic[52] insults, and through afferent nerves arising within the vagus nerve from lungs, heart and great vessels (aorta),[53] giving rise to the 'fight or flight' reaction impelled by nor-epineph-rine secretion. Similar physiological insults invariably give rise to ECE in susceptible subjects.

In a recent review of the physiological properties of the locus coeruleus[54] devoted to behavioural and attentional activities, there was no recognition of any specific relationship with ECE phenomenology. On the other hand, I do assert that the ascending mesencephalic dopaminergic system, whether activated or de-inhibited, is a likely candidate capable of underpinning the ecstatic components of joy and peace which illuminate some NDE reportage.

This is undoubtedly a complex neurophysiological field which offers tantalizing possibilities for further dissection of their relevance to ECE phe-nomenology. At present, more data are needed to clarify many issues (raised by Nelson and colleagues) that are either speculative or unknown. However, the concept of REM intrusion as a factor in ND/OB experiential events is a further welcome step towards an elucidation of their nature: clearly, this is an idea conducive to further prospective examination. Finally, it must be re-membered that the brains of ECE subjects are awaking from major antecedent metabolic insults and, therefore, that the resultant neurophysiological func-tional outcomes are likely to be bizarre. Care should therefore be taken in extrapolating data directly from other case-studies, population surveys, or animal physiological experiments, to the very abnormal circumstances per-taining during ECE generation.

[51] Valentino R, Page M, Curtis A, *Brain Res* 555: 25–34, 1991.

[52] Bodineau L, Larnicol N, *Neuroscience* 108: 643–653, 2001.

[53] Puizillout J, Foutz A, *Electroencephalogr Clin Neurophysiol* 42: 552–563, 1977; Puizillout J, Foutz A, *Brain Res* 111: 181–184, 1976.

[54] Aston-Jones G, Rajkowski J, Cohen J, *Progr Brain Res* 126: 165–182, 2000.

7.2. THE NEUROPATHOLOGY OF DREAM-STATE MODES

The scheme of Hobson and colleagues outlined above has been challenged, successfully in my view, by the neurosurgeon Dr Mark Solms. His studies of brain-damaged patients indicate that the cerebral cortex may indeed be capable of initiating dream sequences, as evidenced from malignant or stroke pathologies that either reduce, or generate, dream-state mentation. He has built his case by collectively studying case-reports of patients with brainstem and cortical lesions, and determining whether, and in what circumstances, REM sleep-mode occurs without dreaming, or the converse. It seems clear, therefore, that dreaming is not the *sine qua non* of rapid eye movement behaviour.[55]

7.2.a. Cortical Pathology and Oneiric (Dream) Competence

Pathologically defined lesions in specific cortical regions provide evidence for Solms' assertion that dreaming is a cortically based phenomenon. Various studies have shown that the REM sleep-mode persists in the absence of its associated dream phenomenology. Global loss of dreaming is due either to unilateral/bilateral parietal lobe pathology,[56] or to deep frontal lobe lesions[57] (Figure 9). Parietal damage is commonly centred on the inferior parietal lobule, specifically the region of the supramarginal gyrus, Brodmann Area 40. The inferior parietal lobule (IPL) fulfils the office of a multimodal association area, being important in its contribution to cognitive perceptions of body-image as elucidated in Chapter 6. Regarding dream mechanisms, the right IPL is concerned with concrete spatial imagery, the left with symbolic representations of spatial cognition.

Deep frontal lobe lesions arise from varied forms of pathology involving both grey and white matter. In a series of ten patients with internal hydrocephalus, dreaming was absent as a result of hydrostatic compression of white matter in the vicinity of the anterior horns (Figure 9). The insertion of ventriculo-peritoneal shunts in five subjects led to a rapid resumption of

---

[55] Solms 1997.

[56] Benson D, and Greenberg J, *Arch Neurol* 20: 82–92, 1969; Jus A, Jus K, Villeneuve A, Pires A, Lachance R, Fortier et al, *Biol Psychiatr* 6: 275–293, 1973; Kerr N and Foulkes D, *J Ment Imagery* 2: 247–264, 1978; Schanfald D, Pearlman C, Greenberg R, *Cortex* 21: 237–247, 1985; Solms 1997, 138, 142.

[57] Solms 1997, 137 (involving 35% of 321 patients).

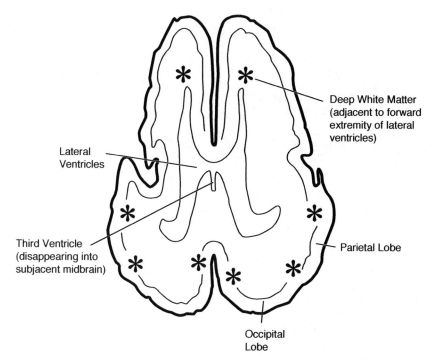

Deep White Matter
(adjacent to forward
extremity of lateral
ventricles)

Lateral
Ventricles

Third Ventricle
(disappearing into
subjacent midbrain)

Parietal Lobe

Occipital
Lobe

Figure 9. This diagram provides an imaginary horizontal cross-section of the cerebral cortex. Asterisks (*) indicate areas where pathological processes inhibit dream competence. Anteriorly, lesions around the anterior horns of the lateral ventricles (containing cerebral spinal fluid) interfere with neuronal fibres (white matter) in this area including those of the ascending mesencephalic dopaminergic tract (see Figure 10). Posteriorly, cortical lesions of the parietal and occipital lobes have similar effects. It is suggested that subjects with cortical pathology in these latter areas would be unable to undergo ECE events.

dreaming, even though the causal brainstem pathology responsible for the raised pressure remained.[58] Solms[59] concluded that relief of the effects of internal cerebral pressure permitted return of the functional competence of the ascending dorso-medial dopaminergic pathways (Figure 10), which, for him, are integral to cortically produced dreaming. This assertion gains further support from lobotomized schizophrenic patients[60] for whom dreaming is

---

[58] Solms 1997, 156. The pathology was variable: left internal carotid aneurysm; pontine medullary astrocytoma; posterior 3rd ventricular tumour; 3rd ventricular colloid cyst; idiopathic hydrocephalus.

[59] Solms 1997, 156.

[60] Frank J, *J Ment Sci* 92: 497–508, 1946; idem, *Psychiatry* 13: 35–42, 1950; Jus et al 1973.

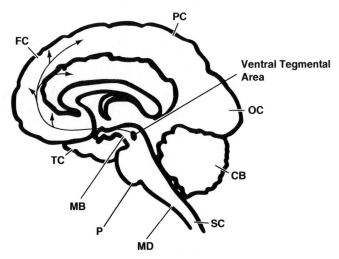

Figure 10. The nucleus concerned with dopamine synthesis and its distribution is located in the basal region (= tegmentum) of the midbrain (MB, or mesencephalon, lying above the pons, P). The entire system is known as the ascending mesencephalic dopaminergic system, being the fourth component of the diffuse amine system of the brain (see Figure 8). The dopaminergic system is restricted in distribution to the frontal cortex. It subserves the 'reward' system of the body, and reinforces certain adaptive behaviours, including drug addiction. This system is very likely to be responsible for the intensely ecstatic highs characterizing the feelings alluded to in some NDE reportings. Such inexpressibly wonderful feelings could occur if the inhibitory controls on this system were inoperative, as would be likely in a brain recovering coordinated physiological functioning following a severe, preceding metabolic insult. This ecstatic phenomenology sometimes occurs with overdoses of the anti-Parkinsonian drug L-dopa. (Nomenclature as for Figure 8.)

either abolished or severely reduced. In such cases, the cut transects the ascending dopaminergic tract. Other data supporting a central dopaminergic input for dreaming reveal its inhibition by anti-dopaminergic drugs, such as Haloperidol,[61] and exacerbation by dopamine agonists (L-dopa) resulting in frequent vivid dreams and nightmares, a side-effect noted with treated Parkinsonian subjects.[62]

So far, we have seen that dream activity is subject to modulation by cortical disease. The latter stems from vascular, traumatic, degenerative, toxic, neo-

---

[61] Sacks O, *An Anthropologist on Mars*, London: Picador 1995, 74.
[62] Sharf B, Moskovitz Ch, Lupton M, Klawans H, *J Neural Transm* 43: 143–151, 1978; Nausieda P, Weiner W, Kaplan L, Weber S, Klawan H, *Clin Neuropharmacol* 5: 183–194, 1982.

plastic insults, or aplasias,[63] surgery and pharmacological influences. But vivid dreaming and recurrent nightmares originate from another cortical irritant, that of temporal or parietal lobe epilepsy.[64] Moreover, these abnormally generated dreams usually occur during SOP stage I, being obliterated by appropriate surgery or suppressed by anti-convulsant therapy.[65] One case of particular interest is a man with temporal lobe epilepsy[66] whose illness evolved through daytime hallucinations, followed by identical dreamed olfactory hallucinations of perfume associated with his wife and a former girlfriend. This case establishes that the same area of the brain provides the basis of wakeful, as well as oneiric, experience.

7.2.b. Loss of Dreaming and Vivid Dreaming

Two further aspects of Solms' approach to dreaming, which are highly relevant to ECE phenomenology, remain: loss of visual dreaming and vivid dreaming. The former encompasses the Charcot-Willbrand-Muller syndrome, related to unilateral or bilateral lesions predominantly affecting the unimodal (visual) association territories of the medial occipito-temporal region including the fusiform gyrus[67] (Figure 4). The predominant outcome is loss of visual dream content that is invariably associated with irreminiscence—the conscious inability to visualize shapes. Accompanying defects may include prosopognosia or failure to recognize faces, topographical agnosia or inability to navigate familiar terrain, visual agnosia or loss of object recognition, and more rarely achromatopsia or loss of coloured vision.[68] Circumscribed pathologies, carbon monoxide intoxication, or trauma involving visual association areas, result in deprived visuo-spatial oneiric content:[69] 'I can dream about a person without seeing him, and can remember the person without having seen him.' These specific forms of visual agnosia occur during wakefulness, indicating that the same areas of cortex employed for full visual conscious comprehension are also recruited for the elaboration of oneiric visual imagery during sleep. It is important to recognize that dream recall is

[63] Solms 1997, 847.
[64] Epstein A, *Arch Gen Psychiatr* 10: 49–54, 1964; Solms 1997, 244.
[65] Boller F, Wright D, Cavalieri R, Mitsumoto H, *Neurology* 25: 1026–1028, 1975.
[66] Epstein A, Freeman N, *Epilepsia* 22: 603–605, 1981.
[67] Solms 1997, 20, 30, 92, 97–101.
[68] Solms 1997, 112ff.
[69] Adler A, *Arch Neurol Psychiatr* 51: 243–259, 1944; idem, *J Nerv Ment Dis* 111: 41–51, 1950; Benson and Greenberg 1969; Brain R, *Proc R Soc Med* 47: 288–290, 1954.

influenced by neither global mnemonic nor dysphasic incompetence consequent upon left-sided temporo-parietal lesional pathologies.[70]

Now in turning to vivid dreaming, I refer to those subjects who present with the difficulty of distinguishing between dream-states and reality, often associated with increased vivacity of dream-content. For some subjects, it is unclear whether they are conscious or in dream-state mode.[71] In the majority of Solms' reported cases (his Table 7, p. 62) there was invariably bilateral anterior limbic damage, with affective disinhibition and the breakdown in the neurophysiological monitoring of what is real and what belongs to the world of dream-state hallucinatory mentation:[72] 'it must have been a dream . . . my mind is playing tricks on me again':[73] or, 'I had the impression that the hospital was built in my house. I even told the doctor . . . I realize that was impossible nonsense . . . it was my imagination'.[74] In other cases, the dreams are not only seemingly continuous as perceived by the subject, but very unpleasant and disturbing in their imagery, and thus analogous to some of the terrifying experiences undergone during ECE.

The occurrence of frequent, vivid hallucinatory nightmares based on recurrent or stereotypical thematic material is an allied phenomenon usually generated by epileptogenesis or brain tumours: some element of disturbed fantasy–reality confusion may be a further accompaniment. Of the nine cases reported by Solms (Table 22.1, p. 208), five were due to bitemporal foci, the remainder to traumatic brain damage or tumours. The dream-hallucinations were often frighteningly real and horrific: in Case 230 (p. 205) the recurrent theme was of disturbing road accidents, dismembered individuals, blood, and broken bodies strewn across the carriageway; in Cases 136 and 357 (pp. 203–204) the subject matter was of verminous animals, insects or reptiles crawling around the room, in the bed, the nightclothes and even within body orifices. Case 31 (p. 206) was chased by 'something horrible' and Case 31 (pp. 207–208) by 'a bull with extremely long horns'.

Three of the epileptics were cured by surgery or anticonvulsant drugs. This suggests[75] that a low seizure threshold relates reality-confusion to increased

[70] Murri L, Arena R, Siciliano G, Mazzotta R, Muratorio A, *Arch Neurol* 41: 183–185, 1984; Arena R, Murri L, Piccini P, Muratorio A, *Res Comm Psychol Psychiatr Behav* 9: 31–42, 1984.

[71] Solms 1997, 60–69.

[72] Whitty C and Lewin W, *Brain* 80: 72–76, 1957; Lugaresi E, Medori R, Montagna P et al, *N Engl J Med* 315: 997–1003, 1986; Gallassi R, Morreale A, Montagna P et al, *Cortex* 28: 175–187, 1992; Morris M, Bowers D, Chatterjee A, Heilman, *Brain* 115: 1827–1847, 1992; Sacks O, *Migraine*, London: Picador 1995.

[73] Solms 1997, 177 (case 106).

[74] Solms 1997, 185 (case 281).

[75] Whitty and Lewin 1957.

dream vivacity and recurrent stereotyped nightmares. Indeed, like the anterior cingulate limbic syndrome, characterized by damage engendering loss of distinction between reality and fantasy, an epileptic discharge in the temporal lobes could overwhelm that system and give rise to the additional features of recurrent dreams of an unpleasant nature.[76] Furthermore, the mechanism for REM sleep is, like temporal lobe epilepsy, an arousal state: external stimuli, if of sufficient intensity, provide a third mechanism of arousal for dreaming.[77] All cause disturbances in sleep, leading to dream mentation. The final common pathway for either is likely to be the meso-limbic dopaminergic system (MLDS). In this respect, we should recall that a global cessation of dream competence ensues with severing or destruction of the ascending mesolimbic dopaminergic system (MLDS).[78]

7.3. THE PAEDIATRIC ECE/DREAM PROBLEM REVISITED

Finally I wish to revisit children's ECE, in order to consider the likely relationships between them and the dream-state mode (see above, Chapter 1, p. 10). The main corpus of paediatric cases derives from the book by Morse and Perry.[79] Importantly, the narratives offered by these children, in comparison with those of adults, are far less composed and far less elaborate. It is part of my overall contention that children's ECE phenomenology is poorly developed because their dream-state mentation is similarly retarded, dependent on age. But that is due to neither an absence of dream mentation, nor an inability to recall it. Rather,[80] it is more directly related to the quality of REM dream-state mentation, which is more impoverished the younger the child. Dream recall is closely related to acquired visuo-spatial capacities, as assessed quantitatively by the Wechsler Block Design protocol, as opposed to verbal proficiency. In children of eight years or below, there is a paucity of substantial dream recall. Beyond eight years, dream recall improves in parallel with increasing visuo-spatial competence, together with a substantially improved contribution from self-agency in the dreams reported.

[76] Solms 1997, 211ff.
[77] Solms 1997, 214.
[78] Solms 1997, 171ff.
[79] Morse and Perry 1990.
[80] Foulkes D, *J Sleep Res* 2: 199–202, 1993; Butler S, Watson R, *Percept Motor Skills* 61: 823–828, 1985; Foulkes D, Hollifield M, Sullivan B, Bradley L et al, *Int J Behav Devel* 13: 447–465, 1990.

Interrogated from this perspective, there is one outstanding deficiency in the childhood ECE cases reported:[81] that is, their overall numbers are very small and thus totally unrepresentative of the childhood age-span. In general, the reported bias is towards older children. From this, it is evident that a closer relational analysis of REM-dream content to reported ECE phenomenology should be undertaken. Such a trial would be prospective, necessarily multi-centred in order to recruit sufficient numbers, and performed in collaboration with child psychologists and experienced paediatric dream-research personnel. Evidence would be accumulated on a year-on-year basis, beginning with 3- or 4-year-old infants, and involving annual cohorts up to the age of about 14 years. That form of study would provide further evidence that ECE phenomenology, like REM dream-state mode, is correlated and dependent on relevant cortical functions and their age-dependent development. Such approaches, and to date entirely novel as far as I am aware, would contribute greatly to understandings of the neurophysiology of childhood dream-states and their relationship to the putative brain-based phenomenology of ECE across this somewhat neglected age-group.

7.4. SLEEP, DREAMING, AND ECE REVIEWED

Dreams are complex neural forms of subconscious mentation which, as I have described, arise from coordinated processes functioning across neocortical and brainstem networks. They are largely generated by the medial frontal lobes together with the association areas of the temporal, parietal and occipital cortices. The parallelism between dream-sleep modes and the formed visual, auditory, emotive and motor imagery of ECE, particularly NDE, should not go unnoticed. The brain scanning data on sleeping subjects may have considerable relevance to NDE phenomenology. In identifying areas of the brain that are metabolically deactivated, or disconnected from other facilitatory or inhibitory control centres, the data indicate possible mechanisms through which the bizarreness and illogicalities of NDE mentation, likewise, could take place and evolve. I part company with Nelson and colleagues[82] who think that NDE reportage lacks the bizarre quality of dreams: they clearly cannot have read the appropriate accounts.

Dreaming, it should be noted, is an ordered physiological process as the nocturnal sleep-cycle unwinds. NDE phenomenology, on the contrary, arises in brains recovering from severe antecedent insults. This is a most important

---

[81] Morse and Perry 1990; Fenwick and Fenwick 1998, 169–185.
[82] Nelson et al 2006.

distinction, and may possibly explain why we do not always have an NDE when waking from ordinary sleep. Moreover, the mentational typologies of NDE, as recalled and narrated, reflect idiosyncratically on the subject and are of twofold origin. Psychologically, the phenomenology rests on each individual's personal life-history and, in particular, on previously held beliefs and varied perceptions remembered in respect of death and the afterlife. And second, from the neurophysiological perspective, the recovery is dependent on the subject's age, degree of cerebral arterial atherosclerosis, pre-existing embolic blocks, thromboses, or congenital abnormalities frequently obtaining within the cerebral vasculature. It is therefore most unlikely to be an ordered recovery akin to dream awakenings. Furthermore, the neural elements which predominate, depending on the biological variables operative at the time at which the NDE is experienced, will orchestrate the successive phases of the phenomenology undergone. The neurological repertoire out of which that phenomenology arises may be ultimately limited, and indeed stereotyped, but its resultant outcome viewed thematically and sequentially need not, and could not, follow a uniform pattern. Any critical perusal of the published ECE narratives makes that clear. There is, and never has been, any experiential 'core' blueprint[83] inexorably tied to an invariant sequence: that is merely a contrived artefact imposed on readers by the authors concerned.

Despite such strictures, the very distinctive parallels between certain dream-state modes and ECE must be considered. Firstly, the twilight mentation of sleep-onset hypnagogic reveries not only involves perception of vivid visual and auditory imagery, but the acquisition of 'complete knowledge' and 'all-knowing states' that is typically representative of NDE narratives. Of further relevance to NDE, as explained in the preceding chapter, are the intrusive vestibular influences of flying, rapid acceleration, being propelled through a tunnel, or being wrenched out of the body.

Secondly, identical motor/vestibular phenomenology attends the REM dream state: indeed flying over water, or falling from a great height, are almost universal features of this type of unconscious mentation, accompanied by formed panoramic coloured vistas, sounds of music, chimes or bells, and sequences of highly affective content and meaning.

Thirdly, hypnopompic dream-offset events usually occur during the shorter periods of sleeping following subjects' first morning awakenings. The dream content is extremely vivid, while the awakening is often accompanied by an abrupt 'startle' reaction, such as the perception of a noise, typically a ringing (telephone or door) bell or a knock on the door. The

---

[83] Moody 1976, 21–23; Ring 1980, 32, 39ff, 102; Grey 1985, 30–55.

subject, on awakening, is unsure of the reality: often it is illusory. There is a marked similarity here between the terminal pictorial vividness of the hyno-pompic dreamlet that gives way to conscious-awareness, and that of NDE and the re-occupancy of the body. Moreover, with that abrupt return to corpore-ality, the physical realities both of gravity or heaviness as opposed to apparent weightlessness, and pain as opposed to a joyfully pain-free and ecstatic affective state while the experience lasts, are forced upon the subject.

Dreams, and NDE, undoubtedly confer a sense of reality on their recipi-ents. Subconscious mentation is as real as ordinary conscious wakefulness:[84] the differences arise partly because in sleep, endogenously stored and newly created material determine the outcome, while during conscious-awareness, externally derived signals prevail.[85] Dreaming subjects[86] cannot reliably dis-tinguish between information gained while awake or dreaming. I suggest that the sense of reality pervading the narratives of NDE subjects is no different. Indeed, my contention is that the phenomenologies of NDE and dream-state modes are analogous forms of subconscious mentation and that, like wake-fulness, they all derive from the same cerebral machinery. I base that conten-tion on the objectively definable coincidence between the termination of NDE and the re-establishment of full conscious-awareness.

The insights culled from the pathological variant, sleep-paralysis (SP) syndrome, are highly relevant to ECE, particularly OBE. This follows from patients' total inability to identify specific objects which they intended to locate in their bedrooms during their SP out-of-body attacks. This conclu-sively indicates that during OBE, subjects being likewise unable to 'see' or 'know', would therefore be incapable of providing a veridical, moment-by-moment account of the unfolding scenes supposedly witnessed.[87] Such inno-cent observations preclude the elaborate experiments proposed by those writing in the field in attempting to prove the opposite. The experiments, aimed at demonstrating that OB subjects would have no difficulty identifying varied items secretly concealed around the inaccessible recesses of operating theatres or intensive care units, are unlikely to be necessary or valid: the SP data have already conclusively deemed them to be redundant.

From another pathological perspective, studies into the narcolepsy-cata-plexy (NC) complex have yielded most interesting insights pertinent to ECE states. There is a breakdown, or loss of state (i.e. sleeping or waking) bound-

[84] Revonsuo A, *Philosoph Psychol* 8: 35–58, 1995.
[85] Purcell S, Mullington J, Moffit A, Hoffmann R, Pigeau R, *Sleep* 9: 423–437, 1986.
[86] Mazzoni G and Loftus E, *Consc Cogn* 5: 442–462, 1996: Mahowald M, Woods S, Schenck C, *Dreaming* 8: 89–102, 1998.
[87] The alternative would be to propose various forms of OBE. In considering the variant types of body image distortion (Chapter 6), such a proposal is more than likely to be invalid.

ary controls during the sleep–wake cycles of NC subjects, possibly orchestrated by lack of stimulation of the wakefulness-promoting locus coeruleus by hypocretin. The manner in which these complex neurophysiological control mechanisms are disrupted is by no means clear at present. However, the observed propensity of surveyed NDE subjects to be open to REM intrusion events, such as sleep paralysis or visual and auditory hypnagogic hallucinations, provides further critical insights into likely neurophysiological mechanisms underlying this form of experiential phenomenology. It is another key example of the way in which an approach to dream-state physiology, and its varied disorders, has enlightened our perceptions as to how OB/ND events could conceivably come about.

The detailed analysis of cerebral pathology by Solms has emphatically revealed that dreams become non-visual with lesions of the medial occipito-temporal cortex, and subject to global erasure with pathology involving the inferior parietal lobule or deep within the anterior frontal cortex. These three sites are critically and exclusively devoted to the creation of specific phenomenological contours of dream-state modes, with particular reference to their visual, spatial and constructional background. Furthermore, that dreams can be generated by epileptic discharges within the limbic system provides further evidence that subconscious hallucinatory mentation is a functional property of the cortex. We might also note[88] that while the cholinergic drive from midbrain may provide the neurochemical milieu upon which dreaming occurs, it may be solely related to the timing of these episodes within the entire nocturnal sleep cycle.

The final common pathway for normal or disturbing dreams may be the ascending dorso-medial limbic dopaminergic system. This observation may be relevant to the hellish ECE noted in Chapter 1, and suggestive of temporary disordered neurological control while recovery from the ECE takes place. We may note that vivid and highly disturbing dreams commonly arise through the use of L-dopamine in the treatment of Parkinson's disease.[89] Indeed, the ascending dopaminergic system may play a contributory role in the undoubted overall vividness of the experiences recalled. Furthermore, the system is probably required for the rapidity and forced nature of the thoughts which race through the minds of ECE subjects, and which is often thought to have 'mystical' or psychical connotations. Such pharmacological background could be responsible for the so-called 'life review' and 'judgement' described by subjects.

---

[88] Sitaram N, Wyatt R, Dawson S, Gillin J, Science 191: 1281–1283, 1976; Sitaram N, Moore A, Gillin J, Nature 274: 490–492, 1978.

[89] Sacks Oliver, *The Man Who Mistook his Wife for a Hat*, London: Picador 1986, 144–145.

In this context, therefore, one cannot help but be reminded of one of Dr Oliver Sacks's Parkinsonian patients and her reported experiences while taking L-dopamine. Sacks recalls her increased psychomotor activity, the heady sexual upsurges remembered from days long spent, as well as a joyful elation in recalling this distant but forgotten effulgent behaviour. This is the neuropharmacology of déjà vu,[90] the 'doubling of consciousness', the resurgence of long-distant memories, and of forced thinking: Sacks employs Zutt's description of how *'thousands of memories suddenly crowded into the patient's mind'*. That sounds very like the so-called life-review-judgement phenomenology that occasionally obtrudes into late-phase NDE (Figure 3), but which, in my view, betokens the imminent return of consciousness, awakening, and the resumption of full mental activity. Clearly, dopamine may play an important role in facilitating these varied phenomenological sub-typologies of NDE, including the life-review that flashes across the subject's mental screen. There is no doubt that this excursion into the physiology and pathophysiology of dreaming opens up many new fascinating insights into the phenomenology of NDE and OBE that are lacking from the canonical literature.

Additional implications pertinent to ECE are derivable from dream-state pathology. It is clear that oneiric capacity is either severely reduced or eradicated by stroke lesions located around the temporo-parietal junctional zone of the cerebral cortex. Since the visuo-spatial aspects of dream mentation, as in wakefulness,[91] require an intact temporo-parieto-occipital (TPO) cortex,[92] I contend that the internal visual imagery and associated auditory and vestibular accompaniments of ECE are largely subserved by the same neurocortical architecture. If that proposition[93] is correct, then individuals with cortical stroke lesions involving this important associative watershed in the brain should have a markedly lessened propensity to experience dreamlike mentation during ECE. A prospectively controlled trial between such victims and age-/sex-matched control subjects would highlight any discernible differences. If that was the result, it would indicate conclusively that the TPO cortex is crucial for the phenomenology undergone by ECE subjects. More importantly, it would clearly demonstrate that ECE phenomenology originates within a disordered brain recovering full functional competence, rather than a cerebral realization of events primarily experienced in some other 'spiritual' or 'mystical' realm, perhaps beyond the known universe.

---

[90] Sacks 1986, 230 n. 16.

[91] Sacks 1986, 144–145.

[92] Llinas R and Pare D, *Neurosci* 44: 521–535, 1991.

[93] The corollary here, I suggest, is that of younger children whose poorly developed oneiric competence seemingly parallels the immature development of their ECE phenomenology. See p. 151, this chapter.

Continuing this theme, it should be immediately evident that other prospectively controlled trials could be organized on pharmacological principles. They would need careful planning to avoid possible interference with resuscitative procedures. Nevertheless there is sufficient evidence, for example from dream research, psychiatric practice and other sources, that drugs can either induce, augment or diminish oneiric activity.[94] On similar grounds, if ECE are derivative of cerebral activity, then clearly their phenomenology, likewise, should be subject to modification by pharmacological intervention. The apparent conversion of a pleasurable ECE to an unpleasant sequela[95] is a tantalizing example of the possible manipulability of these occurrences, and would provide yet further third-party data for their cerebral origin. Yet, still the difficulty remains as to whether stroke victims continue having ECE (and probably not, according to Solms) and whether children's fragmentary ECE narratives reflect their undeveloped competency to dream in REM sleep-mode.

There seems to be no doubt that this excursus into dream-state neurophysiology and pathology has significantly enlightened our further understandings of the quasi-dreamlike phenomenology of both NDE and OBE, and, moreover, offered several additional fruitful avenues of research through which their underlying cerebral mechanisms could be proved or, alternatively, disproved. In the next chapter, I return to the temporal lobe—its function and dysfunction. In the literature analysed in this book, the approach to the temporal lobe as an aetiological agent in the genesis of, or contributor to, ECE phenomenology has been somewhat dismissive: I think that is a mistaken attitude on the part of those authors surveyed herein.

---

[94] Hobson et al 1997; 1998; Vogel G, Buffenstein A, Minter K, Hennessey A, *Neurosci Biobehav Res* 14: 49–63, 1990; Aizenberg D, Modai, *Psychopathol* 18: 237–240, 1985; Hemmingsen R, Rafaelsen O, *Acta Psychiatr Scand* 62: 364–368, 1980; Schlauch R, *Am J Psychiatr* 136: 219–220, 1979; Albala A, Weinberg N, Allen S, *J Clin Psychiatr* 44: 149–150, 1983.

[95] Judson I and Wiltshaw E, *Lancet* 2: 561–562, 1983.

8

ECE and the Temporal Lobe: Assassin or Accomplice?

My purpose in this chapter is to focus specifically on aspects of temporal lobe function other than its role in disturbances of body-image, as outlined above in Chapter 6. I proceed in reviewing other ground related to the temporal lobe and its particular contributions to emotion, cognition, ecstasy and even 'mystical' experiences. However, the possible aetiological role of the temporal lobe in ECE phenomenology as dealt with in the canonical literature, as I shall outline below, has neither been satisfactorily considered nor its likely neuro-physiological contributions effectively developed.

In their longest textual sequence,[1] the Fenwicks offer no referential material pertinent to temporal lobe studies. Sabom, in his earlier work,[2] refers only to Penfield's work and to a local set of collected essays on electrical stimulation of the brain.[3] Ring (1980) solely relies on a previous paper by Sabom and Kreutziger, whose referential material to the temporal lobe is based on Slater and Roth's 1969 *Textbook of Clinical Psychiatry*. Grey (1985) merely relies on Moody, Ring and Sabom thus to conclude, most inappropriately in less than one page, that 'this mechanism [of temporal lobe seizures] is inadequate to explain the complete range of near-death phenomena'.[4] In his later book Sabom[5] has a lone reference on the temporal lobe to a paper by the former eminent London-based neurologist Dr Dennis Williams (1956). Williams's paper comprises a personal collection of 2,000 cases of temporal lobe epilepsy.[6] That material is representative of the current field then existing more than half a century ago. Compared with the rapid advances in neurophysiology that have evolved since then, that material is clearly out of date and entirely unacceptable as a definitive statement on this part of the brain. Given the

---

[1] Fenwick and Fenwick 1998, 218–221.
[2] Sabom 1982, 173–174.
[3] Roberts L, in: Sheer DE (ed), *Electrical Stimulation of the Brain*, Austin (TX): University of Texas Press 1961, 547.
[4] Grey 1985, 176.
[5] Sabom 1998, 179–181, 238.
[6] Williams D, *Brain* 79: 28–67, 1956.

additional wealth of material available to these various authors at their respective times of publication, that is a somewhat unsatisfactory state of affairs.

8.1. THE EXPERIENTIAL OUTCOMES
OF TEMPORAL LOBE PATHOLOGIES

There has been an enormous expansion contributory to our current understandings of temporal lobe neurophysiology and neuropathology. This has been achieved through varied scanning techniques,[7] computerized electroencephalography and the operative deployment of multiple subdural and deep, stereotactically inserted electrodes into the brain.[8] Furthermore, distinctions have been made between deep medial, and neocortical temporal lobe (epileptic) syndromes.[9] In addition, great emphasis has been laid on the recognition of minor forms of injury as aetiological causes of disordered temporal lobe function, including closed head trauma; childbirth trauma; neonatal, childhood and adolescent febrile episodes and/or delirium; and on pre-ictal auras, and inter-ictal behavioural outcomes.[10] Simple pre-ictal auras comprise uninterpretable visual sensations like coloured flashes, scintillations or 'fireworks', or auditory accompaniments such as buzzing, vibrations, noises, all of which arise from their respective primary cortices. Complex auras, offering explanatory insights into the disturbed cortical functioning during NDE, comprise coordinated visual experiences accompanied by music or other intelligible sounds. There is greater recognition that psychical and 'mystical' behaviour, at least in many individuals, represent non-ictal auras arising from disturbed temporal lobe functioning. Below, I offer relevant published case material irrespective of aetiological factors, such as epilepsy, migraine, stroke, the effects of secondary tumour formation, vascular abnormalities, or other developmental and acquired space-occupying lesions (cysts, hamartomas, rests, etc.).

[7] Lamuso S, Ruottinen H, Knuuti J et al, *J Neurol Neurosurg Psychiatr* 63: 743–748, 1997.

[8] Lesser R, Luders H, Klem G et al, *J Clin Neurophysiol* 4: 27–53, 1987; Heath R, *J Nerv Ment Dis* 154: 3–18, 1972; Wieser H, *Neurosci Biobehav Rev* 7: 427–440, 1983; Gloor P, Olivier A, Quesney L, Andermann F, Horowitz S, *Ann Neurol* 12: 129–144, 1982; Pacia S, Devinsky O, Perrine K et al, *Ann Neurol* 40: 724–730, 1996.

[9] Foldvary N, Lee N, Thwaites G et al, *Neurology* 49: 757–763, 1997.

[10] Fenwick P, Galliano S, Coate M et al, *Br J Med Psychol* 58: 35–44, 1985; Daly D, 1975; Waxman S and Geschwind N, *Arch Gen Psychiatr* 32: 1580–1586, 1975.

This extensive case material encompasses the hallucinatory basis of transcendence of space,[11] of time with the accompanying illusions that time is speeding up,[12] and of self[13] including rapid life reviews or memories;[14] of vertiginous sensations of floating or rotating;[15] of auditory hallucinations[16] of buzzing, ringing, or vibrational noises or voices and/or[17] commands given to subjects; of peace,[18] joy, pleasure, or of ineffable ecstasy and euphoria;[19] of observing deceased relatives or friends;[20] of being in a light[21] or of being in the presence of God, Jesus, or other persons;[22] of experiencing 'presences';[23] an OBE,[24] 'pre-currence',[25] pre-cognition;[26] or horrific hallucinations,[27] and ictal and interictal derealizations and depersonalizations.[28]

These case reports, ranging over a century from 1899 to 1996, indicate quite clearly that the repertoire of the experiential phenomenology reported in ECE can be created *in toto* by brains subject to various types of insult, the majority, however, predominantly incriminating the temporal lobe. This repertoire, available within the literature, advances greatly beyond the severely diminished approaches offered by Ring, Sabom, Grey, and Fenwick and Fenwick towards the temporal lobe as an aetiological *factor* in ECE. However,

---

[11] Ionasescu 1960 (Case 2).

[12] Daly 1975, 69.

[13] Ionasescu 1960 (Case 2).

[14] Daly 1975, referring to Jackson 1931; Devinsky et al 1989, referring to Kamiya et al 1982.

[15] Smith 1960; Devinsky et al 1989 (Cases 2, 6, 7, 8, 10); Ionasescu 1960 (Cases 5, 6, 7).

[16] Brugger and Regard 1997.

[17] Mabille H, *Ann Med-Psychol* 9–10: 76–81, 1899 (Observations I–IV); Devinsky et al 1989 (Cases 1, 5–7); Daly 1975; Ionasescu 1960 (Case 2); Halligan et al 1994; Lippman 1954 (Case 1 (migranoid entering darkness and spinning), Cases 2, 5).

[18] Devinsky et al 1989 (Cases 4, 7, 10).

[19] Williams 1956 (Cases 31, 35, 36); Boudoursque J, Gosset A, Sayag J, *Bull Acad Med (Paris)* 156: 416–421, 1972; Cirignotta F, Todesco C, Lugaresi E, *Epilepsia* 21: 705–710, 1980; Viulleumier P, Despland P, Assai G, Regli F, *Rev Neurol (Paris)* 153: 115–119, 1997.

[20] Halligan et al 1994, 465; Ionasescu 1960 (Case 4).

[21] Dewhurst K and Beard A, *Br J Psychiatr* 117: 497–507, 1970 (Cases 2, 4).

[22] Mabille 1899 (Observations I–IV); Waksman and Geschwind 1975 (Case 1); Dewhurst and Beard 1970 (Cases 1, 2, 3); Devinsky et al 1989 (Case 10); Mesulam M-M, *Arch Neurol* 38: 176–181, 1981 (Cases 10, 12); Sedman G, *Psychiatr Neurol* 152: 1–16, 1966; Sedman G and Hopkinson G, *Confin Psychiatr* 9: 65–77, 1966.

[23] Ardila and Gomez 1988; Brugger et al 1996; Persinger M, *Psychol Rep* 75: 1059–1070, 1994; Lippman 1954.

[24] Daly 1975 (Case 5); Brugger et al 1996; Lunn 1970 (Cases 1, 2); Lance J, Cooper B, Misbach J, *Proc Austral Assoc Neurol* 11: 209–217, 1974 (Case 4).

[25] Gowers 1910, quoted by Daly 1975.

[26] Gloor et al 1982 (Case 4); Penfield W, *Proc Nat Acad Sci (USA)* 44: 51–66, 1958 (Case MM).

[27] Williams 1956 (Case 43); Mesulam 1981 (Cases 8, 9); Lippman 1954 (Section 3, Case 1); Kroll J and Bachrach B, *J Nerv Ment Dis* 170: 41–49, 1982 (vision of St Guthlac).

[28] Devinsky O, Feldmann E, Bromfield E, Emoto S, Raubertas R, *J Epilepsy* 4: 107–116, 1991.

at the same time, we must exercise some caution because although an epileptic discharge may seem to originate from the temporal lobe, it is by no means certain that the ensuing spread of electrical activity will respect anatomical boundaries. Therefore, its influence may involve and hence incorporate centres structurally, and functionally, remote from the originating focus of activation.

I am at pains to stress that temporal lobe epilepsy is not being advocated as *cause* of ECE: that would be a totally untenable hypothesis. Furthermore, I resist criticisms that the above case-reported hallucinations are in some instances single events, as opposed to being welded into a sequential phenomenology reminiscent of spontaneous ECE. But that is not my argument. Rather, my case rests on the notion that the temporal lobe and its neural environs can, in a variety of defined circumstances, be held to conjure all aspects of the phenomenologies characterizing ECE. Therefore, ECE could well be emergent phenomena deriving from within the brain's temporo-parietal axis, given the massive contribution which this axial multi-modal associative centre affords to conscious, as well as subconscious, mental awareness. Physiological stresses, as occasioned by ischaemia, hypoxia or other functional aberrant pathologies of which the preceding paragraph treats, are the catalysts most favoured to generate ECE phenomenology. Moreover, because ~80% of ECE occur during life-threatening circumstances,[29] there is no particular reason why such phenomenology should be shrouded with mystical overtones consonant with other-worldly trips, or even glimpses of heaven. The brain dimension must be neither ignored, dismissed, nor underestimated.

8.2. TRANSPORTS OF JOY, LOVE, AND ECSTASY

In developing my theme, I wish to trawl a little more widely to include mesolimbic and anterior cerebral components, in view of their intimate structural and functional connections with the temporal lobe. One such possible outcome is articulated by Fenwick and Fenwick,[30] who at least raise the important question as to why (during NDE) such rapturous 'feelings . . . joy . . . different from ordinary happiness and pleasure . . . should be encoded in the brain'. Consider:

[29] Fenwick and Fenwick 1998, 212.
[30] Fenwick and Fenwick 1998, 72.

I was just in a wonderful peace and wellness [*sic*] in a beautiful landscape setting of grass, lawns, trees and brilliant light, diffused . . . with a feeling of being surrounded by *wonderful love, joy and peace* . . .[31] (My emphases.)

This excerpt speaks for the majority of respondents, I suggest, in terms of the emotionally charged intense 'loving feeling' that invariable enshrines the ND event. In attempting to recapture the underlying neurophysiological essence of that blissful elation, I was struck to note that two respondents used the adjective *orgasmic* to articulate the overwhelming vividness and wonder of such an ineffable uplifting, experienced as an intensive affective backdrop to the accompanying beauty of the panoramas visited. The first is from Ring, concerning a man who came close to drowning in a boating accident.[32] The victim stated:

It's tough. Use euphoric. Use orgasmic. Or use high. It was very tangible, very real. But it was doing magnificent things to me. You know, afterward I looked at that lake and I said, 'That lake made love to me'. It really did, it felt like that.

A similar statement comes from Howard Storm, whom we previously met in Chapter 1, because of a very protracted hellish experience while he awaited surgery in Paris for an intra-abdominal emergency. After praying for an end to that part of his NDE, he entered the light. Storm continues:

and I was aware that the light was a Being. And all these things I knew immediately. That the light loved me. That it knew me. That it was really powerful and good. And we went out of that place, and there was a strong sense of moving upwards very rapidly. And we travelled together and I was in ecstasy . . . if you can imagine having orgasms of every sense and of your intellect . . . that's what I was into. It was wonderful. . . .[33]

Above, I referred to manifestations of disturbed temporal lobe function in subjects who expressed intense episodes of supreme ecstasy which wholly, or in part, comprised pre-ictal auras. In many cases with *latent* dysfunction, the aura occurs without the ensuing motor fit.[34] Such occurrences amply satisfy the Fenwicks' query. The brain can, indeed, conjure appropriate phenomenological expressions of ecstasy, whether damaged, functionally impaired, or not. They should also be informed that of those few signal occasions in life when intense exaltation is experienced, an orgasm is one. Moreover, orgasms are 'hardwired' in the brain. We do not have to be taught how to have one:

---

[31] Fenwick and Fenwick 1998, 75.
[32] Ring 1980, 42.
[33] Wilson 1997, 143.
[34] Williams 1956; Cirignotta et al 1980; Devinsky et al 1989; Vuilleumier et al 1997.

they even occur in children. Usually, they arise naturally and spontaneously, when either men or women are dreaming, and at other appropriate times and circumstances. Unfortunately, none of the latest case-studies that I cited from the literature was subjected to functional brain-scanning techniques, so the precise cerebral loci of their ecstatic auras was not determined. Yet there are additional considerations to be exemplified and drawn out.

In order to explicate further, my emphasis will focus on the neurophysiology of the orgasm, since it provides one heuristic approach to the unravelling of the neurophysiology of ecstatic bliss encountered during NDE, as exemplified by the two foregoing commentaries. Its basis lies in the brainstem's ascending dorso-medial reward system comprising dopaminergic neurones in the ventral tegmental area, VTA, projecting to the orbito-frontal cortex,[35] which is clearly relevant to the overwhelming sense of invincibility gone through during intravenous heroin 'rushes' or sexual climaxes (Figure 10). During these events,[36] brain scanning procedures have revealed increased cerebral blood flow in the mesodiencephalic areas of the upper brainstem, including the VTA, as well as other important neocortical regions.

A further piece of important information relevant to our quest for the ecstatic event, although omitted by all key writers on ECE phenomenology, is that part of the extensive repertoire of temporal lobe dysfunction is to generate orgasmic auras, with or without a subsequent tonic-clonic fit.[37] Conversely the activity involved in sexual intercourse, possibly a result of hyperventilation, will also precipitate an orgasmic psychomotor episode.[38] The literature contains reports of over forty subjects[39] with temporal lobe dysfunction associated with veridical, 'cerebral' orgasmic climaxes. They are to be distinguished from genital auras originating from the medial sensory area located on the inner surface of the parietal cortex (sometimes generated by meningiomas of the falx). The brainstem ventral tegmental

[35] Sell L, Morris J, Bearn J et al, *Eur J Neurosci* 11: 1042–1048, 1999; McBride W, Murphy J, Ikemoto S, *Behav Brain Res* 101: 129–152, 1999; Previc F, *Consc Cogn* 15: 500–539, 2006.

[36] Tiihonen J, Kuikka J, Kupila J et al, *Neurosci Lett* 170: 241–243, 1994; Holstege G, Georgiadis J, Paans A et al, *J Neurosci* 23: 9185–9193, 2003; Bartels A and Zeki S, *NeuroReport* 11: 3829–3834, 2000; Breiter H, Gollub R, Weisskoff R et al, *Neuron* 19: 591–611, 1997.

[37] Hoenig J and Hamilton C, *Acta Psychiatr Scand* 35: 448–456, 1960; Freemon F and Nevis A, *Neurology* 19: 87–90, 1969.

[38] Gautier-Smith P, *Rev Neurol (Paris)* 136: 311–319, 1980.

[39] van Reeth P, Dierkens J, Luminet D, *Acta Neurol Belg* 58: 194–218, 1958; Currier R, Jackson M, Little S, Suess J, Andy O, *Arch Neurol* 25: 260–264, 1971; Crevenna R, Homann N, Feichtinger M, Ott E, Korner E, *Br J Psychiatr* 176: 300–303, 2000; Warnek L, *Canad Psychiatr Assoc* 21: 319–324, 1976; Jansky J, Szucs A, Halasz et al, *Neurology* 58: 302–304, 2002; Jansky J, Ebner A, Szupera Z et al, *Seizure* 13: 441–444, 2004; Fadul C, Stommel E, Dragnev K et al, *J Neuro-Oncology* 72: 195–198, 2005.

area targets the pre-frontal cortex, and limbic anterior cingulate. Therefore disinhibition[40] of GABA-ergic inter-neurones could promote exceptionally heightened activity within the VTA dopaminergic neural network. That could well ensue in a brain during the period of disordered functional recovery. Interestingly, patients on treatment with L-dopa for alleviating Parkinsonian dyskinesia may suffer the unwanted side-effect of uncontrolled hypersexuality.

There is associated activity within the posterior hypothalamus which serves as the neural gateway to the endocrine and autonomic nervous systems.[41] The hypothalamus secretes oxytocin from the paraventricular nucleus, levels of which rise considerably during sexual arousal[42] and which can be inhibited by naloxone, whose influence reduces somewhat the accompanying excitement.[43] There is here a clear neurophysiological relationship between temporal lobe activation and the neurohypophyseal elaboration of oxytocin. Because of its critical role in sexual activity, pair-bonding, lactation and nursing of suckling young, oxytocin contributes significantly to the experiential aspect of the 'deep feelings of love' accompanying these facets of biological behaviour.[44]

Here, we should register another very important corollary arising from many such brain scanning investigations: that the classical limbic system comprising amygdala and hippocampus is *deactivated* during heroin 'rushes' and sexual orgasms. Neither is it activated during the playing of 'spine-tingling' music,[45] arousals secured through the portrayal in film clips of pornographic material and sexually explicit activities, or when pictures of loved ones are being observed.[46] Little more can be said at present, because the neurophysiological and neurochemical backgrounds to these experiential qualia await more extensive exploration. Still, care needs to be taken in ascribing all ECE-related pleasure to the limbic system alone. Of further interest is that in temporal lobe epileptics, involvement of the meso-temporo-amygdaloid complex invariably causes widespread feelings of fear, disgust, and anxiety,[47] but very rarely sensations of pleasure—a pointer indicating that this type of brain

---

[40] Sell et al 1999; Bocher M, Chisin R, Parag Y. et al., *NeuroImage* 14: 105–117, 2001.
[41] Redoute J, Stoleru S, Gregoire M-C et al., *Hum Brain Mapp* 11: 162–177, 2000; Arnow B, Desmond J, Banner L et al., *Brain* 125: 1014–1023, 2002; Karama S, Lecours A, Leroux J et al, *Hum Brain Mapp* 16: 1–13, 2002.
[42] Carmichael M, Warburton V, Dixen J, Davidson J, *Arch Sex Behav* 23: 59–79, 1994.
[43] Murphy M, Checkley S, Seckl J, Lightman S, *J Clin Endocrinol Metab* 71: 1056–1058, 1990.
[44] Insel T, *Psychoneuroendocrinol* 17: 3–35, 1992.
[45] Blood A and Zatorre R, *Proc Nat Acad Sci (USA)* 98: 11818–11823, 2001.
[46] Bartels and Zeki, 2000.
[47] Rauch S, Shin L, Wright C, *Ann NY Acad Sci* 985: 389–410, 2003.

pathology or dysfunction may not be directly related to ECE, or NDE in particular.

Conversely, attempts at increasing orgasmic intensity are witnessed in erotic hangings. The partial cerebral ischaemia/hypoxia induced with a controlled self-hanging event during autostimulation, achieves that end: unfortunately, mistakes lead to the death of the subject by asphyxiation.[48] Another means of achieving exhilaration at the point of orgasm[49] is to inhale amyl nitrate: the resultant generalized vasodilatation induces mild hypotension, a reduction in cerebral blood flow, but a heightened sexually dreamy and euphoric blissfulness. These observations are relevant to the perceived vividness and accompanying ecstatic affective sensations of the NDE, indicating that temporary arterial hypotension (as the brain recovers) is a further contributory factor in their genesis, and to their obvious intensity. We should also recall the greatly enhanced vividness of perceived colours during NDE consequent upon cortically induced ischaemia, as elucidated in the succeeding chapter. I thus conclude that the ecstatic transcendence associated with NDE is more likely to reside in the upper diencephalon rather than necessarily within the limbic-amygdaloid system. That conclusion is, of course, open to further experimental verification.

These considerations obviously open up entirely new vistas and insights derived by my bringing to notice these specific orgasmic-ecstatic temporal lobe auras, in addition to the activity and disinhibition of the mesolimbic dopaminergic reward system, in the physiology of heightened erotic and ecstatic pleasure. My view is that the temporal lobe and the ascending mesolimbic reward system may come to offer crucial links to ECE phenomenology, as manifested by the intensity of the ecstatic feelings of joy, love and longing thereby generated, and which so incisively demarcate those responses. Time will come when the neurophysiological basis of these experiences will be more finely discerned and explained.

8.3. THE EMERGING CRITICAL RELEVANCE OF LATENT TEMPORAL LOBE DYSFUNCTION

In a study of apparently healthy young individuals (n = 1,096) drawn from a university undergraduate population, the results of a questionnaire revealed

---

[48] Resnik H, *Am J Psychother* 26: 4–21, 1972.
[49] Louria D, *Med Asp Hum Sex* 4: 89, 1970.

that 45% of those sampled claimed to have experienced repeated clinical symptoms suggestive of latent temporal lobe damage.[50] The damage was related to previous episodes of closed head trauma or severe febrile illnesses throughout childhood and adolescence. From an additional series (designated Study 3) of 600 consecutive hospital-based referrals, 15 patients were selected for further evaluation of temporal lobe dysfunction. Seven of those patients gave past histories of closed head injuries, another seven had been subject to febrile illnesses, and one was exposed to a lightning strike. All fifteen patients demonstrated symptoms indicative of temporal lobe-related seizural activity. In two other independent studies, similar forms of symptomatology responded to specific anti-epileptic drug therapy with carbamazepine, strongly suggestive of originating focal temporal lobe discharges in these subjects.[51]

In another study, a large, heterogeneously selected group of subjects (n = 1,071), comprising undergraduates, artistic people and clinically relevant patients with either post-traumatic stress disorder, anxiety-depression, exotic dissociation or temporal lobe epilepsy, was investigated prospectively over a 10-year period. Each recruited subject completed a set of questionnaires[52] based on phenomena previously reported by another cohort of subjects[53] and correlated with electroencephalographic activity over the temporal lobes. Responses included memory fragments, vivid visual and auditory hallucinations, intense personal meaning given to the experiences reported, vibrations, sudden insights, ego-alien intrusions, and mystical encounters.[54] Each group was given a 'T' score, the calculation of which is, unfortunately, not clear from Persinger and Makarec's paper. The data revealed increasingly abnormal scores, in comparison with age-/sex-matched controls for whom 'T' = 50 ±10: m±sd, through the artistic people to the clinical groups. The latter exhibited the greatest 'T' values, those with suspected partial temporal lobe seizure activity achieving the highest scores. Thus a spectrum of personality changes and dispositions, related to 'T' score, was demonstrated indicating a progressively greater influence of the temporal lobe, together with its accompanying intrinsic latent damage, on the dispositions and natures of the subjects examined. The issue here, of course, is whether all these substantial

[50] Roberts R, Varney N, Hulbert J et al, Neuropsychol 4: 65–85, 1990: their Studies 1 and 2.
[51] Tucker G, Price T, Johnson V, McAllister T, J Nerv Ment Dis 174: 348–356, 1986; Neppe V, Kaplan C, Clin Neuropharmacol 11: 287–289, 1988.
[52] Persinger M and Makarec K, J Clin Psychol 49: 33–45, 1993.
[53] Makarec K and Persinger M, J Res Personal 24: 323–337, 1990; Makarec K and Persinger M, Percept Motor Skills 60: 831–842, 1985.
[54] Gloor et al 1982; Wieser 1983.

groupings are a representative microcosm of society at large. It is certainly a possibility.

Without doubt, these two studies by Roberts, and by Persinger, are important and deserve our attention. They provide the first, definitive empirical evidence for a possible mechanism which could explain why only a small proportion of the general population has a propensity to undergo NDE. Indeed, the hypothesis could be offered that temporal lobe stimulation, through either electrical stimulation or spontaneously through auras, with or without the subsequent ictal phase and triggered by other extraneous factors, plays a contributory role towards a variety of mystical and other experiences analogous to NDE phenomenology.[55] The baseline electrical sensitivity within deep temporal lobe structures is a reflection of the activity at any given time of its neuronal networks in each individual.[56] That sensitivity or liability to activity[57] is evidently related to previous traumatic insults, such as closed head injury, hypoxic episodes, high fever and delirium, and the stresses of daily life (including accidents, heart attacks, bereavement, suicide bids, severe allergic reactions, etc.), and, hyper-ventilation,[58] which is one form of breath control (e.g. *anapanasati*) common to certain eastern meditative practices.[59] These extraneous factors increase the predisposition to the experiencing of symptoms deriving from the temporal lobe. Since in general, the psychological and behavioural characteristics[60] of an individual at any time are dependent on the metabolic activity of particular brain centres or networks, factors that impinge on pre-existing temporal lobe damage may define an increasingly abnormal spectrum of psychical and mystical experiential beliefs and behaviour throughout any population. Indeed, such stresses may hypersensitize neurons to lower seizure thresholds:[61] this is demonstrable during deep sleep,[62] at which time there is some degree of hypoxia.

[55] Penfield 1958; idem, *J R Coll Surg Edin* 5: 173–190, 1960; Jasper H and Rasmussen T, *Res Publ Assoc Res Nerv Ment Dis* 36: 316–334, 1958; Persinger and Makarec 1993.

[56] Persinger M, *Percept Motor Skills* 59: 583–586, 1984; idem, *Percept Motor Skills* 64: 1112–1114, 1987.

[57] Fenwick et al 1985; Rocca W, Sharbrough F, Hauser W, Annegers J, Schoenberg B, *Ann Neurol* 21: 22–31, 1987; Guidice M and Berchou R, *Brain Injury* 1: 61–64, 1987.

[58] Gotoh et al 1965; Allen T and Agus B, *Am J Psychiatr* 125: 632–637, 1968; Kennedy R, *Am J Psychiatr* 133: 1326–1328, 1976 (Case 1).

[59] Laughlin C, McManus J, d'Aquili E, *Brain, Symbol and Experience*, New York: Columbia University Press 1992, 211 and 303.

[60] Chugani H and Phelps M, *Science* 231: 840–843, 1986; Posner M, Peresen S, Fox P, Raiche M, *Science* 240: 1627–1631, 1988.

[61] Benviste H, Drejer J, Schousboe A, Diemer H, *J Neurochem* 43: 1369–1374, 1984.

[62] Malow B, Lin X, Kushwaha R, Aldrich M, *Epilepsia* 39: 1309–1316, 1998.

Now, it is on that background that Britton and Bootzin[63] investigated, for the first time, 23 ECE subjects and compared them with 20 age/sex-matched controls without a pre-existing history of stress-related life events. Those within the NDE group revealed more (20%) inter-ictal epileptiform waveforms in their electroencephalograms in comparison with the control group (6%). They also showed highly significant differences on the Complex Partial Epileptic Signs ($p < 0.01$) and Temporal Lobe Symptoms ($p < 0.005$) Inventories. On the Dissociation Experiences Scale,[64] there was less of a detectable difference between control scores ($m = 7$) and NDE subjects ($m = 11$: $p < 0.1$) in comparison with subjects with post-traumatic stress disorder ($m = 30$) or dissociative disorders ($m = 35$). This work indicates that NDE subjects do not necessarily constitute a specifically dissociative group of individuals, a conclusion endorsed by Greyson's recent analysis.[65] The NDE group, however, revealed EEG evidence of abnormal inter-ictal spiking (22%) and reported more temporal lobe epileptic symptoms than their age/sex-matched controls (6%).[66] In that regard, they exceed the prevalence of allied symptomatology in other reported 'normal' control populations[67] (0.4%), non-epileptic clinical subjects (2–3%), and even individuals with a previous history of head trauma and loss of consciousness (~6%). Notably, the EEG abnormalities were left-sided.[68] The obvious difficulty here is that the original sample numbers were very small. Furthermore, based on detailed reviews of published cases, Blanke and Mohr[69] found that ~70% OBE occurred with right-sided temporo-parietal forms of pathology.

Despite that, the studies of Britton and Bootzin are of enormous value in being the first to demonstrate latent cerebral pathology, not only related to OBE, but also in a significant proportion (~20%) of NDE subjects. The data seemingly indicate that proneness to subclinical complex partial auras arising from the temporal lobe (and in the absence of ictal development) identifies a cohort of individuals possibly at risk for NDE in response to a variety of stress-inducing circumstances.

These are but preliminary observations. Nevertheless, they provide novel grounds on which further prospective studies should be based. Indeed, it is from that kind of future study that we should now be expectantly anticipating further insights into those triggers relevant to ECE phenomenology. The

---

[63] Britton W and Bootzin R, *Psychol Sci* 15: 254–258, 2004.
[64] Stewart and Bartucci 1986; Carlson E and Putnam F, *Dissociation* 1: 16–27, 1993.
[65] Greyson 2000.
[66] Britton and Bootzin 2004.
[67] Shintani S, Tsuruka S, Shiigai T, *J Neurol Sci* 182: 129–135, 2001.
[68] Stewart and Bartucci 1986; Carlson and Putnam 1993.
[69] Blanke and Mohr 2005.

contribution of the empirical data now to hand concerning aberrant functioning of the temporal lobe provides much-needed impetus for investigating afresh those experiential expressions of NDE of which so many respondents speak. We need further scientifically organized study of NDE phenomenology to consolidate these recent neurophysiological advances. As an ancillary study, it would be useful to subject the narratives of temporal lobe epileptics, ECE experients, those with known cerebral vascular insufficiency, migraineurs, and subjects able to recall their dream-state modes to a panel of 'blinded' judges, to determine to what extent each sample of experiences is separable, or distinctive. The methodological techniques used by dream-state researchers would be invaluable in this type of analytical setting.

We are now witnesses to a revolutionary scene regarding the neurophysiology of the temporal and parietal lobes which, over 50 years ago, would have been inaccessible to Dr Williams at the National Hospital, Queen Square, London. As should be likewise evident, the material and views which I have expressed expand greatly the diminutive contributions to possible aetiology provided by Ring (1980), Sabom (1982; 1998), Grey (1985), and Fenwick and Fenwick (1998). Their books remain standard texts regarding the phenomenological and mechanistic background to ECE. My account illustrates their defective evaluations in excluding much work regarding disturbed temporal lobe function, much of which was in the public domain before their respective times of publication.

In the following chapter, I return to familiar territory already inhabited by these key authors, in elucidating other possible neurophysiological aetiologies of ECE. These include such items as endorphins, hypoxia, nitrous oxide, and carbon dioxide narcosis, and whether the anaesthetic agent ketamine could be considered to be a credible mediator of ECE phenomenology.

9

Other Neurophysiological Aspects Pertinent to ECE Phenomenology

In this chapter, we travel beyond states of consciousness, sleep, dream-states, the neurophysiological constructs of body-image, the pathologies of overt and latent temporal lobe disease, and their contributions to our understandings of OBE and NDE phenomenology. The further spheres of neurophysiology to which we now look have been visited previously by the key authors under consideration in this book.

My aim in revisiting this territory is to effect more detailed, efficient evaluations since the extent to which each has been discussed previously varies widely between my group of selected authors. Furthermore, their levels of engagement with basic neurophysiological mechanisms has, in my view, been extraordinarily indifferent. First, I deal with intrinsic mechanisms, related to endorphin metabolism, and then extrinsic factors such as hypoxia, anoxia, hypercapnia (or an elevated CO_2 level in the body), and the anaesthetic agent ketamine. These, to my mind, are the most important key themes that require further evaluation.

Second, I wish to deal with the vivid tinctorial vistas perceived by subjects during their NDE in comparison with neuropathological vascular disturbances in the brain. I revisit this scene because of the impression given by previous authors that such heightened perceptions of colour during ECE point to something extraordinary, and thus 'other-worldly'. I wish to take issue with that view on the grounds that such implicit relationships by no means necessarily hold.

9.1. INTRINSIC MECHANISMS

9.1.a. The Role of Endorphins

Dr Daniel Carr proposed[1] that the experiential phenomenology of ECE could result from the endogenous secretion of opioid-like endorphins, due either to

---

[1] Carr D, *Lancet* 1: 390, 1981; idem, *J Near-Death Stud* 2: 75–89, 1982.

limbic system activation as might be effected through the temporal lobe, intrinsically by epilepsy, or extrinsically through electrical stimulation of its outer cortex.[2] Limbic activation is predominantly manifested through β-endorphin receptors which are concentrated throughout the upper diencephalic regions of the brain and beyond, including hypothalamus, hippocampus, amygdala, thalamus and reticular formation. β-endorphin, together with many other peptides, are released during the physiological stresses resulting from hypotension, hypoxia, hypoglycaemia, endotoxaemia, psychological trauma, or during ether and N_2O anaesthesia, the resultant effect leading to sedation, analgesia and passivity. Carr's thesis is that endorphins induce hallucinatory states reminiscent of NDE reportings. There is some overlap here with another independent proposal[3] involving the temporal lobe from which an opioid-induced electrical discharge to the limbus, hippocampus, amygdala and neocortex results in NDE.

Sabom dismissed a central role for β-endorphin on account of its prolonged action, thus exceeding the interval during which an NDE might be expected to have taken place.[4] This view, however, is based solely on one report which details the application directly into the cerebro-spinal fluid of β-endorphin in terminal cancer patients. The problem here is whether, after the injection, the resulting tissue levels within the brain were comparable to those realized through endogenous physiological secretion.[5] Nevertheless, the persisting effect of endorphins beyond the stressful crisis precipitating their release, and their failure to reproduce the ecstatic bliss that is a recurrent theme of NDE reports, suggests that their aetiological role, if any, is ancillary, rather than primary. However, endorphins should not be dismissed outright. They are endogenously secreted during stress, and thus could provide one important factor in activating latent temporal lobe dysfunction, given that β-endorphin causes non-convulsive limbic epileptiform disturbances.[6] It would be useful to sample jugular venous (bulb) blood during ECE in order to perform assays for endorphins and thus attempt to shed more light on this intriguing proposal. I am surprised this appears not to have been a priority in the minds of previous investigators.

Another difficulty is that the pharmacologic effect of endorphins cannot explain the OBE, the visions of religious people,[7] or the 'tunnel' which, it is

---

[2] Penfield and Perot 1963.

[3] Saavedra-Aguilar J and Gomez-Jeria J, *J Near-Death Stud* 7: 205–222, 1989.

[4] Sabom 1982, 171.

[5] Oyama T, Jin T, Yamaya R, *Lancet* 1: 122–124, 1980.

[6] Henricksen S, Bloom F, McCoy F, Ling N, Guillemin R, *Proc Nat Acad Sci (USA)* 75: 5221–5225, 1978.

[7] Saavedra-Aguilar and Gomez-Jeria 1989.

claimed, are due to after-discharge in primary visual cortex. I reject entirely previous suggestions, as reviewed elsewhere,[8] that the tunnel represents either some transition to higher consciousness, a rite of passage, a literal geocentric translocation, or a revisitation of the birth canal at one's natal origins. What then of a possible neurophysiological account?

9.2. THE TUNNEL AND RELATED PHENOMENOLOGIES

The initial sense of darkness, referred to by many experients, is representative of the first glimmerings of a return to conscious-awareness and, as such, yields only to the vaguest form of verbal capture. The experience is analogous to an incipient fainting attack or loss of consciousness, and the initial recall of a vague grey darkness as conscious-awareness begins to return. The perception of darkness, together with its varied, and in some cases extraordinarily dramatic, subjective descriptions, may then be followed by the tunnel sensation proper and perception of a distant light that rapidly enlarges. The latter suggests a return of visual competence, a view corroborated by the physiological evidence from acute occlusion of the neck arteries[9] or during G_z-enforced acute cerebral ischaemia.[10] Peripheral vision is first lost yielding subjective sensations of grey-out, while macular central vision remains for about another second before consciousnesss is completely erased as retinal artery perfusion dwindles. The retina is a little less sensitive to a reduced blood flow than the cortex because of its higher perfusion pressure[11] $\sim$20mm Hg above cerebral pressure. Conversely, the restoration of retinal blood flow would be a reversal of the pattern experienced as consciousness wanes, that is, a bright central photoma (circle of light) heralding return of macular competence followed by a spreading of light as peripheral retinal field function returns. Furthermore, we do not 'see' with our retinae but by means of the higher cortical visual representations in the multimodal association areas of the temporo-parietal cortex. In other words, the sequence of the enlarging light is a viewing of the retinal fields of view by the cortex as *both* become re-vascularized.

---

[8] Blackmore S and Troscianko T, *J Near-Death Stud* 8: 15–28, 1989; Kellehear A 1993; Drab K, *J Near-Death Stud* 1: 126–152, 1981.

[9] Rossen R, Kabat H, Anderson J, *Arch Neurol Psychiatr* 50: 510–528, 1943.

[10] Whinnery and Whinnery 1990.

[11] Lambert E and Wood E, *Med Clin N Am* 30: 833–844, 1946; Woerlee G, *Skeptical Enquirer* 28: 28–33, 2004.

Contra Blackmore,[12] I suggest that the experience of the light cannot come from the primary visual cortex because either (electrical) stimulation in that region or vascular insufficiency give rise to coloured scintillating auras such as 'lightning flashes' or 'fireworks', rather than the cognitively interpreted, multi-coordinated visual, auditory and affective perceptions that specifically characterize ECE. I therefore cannot agree with Blackmore and Troscianko, who suggest that 'scintillations', interpreted as increasing noise in their computerized model of the retina as the intensity of the spots increases into the peripheral fields, satisfy the criteria for light at the end of the tunnel. Scintillating photomas (visual 'fireworks') imply activation of primary visual cortex.[13] However, the experiential imagery recalled indicates quite clearly that the perceived image is not only formed, but accompanied by intelligible sounds and vestibular symptomatology. Therefore, these multi-coordinated events would presumably need to be located far more anteriorly in the cortex,[14] in the heteromodal association areas of the temporo-parietal region. Admittedly, some of the earlier sounds likened to hissing or the rumble of machinery accompanying the darkness phase do suggest an emanation from the primary auditory cortex in the temporal lobe cortex.

Nevertheless, the combination of perceived darkness, of vestibular-induced motion, together with the illusion of a distant light-source, provide the three contributory ingredients for the later recalled interpretation of illusory 'motion' along an illusory 'tunnel' at the end of which is a bright, rapidly enlarging 'light'. The increase in size of the cortically perceived retinal image, and the illusory vestibular (Chapter 6) component of forward movement, rotation or linear acceleration, provide the necessary basis for the post-experiential interpretation of having traversed an imagined tunnel from blackness thence to have been catapulted into an intense, enveloping light.

It is evident that the tunnel represents a retrospective, interpretative synthesis of two concurrent inputs—visual and vestibular. Clearly, such an illusory construct can have no precise geomorphic coordinates, and since more than 70% of subjects never experience this event it cannot be regarded, from any perspective, as a specialized entrance to any kind of 'higher' consciousness, nor to any other type of notional plane of 'elevated' existence. Finally, we should note the markedly idiosyncratic and subjective variations

---

[12] Blackmore and Troscianko 1989; Blackmore 1993, 67ff.

[13] Sveinbjornsdottir S and Duncan J, *Epilepsia* 34: 493–521, 1993.

[14] Purely visual hallucinations can be formed in the ventral occipital cortex (e.g. visual areas 4/8 for coloured scenes) in patients with Charles-Bonnet syndrome (interested readers please see ffytche et al, *Nature Neuroscience* 1: 738–742, 1998). The tunnel involves the additional percepts of touch, vestibular accompaniments of rapid movement or gyrations, and sound, thus implying a location to the temporo-parietal association areas.

in the manner by which the tunnel phenomenon has been portrayed in recall. There are, like ECE reports in general, as many tunnels as there are subjects willing to testify to this particular type of experiential phenomenology.

The variable spread of these experiences is dependent on the underlying cause for the loss of consciousness or hypotensive episode; the duration of the crisis and the speed of recovery in re-establishing an effective cerebral blood flow. More generally, recovery will reflect the age of the patient, mean blood pressure, and degree of atheromatous degeneration of the cerebral arterial tree, bearing in mind Drab's observation that many tunnellers will have suffered cardio-pulmonary collapse. Recovery, seen in terms of re-vascularization, will be strongly influenced by the state of the intra-cerebral vessels, their degree of narrowing and the effectiveness of the cross-circulation through the circle of Willis, and any previous history of hypertension. Atheromatous plaques will result in maldistribution of blood leading to a patchy return of activation in all critical areas of the brainstem and cortex. That could certainly account for the non-uniform perceptions of the tunnel phenomena in the few subjects experiencing them: there is no canonical description that defines the event. For the remaining non-tunnellers, the pattern of cerebral blood flow could mean a bypassing of this initial recovery phase, if re-vascularization were more rapid, especially in younger subjects without a prolonged loss of circulatory competence, as during childbirth, eclamptic seizures or febrile incidents. Consideration of these many and varied circumstances offers a plausible account of the tunnel—in its fullest representations, in its myriad partial descriptions as given in later recalled narratives—as well as, for the vast majority of ND subjects, its absence.

9.3. EXTRINSIC FACTORS

Next, I consider some of the extrinsic factors capable of influencing brain physiology in respect of ECE. These include O_2, CO_2, and the anaesthetic agents ether, N_2O (nitrous oxide or 'laughing gas') and ketamine. It is worth remembering that much ECE phenomenology occurs while subjects are in some kind of subconscious state. This applies to ~70–90% of cases[15] since many are undergoing surgery, an acute crisis with cardio-respiratory arrest, or the effects of acute hypotension consequent upon severe haemorrhage. In this hospitalized setting the use of many ancillary drugs and anaesthetic agents

---

[15] Fenwick and Fenwick 1998, 205; Stevenson I and Greyson B, *J Amer Med Assoc* 242: 265–267, 1979.

could confuse the picture. In general, such possible explanatory contributions are usually dismissed, because similar factors are thought to be equally operative in the majority of cases ($\sim$80%) in which, under identical clinical settings, ECE are not experienced. But great caution is required before the acceptance of such simplistic claims can be justified. Since the majority of those latter subjects are not prone to experience an ECE, the sample does not comprise a valid control population against those who are susceptible, nor can it support the conclusions usually drawn from the comparison.

9.3.a. Cerebral Hypoxia

Moody and Ring[16] dismiss hypoxia as an aetiological factor on the grounds that not all ECE subjects suffer hypotensive episodes occasioned by severe haemorrhage or cardio-pulmonary collapse. There has also been a failure to distinguish between anoxia and hypoxia: '[A]noxia does *not* mean hypoxia':[17] these are not interchangeable terms. Anoxia means complete absence of a source of molecular oxygen for uptake into cellular metabolic processes. Hypoxia implies a reduction in ambient arterial oxygen levels (PaO_2), and is dependent on many factors including alterations in regional cerebral arterial blood flow, vascular resistance within the arterioles, arterial CO_2 levels ($PaCO_2$), supplies of inspiratory oxygen, cerebral oxygen-extraction rates and, hence, on the metabolic rate of the brain, and on the presence of metabolic toxins or inhibitors. We know nothing about these factors operative *locally* within various parts of the brain during ECE. In migraine, for example, rCBF may be severely compromised for as long as 60 minutes[18] even to ischaemic levels but without evidence of intra-neuronal acidosis (reduced pH_i)[19] or resultant damage detectable at clinical level in the post-headache/aura period.

Vague statements and assumptions, then, about conditions of cerebral 'hypoxia' or 'anoxia' within the brains of ECE subjects, without any reliable data concerning local physiological variables pertaining at the time, are not particularly informative and offer no proof as to whether, or to what extent, these factors contribute to the problem. Indeed, it is patently obvious that the brains of most of these subjects could never have been severely anoxic, for, if they had, the experients would have suffered long-standing neurological

---

[16] Moody 1977, 109; Ring 1980, 213.
[17] Fox Mark, *Religion, Spirituality and the Near-Death Experience*, London: Routledge 2003, 147.
[18] Olesen J, *Cerebrovasc Brain Metab Rev* 3: 1–28, 1991.
[19] Welch K, Levine S, D'Andrea G, Helpern J, *Cephalalgia* 8: 273–277, 1988.

defects. Despite that, many subjects investigated have displayed some form of circulatory disturbance compatible with variable degrees of hypoxic insult to the brain.

The effects of induced cerebral hypoxia,[20] either by the inspiration of progressively O_2-depleted air samples, or from acute carotid arterial occlusion, or through induced cerebral ischaemia following centrifugation, all reveal a slowing of subjects' physical and mental activity, ultimately leading to convulsions and loss of consciousness. That train of events is exemplified by a progressive 'muddling and confusion of cognitive ability' in contrast to the sharpness of cognitive insight evident during ECE.[21] Moreover, this sequence of events does not reproduce the typical evolution of ECE, as testified[22] to by a pilot who had experienced both acute (aerial) hypoxia and an ECE. In line with these observations, my proposal gains considerable validity in stating that ECE occur as conscious-awareness is being regained, that is, as the brain is being revascularized and re-oxygenated, as is the conclusion to be drawn from the centrifuged aircrew studied by Forster and Whinnery.[23] Therefore, hypoxia, although relevant, cannot be a lone aetiological factor. Sabom records a patient who, after a massive heart attack, exhibited high O_2 and low CO_2 levels in his blood.[24] Despite the widespread use of this information against an aetiological role of hypoxia, we must remain aware of the difficulty that those peripheral arterial gas measurements may not have been at all reflective of intra-cerebral tissue levels obtaining at the time in Sabom's patient.

9.3.b. Hypercapnia—Cerebral Effects of Elevated Levels of CO_2

An altered state of consciousness may be brought about by carbon dioxide (CO_2) intoxication. Some degree of hypercarbia, that is an elevated level of CO_2 in the cerebral blood, may follow a cardiac arrest. The experience of inhaling a 30:70 (v:v) CO_2:O_2 mixture was examined by LJ Meduna,[25] whose subjects comprised 150 psychiatric patients and 50 controls. After continuously inhaling this mixture for some minutes, the occurrence of severe

[20] Henderson Y and Haggard H, Noxious Gases And The Principles Of Respiration Influencing Their Action, New York, Reinhold Publ Corp 1943; Rossen et al 1943; Forster and Whinnery 1988.
[21] Sabom 1982, 176.
[22] Fenwick and Fenwick 1998, 213.
[23] Forster and Whinnery 1988.
[24] Sabom 1982, 178.
[25] Meduna LJ, CO2 Therapy: A Neurophysiological Treatment of Nervous Disorders, Springfield: Thomas 1950.

neurological compromise in these patients was indicated by the appearance of certain physical signs (upwards conjugate deviation of the eyes, opisthotonus, tonic extension of the extremities, and hyporeflexia). Other bizarre features experienced by these patients, such as having illogical compulsions, apprehending frightening figures and shapes, and the perception of complex geometric shapes, are notably unlike the phenomenology of ECE. Meduna rightly concluded that such phenomena were not idiosyncratically related to each of his subjects but to the generalized effect of CO_2 intoxication on the brain.

9.3.c. Inhalational Anaesthetic Gases

While acute lack of inspired O_2, or the inhalation of CO_2, fail to induce altered states of consciousness reminiscent of ECE, this is not the case with the inhalational anaesthetic gases ether and nitrous oxide, otherwise N_2O or 'laughing gas'. During the nineteenth century, when these gases were first prepared, there was a widespread vogue for inhaling them in order to discover their properties. A particular account is attributed to Oscar Wilde's visit to his dentist in Broad Street, Oxford, May–June 1895, during which he received ether anaesthesia.[26] He observed a reduction of conscious-awareness during which he knew everything and experienced a rush of thoughts which solved all his pre-existing problems:

I seemed to see myself as in a dream, a space of light about 4 or 5 inches in diameter. Surrounding this space a non-existence, a thick, heavy material darkness which steadily encroached upon the limits of the light . . . this luminous space seemed to be in the form of a funnel, and gradually to decrease in size until it became a point of light . . . .

Ernest Dunbar[27] reviews his experiences with ether, which are different from Snow's rather more prosaic clinical account.[28] Dunbar's thoughts 'raced like a mill-wheel . . . every trifling phenomenon seemed to fall into its place as a logical event in the universe. I began to realize that I was the One.' Having asked surgical patients of their experiences during ether anaesthesia, 80% recalled rushing into a dark tunnel, experiencing singing in their ears, and a flashing of lights in their eyes. Their sense of time was also disturbed, as with N_2O. His call for all these reactions to be recorded appears to have gone

---

[26] 'I.B.', *Psychol Rev* 6: 104–106, 1899: and see Smith PB, *Chemical Glimpses of Paradise*, Springfield: Thomas 1972, 38ff.
[27] Dunbar E, *Proc Soc Psychic Res* 19: 62–77, 1905.
[28] Snow J, *On Inhalation of Ether in Surgical Operations*, London: Churchill 1847.

unheeded: that is a pity, because much of the phenomenology recorded reflects that undergone by subjects experiencing an ECE. Modern anaesthetic techniques have now rendered the possibility of retracing those early experiences redundant.

Humphry Davy (1799) was the first to record the effects of N_2O inhalation, during which there was a very heightened sense of audition, a loss of connection with external realities, and a rapidity of thought processes (as with ether and during ECE). 'I existed in a world of newly connected and newly modified ideas'.[29] A fusion of antitheses was experienced by William James.[30] He concludes:

the keynote of the experience is the tremendously exciting sense of an intense metaphysical illumination. The mind sees all the logical relations of being with an apparent subtlety and instantaneity to which its normal consciousness offers no parallel... It is impossible to convey an idea of the torrential character of the identification of opposites as it streams through the mind in this experience...

N_2O parties were often held during those earlier times, much as drug parties are held today. But here are some excerpts from a recent orgy[31] at which modern gas cylinders were used as a source of N_2O:

often, during the N_2O exhilaration, one experiences sensations of floating, whirling or flying, The setting of these sensations is frequently an infinite vacuum or void, astral blue or neutral grey. More often than a floating sensation, I have experienced a rushing feeling—I am being propelled upright, through unidentifiable time and space at an extremely high rate of speed—only to arrive back at my nitrous oxide party.[32]

Another experient writes:

as more gas is inspired a loss of ego and subsequent sense of unity—the cosmos is one and interrelated—as experienced in a mystical state of consciousness, is achieved. There is a certain point of the mind from which life and death, the real and the imaginary, the past and the future, the communicable and the incommunicable, the high and the low, cease being perceived as contradictions.[33]

Moody records the experience of a patient at the dentist: 'as [N_2O] began to take effect, she felt herself going round in a spiral—as if the chair was moving

[29] Davy, Humphry, *Researches Chemical and Philosophical, chiefly concerning Nitrous Oxide and Its Respiration*, London 1799–1800.

[30] James W, *Mind* 7: 186–208, 1882.

[31] Sheldin M, Wallechinsky D, Saunia S, *Laughing Gas (Nitrous Oxide)*, California: And/Or Press 1973. Note: this is an extremely dangerous practice that can result in subjects' deaths.

[32] Lopez W, The Effects of Nitrous Oxide, in: Sheldin et al 1973, 20.

[33] Kaplan D, Nitrous Oxide and the Surreal Condition, in: Sheldin et al 1973, 36.

and spiralling upwards—up and up and up'.[34] Another example describes a woman in her third labour who was quite obviously intoxicated by her N_2O inhalations.[35] In her hallucination, she sees herself floating down the corridor above her trolley and then undergoing a Caesarian section with the birth of a new daughter. She thought she had transferred into her own body, and gone to sleep. She was then aroused by some very much alive, muscular midwives who now exhorted her to push, resulting in the arrival of the real, non-hallucinatory baby. These accounts of the phenomenological experiences associated with the inhalation of N_2O are important for two reasons. First, because in no account has any author previously considered the inhalation of this agent as a precipitant of ECE, for example, during childbirth in a susceptible subject (as opposed to other antecedent causes such as pain, haemorrhage or a full eclamptic fit). Second,[36] because N_2O has been shown to fulfil criteria of a 'dissociative' anaesthetic agent, that is, causing a loss of reality in self and of spatial orientation.

Anaesthetic agents can be broadly divided into those acting through the inhibitory neural transmitter GABA ($\gamma\text{-NH}_2\text{-n-butyric acid}$) such as barbiturates, halothane and valium-like compounds. The others block the glutamate neuro-excitatory receptor NMDA (n-CH_3-D aspartate) such as N_2O and ketamine. These latter agents can also block NMDA receptors on GABA-ergic neurones, thus abolishing their glutamatergic and cholinergic inhibition resulting in neurotoxicity and neuronal cell damage. The importance of these recent neurophysiological discoveries concerns the NMDA-receptor antagonist and anaesthetic, ketamine. Ketamine probably acts through selective inhibition of thalamo-cortical neural networks, and stimulation of limbic systems.[37]

9.3.d. Is Ketamine the Ideal Paradigm of ECE Phenomenology?

After sub-anaesthetic doses, ketamine induces awakening ('emergence') phenomena, akin to ECE, such as lively dream activity, sensory distortions and hallucinatory phenomena. They can be categorized as a sensation of bodily lightness and of floating, an aberrant sense of body composition (like foam rubber or plastic) or shape (micro-/macrosomia), vividly coloured imagery (a conviction of seeing coloured shapes, or movement through differently

---

[34] Moody 1976, 158.
[35] Fenwick and Fenwick 1998, 198–199.
[36] Jevtovic-Todorovic V, Todorovic S, Mennerick S et al, *Nature Med* 4: 460–463, 1998; Pang E and Fowler B, *Psychophysiol* 36: 552–558, 1999.
[37] Hansen G, Jensen S, Chandresh L, Hilden T, *J Psychoact Drugs* 20: 419–425, 1988.

coloured rooms), a feeling of utter timelessness (eternity), the acquisition of all knowledge or insight into perplexing problems, emotional 'highs' and fusion with other people or objects in the environment; and OBE. Similar experiences are reported for patients receiving full ketamine anaesthesia for formal surgical procedures.[38] These phenomena have engendered the proposition that ketamine is a model 'dissociative' paradigm for ECE.[39] This proposal depends heavily on the notion that an endogenous blocker of the NMDA receptor, akin to ketamine's actions, is released by the brain during events conducive to brain injury, and ECE, such as epilepsy, hypoxia, hypotension, and acute hypoglycaemia. At present, there seems to be little hard support for this radical, but interesting, concept.

In 1984, a breakdown product of L-arginine called agmatine was shown, like ketamine, to block the PCP sub-unit of NMDA. Another agent, 'β-endopsychosin'[40] was shown to attach to another sub-unit (σ) of NMDA, but this may not have any influence on subconscious brain activity. However, the paper which Jansen (1990) cited to further support the role of these ketamine-like NMDA blocking agents is highly critical of previous findings. It cautions: 'rigorous studies are needed to determine if "endogenous ligands" [in this context meaning receptor blocking agents such as agmatine] have a real physiological significance, or whether they are merely extraction artefacts'.[41] A recent review of agmatine fails to mention such a pioneering role for this polyamine.[42] Whether agmatine or any other putative endogenous NMDA blocking agents are released during ECE, what their specificity for its multiple receptor sub-units[43] could be, and hence what effects might ensue from such particular forms of blockade, remain to be determined. The widespread distribution of the various combinations of NMDA receptor sub-units throughout the central nervous system confers a diversity of pharmacological sensitivities to a variety of agonists and antagonists. That remains a fundamental, and as yet relatively unexplored, problem for any further understanding of a possible role for generating ECE through this type of mechanism.

At sub-anaesthetic dose levels, ketamine interferes with dopaminergic pathways in the pre-frontal cortex. This effect, through activation of other

---

[38] Collier B, *Anaesthesia* 27: 120–134, 1972.

[39] Rogo D and Scott J, *J Near-Death Stud* 4: 87–96, 1984; Jansen K, *Med Hypoth* 31: 25–29, 1990.

[40] Jansen K, 2000; Jansen K, *Br Med J* 298: 1708, 1989.

[41] Sonders M, Keana J, Weber E, *Trends Neurosci* 11: 37–38, 1988.

[42] Berkels R, Taubert D, Grundemann D, Schomig E, *Cardiovasc Drug Rev* 22: 7–16, 2004.

[43] Moghaddam B, Adams B, Verma A, Daly D, *J Neurosci* 17: 2921–2927, 1997; Haberny K, Paule M, Scallet et al, *Toxicol Sci* 68: 9–17, 2002.

forms of glutamergic receptors leading to increased tissue levels of dopamine,[44] is particularly marked with the S-type enantiomer of ketamine.[45] The effect resembles the metabolic hyperfrontality seen in acutely psychotic schizophrenic subjects, including ego-disintegration and hallucinations.[46] Other studies point to widespread impairments in frontal lobe activity, including the fronto-medial cortex, anterior cingulate gyrus; left inferior, middle and medial frontal gyri and right middle frontal gyrus: also the thalamus, parietal, sensorimotor and temporal cortex.[47] These lead to poor memory and attention, thought disorders, depersonalization, lack of time perception, and severe emotive withdrawal.[48] These are parts of the brain which have figured greatly in our preceding discussions pertaining to ECE phenomenology, yet the cognitive and psychological perturbations recorded with ketamine embrace a much wider constellation of defects not generally recognizable as those associated with ECE.

Despite these several pertinent drawbacks, it is noteworthy that the ketamine-associated dissociative episodes are emergent phenomena,[49] occurring as subjects recede from its pharmacological influence to regain conscious-awareness. That is analogous to my claim that ECE likewise are emergent phenomena, but in the latter case as the brain is receding from a subconscious state.

But there are troublesome differences between ECE and ketamine-induced psychological outcomes. First, recurrent hallucinations occur from one week to more than one year post-ketamine anaesthesia[50] thus more resembling the flashbacks associated with LSD usage[51] rather than ECE. Second, 8% of anaesthetized subjects[52] were perturbed by unpleasant visions, a figure greatly in excess of the fewer unpleasant events recorded by ECE subjects. Third, one patient underwent a transcendental ascent into heaven during which God was seen, and after which he thought he had been reincarnated in Italy. This

---

[44] Moghaddam et al 1997.
[45] Vollenweider F, Leenders K, Oye I, Hell D, Angst J, *Eur Neuropsychopharmacol* 7: 25–38, 1997a.
[46] Vollenweider F, Leenders K, Scharfetter A, Maguire P, Missimer J, *Eur Neuropsychopharmacol* 7: 9–24, 1997b.
[47] Vollenweider et al 1997a.
[48] Krystal J, Karper L, Seibyl J, Freeman G, Delaney R, Bremner J et al, *Arch Gen Psychiatr* 51: 199–214, 1994; Malhotra A, Pinals D, Weingartner H et al, *Neuropsychopharmacol* 14: 301–307, 1996; Adler C, Goldberg T, Malhotra A, Pickar D, Breier A, *Biol Psychiatr* 43: 811–816, 1998; Breier A, Malhotra A, Pinals D et al, *Am J Psychiatr* 154: 805–811, 1997.
[49] Hansen et al 1988; Perel A and Davidson J, *Anaesthesia* 31: 1081–1083, 1976; Collier 1972.
[50] Perel and Davidson 1976; Johnson B, *Br Med J* 4: 428–429, 1971.
[51] Horowitz M, *Am J Psychiatr* 126: 565–569, 1969.
[52] Collier 1972.

illusion persisted for over two hours in the awake post-operative period, throughout which the subject was convinced he was speaking Italian (ibid.). That does not occur with ECE, since the transcendental voyage ends abruptly at the point when conscious-awareness is regained.

The effects of ketamine and its cogener phencyclidine ('angel dust'), (both of which non-competitively block the PCP sub-unit of the NMDA receptor), have been known for over forty years.[53] Yet the apparent importance of these substances for a greater understanding of the mechanisms of ECE has had little impact in the literature. Of all the predominant ECE authors dealt with here, only Moody[54] gives ketamine a mention as an agent capable of reproducing some of the phenomenology of these events. But he ultimately dismisses anaesthesia, and drugs in general, like Ring, Sabom and Grey,[55] since many of their respondents interviewed had putatively never received medications of any kind. That may, in part, be correct, but it is also important to stress that the administration of CO_2, N_2O, ketamine, or even ether, perturbs the brain in a manner analogous to ECE. Therefore, their mechanisms of action require investigating, and not to be ignored or only superficially perused, so that further insights may be brought to ECE phenomenology. I have already pointed out that, in my view, a failure of these authors to have seriously engaged with the neurophysiology of the various dream-sleep modes, the phantom limb phenomenon, and body-image, likewise, missed important opportunities for gaining a fuller appreciation of ECE at neuronal and molecular levels.

Nevertheless the observations, however complex and presently unresolved, are of great importance for neurophysiology and for a possibly greater understanding of the molecular basis of ECE. More information is needed as to why ketamine induces impairments of cognitive and memory recall and emotional negativity which are foreign to the ECE typology. Second, Collier[56] found that although many patients enjoyed the pleasantness of ketamine anaesthesia, 60% of her sample did not wish to repeat the experience. That is not the impression given by ECE subjects, many of whom express great reluctance at having to return to earth. Third, in comparisons with ketamine anaesthesia, ECE subjects rarely experience a marked slowing of time and thought processes, a feeling of death as that of an internal emptiness, paranoia, micro-/macrosomia, or a convergence of visual perception rather than the beautiful panoramic vistas usually reported by them. Fourth, the

---

[53] White P, Way W, Trevor A, *Anesthesiology* 56: 119–136, 1982.
[54] Moody 1976, 157.
[55] Ring 1980, 210; Sabom 1982, 168; Grey 1985, 174.
[56] Collier 1972.

ketamine model of ECE fails to explain why only ~20% of the population is prone to these events. Despite Jansen's requirement[57] that every person, subject to an ECE and likely to suffer excitotoxic (glutamergic) neuronal damage, should elaborate an endogenous neural protector to occupy the NMDA receptor, the low percentage of actual susceptible subjects needs another explanation. We must conclude that ketamine does not fulfil the criteria of the ideal paradigm of ECE.

9.4. INSIGHTS INTO THE BRILLIANTLY COLOURED HEAVENLY PASTORAL

Most impressive are accounts of the vivid tinctorial panoramas incorporating radiant yellows, greens and particularly blues, which figure in the narratives of many respondents. They are likely to have arisen because of impaired circulation to the region of the temporo-parietal-occipital cortex. These illusory auras reflect dysfunction of more rostral parts of this associative cortical region, since the colours reported are simultaneously coordinated with sounds of music and bodily movement like walking. Whitmarsh saw a blue train,[58] was impressed by the intensity of blueness of the sky, and thought he was wearing a blue gown just like the passengers on the illusory train. Darell, as he faded into unconsciousness following the first of a series of rapid cardiac arrests, was enshrouded in sky blue.[59] Or another woman respondent: 'and I went on to this lovely land, green grass, blue sky ... [then] I started down [a vestibular influence] this hill by the stream'.[60] Similar reports abound: 'At the end of this deep well I could see a wonderful blue light which was coming up and enveloping me';[61] 'A blue-gold light appeared and grew brighter and brighter' (idem, p. 47); 'by now the tunnel is behind you and before you is this magnificent, blue-white light' (idem, p. 47); and 'I [saw] a lot of beautiful blue ... on all sides of us was this beautiful blue. You can't even call it a sky, but it was a deep blue—a beautiful colour. I've never seen a blue like it';[62] 'before you ... is this gorgeous ... blue-white light'.[63]

[57] Jansen 2000.
[58] Fenwick and Fenwick 1998, 93.
[59] Sabom 1998, 20.
[60] Fenwick and Fenwick 1998, 104.
[61] Grey 1985, 46.
[62] Sabom 1982, 54.
[63] Ring 1980, 57.

But let us consider the following: 'For instance, he thought of fire-crackers, and suddenly these were seen in sunset colours of blue and purple'. This young epileptic boy had extensive left hemispherical atrophy involving temporal, parietal and occipital lobes.[64] And: 'his final hallucinatory experience was of a large bluish inkspot with gold rim around it', or, 'She described a lady in a blue dress'.[65] Both individuals had undergone strokes (infarctions of the right parieto-occipital cortical areas), related to vertebro-basilar arterial insufficiency. Another 73-year-old woman[66] while sitting quietly at home saw 'beautiful scenes—a tropical shore with white sands, a blue sky and brilliant flowers, *more lovely and more vivid* than she could have believed possible' (my emphases). At a subsequent post-mortem, a thrombus of the basilar artery was demonstrated. Another lady experienced hallucinations of 'verdant Elizabethan gardens, with peacocks [bluish-green feathers] and lovely flowers . . . brightly coloured stars and fireworks . . . which became more vivid and more lovely as time [the passing years] went on'. She gave a ten-year history of severe migrainous headaches with a variety of preceding auras. Michael Perry, in his recent book, refers to a man witnessing blue smoke rising up from a church floor during a service, presumably as a result of some kind of trance.[67] 'But . . . it was not smoke, but an impalpable . . . haze of violet colour.' The 'luminous blue haze' which 'then engulfed him was transformed into golden glory'.

Price and colleagues[68] emphasize the prolonged perception of golden light which symptomatically typifies basilar arterial insufficiency. My call for 'blinded' judges to review hallucinatory/illusory narratives, such as these, in comparison with ECE narrative encounters assumes a greater significance as we ponder what the brain evidently conjures in the presence of progressive (arteriosclerotic) vascular damage and its resultant ischaemia. The illusionary perceptions are all very much of a piece, despite their varied aetiologies, and that includes ECE.

It is especially important to appreciate that reduced cortical blood flow due to thrombotic or embolic events and involving the vertebral-basilar-posterior cerebral arterial supply can produce identical 'auras' of golden light to those experienced by NDE subjects as they regain conscious-awareness. There can be little functional difference between golden yellow/blue auras of light arising from a partial *reduction* of blood flow due to longstanding arterial blockade,

---

[64] Karagulla and Robertson 1995 (Case 3C, p. 751).
[65] Lance J, *Brain* 99: 719–734, 1976; Lance et al 1974.
[66] Williams D and Wilson T, *Brain* 85: 741–774, 1962 (Cases 8, 9, p. 755).
[67] Perry M, *Psychical and Spiritual,* Louth (Lincolnshire): Churches' Fellowship for Psychical and Spiritual Studies 2003, 72.
[68] Price et al 1983.

and that resulting from a partial *restoration* of blood flow, as would necessarily occur during the recovery phases from an NDE consequent upon a period of prolonged acute circulatory arrest.

Vivid, lively visual hallucinations[69] of people, scenes and animals with affective concomitants are associated with another condition originally recognized by L'Hermitte and termed '*peduncular hallucinosis*' (PH) by van Bogaert.[70] This is not directly concerned with the (cerebral) peduncles themselves[71] but presumably involves critical neuronal pathways passing through the peduncles between upper brainstem, thalamus and cortex. Pathologies involving these tracts include various encephalopathies, tumour,[72] phenobarbitone toxicity which has a predilection for structures in the upper brainstem,[73] multiple sclerosis, and especially vascular disturbances,[74] either obliterative, haemorraghic, or structural.[75] The case of Taylor[76] revealed demyelination in the periaqueductal grey, indicative of a disruption of multi-sensory projections to the multi-modal association cortex and their feedback controls, resulting in visual and auditory hallucinations. Interruption to the ascending reticular formation may be very relevant to the phenomenology experienced.

One case-report demands further detailed consideration.[77] A woman was referred with left-sided symptoms suggesting a (contralateral) right hemisphere lesion. An attempt to define the lesion by carotid artery angiography resulted in erroneous cannulation and the resultant delivery of the full dose of contrast medium into the vertebral artery. Following this error, there arose a series of extremely vivid, colourful hallucinations: 'a garden planted with trees and flowers of all colours—the scene was lovelier than in nature'. Many of the scenes hallucinated involved vivid blue or green hues: 'I saw a green colour which dissolved into a field of corn [yellow] waving faintly in the breeze'. And: 'There was a pretty blue colour transformed into a sea scene—on both sides of the horizon there rose up high massive mountains. All the images appeared in colours brighter than nature.' After two to three weeks these hallucinations

[69] L'Hermitte J, *Rev Neurol (Paris)* 38: 1359–1365, 1922.
[70] van Bogaert L, *Rev Neurol (Paris)* 40: 417–423, 1924.
[71] Feinberg W and Rapcsack S, *Neurology* 39: 1535–1536, 1989; Catafau J, Rubio F, Serra J, *J Neurol* 239: 89–90, 1992; Jones E, *J Comp Neurol* 162: 285–308, 1975.
[72] Dunn D, Weisberg L, Nadell J, *Neurology* 33: 1360–1361, 1983.
[73] Trelles J and Lagache D, *Ann Med Psychol* 90: 565, 1932.
[74] Caplan L, *Neurology* 30: 72–79, 1980; Tsukamoto H, Matsushima T, Fujiwara S, Fukui M, *Surg Neurol* 40: 31–34, 1993; Kumar R, Behari S, Wahi J, Banerji D, Sharma K, *Br J Neurosurg* 13: 500–503, 1999.
[75] Bossi L, Nobili M, Benedetto P, *Arch Sci Med* 137: 347–350, 1980.
[76] Taylor K, Brugger P, Schwarz U, *Cogn Behav Neurol* 18: 135–136, 2005.
[77] Rozanski J, *Neurology* 2: 341–349, 1952.

became less obtrusive and thus were unlikely to have been precipitated by the original (undiagnosed) right hemisphere pathology, rather than the injection. The contrast medium injected may have temporarily occluded vascular terminals in the brainstem, and other cortical areas beyond, thus impairing the function of the territories involved.

The importance of this syndrome is that disturbances of presumptive visual connections between thalamus and cortex, often due to vascular causes, lead to perceived phenomenology analogous to that of ECE. The point should be made that coloured panoramic scenes, in which the perceived hues are more intensely vivid than those naturally perceived, as is usually reported for NDE, together with pleasurable feelings and even auditory commands[78] can be hallucinated by subjects whose brains are compromised, either through space-occupying pathology, inflammatory conditions or, most commonly, obliterative vascular disturbances due to either atheroma, embolus or haemorrhage. Much of the pathology discussed in many case reports seems to be centred on, or in near proximity to, the upper midbrain. On these grounds, I suggest that there is warrant for supposing that reduced vascular flow rates, particularly in the posterior cerebral circulation, could reasonably be held responsible for, or contributory to, the phenomenologies of ECE, as well as peduncular hallucinosis. It is of particular relevance to ECE events that in another case report[79] of peduncular hallucinosis the lady, having been thrown by men in pin-striped suits into a pit containing cobras, immediately found herself in a tunnel at the end of which was a golden gate. No hints are given, however, that she was about to enter the afterworld.

9.5. MOVING ONWARDS—THEOLOGICAL PERSPECTIVES ON ECE

As already foreshadowed in the previous chapters, ECE exhibit complex, two-sided phenomenologies comprising other-worldly and this-worldly perspectives. Interpretations of the other-worldly perpective can be accomplished through two additional criteria. First, from a this-worldly perspective, there arises the need to assess how subjects themselves interpreted their experiences and what meanings they derived from them. From that position, we may determine how their lives were subsequently modulated and conditioned.

---

[78] Manford and Andermann 1998.
[79] Manford and Andermann 1998, 1822 (Case 2).

Neither of these issues has been addressed in a considered or systematic way in the literature considered in this book.

Secondly, we need to consider whether ECE can be deemed to be true spiritual experiences, and furthermore, how they relate to Christian concepts of death and eschatology based on scriptural and doctrinal evidence. These issues are evaluated in the three succeeding chapters.

10

Anthropological and Eschatological Considerations of ECE Phenomenology

So far, I have argued that ECE phenomenology is an illusory product of brains awakening from severe antecedent insults. In this chapter, it is my intention to consider the claims by ECE subjects to experience an other-worldly domain and thereafter to report on it. I evaluate the validity of this recall of another world from the perspective of Christian eschatology, with its variety of notions about the soul and resurrection, and from the biblical viewpoint of the anthropological nature of the person.

Problems about the nature of personhood and persons continue to exercise theological as well as philosophical and scientific minds: 'It is the ultimate question.'[1] The crux of the problem may be more easily discerned through the Greek Orthodox theologian John Zizioulas, Metropolitan of Pergamon.[2] He stresses that a proper definitional approach to person derives from the question 'Who am I?', and not 'What am I?' The latter is a common and rather superficial means of pointing out the distinguishing features of one individual from the other ('Oh! he's a doctor', or 'Yes, she's the blonde who drives the Porsche'), an approach which does not succeed in embracing the true essence of personhood, that is, the one who is. Although talk about 'Being' certainly transcends the being of individual persons, the individual participates in Being, and Being can only be known in particular beings. Speaking of 'the one who is' thus encapsulates what is unique to every person. The is offers that sole claim to uniqueness, a reality which is unrepeatable. It embraces each hypostasis ('distinct reality'), with its 'is-ness' or 'who-ness', as opposed to a 'what-ness' which derives from a sharing of characteristics with others, and which is therefore repeatable. Here, then, is an echo of God's self-definition, 'I am who I am' (אהיה אשר אהיה)[3]

---

[1] Tillich Paul, *Systematic Theology* (vol 1), London: SCM Xprint 1997, 164.
[2] Zizioulas John, in: Schwöbel Christoph and Gunton Colin (eds), *Persons Divine and Human* Edinburgh: Clark 1999, 33ff.
[3] Exod 3: 14.

and a parallel with the three Trinitarian hypostases which are constitutive of one divine Being.[4]

10.1. BIBLICAL ACCOUNTS OF HUMAN ANTHROPOLOGY

10.1.a. The Jewish Background

Current perceptions of the person as a unitary body and mind, and its abrupt cessation at death, align themselves with early Hebrew notions of the person. In the 'P' (*c.*600–500 BCE) version of Genesis[5] humankind is created in God's *image* (בצלמו), both male and female, to live as His viceregents on earth, in harmony with each other in an exclusive relationship with Him (Gen 1: 26). In the older 'J' (Yahwist) tradition (dating from *c.*1000 BCE), the breath of life (נפש חיה) vitalizes the earthen vessel destined for humanity (Gen 2: 7) thereby establishing both a physical origin, and an end (חיה-מת) as God's breath (רוח) departs the corpse (Gen 35: 18). There is no perception of immortality. The hovering in the 'lower pit' (שאול) of weakened bodily 'shades' (רפאים) from which the breath (נפש) had withdrawn, was a vague concept never elaborated further in the pre-exilic period. A future existence was never envisaged.

The ontological anthropology here is of being resolutely tied to that of a fulsome life lived to old age (Ps 128). This is the prayer of a peasant people: to work the inherited lands of one's father, to have many sons at one's side, to see the fruit of one's toil and to be fulfilled in the abundance of one's reaping and gathering.[6] Any sense of continuity emerged through embodiment of one's name, through one's sons, in perpetuity, thus to contribute to the collective prosperity of Jerusalem. Interestingly, there was no definitive word for a body in biblical Hebrew: over eighty body parts[7] are described, each of which, by synecdoche, is capable of alluding to the entire person.[8] Here, then, 'man is

---

[4] MacKinnon Donald M, in: Sykes S and Clayton J (eds), *Christ, Faith and History,* Cambridge: Cambridge University Press 1972, 279; Zizioulas J, in: Schwöbel Christoph (ed), *Trinitarian Theology Today,* Edinburgh: Clark 1995, 47–49.

[5] Gibson J, *Language and Imagery in the Old Testament,* London: SPCK 1998, 37.

[6] Martin-Achard Robert, *From Death to Life: A Study of the Development of the Doctrine of the Resurrection in the Old Testament,* London: Oliver & Boyd 1960, 3ff (ET: J Penney-Smith).

[7] Robinson John, *The Body: A Study in Pauline Theology,* London: SCM Press 1957, 11.

[8] Johnson Aubrey, *The Vitality of the Individual in the Thought of Ancient Israel,* Cardiff: University of Wales Press 1964, 37ff.

conceived, not in some analytical fashion as a "soul" and "body", but synthetically as a psychophysical whole'.[9] Furthermore, the person is never isolated, individualized or regarded as a thing, but lives in continuity with others—the so-called corporate nature or corporate personality of Israel.[10]

In moving into first-century Palestine and the Diaspora, we enter the milieu of Hellenistic culture and philosophy and its interactions with Jewish thought-forms and the new Christian thinking. Are new vistas encountered in giving account of Pauline and other New Testament anthropologies? David Stacey, for example, notes the large number of Greek words adopted into contemporary Hebrew writings, including thirty in the Mishnah: even Josephus was forced to learn Greek in order to keep up with commerce and officialdom in this widening environment.[11]

In entering this new territorial domain, one major interpretative difficulty now entails critical adjudications on meanings of important word usages such as σῶμα, σάρξ, ψυχή and πνεῦμα, and their construal with Hebrew concepts embodied in words already met, such as נפש, רוח and בשר particularly within the Pauline corpus and later gospel accounts.

10.1.b. New Testament Perspectives—The Pauline and Non-Pauline Corpus

For these interpretative reasons, the Pauline view of mankind is not the easiest to discern from a twenty-first-century perspective. Although Paul was a staunch Hebrew and subject to a strict upbringing in the synagogue, he was raised in a Greek-speaking milieu (which language would have been his first tongue), and Christianity rudely intruded into his life to interrupt it forever. In his writings the Greek words he uses are to be construed not necessarily in their native meanings, but in the special understandings which he attributed to them in enabling him to disseminate the gospel. Yet his outlook was neither analytic[12] nor 'partative',[13] but conclusively and consistently emphatic of the

[9] Johnson Aubrey, *The One and the Many in the Israelite Conception of God*, Cardiff: University of Wales Press 1961, 1–2.

[10] Johnson 1961, 8; Wheeler-Robinson H, *Corporate Personality in Ancient Israel*, Edinburgh: Clark 1981; Num 21: 4 'And [Israel] journeyed from Mount Hor . . . and נפש-העם became impatient on the way'. The collective noun for the people (body) of Israel is singular. Such a view, however, has been contested by Rogerson, JW, *J Theol Stud* 21 (NS): 1–16, 1970. And see Cyril Rodd's introduction to Wheeler-Robinson 1981, 1–14.

[11] Stacey David, *The Pauline View of Man, in Relation to its Judaic and Hellenistic Background*, London: Macmillan 1956, 26–27.

[12] Stacey 1956, 222.

[13] Dunn James DG, *The Theology of Paul the Apostle*, Edinburgh: Clark 1998, 54.

unitary nature of mankind, thus reflecting the underlying Semitic cast of his mind. As a Jew, and a proud Benjamite who had excelled in his studies,[14] Paul's thinking was centred on God, not on man *qua* man in reflecting the prevailing Hellenistic temperament. Having discovered a new view of God on the Damascus road, his subsequent task was to articulate that recently acquired perception of God in Christ as determinative, in part, of his future anthropological understanding of the human person.

$\Sigma \acute{a} \rho \xi$ and $\sigma \hat{\omega} \mu a$ are both employed by him, over a wide spectrum, to refer to the whole person: $\sigma \hat{\omega} \mu a$ has no immediate Hebrew correlate, while $\sigma \acute{a} \rho \xi$ does not necessarily equate to flesh or נֶפֶשׁ. While $\sigma \hat{\omega} \mu a$ can refer to self, bodiliness and relationality (or corporateness, as in 'the Body of Christ'), $\sigma \acute{a} \rho \xi$ denotes the weakness of the natural person, while connoting its propensity to temptation and mortality. According to Dunn[15] $\sigma \hat{\omega} \mu a$ refers to a person in the world while $\sigma \acute{a} \rho \xi$ is more suggestive of a person belonging to the world. The next pairing of difficult words involves $\psi v \chi \acute{\eta}$ and $\pi v \epsilon \hat{v} \mu a$. Paul uses the former on thirteen occasions compared with 146 occasions for the latter.[16] For Paul, $\psi v \chi \acute{\eta}$, is equivalent to נֶפֶשׁ (OT) and $\psi v \chi \acute{\eta}$ (LXX). Although $\psi v \chi \acute{\eta}$ may be construed as 'immortal soul' if read in a Platonic sense, it seems more likely that Paul's concern was in expressing the reciprocal interplay between humankind's, and God's, spirit.[17] Hence, his emphatic usage of $\pi v \epsilon \hat{v} \mu a$ that underpins the apostle's determined movement away from any concept of 'soul' as separable from body and the ideology pertaining to immortality. Thus $\sigma \hat{\omega} \mu a$ $\pi v \epsilon v \mu a \tau \iota \kappa \acute{o} v$ is a Godly spirit-imbued person, while $\sigma \hat{\omega} \mu a$ $\psi v \chi \iota \kappa \acute{o} v$ is a this-worldly engaged individual.[18]

In Paul's anthropology (following Dunn's analysis), living beings reflect embodied and relational ($\sigma \hat{\omega} \mu a$) attributes with the quality of judgement and discernment[19] as part of mind ($v o \hat{v} \varsigma$) with a natural tendency towards the spirit of God ($\pi v \epsilon \hat{v} \mu a$) as opposed to non-spirituality ($\psi v \chi \acute{\eta}$), but endowed with a fleshly body ($\sigma \acute{a} \rho \xi$) redolent of mankind's intrinsic frailties, open vulnerability to temptation, and ultimate demise through bodily corruption and death. So Paul's approach seems to be Hebraic rather that

---

[14] Rom 11: 1; Phil 3: 5–6; Gal 1: 14.

[15] Dunn 1998, 72–78.

[16] Stacey 1956, 145.

[17] Stacey 1956, 121; 1 Cor 6: 17—'But he that is united with the Lord is one with him in spirit' ($\check{\epsilon} v$ $\pi v \epsilon \hat{v} \mu \acute{a}$).

[18] Dunn 1998, 78; Dahl Murdoch E, *The Resurrection of the Body*, London: SCM Press 1962, 15.

[19] Stacey 1956, 199.

Hellenistic, recognizing 'that the terms body, spirit and soul are not different, separable faculties of man, but different ways of viewing the whole man'.[20]

The non-Pauline documents provide little material on anthropology, much as they present little on the topic of resurrection.[21] One suggestive reference to a dualistic concept is Matt 10: 28: 'Do not be afraid of those who kill the body (τὸ σῶμα) but cannot kill the soul (τὴν ψυχὴν). Rather, be afraid of the One who can destroy both soul and body (καὶ ψυχὴν καὶ σῶμα) in hell.' John Cooper[22] concludes that this pericope, in its talk of a body and a soul, cannot be referring to the same entity and therefore articulates dualistic thought-forms. Wright,[23] however, cautions against Platonistic readings: that is, the 'point of telling people not to be afraid of being killed is if there is an afterlife beyond bodily death'. Or, fear God if he does not resurrect you.[24]

Revelation 6: 9 also needs consideration in reference to the verse: 'I saw beneath the altar the souls (ψυχάς) slain on account of the word of God.' This, in direct parallel to Temple slaughterings, suggests that the martyrs' lifeblood was poured out, indicative of bodily death as the life force drained away (Deut 12: 23; Lev 17: 14), rather than discarnate 'souls' awaiting resurrection.[25] Despite such a brief review, I nevertheless conclude for the purposes of my theme that few references to a Hellenistic dualism are offered in the NT: rather, humankind continues to be regarded as a unitary construction of a fleshly body and an immortal soul. The difficulties begin in regard to resurrection—are we bodies or souls, and what persists and what perishes?

10.2. THE PERSON, DEATH, AND A FUTURE HOPE

Eschatology can easily become hostage to the somewhat mechanistic cate-chetical definition of the 'Last Things': death, judgement, heaven or hell, eternity. The late Professor Colin Gunton[26] has rightly complained of such a cramped and errant theology. Cramped because the view on offer is so

---

[20] Ladd, George Eldon, *A Theology of the New Testament*, Grand Rapids (MI): Eerdmans 1975, 457.

[21] Wright NT, *The Resurrection of the Son of God*, London: SPCK 2003, 401.

[22] Cooper 2000, 117.

[23] Wright 2003, 431.

[24] Cullman Oscar, Immortality of the Soul or Resurrection of the Body, in: Stendahl Krister (ed), *Immortality and Resurrection*, New York: Macmillan 1965, 27.

[25] De Silva Lynn, *The Problem of the Self in Buddhism and Christianity*, London: Macmillan 1979, 83, 168 n. 36.

[26] Gunton Colin, *The Christian Faith*, Oxford: Blackwell 2002, 157ff.

limited, and errant because although eschatology has a directional future, it starts not with death but surely with Jesus' proclamation of the Kingdom (Mark 1: 5, 13) as adumbrated in Jewish scripture as '*The Day of the Lord*' (Joel 2: 1ff). Both are eschatological, denotative of καιρός—a significant divine event anticipated, or imploding, into historic time, χρόνος. Much theology is weakened in isolating death from reference to resurrection, or implying eternal life effected through the agency of an immortal soul capable of penetrating the barrier of death.

10.2.a. Death: The Incompleteness of the Personal Project

We should take death seriously. Unfortunately, we inhabit a death-anaesthetized society in which the prospect of mortal finitude is air-brushed out of main-stream concerns—the commerce of private and communal living. Society has no apparent qualms about abortion,[27] while euthanasia may inexorably come to be an accepted, standard package for disposing of those no longer fit and healthy, their lives being now adjudged a burden on society and not worth prolonging. Moreover, for many in today's scientifically conditioned society, the secularists, humanists, reductionists and non-believers, death is the end of existence.

Eschatologically, death needs to be firmly grasped, confronted and taken more seriously. Death is surely 'not just the cracking of an outer shell of flesh so that the butterfly of an immortal soul may emerge'.[28] Thus, for some philosophers and theologians, to grapple with the meaning of death informs us about the true nature of personhood. For Paul Tillich, for instance, the limit of death is a key expression of the 'non-being' which threatens our being; it prompts a sense of self-transcendence, of belonging to that which is beyond finitude:

The fact that man is never satisfied with any stage of his finite development, the fact that nothing finite can hold him is indicative of the indissoluble relation of everything finite to being-itself. Being-itself manifests itself to the finite being in the infinite drive of the finite beyond itself.[29]

In his trilogy on God, Christ and Man, the late John Macquarrie picked up the notion of 'becoming' in the volume on mankind: *In Search of Humanity*. It is not just that we are human *beings*, but humans in process of *becoming*.

---

[27] For the EU, UK and USA, current abortion rates are in excess of 300,000 per annum.

[28] Fiddes Paul, *The Promised End*, Oxford: Blackwell 2000, 66: and see Pannenberg Wolfhart, *Systematic Theology* (vol 2), Edinburgh: Clark 1994, 181ff.

[29] Tillich Paul, *Systematic Theology*, London: SCM Xprint 1997, 1.191ff.

He envisages the sense of our human nature deriving from the Latin meaning to issue forth or to develop: 'Keeping and making humanity human' is not a tautology as if applied to cats or dogs.[30] But within that lifelong process of becoming is implied the incompleteness or unfinished aspect of the human project. In considering death, we see a reflection of the meaninglessness and failure that imposes itself upon life, thereby inevitably dogging much of human existence. Gunton, in considering the final enemy,[31] sees this incompleteness, or even failure, in life's accomplishments in the many published obituaries even of prominent men and women. He continues:

Certainly, every life is highly particular, bearing its achievements and failures in different ways. If eschatology is to bear upon the way in which we envisage our human particularity, it is especially relevant at this place, where we face not only the question of relative failure of those who die full of years and sometimes of honour, but also the lives of those who die apparently before their time, especially young children and young people. In that sense, it is death that defines the limits and so the eschatological reality of each human life.

In another context, John Zizioulas[32] describes death as 'the tragic "self-negation" of the natural hypostasis (body and personality) which in trying to affirm itself discovers that its nature has led it along a false path towards death'.

Taking death seriously means not only being alerted to the incompleteness of the human project, leading to hopes of completion beyond death, but reckoning with the decisive impact of death upon the human person which—according to the biblical witness—is an indivisible whole. In this connection, we notice that ECE literature curiously bears a thin, superficial reference to Christian theological perceptions of death and what might comprise the afterlife. It portrays immortality as a direct continuity of the person, and offers glimpses of a heaven-like realm and sight of individuals glossed with a quasi-divine status. Continuity of personhood is assumed to take the form of the escape of free consciousness from a physical brain which is purportedly undergoing its agonal death throes, or, in Sabom's estimation, as release of soul from corporeal bondage. Thus it is notable that most authors (Ring, Grey, Fenwick) are prepared to propose an immediate immortality, even if only momentarily sampled, envisioned as an escape of mind or soul from the body and onwards into the heavenly realm.

---

[30] Macquarrie John, *In Search of Humanity*, New York: Crossroad 1983, 1–3.
[31] Gunton 2002, 160.
[32] Zizioulas John, *Being as Communion*, Crestwood (NY): St Vladimir's Seminary Press 1993, 51.

It is difficult for us, as humans, to envisage ourselves as we shall be in the afterlife. Will our new 'being' be that of complete disembodiment, or is it likely that we will have similar bodies to the ones we now inhabit on earth? It is difficult to imagine ourselves being other than body and mind, or finding ourselves in a similar carbon-based habitat. So for the believer, the reality of eternity rests on faith and hope in the revelation that has been given to us through scripture and the reflections of the church upon it. It is part of the radical nature of death, a consequence of taking death seriously, to forbid us simply to extend our present experience of life. But, however unknowable it may be, the eschaton need not be envisaged as bleak or devoid of promise beyond our demise. One clue is offered by Macquarrie[33] as 'learning that love...loses itself by pouring itself out'. He continues by saying that any worthwhile account of our future destinies must be purged of all egocentricity. This purging, he explains, should not result in personal extinction or annihilation because that would violate the process of movement from *creation* to *reconciliation* and to *consummation*; it would also deny the generous expenditure of love on us by others, that has made us what we are. Rather, that which *is* should advance into yet further potentialities of being, that is of *becoming*, thus contributing to a more fully diversified and complete unity— one more valuable than its predecessor. The end, a commonwealth of love, would comprise free, responsible beings united in love. And that is only achievable for its existents with the preservation of some kind of identity and their being graced through and by the Creator.

Although there is no necessary parallel between Jesus' death and resurrection and our own destiny, the event is the basis of the hope which dashes the materialist's view that death signifies the end of all corporeal, earthbound existence. There is no doubt that, for Christians, Jesus' resurrection is a special and unique eschatological case, but it can still be foundational and catalytic for personal resurrectional faith and (credal) belief. For these reasons, Jesus' resurrection must be carefully considered: it is to this subject that we now turn.

10.2.b. Jesus' Resurrection as Proleptic Sign

Jesus' resurrection does matter: first, for belief in Christ, and secondly, because of our own future destinies. Thus Paul writes: 'For if the dead are not raised, then Christ is not raised. And if Christ is not raised, your faith is worthless, and you are still in your sins' (1 Cor 15: 16–17). That is a radical

---

[33] Macquarrie John, *Principles of Christian Theology*, London: SCM Press 1966, 321ff.

critique of Christian faith, a critique requiring a demanding analysis if the basis of a resurrection of the dead is to be firmly undergirded.

Jesus' resurrection does matter,[34] not because it shows that God has the relevant power, or that it provides grounds for the afterlife, or that it represents Jesus' exaltation to God's right hand on high, or that it manifests a singular 'kairos-event'—an eschatological sign that the 'End-Time' is upon us—or even because it was the 'Son of God' who was raised. These interpretations of the resurrection are incomplete without an aspect that John Barton finds the most telling: it is the vindication of Jesus' supreme and absolute moral goodness, as man *qua* Man, that so pointedly avoids the entire episode dissolving into folksy mythology (of which we have seen some hints and traces above). Jesus is very God of very God, but incarnately fashioned into the perfection of a human person on earth. That is the key element so acutely expressed by John Austin Baker[35] in *The Foolishness of God*:

if Herod the great had risen from the dead [that would indicate] a God who ratified monstrosity [but] could never satisfy us as a source of goodness. Jesus' vindication alone supplies the crucial testimony.

The preceding considerations point to significant aspects of Jesus' resurrection—salvific, miraculous, eschatological and so on. But there is one further, crucial aspect of the gospel narratives on which Barton puts his finger: the demonstrable continuity between the earthly Jesus and the risen Christ, as paradigmatically revealed 'most heart-stoppingly in the story of the walk to Emmaus (Lk 24: 13–35) . . . the recognition of the stranger as the Jesus already known'.[36] This, and the other appearance stories, are of great importance in that Jesus was only recognized after performing a sign—his call by name to Mary in the garden, the breaking of bread in a travellers' inn, the public exhibition of his wounds—thereby linking him to the former Jesus known to his circle in Galilee. Jesus' 'resurrection body' was undoubtedly changed, different, and not immediately recognized for what it was. In the synoptic stories this changed body is expressed by its appearing and disappearing through walls and locked doors. Whatever the true nature or essence of Jesus' resurrection body, it necessarily had to be recognizable and so viewable by the disciples.

[34] Barton John, Why Does the Resurrection of Christ Matter? in: Barton S and Stanton G (eds), *Resurrection*, London: SPCK 1994, 108.

[35] Baker John A, *The Foolishness of God*, London: Darton, Longman & Todd 1970.

[36] Barton 1994, 113; and see Williams Rowan, *Resurrection: Interpreting the Easter Gospel*, London: Darton, Longman & Todd 1982, 83.

Now, dispute arises as to how that visibility came about.[37] If one rejects the view that the belief about Jesus' resurrection was already implanted in the minds of the disciples and others, on grounds that question how that kind of belief could have originated, two remaining possibilities are left. Either they were true sightings, or they were hallucinatory. It is the latter possibility which I now wish to consider further. And so, in the context of the theological implications of extra-corporeal phenomenology which is our present interest, we turn to current perceptions of the resurrection of Jesus as considered by Professor Paul Badham, and later to the implications of this for the nature of persons in general.

Badham is very sceptical about the empty tomb narratives since Paul's account (1 Cor 15) fails to mention this detail. In response we should observe that because Paul[38] was reacting to questions posed by the Corinthians around 53–54 CE, twenty years or more after the event, reference to the tomb may no longer have been a necessary or, indeed, immediately relevant part of his answers to this fractious community. Secondly, Professor Badham mentions that the gospel reports are internally incoherent, and so lack the kind of uniformity suggestive of true historicity, rather than a mythology concocted later on by the Christian communities reflecting on what could have transpired. He sides[39] with Lampe, who regards the prominent role played by the angels as inimical to acceptable valid, historical testimony.

Thirdly, Badham claims that the resurrection appearances were not objectively real, but were projected onto the observers as 'veridical hallucinations' (although this term seems obscure, as J. Muddiman points out[40]) by means of telepathic communication from Christ's risen soul. Much is made of the

---

[37] Muddiman John, 'I Believe in the Resurrection of the Body', in: Barton S and Stanton G (eds), *Resurrection*, London: SPCK 1994, 133.

[38] Barrett CK, *The First Epistle to the Corinthians*, London: Black 1992, 5. That Paul's mentioning of the empty tomb would have been redundant, see Borg MJ and Wright NT (eds), *The Meaning of Jesus*, San Francisco: Harper 1999, 119. It is of interest to refer to the imaginative reconstruction by Richard Hays of 1 Cor 7 in which the supposed Corinthian questions and Pauline responses are interwoven: the warning here, maybe, is not to read too much into a one-sided conversational exchange: see his *The Moral Vision of the New Testament*, Edinburgh: Clark 1997, 47.

[39] Badham 1976, 33ff, esp 37–38; idem, The Meaning of the Resurrection of Jesus, in: Avis Paul (ed), *The Resurrection of Jesus Christ*, London: Darton, Longman & Todd 1993, 32; Lampe GWH, Easter, in: Lampe GWH and MacKinnon DM, *The Resurrection*, London: Mowbray 1967, 46ff. But see Williams Rowan, Between the Cherubim: The Empty Tomb and the Empty Throne, in: D'Costa G (ed), *Resurrection Reconsidered*, Oxford: Oneworld 1996, 87. Note also Sanders' trenchant remark that too much collusion among the gospel writers to produce uniform accounts would have been counter-productive, see his *The Historical Figure of Jesus*, London: Penguin 1995, 280.

[40] Muddiman 1994, 133, including reference to other theories.

aorist passive ὤφθη,[41] as a deponent, to indicate a spiritual (non-retinal) receptivity of the appearances. That is, Christ let himself *be* seen, rather than *was* physically seen. These effects, he says, parallel Paul's experience on the Damascus road, grammatically and experientially.[42] But, according to the Gospel account, did Mary not objectively see Jesus after recognizing him only after his second call to her in the garden on that disturbing Sunday morning? Can it possibly be that the disciples, according to Luke, only saw an externally imposed hallucinatory glimpse of the risen Jesus displaying his crucifixion wounds? Here, Jesus is portrayed as reassuring his followers that earthbound 'ghosts' lack real flesh and bones, and in doing so, provides a welcoming invitation to come, look and touch his hands and feet, almost imperceptibly overshadowed by the messianic 'I AM HE'.[43] And was it no more than a hallucinated spectre of Jesus which shimmered up the Emmaus road from Jerusalem in company with two of his followers, offering them on the way a deep account of the scriptural anticipations of his passion and resurrection, then to break bread before vanishing out of the back door? Whatever reality these gospel stories reflected, they most emphatically do not fit well with the idea of hallucinatory phenomena.

Indeed, the case that the post-resurrection appearances were caused by single or mass hallucinatory phenomena[44] is, to my mind, an unconvincing explanation. Was Jesus, for example, simply playing on the minds of these men, in circumstances when the future of 'Christianity' and of the church hung so critically on his resurrected appearances being perceived as truly veridical? Given the profundity of the occasion, we would think not. Moreover, in these stories, the identity between the 'appearances' and the Jesus known to his followers in Galilee seems to be crucial. By contrast, when people are apparently returned to an 'earthly presence' in a hallucination, they are recognized immediately, as for example, the chimaeras of recently dead relatives or spouses. I know of no evidence that it has been thought necessary for

---

[41] Marxen W, The Resurrection of Jesus as a Historical and Theological Problem, in: Moule CFD (ed), *The Significance of the Message of the Resurrection for Faith in Jesus Christ*, London: SCM Press 1968, 26; Carnley Peter, *The Structure of Resurrection Belief*, Oxford: Clarendon 1993, 206ff and 223ff; Badham, The Modernist Understanding of the Resurrection of Jesus Christ, in: *The Contemporary Challenge of Modernist Theology*, Cardiff: University of Wales Press 1998, 108; idem, The Meaning of Resurrection and Immortality, in: Badham Paul and Badham Linda, *Immortality or Extinction?* London: Macmillan 1982, 22.

[42] Is Badham somewhat bold to assert that ἐν ἐμοί (Gal 1: 16) can only denote a spiritual inwardness? Since ἐν is one of the most slippery prepositions to translate from the Greek, the implicit meaning could simply be 'in my case', or 'in my presence'.

[43] Luke 24: 39 ἴδετε τὰς χεῖράς μου καὶ τοὺς πόδας μου ὅτι ἐγώ εἰμι αὐτός: Ψηλαφήσατέ με καὶ ἴδετε ὅτι πνεῦμα σάρκα καὶ ὀστέα οὐκ ἔχει.

[44] Badham 1976, 30ff.

these hallucinatory persons to perform signs in order to secure recognition and linkage to their previous bodily existence. In other words, it is not usually the case that the person or persons 'seen' are required to perform signs in order to affirm their identity. For instance, after a close reading of the pertinent literature, it is clear that with near-death experiences the recognition of the dead, and even other 'heavenly persons', is thought to be both immediate, and certain. These are reasons why, on the basis of the material discussed above, I am more inclined to follow John Barton's view as against Badham's.

Finally, we might pick up the point made by Professor Badham regarding the confusional reportings of the resurrection in the gospels. For Barton,[45] on the contrary, this is the telling feature of authenticity—of non-collusion so as to present to the world a non-fabricated account. Beyond that kind of debate, another observation is highly relevant. CFD Moule[46] asks why such a 'medley' of biblical canonical writings should have assumed such importance, and answers that despite all the differences and varieties, there was a unity under-pinned by the firm conviction that the historical Jesus was, indeed, the Messiah and Lord. The question is whether a 'hallucinatory' appearance could have given rise to that conviction. Similarly, Martin Hengel remarks on how, historically, the term $\chi\rho\iota\sigma\tau\acute{o}\varsigma$ within 'an amazingly brief period (by ca. AD35–40)' had become synonymous with the Messiah and firmly linked with Jesus of Nazareth. He also notes the occurrence of other well-entrenched formulaic confessions that were assumed into the earliest Pauline epistles, and that may be collectively summarized as 'Christ suffered, was crucified and died for us, was buried, and raised by God on the third day'.[47]

The gospel accounts of the resurrection of Jesus are, then, the positive foundation of a Christian hope for life beyond death. Moreover, I have argued that, negatively, the stories offer no support for the idea that resurrection is a mere image for the survival of a soul, detached from the body, which might have powers of communication with other persons. It is, of course, just this kind of disembodied soul that is assumed by ECE literature.

10.2.c. Personal Hope for an Afterlife

What, then, is humankind's hope for an afterlife? The New Testament scholar Tom Wright[48] maintains that the hope of the afterlife is firmly embedded in

---

[45] Barton J, in Barton and Stanton 1994, 114.
[46] Moule CFD, *The Birth of the New Testament*, London: Black 1966, 9.
[47] Hengel Martin, in: *Studies in Early Christology*, Edinburgh: Clark 1995, 1–72.
[48] Wright NT, *The Resurrection of the Son of God*, London: SPCK 2003.

resurrection, and he insists on an understanding of resurrection which involves the whole person. Wright is critical of much modern writing in which resurrection is used as a synonym, simply, for the vaguer concept of life-after-death, thus aligning itself with the populist notion of 'dying and going straight to Heaven'[49]—an idea that characterizes some ECE reportage. Rather, he insists that resurrection is definable as 'life after "life after death"': that is, resurrection is what happens after bodily death has been succeeded by an interim period of 'death-as-a-state'. After this period, at what the New Testament calls the 'end-time', manifest by the coming of the Lord 'on the clouds', judgement will be effected, and, through the general resurrection people will be ultimately raised to a 'glorious spiritual body' with the establishment of God's Kingdom.[50] Above, we saw the early Hebraic notion of Sheol. But later, post-exilic Jewish expectations surrounding death did not remain so narrowly focused or underdeveloped. There was widely present in many Hebrew[51] and intertestamental apocalyptic[52] writings a progressive yearning both for the need for martyrs to receive justice (2 Macc 7: 9, 14; Dan 7: 14, 18) and for the ultimate restoration of Israel. This hope took the form of resurrection. As the Christian church evolved from its Judaic background, an additional caveat to the general scheme became necessary, in that Jesus' own resurrection demanded a new understanding and acceptance that he, uniquely and singly, had been raised ahead of the end-time by God from the tomb.[53] Later we are going to ask how we might give weight to these New Testament images in considering the hope we might have for the life of the human person beyond death.

10.3. PERSONHOOD, THE AFTERLIFE, AND THE SOUL

It is to theological exploration of the nature of the afterlife for humankind that our attention must now turn. In view of what has just been written, our future hopes do have a relationship to the resurrection of Jesus. That focus,

---

[49] Wright 2003, 3.
[50] Wolfson 1965, 63–73; Kelly JND, *Early Christian Doctrines*, London: Black 1968, 469–479; Cooper 2000, 7ff.
[51] Ezek 37: 1–14; Hos 6: 1–2; 13: 14; Isa 26: 19; 40: 5; 52: 3; Dan 12: 1–3; Pss 16: 10–11; 49: 15; 73: 23–28.
[52] I Enoch; 4Ezra 7:25–32; Test. 12 Patriarchs [T.Jud 25:1; T.Abr 20:14; T.Zeb 10:2]; 4Macc 18:23, in Charlesworth, James H, *The Old Testament Pseudepigrapha* (Vol 2), New York: Doubleday 1985.
[53] Wright 2003, 415; also 448, 551.

according to the gospel stories, is grounded on the visual experiences of seeing someone or something—a travelling companion, a gardener, bread lying broken on a tavern bench, the blood-caked, gouged-out muscle—leading to the dawning recognition that through such signs the sightings were of Jesus himself; this in turn prompted a synthesis of the pre-and post-resurrection data, including the predictions which had entirely escaped the comprehension of stumbling disciples at the time, followed by the final triumphant conclusion that Jesus had been for real, and, that they—the Apostles—would now be empowered by the Spirit to evangelize to the ends of the earth:

A meeting with Jesus who had been dead but was now alive could mean . . . that God has begun to raise the dead . . . that the Kingdom was in the here and now: winter was over and the spring arrived . . . the first sheaf of the harvest [עומר] had been reaped.[54]

With those signs of continuity between Christ's earthly and post-resurrection existence comes the hope of a similar continuity between our human life and that expected in the afterlife. Yet that continuity could be understood in different ways, summed up in two strands of belief within the Christian tradition: that is, continuity of personhood might be delivered through immortality of the soul, or it might be created anew in resurrection—or indeed there might be a combination of the two. The historical developments and evolution of beliefs in a soul are beyond the scope of this work. I therefore do not want to enter into a 'metaphysics of the soul', whether based on Plato's view of a substance capable of inhabiting successive bodies, on the Aristotelian entelechy which enlivens the flesh, or on Aquinas' appropriation of the latter as an ecclesial account of spiritual immortality.

Far more relevant to our theme are contemporary developments in which the soul is perceived in neuropsychological terms. Our discussion thus turns on these modern understandings of soul and the approaches employed in defence of the soul as agent of continuing existence into the hereafter.

10.3.a. The Evolution of a Modern Epistemology of 'Soul'

An account of soul could be made in terms of the emerging development of each person. That development begins *in utero* and continues throughout the earthly life. As we have seen from Macquarrie's approaches in *In Search of Humanity*, possibility and potential lie at the very foundations of each person's existence and lifetime evolution.[55] At birth (and from about the

[54] Barton 1994, 47.
[55] Macquarrie 1966, 257ff.

25th week of gestation,[56] probably even earlier) the human infant is conscious despite its marked cerebral immaturity. Consciousness seems to be basic: it is either present or not. The ensuing changes wrought upon that pre-existing, basic consciousness are manifested through the progressive acquisition by the brain of higher-order attributes, attributes dependent on its continued growth and the maturation of the neuronal networking, especially of expanding synaptic connectivity. The mental capacity of the neonate may hardly differ from that of a goldfish. The difference lies post-natally and beyond, during which the new human individual is subject to intensive training and prolonged conditioning through maternal, familial, societal and environmental influences. The development of mature mental capacity (or 'mind') and a fully grown brain requires at least one-quarter to one-fifth of expected life-expectancy. That could be viewed, biologically, as an extreme, costly evolutionary gamble: but within that gamble could be perceived possible divine intent.

The gradual emergence of an individual's mind entails possession of personal self-awareness, self-consciousness and the capacity for embarrassment (and its physiological correlate blushing), the ability to engage in abstract thought and logical reasoning, thus to initiate purposive aims and actions, and the use of language which permits the establishment of personal relationships without which any semblance of 'personhood', or human 'becoming', could never arise.[57] Moral reckoning serves to condition and thus modify personal and social behaviour while memory, both declarative (or knowing *that*) and procedural (or knowing *how*), serves to anchor the person historically and socially.

Self-awareness affords a certain understanding of person or 'I-ness' which subsumes one's sense of corporeality and body-image that, with the additional attributes of mind and the influence of time, creates an integral sense of personal uniqueness. Thus there is an introspective wholeness perceived to be complete, unified and exclusive for each individual. In addition to speech and language, other characteristics demarcate humans from animals. These include the realization of personal mortality, the anticipation of and planning for the future, asking questions about a life beyond death, as well as posing (as Zizioulas suggests[58]) the question 'Who am I?' Religious believers will want to add to this list the ability to behave spiritually in an apprehension of the divine and of other-worldly spheres. Other features considered by Warren

---

[56] Flower M, *J Med Philosoph* 19: 237–251, 1985.
[57] McFadyen Alistair, *The Call to Personhood*, Cambridge: Cambridge University Press 1990, 69ff.
[58] Zizioulas J, in Schwöbel and Gunton (eds) 1999, 33ff.

Brown[59] are a capacity for sin and guilt, acceptance of redemption, receipt of grace, and a life in the Spirit in the full recognition of God's revelation. The after-effects of experiencing an NDE, as we have seen, also shape the experient's search for meaning in life and the hereafter.

Various writers, working from theologically based perspectives,[60] have suggested that soul approximates to the attributes of 'personality' for each individual. By personality, I understand this to comprise the totality of mind, together with the additional characteristics of the individual's disposition, considered as conscientiousness, openness to other opinion, demeanour, degree of intro-/extraversion and the expression of stability or lability of affect, determination and drive, physical vitality, and spiritual orientation. On this construction, soul would be conceived as an emergent property of cerebral activity and of the outcome of personal becoming in relationship with other humans; 'soul' in this sense can be conditioned by divine grace through sacramental action in communion with the divine. The implication is that at death, the soul, being thus defined as derived biologically and socially, would cease unless—in some way—salvaged by God. Death remains a certain, and radical, disjunction between earthbound existence and any eventuality of a future existence.

10.3.b. Immortality Viewed as a Function of Soul

The propensity to be aware of, and to reflect upon life, one's bodily mortality, who one is, and the possibility of a future eternal life, raises questions about whether the soul is a realistic model upon which to predicate a potential locus of immortality. Here, again, I shall be considering the thoughts of Professor Badham in particular, not as a special target, but because his writings over many years have consistently linked an understanding of the immortality of the soul to his acceptance of the validity of the experiential phenomenology of extra-corporeal events, and other paranormal and psychical happenings. Therefore, his views have a special relevance to the theme of this book and need to be considered. Recognizing the obvious and passionate sincerity with which he writes, we can usefully analyse his major claims. In terms of

[59] Brown Warren S, Cognitive Contributions to Soul, in: Brown W, Murphy N, Malony HN (eds), *Whatever Happened to the Soul?* Minneapolis: Fortress 1998, 101; and see Pannenberg Wolfhart, *Anthropology in Theological Perspective*, London: Clark 2004, 27, 48, 241.

[60] Macquarrie 1966, 64–6; Hanson Anthony and Hanson Richard, *Reasonable Belief*, Oxford: Oxford University Press 1981, 201; Swinburne Richard, *The Evolution of the Soul*, Oxford: Oxford University Press 1997, 161, 262; Ward Keith, *In Defence of the Soul*, Oxford: Oneworld 1998, 134; Jeeves Malcolm, *Mind Fields*, Leicester: Apollos 1994, 132ff.

immortality, the thrust of his argument is that the idea of soul is the only logical construct capable of guaranteeing continuity of personhood into the afterlife. This conviction (as we noted above) is predicated on his profound scepticism about the empty tomb narratives, the physical reality of Jesus' post-resurrection appearances, and credal professions of a general resurrection of the flesh or body.

Professor Badham continues that 'any adequate possibility of continued personal identity—and the sine qua non for any new life—continues to require continuity of my soul through death'.[61] But what of the soul and its origins? He continues: 'It is an emergent property [of brain] that comes into existence in the course of life',[62] and defers to the Roman Catechism:[63] 'that every soul is created immediately by God—it is not produced by the parents—also that it is immortal: it does not perish when it separates from the body at death, and will be reunited with the body at the final Resurrection'. That defines 'when?' (at conception) and 'how?' (by God) but does not explain 'what?' (its structure, location, function, 'essence'). Here Badham seems to rely not on the Catechism but on Richard Swinburne and Keith Ward.[64] The implication from their writings is that the soul equates to each individual's personality and is intimately dependent on the brain. Further, it is striking that neither Badham, Swinburne nor Ward are prepared to assert dogmatically that this biological soul (= 'personality') can survive the *death of its brain*. A wavering doubt remains whether the soul in its vehicular role provides, or is guarantor of, a future afterlife. Of course, there can be no certainty and the subjunctives and optatives employed by them indicate that dilemma.

So we find Badham writing that: 'Throughout life [the soul] interacts with the body, but *in principle* it is separable from it, and *perhaps* at death separation *can* occur.'[65] Swinburne asserts that: 'The soul may be said to function *when* it has conscious episodes (sensations, thoughts, or purposings) [which] *depend* on the operation of the brain.'[66] Ward concurs:

When the brain reaches a certain stage of complexity the power of conceptual thought, of reasoning and thinking begins to exist; and that is when the rational

[61] Badham Paul, *The Contemporary Challenge of Modernist Theology*, Cardiff: University of Wales Press 1998, 122.

[62] Ibid, 123.

[63] *Catechism of the Catholic Church*, London: Chapman 1994, 83.

[64] Badham 1998, 123.

[65] Badham 1998, 123, my italics.

[66] Swinburne 1997, 174ff, my italics.

soul begins to be. This is known through introspection. It is *separable* from the body and *could exist* in an imperfect way without it.[67]

Unlike Badham, Swinburne rejects parapsychological explanations—of reincarnation, of spiritualism, or of ECE (OBE or NDE) phenomenology—as pointers of immortality.[68] Indeed, Swinburne rightly points out that in the case of neither OBE nor NDE has it been shown that the brain was *not* working. What becomes evident from such case reports is that the soul can function 'in the absence of normal sensory input'. I should not wish to dissociate myself from that claim. Furthermore, Swinburne rejects the dualist claim that a soul could survive on its own—'under its own steam'—by virtue of its having an immortal nature. Thirdly, however, Swinburne knows of no psychophysical law which, of necessity, *requires* a brain or some other 'material system' for the functioning of a soul. 'There are no natural laws which dictate what will happen to the soul after death.' Thus having rejected these three possibilities, Swinburne can only seek refuge in a metaphysical process through which the soul could be salvaged by something beyond the natural order—that is, God. Thus, while in its earthly existence the soul is 'plugged into' the brain as its source of power, it could be 'plugged into' an alternative, non-neural source of power equivalent to a physical brain, he affirms, or the power could even be supplied by God himself, at least for a period. Either process, we notice, rules out the possibility of any intrinsic or inherent immortality.

We may certainly agree that post-mortem survival is in God's hands, and effected entirely by God's own actions and intentions. But the possibility that this intention might include the soul's deriving its power-supply directly from God portrays the soul as a 'thing' that can be 'plugged into' a power source, and which survives death intact, ready to be so attached. That surely is not what a soul is. My definition of soul rests on the evolving personality of the subject; while 'soul' is evidently more than mere body or brain, it is an evolving outcome encompassing not only mind and physique, but also important features such as demeanour, vitality, presence, conscientiousness, and so on.

For Badham, belief in a soul which is separable from the body rests on four criteria: rational thought, paranormal events, near-death experiences, and spiritual encounters with God.[69] Neither cognitive activity nor experience of the divine can, however, sufficiently underpin the occurrence of an immortal

---

[67] Ward 1998, 56, 107, 136, 145, 148, my italics.
[68] Swinburne 1997, 301–310.
[69] Badham 1998, 123–125.

soul: his chief evidential focus rests on telepathy and out-of-body experiences. From the evidence adduced in my Chapters 3–7 above, that reliance may, in fact, be extremely precarious, if not totally uncertain. We should observe the warning flag. In addition, I have already pointed out that OBE and NDE are separate neurophysiological constructs arising out of sick brains. Can Badham's certainty of the soul as the *unitary* agential representative of the whole person in immortality, rest on such an uncertain and experientially divided evidential base?

We do not, in fact, have firm grounds for believing that the soul is immortal or that it is the undoubted agent which guarantees continuity of personal life into the afterlife. Indeed, if the soul is the outcome of cerebral and bodily function, then the kind of separatist dualism implied in an immortal soul lacks conviction, since it seems to undermine the unity of person as a tight psychophysical unit of beliefs, emotions, action and intentions. Furthermore, it is difficult to see how communication between disembodied souls and between those souls and God might be effected. Does an answer lie in telepathy—as strongly envisioned by Badham based on his understanding of Jesus' appearances to the disciples? Or in the kind of dream-world envisioned by Price[70] as subconscious imagery accompanied by telepathic interpersonal communication? Given that the soul is the outcome of both cerebral and bodily function, it is hard to conceive how a physically based soul—the 'emergent property of brain and body'—could continue functioning without corporeality and neurophysiological process, and in the absence of those basal structural features (voice, vision, audition, memory) without which the means for personal interaction, recognition and society are inconceivable.

10.4. PERSONHOOD, THE AFTERLIFE, AND THE RESURRECTION OF THE BODY

10.4.a. The Person, the Afterlife, and Resurrection

'I believe in the resurrection of the body and the life of the world to come'. In support of his insistence on the soul being the agent of personal survival into the afterlife, Professor Badham finds belief in a general resurrection at an end-time totally incomprehensible, and inconsistent with modern cosmological

---

[70] Price HH, Survival and the Idea of 'Another World', in: Smythies JR (ed), *Brain and Mind*, London: Routledge & Kegan Paul 1965, 1–24.

theory.[71] He lampoons the idea of congregations getting to their feet and declaring, literally: 'I look for the standing-up-again of the corpses'.[72] Maybe, but if we cast our minds back to the era in which these words were originally written, it would not in the least have seemed strange. Getting out of bed each day after waking in order to clear the same space for daily living would have provided a most admirable way in which to speak of resurrection—as a new rising to life from 'sleep'.

Professor Badham views such a credal declaration to be a

ruthlessly physical doctrine [which has dominated] Christian thinking from the 2nd– 17th Centuries, based on the deliberate understanding that Jesus' resurrection body was just a resuscitated corpse [thus] supersed[ing] the original understanding (like St Paul) of a spiritual event.[73]

Next he suggests that a general resurrection is an absurdity. Heaven is not above the clouds nor the crystal spheres, an ancient view which modern cosmology has demonstrated to be erroneous. So, could we be looking (with John Hick) for another universe, indeed multiple earth-like planets so many light years away thus to be rendered immune from future daytrippers coming via spaceship from earth?[74] But that presupposes a new life that is carbon-based: we do not know that. It presupposes another universe identical in being nuclear-powered by stars as sources of energy and carbon: but we really do not know that either. Our current universe, whether or not of a recurrent cycle, is a vast heat engine subject to the Second Law of Thermody-namics: it will eventually die down, despite occasional chaotic eruptions leading to other complex higher-order systems. It therefore seems unlikely that the New Creation is to based on an identical blueprint to the one we are accustomed to. A general resurrection could not take place on earth nor in some other locus of the universe as currently conceived. Moreover, if we all have something closely akin to earthly bodies a great deal of space will be needed, for there will be billions upon billions of individuals needing imme-diate accommodation. But will the New Creation be of the space-time type to which we are now accustomed? That is a question we really cannot answer.

These considerations appear to support Badham's scepticism. But we need not give up the image of 'resurrection' so easily. That life in the hereafter, in response to Sadducean taunts, will be radically different is indicated by the gospel's response given by Jesus (Matt 22: 23–32). There will be no marriage,

---

[71] Badham 1998, 101ff.
[72] Badham 1998, 113.
[73] Badham 1998, 113.
[74] Badham 1976, 78–79.

nor the implied sexuality beyond the grave. Whatever that gospel exchange means, we can assume that life in the hereafter will not be an exact re-run of earth-like corporeality beyond death. Life as we know it on earth cannot go on for ever: death is final. Resurrection faith means, as Brian Hebblethwaite suggests, 'a new creation, receipt of a new incorruptible "body", a taking up into a "World" that is entirely new, unambiguous and imperishable, and in which the community of those raised to be in Christ will find an everlasting home'.[75] It emphasizes that it is God who is, and will be, the source of that future life, although we hardly have a glimmer of insight into how our 'selves' will be ultimately reconfigured in the new creation: we really do not know.

A further approach to resurrection, seen from a literary perspective, is articulated by Paul Fiddes.[76] Having reminded us that we must take death seriously, he continues by elucidating how we can account for personal identity in the afterlife. Of relevance here is his appeal to community within the Body of Christ. Fiddes envisions an eschatologically corporate, interpersonal life in non-competitive sharing in, and with, one another. We may add that this is precisely the often neglected action of the risen Christ, his Body evoking the spiritual locus of the believing community:[77] 'For we were all baptized by one Spirit into one body' (1 Cor 12: 13). This is not a suprapersonal collective, but a specific personal organism.[78] We each contribute an executive role to its functions[79] and belong eucharistically in sharing the one bread which is its earthly manifestation ('we who are many are one body because we share of the one loaf': 1 Cor 10: 17; 'Therefore, whoever eats the bread . . .': 1 Cor 11: 27–29). Paul, in particular, maintains the Hebrew fluidity of understanding between the person and the collective group. Therefore, if resurrection is centred in, and on, Christ 'then there can be no separate resurrection bodies existing on their own: we shall be inseparable from the inclusive resurrection of Christ, which has cosmic scope'.[80]

This confronts head-on the view that afterlife will just be another sequential chapter in the continuing saga of life on earth. Such is an earthly oriented view frequently depicted throughout the ECE narrative collective. Death is a radical disruption to that imagined continuity. We must take death seriously;

---

[75] Hebblethwaite Brian, *The Essence of Christianity: A Fresh Look at the Nicene Creed*, London: SPCK 1996, 189–190.

[76] *The Promised End: Eschatology in Theology and Literature*, Oxford: Blackwell 2000, 53ff, 76ff.

[77] 'But he who unites himself with the Lord is one with him in the Spirit' (1 Cor 6: 17); 'Now you are the body of Christ and each one of you is part of it' (1 Cor 12: 27).

[78] This is Christ's risen σῶμα its metaphorical force emphasized by Robinson 1957, 50–51.

[79] 1 Cor 12: 12–26.

[80] Fiddes 2000, 98.

there will be no stoking of old embers; death is a radical break between now and the hereafter.

Furthermore, such an approach reverses the trend which sees translation into the afterlife from a very human and individualistic perspective, rather than the more realistic view that resurrection comes entirely from God. Christians believe that God has secured our salvation through the Son's death and resurrection. God is thus the object of our hope for any continuity of identity after death. God is our salvation through our faith, not abilities or achievements. God alone can justify us and preserve us for who we are. God therefore will recreate us when renewing the entire cosmos. That New Creation, of us and of the universe, will be in his hands alone, through his grace alone. Resurrection means renewal of the physical environment as well as the universal spiritual consciousness. This entails 'a bringing of truth to light, an eschatological judgement, which cannot take place as each individual dies'.[81] By contrast, in the ECE mythology a so-called judgement is sometimes alleged to occur on the point of presumed death, which is what I now wish briefly to examine.

10.4.b. On Judgement

The theme of judgement has received scant coverage in the assessment of NDE phenomenology, relative to other aspects. But Moody, for instance, writes that:[82]

Again and again, my near-death subjects have described to me a panoramic, wrap-around, full-color, three-dimensional vision of the events of their lives . . . [for some,] major events . . . [for] others, . . . every single thing they had ever done or thought . . . the good things and all the bad . . . instantaneously . . . frequently in the presence of a 'being of light' whom some Christians have identified with Christ [who asked], 'What have you done with your life?' . . . [a]t this point . . . a kind of judgement took place: when people saw selfish acts they felt extremely repentant [and] when gazing upon those events in which they had shown love or kindness they felt satisfaction . . . the judgement came from within the individual being judged.

This is how respondents expressed the event:

everything in my life just went by for review . . . I was really very, very ashamed of a lot of the things that I experienced . . . that the light was showing me what was wrong, what I did wrong. And it was real . . . It was like there was a judgement being

---

[81] Fiddes 2000, 99.
[82] Moody 1977, 31–35.

made ... [then] ... the light became dimmer and there was a conversation—but in thoughts ... it showed me not only what I had done but even how what I had done had affected other people.

Or:

there was instant communication. My entire life was like that [snapping fingers] ... things that, I mean, He, God knew. Right off the bat. I felt ashamed, I was ashamed of certain things ... that were wrong: these things just came back. I was encompassed by the greatest feeling of love ... instant communication.[83]

It should be observed that for other authors, the 'life review' of many of their subjects lacked judgemental character. The reviews varied from vivid to meagre recollections of occasional historical moments. Further, events characterized by some kind of judgement were personally idiosyncratic, being experienced by 25%,[84] 15%,[85] and 2%[86] of the respective samples analysed. Therefore, 'judgement' is by no means an expected aspect of ECE phenomenology: indeed, it is a minimalist aspect of the entire recorded oeuvre of that phenomenon.

Judgement, theologically, entails far more than the brief personal encounter characterized by the NDE. Christian faith envisages a judgement of the nations and of the cosmos.[87] Moreover, personal judgement cannot always be purely individualistic, since individuals are in relation to others. We are free people (within certain physical, legal and social constraints), we can make choices, live and learn to regret those choices and past actions: so can peoples, kings, rulers and politicians. Thus groupings become of serious eschatological relevance and importance.[88]

The New Testament declares that humankind has already been judged in the event of the cross, with Jesus as the representative of all humanity; in Christ, human beings can pass 'from death to life' here and now (Rom 8: 1–4; 1 John 3: 14). The judgement that remains is a revelation of the truth about our lives which provokes repentance and has a transforming impact on those who receive it. So the Apostle Paul describes the unworthy work, and not the worker as being consumed with fire (1 Cor 3: 15). Judgement will be an ongoing process during life, and the final judgement (as a cosmic event rather than an individual trial after death) will result in transformation, a

---

[83] Grey 1985, 82.
[84] Ring 1980, 67.
[85] Fenwick and Fenwick 1998, 113.
[86] Sabom 1982, 50.
[87] Macquarrie 1996, 315; Gunton 2002, 161ff.
[88] Gunton 2002, 167.

resurrection into a new body, as Christ's earthly body was likewise transformed into another type of body: 'We shall all be changed . . . ' (1 Cor 15: 51–52). In reported ECE sequences judgement is simply an individualistic event that happens after a supposed arrival in heaven.

There are, then, several features of NDE testimony which militate against an authentic eschatology, compared with the Christian theological account. The narratives reveal subjects in a passive role; there is a noticeable absence of expressed repentance or penance; and there is no implied resurrectional transformation whatsoever. In a few cases there is a sense of remorse, but this is invariably taken as heralding the return of conscious-awareness, since the 'review of life' often coincides with the imminence of the return to earth, and the pressing need to shoulder one's responsibilities to family and workplace again. The latter, as noted above (Chapter 5), reflects the burgeoning influence of conscious-awareness on the subject's mentation, and with it, the increasing intrusion of moral sensibility. In accord with this view of reviving consciousness, I pointed out the reluctance of individuals, at this late-phase stage in the NDE, to traverse physical barriers which they seem to have had no difficulty in traversing as the initial early-phase escape from body was commencing. I am therefore of the opinion that the component of 'life review and judgement' in NDE, in the exceptionally few people in which it occurs, is not a paradigmatic depiction of any realistic Christian eschatology.

10.5. ECE AND AFTERLIFE: NOT AN ENLIGHTENING ESCHATOLOGICAL PARADIGM

Can the narrative phenomenologies of ECE, reviewed throughout Chapters 3–7, constitute legitimate grounds for supporting belief in life after death? Do these so-called extra-corporeal phenomena provide supporting evidence for an immortal soul, that a mental life is possible beyond death without a functioning brain, and do they underpin the Christian construal of eschatology? These are important theological questions in light of the progressive incursion into the wider public consciousness of the realms of 'paranormal' and 'psychical' happenings. To ask these questions is my aim for this chapter and the two chapters following.

Central to any understanding of these problems is the establishment of an anthropology based on perceptions biblical and modern. The former is holistic but aligns with modern scientific and philosophical understandings which envision persons as tightly bound psychophysical units of body, brain and mind. Emergent as a property of that biological unity is 'soul', that is, the psychophysical ontology of 'personality'. The Platonic and Cartesian notions of soul as completely separable from corporeality are inconsistent with current neurophysiological opinion and from much current philosophy, and philosophical opinion, and widely doubted as representing an agent guaranteeing immortality.[89] Throughout much of (post-medieval) Christian history there have been arguments and counter-arguments concerning the status of soul and its relation to a future resurrection of the body of which we should be aware,[90] but that is not my concern here.

Next, we need to consider death. My assertion, in line with Fiddes, Muddiman and Macquarrie, is that death is essentially a radical rupturing between earthly life and the hereafter. From what I have written above, two consequences follow. First, that if 'soul' is an emergent property of body and brain, then, by its nature, it cannot be deemed to be immortal, escaping the impact of death. Despite that, there are important attempts arguing that the biologically determined soul in its entirety could, through the will and power of God, survive death. Or, it has been suggested[91] that it is at least a 'logical possibility' that this could come about. Such views suggest simply the carrying over of the same entity, in its entirety, into the New Creation and lay the *emphasis* on continuity rather than look for a *sufficient* continuity required for identity. That is a view which I take to be incorrect, taking seriously the Pauline hope that 'we shall all be changed'. For the same reason, other ideas from respectable voices proposing models of either teletransportation or the fashioning of replicas[92] fail to offer new insights into how we shall be reconfigured in the new creation. These models are intensely anthropomorphic, mechanistic, and entirely devoid of the corporate theme of resurrectional life within the Body of Christ and the Triune Godhead.

[89] Murphy Nancey, *Bodies and Souls, or Spirited Bodies?* Cambridge: Cambridge University Press 2006, 39; Brown W, Murphy N, Malony H (eds), *Whatever Happened to the Soul?* Minneapolis: Fortress 1998; Pannenberg 1994, 2.194.

[90] Burns NT, Christian Mortalism from Tyndale to Milton, Cambridge: Harvard University Press 1972; Vidal Fernando, Critical Inquiry 28: 930–974, 2002. I acknowledge Professor John Brooke for these various insights.

[91] I am glad to see that both an agnostic and a Christian philosopher bluntly reject the plausibility of 'logical possibility' as a coherent, decisive form of argument. See Nielsen Kai, in Davis 1989, 18; Professor John Cottingham almost sneers at the 'weasel-phrase . . . that delights in quibbling refutation rather than offering serious alternatives', in *The Spiritual Dimension*, Cambridge: Cambridge University Press 2005, 148.

[92] Indeed, John Knox in his article 'Can the Self Survive the Death of its Mind?' (*Rel Stud* 5: 85–97, 1969) demolished the viability of the replica model: if I suffered complete amnesia yet saw my twin brother attempting to deputize for me, I should immediately recognize the deception (p. 90).

An alternative view that psychical or parapsychologically based mechanisms afford some evidence for a soul have been firmly rebutted by the neuroscientific data offered here in earlier chapters. That consciousness appears to reside in an out-of-body mirage does not confirm the existence of a soul, its immortality, or its ability to spontaneously evade the confines of corporeality. That position is even further undermined by heautoscopic phenomenology, during which consciousness rapidly oscillates between subjects and their illusory chimaeras. Such happenings hardly accord with catechismal definitions of a soul which, in its release from corporeal bondage, flies back to its creator God. Current neurophysiological research has conclusively shown these experiences to result from aberrant functioning of the mechanisms underpinning ego-/paracentric body space and body-image.

By contrast, the image of resurrection points to a re-creation of ourselves, since death is the end of the corporeal finitude we know. In today's climate, much opinion is resolutely against the concept of a soul as a divinely implanted essence, and against its putative role in effecting the transmission of personal continuity into the afterlife. If death is totally irrevocable and a radical disruption of our physical lives and activities, then a continued existence in the afterlife demands some kind of re-creation of us in the world to come. Further corollaries follow from another dimly perceived but important fact: the widespread occurrence of dementia, foetal and infant deaths, and severely handicapped children for whom the possibility of either achieving, or retaining a full personality and truly mature relational interactions with others is beyond any possible reach. These 'souls', discarnate, would be gravely dysfunctional and incapable of any sensible activity in the afterlife. Likewise others whose lives had been marred by many of life's catastrophes might find truer meaning and recompense in a re-created body within the Godhead.

All hope of Christian aspiration to a resurrected existence in the hereafter is ineradicably predicated on Jesus Christ raised from the dead and, most important, on his post-resurrectional appearances to the disciples. Because of its centrality to understandings of resurrection faith and to the interpretation of ECE phenomenology, I have dealt with this at length. Problems, however, arise when debates about the resurrection take a narrow (or out-of-context) focus only on the empty tomb and the appearances. Such a restricted view fails to encompass the fullest cosmic dimensions of the understanding of resurrection, resulting in a certain 'thinness' of interpretation. As Wolfhart Pannenberg has shown, a more robust, thorough-going approach demands comprehensive accounts of Second Temple and inter-testamental beliefs which ground resurrection within current thought forms and future expectations of the time, and calls for a detailed evaluation of the cosmic implications that are relevant to, and reflect back upon, the image of resurrection.[93] Without those ideals, the resulting inferences may be of doubtful provenance and risk erroneous interpretations, resulting in mythologies which evaporate the fullest meanings of the Easter event. It is in the context of these ideals that we can best accommodate the seemingly illogical, antithetical juxtapositions and grinding abruptness between this-worldly and other-worldly events, of head-on impacts between the physical and historic on the one hand and the transcendental and spiritual on the other, the conflicting aspects of Jesus' appearances, and of continuity and discontinuity in such images as a 'spiritual body'.[94] In short, and in the words of a New Testament scholar, the New Testament 'witness to the resurrection of Jesus . . . re-describes earth in terms of heaven, and history in terms of eschatology'.[95]

Earlier I drew attention to a significant aspect of the resurrection story of Jesus: there is an observed continuity between his earthly person and his post-resurrection appearances, manifested through certain signs. Continuity is obviously a key issue in our own hope of life beyond death. If our dead bodies and brains, and hence the personality deriving therefrom, are annihilated at death, what remnant of personhood could emerge in the afterlife? That would clearly entail some transference of memory, personal identity and agency into the afterlife, and would necessitate action by God. Through our current understanding of brain wiring and functional circuitry, it could be effected by way of memory traces held by God during the interim period until the uniting of these with a new and glorified resurrection body.[96] In other words, the position we must argue for demands both continuity and radical discontinuity.

It might be objected that in requiring continuity, and in appealing to 'memory traces' of the person in God, I have smuggled in a disembodied soul under the guise of computerized information technology. To so object, however, would be false. I have argued firmly against the construal of soul as agent of complete continuity between old and new creation. 'Soul',

[93] Pannenberg Wolfhart, The Task of Christian Eschatology, in: Braaten CE and Jensson RW (eds), *The Last Things*, Grand Rapids: Eerdmans 2002, 1; Rowland Christopher, Interpreting the Resurrection, in: Avis (ed) 1993, 68; idem 2002, 183ff; Wright 2003. See also Hengel Martin, *The Son of God*, London: SPCK 1976; idem, *Studies in Early Christology*, Edinburgh: Clark 1995.

[94] Don Cupitt complains that 'spiritual body' is a logical hybrid (Badham 1998, 106–107): but I think we get what is meant, surely? We do not seem to have trouble with 'bread of Heaven', 'God our Father', 'disembodied soul', 'holy water', 'Mystical Rose', etc.

[95] Bockmuehl Marcus, Resurrection, in: *The Cambridge Companion to Jesus*, Cambridge: Cambridge University Press 2001, 102.

[96] Jeeves 1994, 132; Polkinghorne John, *The God of Hope and the End of the World*, London: SPCK 2002, 107ff.

neuropsychologically, represents the emergent personality dependent on brain, mind and body reckoned as a tightly knit unity. This is why I do not ascribe to the view of a complete transferral of mind by way of replicas or teletransportation. To speak of 'memory traces held in God' does not imply the storing of a complete personality or total pattern of personal characteristics, ready to be implanted into a body. There are individuals, especially neonates and young children, who have little or no prospects of acquiring or developing any marked sense of personhood which could in itself constitute a continuing identity.

Man does not *have* a soul: he *is* a soul, his total nature, internal and external, being characterized by it.[97] This contradicts the catechetical, and even Papal definitions, referred to by Badham,[98] which imply dualistic anthropologies and which run into dilemmas over twinning or cloning.[99] Using our imaginations, we might suppose that after death, part of the re-created 'I' may feel strange to some degree, perhaps, rather like starting a new life in a distant city, or especially in a foreign land.[100] To take an everyday analogy, how certain can we be that on waking we are the same persons as yesterday? Or, how certain can we be that after recovering from an anaesthetic we are the same self? It is usually the case that things appear to be the same, and that 'I' appear to be identical with whom I was before. But that is not always so, for some people are considerably changed after awaking from a period of unconsciousness, as for example a shell-shocked soldier whose personality is never the same, as he and those near him subsequently recognize. The same may be true of the post-experiential NDE subject—a most important issue which is discussed in a later chapter. So, likewise, come the final resurrection we will be the same and yet we will be somehow different. That is one reason why models about teletransportation, replicas or even transfer of software are so wooden and unrealistic: they fail to embrace the essential plasticity which characterizes behaviour and psychological demeanour from one time to another throughout earthly life and so—by extension—in the continuity between this and a future life. 'We shall be changed', but we

---

[97] Jeeves 1994, 134; *New Dictionary of Theology*, Leicester: IVP 1988, 653.

[98] Badham 1998, 122.

[99] See Knox, n. 93 above; Badham 1998, 122.

[100] An analogous paradigm is recorded in Frankl's account of the abject de-personalization of Holocaust Jews, in being reduced to a mere number tattooed onto their arms. Yet survival, Frankl showed, was dependent on the *freedom of choice to respond*, by a focus on one aspiration—of rejoining a child, working through a previously incomplete project, and even of just watching (through a chink in a hut wall) branches coming into blossom with each passing season. The past was least significant: it was the *future* and maintaining a spirituality that were crucial in keeping people not only alive but able to survive: Frankl Viktor, *Man's Search for Meaning*, New York: Pocket Books 1985, 90ff.

do not know how. We do not know how God will unite traces of our present memory with something corrresponding to a body, so that something new emerges as personality or 'soul'.

From this anthropological, resurrectional and eschatological background, can a realistic case be made out that ECE phenomenology, as we have it, provides a coherent and dramatically new insight into the afterlife, such as to convince everyone that an afterlife is a real possibility, and not a forelorn hope by religious folk or those wishfully seeking more than was obtainable in this life? Implied by ECE 'eschatology' is an escape either of soul (proposed by Sabom), or of free consciousness (proposed by Ring, Grey, and Fenwick), from brains supposedly moribund, if not 'dead'. Although we have no comparative data, it is not difficult to construct the typical narrative of the subject once he has arrived in the afterlife. Such narratives offer extraordinarily vivid and coloured panoramic scenes of heaven and of God or Jesus.[101] Those depictions seem to be far too simplistic, redolent more of half-remembered truths from childhood impressions or vicariously acquired through life's journey, too geocentric, and too anthropomorphically oriented to presuppose any serious claim to an authentic 'eschatology'. However real the encounters experienced by ND subjects seem to them, their accounts do not afford such newer or original insights that would compel us to review traditional doctrinal assertions, uncertain though the latter evidently are. I have briefly shown above that the eschatology of real, in-depth Christian theology has a different articulation pertinent to the wider significance of the hereafter and the role played by God, its author, and by Christ, its Redeemer and Judge.

Despite these obvious strictures, I do think it is difficult for us as humans resident in the earthly domain to envision the eschaton without a certain sense of the personal, or a temporal feeling of sequence. If we were to take the NDE account as typical, its eschatology would embrace, whether preceded by the tunnel artefact or not, the experient's arrival in a realm of great beauty—scenically and often musically—conveying both a sense of heightened ecstasy, light and warmth and an encounter with spiritual beings. In some instances there is an experience of marked horror and torment accompanied by threatened physical attack, or pain or humiliation, invariably succeeded by repose in a heavenly place. Or the encounter with heaven-bound beings may involve conversation, although such exchanges are somewhat monosyllabic and particularly unenlightening. Other verbal encounters are more forthright, whether with ethereal beings or past family members, but invariably persuading subjects to return to earth.

---

[101] For these, see descriptions collected from the various books and illustrated above (p. 82).

Some subjects undergo 'flashbacks' of their previous lives and experience a form of guilt as if subject to a judgement followed by a pressing desire to return to earth and resume former responsibilites. However, from the material presented at the head of the section on judgement above, the forensic interrogation fails to embody a serious encounter with the subject's previous moral life or failings, if that is what judgement is about. Furthermore, it occurs quickly and is inconsistent with the view that judgement will be collective at the end-time. Judgement[102] will be less about sitting in a criminal court or assize: we have already, in part, been 'saved'. Surely the emphasis will be on reparation, a restoration of righteousness, the undoing of previous hurts, quarrelling, disputes with our forebears. As an act of God, it will involve the putting to right of the accumulated injustices of history and of the community. Then 'it will be no longer "unthinkable" to accept repentance, provisionality, openness to judgement [or acknowledge] failure'.[103] Thus will be established a universal and perfect justice, and a community of perfect universal love. Each citizen in the Kingdom will be enabled to live in love as reflection of the Love emanating from and interpenetrating within the divine Trinity.

While Christian faith affirms the elements of death, some continuity, and rebirth in a new, resurrected body by God's action through God's own hands, we really do not know to what extent and in what manner. Vernon White in his recent Sarum Lectures usefully reminds his readers[104] of the hope that God will do a 'radically new thing... [f]or whenever God creates, this is always a radical act... not just recycling, repetition. Instead, divine creation always includes real difference as well as some continuity: otherness as well as connection.' White notes the apocalyptic language of Isaiah or Revelation that is 'deliberately extravagant, vivid... [and] throws up wonderful juxtapositions, oxymorons and impossible contradictions'.

Such imperatives—the end of dying, of pain, and of incompleteness—demand a state in which completion, rest, fullness, and love-in-relation, obtain. And that demand is for something more and, after Donne,[105] like 'a house of God where there shall be no noise or silence, but one equall musick, no fears nor hopes, but one equal Possession, no foes nor friends, but one equall Communion and Identity, no ends nor beginnings, but one equall

---

[102] Jenson Robert W, The Great Transformation, in: Braaten and Jenson (eds) 2002, 38–39.

[103] Williams Rowan, Resurrection and Peace, in: *On Christian Theology*, Oxford: Blackwell 2000, 271.

[104] White Vernon, *Life Beyond Death*, London: Darton, Longman & Todd 2006, 50ff.

[105] Sermon VIII: 7, 645–650 (1628): Moses John, *One Equall Light*, Grand Rapids (MI): Eerdmans 2004, 316.

Eternity'. In addition, as John Polkinghorne insists,[106] 'it is not just you and I who will have a destiny after death, but also the universe. The universe has not merely been a backdrop to the human drama taking place after an overture lasting fourteen billion years: it itself will have a destiny beyond its death.'

My conclusion, therefore, is that the corpus of reported ECE material lacks conviction and hardly offers serious perspectives on the afterlife from which newer insights and reflections might follow, or even command attention. If the opposite were true, we might have before us cogent guidelines on how to conduct ourselves in addition to what we know from the scriptures. Given such guidelines, there may have arisen a new movement, either within Christianity or without, in which this new knowledge might have served as blueprint for a changed moral climate. Not surprisingly, that seems not to have occurred. The lesson surely to be drawn is that ECE phenomenology has not contributed anything significantly new to our present cloudy under-standings about the afterlife and our future resurrectional abiding in the life of the Trinity. Further, its implied claims about the nature of the soul are in conflict with much of the Christian understanding that there is at present.

---

[106] Polkinghorne John, Is there a Destiny beyond Death? Perth: St George's Cathedral 2003, 3.

11

ECE, Revelation, and Spirituality

Since ECEs are widely alleged to offer new insights into phenomena exemplary of the afterlife, there is an imperative to examine these experiential claims. My approach comes from within the framework of Christian orthodoxy, a comparison hitherto not made by the core authorship of ECE literature considered throughout this book. In this chapter, my approach examines whether ECEs can justifiably fulfil criteria of divine disclosure, and thus be construed as truly spiritual events. This is an important issue, raising the problem how God communicates with earthbound subjects and, importantly, how the brain is involved.

We may identify a spectrum of views about claims to divine revelation. At one extreme end, it might be maintained that all claims to communication between human beings and the divine are hallucinatory, having their origin in abnormal cerebral conditions. It might be said that this state is exemplified by the schizophrenic, migraineur or temporal lobe epileptic; in such cases, it is urged, it is reasonable to assume that there is an internal, aberrant source of 'divine messages' which are entirely brain-generated. However, that there certainly are many such cases does not entitle us to conclude that there can *never* be a combination of brain abnormality and divine influence. There may sometimes be a difficulty in discerning what kind of case we are dealing with, and here one test is a moral one. If, for example, a schizophrenic subject in response to a supposedly divine call immediately goes out and murders an innocent victim, as from time to time occurs, society rightly requires that person to be remanded to a secure forensic unit. The assumption, of course, is that the message is entirely internal. Another kind of test is more contentious, but it is one to which I myself hold. That is, the message is *likely* to be entirely internally generated if it can be suppressed or eradicated by appropriate medications or surgery. I recognize, however, that this test is not absolute, since drugs or medical interventions might have the effect of cancelling out genuine divine activity, or God might wish to wait for a period after therapy before making further disclosures. Nevertheless, while this test can only be a matter of probability, I regard it as part of a cumulative case, as I shall explain later.

At the opposite extreme from internally generated 'revelation' is a particular interpretation which is sometimes brought to the claims about revelation made by the holy scriptures of various world religions: that is, the proposal of divine dictation. For example, we read of divine commands which have allegedly been given to, and received by, the prophet Muhammed, or St John while exiled to the island of Patmos. For the latter, one 'like the Ancient of Days' appeared, commanding him to write ($\Gamma\rho\acute{\alpha}\phi o\nu$) the words comprising epistles destined for each of seven churches in western Turkey. In such cases it has sometimes been supposed that the brains of the subjects involved were employed by God merely as means of transmitting holy dictations onto parchment. Any original cognitive contribution by these agents towards the material they wrote is deemed to have been minimal. It should be observed, however, that even if a 'dictation' theory is adopted, the recipients of a message have to understand to some degree the nature of the material presented to them and then carry out the associated intentional motor act in writing the words received and in disseminating them. We notice that children in a dictation test must understand what words are being spoken by the teacher, and be able to write down each letter or word into an intelligible script, on which they may then be questioned about comprehension.

These views—mere internal mental generation or external divine dictation—are antithetical extremes. Between the ends of the spectrum there is a broad middle ground of possibilities. From this perspective, God is widely understood to have addressed humankind through the sending of his word, and implicit in these interactions is the recipient's clear understanding of the word, and the making of a human contribution in the interpreting and shaping of it within a particular context and social conditions. If revelation is understood to be the impartation of a 'message', then neurophysiologically it is unlikely that there is a specific centre, chosen to be the site of 'implantation' of a divine word in order to effect a necessary outcome. The varied pathologies of schizophrenia, migraine or temporal lobe epilepsy make that clear. In my view, the issues of divine–human interaction cannot be clarified with the aid of neural science, beyond acknowledging that somehow a revelatory message enters the conscious-awareness of persons whom God has chosen to speak in sympathy with the divine word. The perception of the entry of divine truth into the mind may be immediate, or evolve temporally. Such effects could apply internally as with a sudden thought, or as a cognitively perceived series of ideas or realizations becoming apparent over time. I conclude that there is no specific cerebral locus nor mode of thinking which distinguishes secular from religious cognitive receptivity, understanding, or its consequentially dependent actions, or self-expression. This conclusion is even more self-evident if revelation is understood not essentially as the communication of a message, but as the self-unveiling of the divine to which human beings respond with concepts of their own.

Within this framework of thought, it might be claimed that NDEs provide some direct transmission of information. Another possibility is that NDEs could be analogous to the biblical dream through which God manifests himself to humankind. From Joseph bar-Jacob (Gen 37: 5ff) to Joseph, son of another Jacob and husband of Mary (Matt 1: 16, 19), there have been many accounts of dreamers believing, through these means, to have been in receipt of a message from God. Recorded dreams of this type often figure as literary devices permitting the writer a means of articulating divine interaction with the world and the minds of humankind. But we should notice that the Bible also requires us to be cautious about dreams. The prophet Jeremiah, for instance, railed against false prophets who claimed to have received visions and dreams which communicated God's message to Israel (Jer 23: 16–32).

In earlier chapters, we came to an initial conclusion that no divine messages of any apparent worth, whether from God, Jesus or supernatural persons, seem to be vouchsafed to experients while undergoing an ECE. We recall that conversations recorded are invariably monosyllabic, usually involving pro-hibitive and somewhat crude commands or urgent coercive demands for the experient to return earthwards. All too often these 'divine' commands are relegated to proxies, usually a grandmother or parents who also, unrealistical-ly, force their offspring to return to earth.

The basic presupposition is that God wishes to bring certain people to 'heaven' and reveal its contours to them. We have already observed the awkward fact that these supposed contours are utterly anthropomorphic and geocentred. Are reports of English green fields, cottage gardens, the tinctorial displays of brilliant floral borders, or sightings of deceased relatives wearing the same old daytime clothing, to be sensibly believed as truly revelatory encounters with 'heaven' and Almighty God, given the marked idiosyncratic variations accompanying each description given? But, in addi-tion, other basic questions arise. Why should such a revelation only be given to those who think they are dead (leaving on one side the question as to whether they are actually dying at all)? Further, why should the revelation be given to only a very small percentage of those who are brought near to death?

These have been some of my initial conclusions and questions, which cast doubt on claims that ECEs are revelatory. But now we must probe further into claims that the reports are a source of evidence that there is a real life to be sampled after death. My method is first to compare the ontological and epistemic aspects of ECE, as derived from subjects' recalled narratives, with those of 'classical' spiritual experiences. By that means, I wish to determine if ECEs are assignable to the same category, that is, a metaphysical experience or, indeed, a true manifestation of God. Here I refer to the material offered in William James's classical account and in William P. Alston's more recent exploration *Encountering God.* Second, I want to consider the extent to which these narrative accounts can be deemed to reveal a supernatural, eternal realm by comparing them with other cases which purport to be encounters with the divine, but which are most likely to be illusions, due solely to internal neuropathology. That this *is* their probable causation, I have already suggested, is shown by their susceptibility to appropriate therapies which target the brain.

However, before embarking on these analyses, it will be useful to examine what forms of 'spirituality' or other like phenomenologies exist in those populations neither specifically concerned with, nor caught up in, ECE phenomenology.

11.1. 'SPIRITUAL' DIMENSIONS IN A SECULAR WORLD

'In all traditions . . . the underlying implication is that there is a constituent of human nature which seeks relations with the ground and purpose of existence, however conceived'. Thus Gordon Wakefield introduces his *Dictionary of Spirituality*.[1] This rather open definition contrasts with the more recent, measured approach of the philosopher Professor John Cottingham.[2] He notes that spirituality does not provoke the immediately polarized reaction effected by the word 'religion' or propositional stances regarding belief in God. It is not that spirituality is without its attendant sense of 'purveying . . . heterogeneous . . . products, from magic crystals, scented candles and astrology'. But in its richer (and not contested) dimensions, spirituality offers 'certain kinds of intensely focussed moral and aesthetic response[s] . . . the search for deeper reflective awareness of the meaning of our lives and [of] our relationship to others and to the natural world'. Thus, for Cottingham, spirituality embodies activities filling the creative and meditative space beyond the material satisfaction afforded by science and technology. Spirituality, then, is concerned with activities rather than theory, ways of living rather than doctrinal allegiance, praxis rather than belief.

---

[1] Wakefield Gordon, *Dictionary of Spirituality*, London: SCM Press 2003, Preface.
[2] Cottingham John, The Spiritual Dimension, Cambridge: Cambridge University Press 2005, 3ff.

11.1.a. Having that Certain Kind of Feeling:
Perceptions of the Divine

Among differing instances such as aromatherapy, zen, and the high, meditative praxis of apophatic mysticism, what is the spirituality of the ordinary person? To obtain answers, we embrace the studies of David Hay,[3] although his definition of spirituality is singularly vague: 'known when seen'. This is reminiscent of Walter Brueggemann's attempt at defining 'Modernism'.[4] But I continue with Hay's approach, since it enlarges on the responses of ordinary folk to the question whether their lives were ever influenced by something—a 'power' or 'God'—different from one's everyday self, and, consequently, what it was like.[5] Here, of course, we are concerned more with 'transcendence' than the more narrowly perceived connotations of spirituality.

Encounters of this type increased remarkably in frequency in surveys conducted during 2000 compared with those conducted thirteen years before in 1987. Classified, the reported phenomenology gave significant meaning to the synchronicity or simultaneity of relevant happenings (55%), feeling God's presence (38%), the answering of prayers (37%), and an awareness of a sacred presence in nature (29%), or of the dead (25%), or of evil (25%).[6] These figures are astounding on account of the marked decline in church attendance during the same period, and the associated stigmatization and taboos immediately attached to those expressing or pursuing a religious stance and the resultant fear of the public articulation of such experiences. Similar inhibitions, we should note, must attend people recounting ECE.

Yet privately, or in small groups, subjects spoke most volubly or even vehemently about the meaning and value of the spiritual intrusions into their lives. Moreover, depending on previous background and upbringing, almost all respondents saw such intrusions coupled to the wider background of fear or apprehension of death, the beauty of nature, confrontations with suffering, and the immediacy of prayer—if only at moments of joy, unhappiness, a threatening event, or pain. Despite their uncertainties and ambivalence towards God, the role of religion and usefulness of the church, these people

---

[3] Hay David, *Something There: The Biology of the Human Spirit*, London: Darton, Longman & Todd 2006, 130.

[4] 'Its like pornography: I know it when I see it', *Texts under Negotiation*, Minneapolis: Fortress Press 1993, vii.

[5] Hay 2006, 9.

[6] Hay 2006, 115ff. Figures even more marked than data (~35%) from similar questions asked in the UK and USA during the 1960s—see: Hay David, *Exploring Inner Space*, London: Pelican 1982.

exemplified a palpably strong, pervasive and ineradicable belief that there was 'something there'.

Even more fascinating, perhaps, was Hay's conjoined study with Rebecca Nye of children aged 6–10 years.[7] In conducting this field survey they employed a different approach, related to pre-existing studies and data from America and Scandinavia, eliciting responses from each child offered evocative pictures—of a child . . . upset, surveying a dead pet, looking wistfully at dying embers in a hearth, contemplating the nocturnal heavens through a bedroom window. Classified, the reactions revealed an acute and sensitive awareness of the here-and-now, of mystery, and of value.[8] They also noted that the intrinsic spiritual sensitivity denotative of phenomena beyond the immediate habitat would be lost once children, on embracing the more rigorous intellectual climate of upper schooling, acquired the practices of rational thought associated principally with mathematically based science. Indeed, throughout later teenage years that intrinsic, uninhibited and spontaneous spirituality so noticeably characteristic of earlier chilhood would undergo progressive effacement if not erasure.[9] In a microcosm of the Enlightenment, we observe rational scepticism gradually gnawing away at the individual's inherently perceived spirituality and its natural expressivity.

How might these phenomena in children and adults be accounted for? Hay follows Alastair Hardy in interpreting the sense of there being 'something there' as an evolutionarily determined outcome beneficial to society and individuals. Beyond the gene/nurture interaction there is an extrinsic divine power contributory to the shaping and informing of personal behaviour— a direct encounter with the divine through the expression of life, its events and interpersonal relationships, and nature. The circumferential delimitation of these influences is what Hay deems 'Relational-Consciousness', although I think 'awareness' would be an improvement on his use of the word consciousness.

The genetic-cultural factors pertinent to the nurturing of religious behaviour derive from the most popular studies available, albeit performed on American subjects.[10] None deal specifically with spirituality or ask the questions employed by Hay. It would therefore be useful to repeat his work on

---

[7] Hay David and Nye Rebecca, *The Spirit of the Child*, London: Fount 1998, especially 79ff.
[8] Idem, 112ff.
[9] Hay 2006.
[10] Waller N, Kojetin B, Bouchard T, Lykken D, Tellegen A, *Psychol Res* 1: 138–142, 1990; Bouchard T, McGue M, Lykken D, Tellegen A, *Twin Res* 2: 88–98, 1999; D'Onofrio B, Eaves L, Murrelle L, Maes H, Spilka B, *J Personality* 67: 953–984, 1999; Kirk K, Eaves L, Martin N, *Twin Res* 2: 21–28, 1999; Comings D, Gonzales N, Saucier G, Johnson J, MacMurray J, *Psychiatr Genet* 10: 185–189, 2000.

monozygotic/dizygotic twins reared either together or apart, to establish more clearly the interplay between genes and cultural influences in the generation of spirituality. Nevertheless, the genetic contribution to religious behaviour overall is, in general, modest (<50%). I have no intention to pursue these issues further. Having outlined the characteristics of spirituality within the general public, I next proceed to consider complementary studies aimed at quantifying the frequency of what might be termed parapsychological experiences—hallucinations and other so-called psychical experiences—in varied adult populations.

11.1.b. The Parapsychological Dimension to Human Behaviour

There is a general acceptance, at the mundane level, of the many ways through which conscious-awareness is directly influenced when brain metabolism is altered. Some people deliberately use recreational drugs to achieve ecstatic 'highs'. Analgesics dull somatic pain, neurochemical modulators relieve depression or suppress mania, while other pharmaceuticals dampen epileptic seizures. Anaesthetics in raising pain thresholds and securing agnosia permit the execution of unpleasant surgical procedures. Yet from another standpoint, it is evident that hallucinatory and psychic phenomena, not necessarily denotative of serious underlying neural pathology and yet seriously affecting conscious-awareness, are commonly experienced within the general population.[11]

Ohayan[12] questioned over 13,000 unselected British, German and Italian correspondents (representing 0.1% of the total population of the three nations) and found an overall hallucination rate of ∼40%. For daytime hallucinations, 3.2% were visual, 3% sensory, and 0.6% auditory, being often related to anxiety, psychosis, recreational drug usage, or accompanying toxic/organic disorders. About 6% of subjects experienced OBE, those occurring most frequently being related to psychiatric disorders or prolonged somnolence. Nocturnal hallucinations (∼2.5%) arose most frequently at sleep-onset (hypnagogic) associated with vestibular sensations of falling down, or of a 'presence'. Hypnopompic hallucinations (7%) comprised sensations of falling into an abyss, being physically attacked, or awareness of a 'presence'.

---

[11] Palmer J, *J Am Soc Psychic Res* 73: 221–51, 1979; Kohr R, *J Am Soc Psychic Res* 74: 395–411, 1980.
[12] Ohayan M, *Psychiatr Res* 97: 153–64, 2000.

From another slant, Mott and colleagues[13] conducted a comparative analysis of hallucinations in three samples (each n = 50) of alcoholic, general medical, and acute schizophrenic patients. The alcoholics with acute-on-chronic brain degeneration revealed the highest prevalence of hallucinations (auditory 76%; visual 70%; sensory 8%) comprising encounters with spiritual persons, persecutions, and verbal instructions. Of acute schizophrenics, 76% declared the occurrence of hallucinations (auditory 66%; sensory 28%; visual 24%) involving external persecutions and controlling instructional commands. Only 34% of general medical patients described hallucinations (auditory 32%; visual 18%; sensory 10%) which concerned spiritual persons or sightings of dead relatives. Although only 21% of all subjects believed their auditory and visual hallucinations to be veridical, there was widespread engagement with people seen (70%) or heard (60%), despite being thought unreal by the remainder of the subjects studied.

Each of the studies reported above could be criticized on the grounds that no systematic investigations of possible underlying local brain damage or pathology were sought, or excluded. The varied aberrant experiences drawn from wide-ranging groups of individuals raise issues of critical importance. First comes the problem of deciding whether some of these phenomena could have been due to externally generated divine influences beyond the effects of drug usage, illness and alcohol. Second, there is the question of how much they were due to internal, brain-generated processes. In the latter case, we should ask whether the outcome was physiological, as with hypnagogic or hypnopompic hallucinations, and OB events, or whether it was due to some form of underlying neuropathological state, either latent or overt. In respect of latent or overt neuropathological processes, there are numerous examples of subjects with temporal lobe disease, or migraine, whose auras involved either visions and/or auditions of God, visits to heavenly realms or the apprehension of celestial scenes and other related artefacts, and who believed these experiences to be indisputably veridical.[14]

Nevertheless, the real issue is not that of discerning between the polarities either of spiritual experiences arising directly from brain-based pathology, or of messages directly implanted by God into the mind of the subject. The difficulty with that approach is the violent extremes posed by both possibilities: that is, an either/or outcome. As I noted in the opening paragraphs to this chapter, there is a wide range of intermediate opportunities whereby a divine self-disclosure could take place and be perceived and understood. There is the possibility that latent or overt brain pathology facilitates an

[13] Mott R, Small I, Anderson J, *Arch Gen Psychiatr* 12: 595–601, 1965.
[14] Dewhurst and Beard 1970; Devinsky et al 1989.

encounter with the divine, or that God uses such a pathology as the medium through which to disclose himself, especially where revelation is understood as the self-unveiling or self-presencing of God rather than as a communication of a message. We might regard such an event as a state of nature which is being 'graced' by the self-giving of God.

Let us, for example, consider Hildegard of Bingen, entered by her parents into a life of monastic servitude as a child-oblate when aged 8 years. She had visionary experiences throughout her life, beginning when she was 3 years old and 'saw an immense light that shook her soul'.[15] These luminous visions continued intermittently until she died, aged 82 years, in 1180. Charles Singer and the neurologist Oliver Sacks are in no doubt of the diagnostic category, migraine.[16] This view is buttressed by her paintings, which simulate structural peculiarities typical of work created by current members of the Migraine Society. Here, then, are intensely vivid hallucinatory visual auras which, for Hildegard, were considered to be divine interventions. Despite their infrequency, they were clearly instrumental in facilitating, driving and giving exquisite meaning to her life, already dedicated wholly to the monastic ideal in the worship of God. For her, those auras provided a 'substrate of supreme ecstatic inspiration' for her onward work and impressive accomplishments.[17] In this case Hildegard's auras did not constitute, for her, 'proof' of God's existence, but provided an ancillary buttress to her pre-existing grounds for faith, belief and praxis.

We should be ever reminded of the fact that much of this aberrant phenomenology, within the general population, often does not involve God, Jesus or apparent insights into the structural terrain of the afterlife. Its subject matter is invariably banal and, therefore, may be of little apparent spiritual, or eschatological, significance to the subjects undergoing such phenomenology. Some experiences may be weak or shadowy, especially when compared with more full-blooded encounters typifying much ECE narrative. The two studies of Ohayan and of Mott outlined above suggest that the majority of experiences would have been of little significance to subjects in their subsequent personal lives. Indeed, it is unlikely that many of those subjects would have interpreted their experiences as spiritually important. I shall be returning to this subject below. However, having introduced the topic, and illustrated the range of spiritual and other 'psychic' experiences undergone and reported by varied groups of subjects, and the relationship of cerebral activity to

---

[15] Maddocks F, *Hildegard of Bingen*, London: Headline 2001, 54.
[16] Singer C, The Visions of Hildegard of Bingen, in: *From Magic to Science*, New York: Dover 1958, 199–239; Sacks O, *Migraine*, London: Picador 1995, 299ff.
[17] Sacks 1995, 301.

commerce between the divine and the subject, I now turn to evaluating the spiritual content of ECE phenomenology in comparison with other published accounts of spiritual encounter.

11.2. ECE PHENOMENOLOGY CONSIDERED AS SPIRITUAL EVENT

If we proceed to focus specifically on ECE phenomenology, we are dealing with certain individuals who, like Hildegard, actually regarded themselves to have seen God or Jesus, or believed that they had been in 'heaven'. Here I stress that the proportion of individuals confessing to such encounters is, apparently from the narratives recorded, extremely small. But I take these particular accounts to represent the high-water mark of ECE phenomenology, thus being usefully comparable to the 'mountain top' perceptions of the divine described by William P. Alston.[18] In addition, I refer to the classic study of William James[19] published at the turn of the last century. The examples quoted by both authors, together with James's criteria of veridical spiritual encounter, form the basis upon which my comparisons with ECE are based.

11.2.a. ECE Considered with Regard to the Studies of James and Alston

In his essay *Perceiving God*, Alston suggests that in exactly the same way that sensory perception is invariably a veridical expression of the world about us, despite the complicating factors of events or alleged artefacts like mirages, UFOs, crop circles, telephone-mast radiosensity and the like, so also spiritual perception could be a direct veridical presentation of divine presence or revelatory disclosure to the subject, despite disputes over telepathy, telekinesis, psi-phenomenology and so on. Alston's criteria for veridical spiritual presentation may be deployed in comparatively evaluating ECE phenomenology from the same perspectives, while ECE testimonies may also be compared with the example of Hildegard given above. Alston's exemplary testimonies,

[18] Alston WP, *Perceiving God: The Epistemology of Religious Experience*, New York: Cornell University Press, 1993.
[19] James W, *The Varieties of Religious Experience*, New York: Longmans, Green & Co 1902.

some taken from William James's 1902 Gifford Lectures, are given below, abbreviated and abridged.

All at once I felt the presence of God . . . as if his goodness and power were penetrating me altogether. I begged him ardently that my life might be consecrated to doing his will . . . I felt his reply . . . [that of] doing his will in humility, poverty. Then slowly the ecstasy left my heart . . . [it] had neither form, colour, odour nor localization. God was present, though invisible; he fell under no one of my senses, yet my consciousness perceived him. (Anonymous experient, James 1902, 67–68)

One day when I was at prayer . . . I saw . . . or was conscious of . . . Christ at my side . . . I saw nothing with my eyes [external eyes or internal soul]. (Life of St Teresa of Avila, Alston 1993, 13)

God surrounds me like the physical atmosphere. He is closer to me than my own breath. In him, literally, I live and move and have my being. (James 1902, 71)

He [God] sheds his sweetness, but does not display his brightness . . . his beauty is not seen. He is surrounded by darkness . . . for he does not yet appear in the light . . . he appears in the fire, it is the fire that warms rather than illumines. (Richard of St Victor, Alston 1993, 52)

In comparison with the above, ECE testimonies differ vastly. Let us remind ourselves of some randomly selected narratives, as referred to in my previous chapters, in order to drive home the differences:

At the end of the tunnel was a glowing light . . . like the sunset in the afternoon. I remember hearing voices . . . I think it was Jesus Christ who was talking to me. (Sabom 1982, 40)

I couldn't see myself but I was standing on something high . . . below was just the most beautiful greenest pasture . . . looking down on cattle and sheep and shepherd. It was a bright sunny day and he was standing on a round knoll. He had his back to me, but like you see in the bible [sic], . . . He had on this long robe and a cloth over his head with a band around it. (Sabom 1982, 45)

I could see mother and Christ saying 'Come home' and waving their hands at me. She had a long sparkling silver gown on, and so did Christ . . . long hair . . . long beard . . . they were both smiling. (Sabom 1982, 169)

I was aware of moving down a dark country lane with high hedges. At the bottom of the lane was a small cottage with a light on in the window. (Fenwick and Fenwick 1998, 51)

I seemed to find myself in some type of building . . . pervaded by this beautiful golden light. Many people about me were milling about. I saw my parents approaching [saying] 'We've been waiting for you'. It was telepathic communication. The surroundings appeared to be marble . . . a crypt and stairs. I arrived at a place . . . I can only describe it as heaven . . . more a bustling city than a lonely country scene. I felt enlightened and cleansed. I saw Jesus Christ. I recognized my [deceased] mother [and St] Peter [and St] Paul [and] Wilson Carlisle [founder of the Church Army]. In heaven there is light, peace, music, beauty, and joyful activity, but above all, love. (Grey 1985, 51–52)

Alston's analytical critique of the marks of spiritual perception[20] sees them as an appearance of God within the experient's consciousness, just as an object X would similarly present itself to an observer within the physical world of sensible perceiving. Either form of perception differs from other modes of cognitive apprehension of X—such as thinking about, forming mental images of, analysing the properties of, remembering, or deriving beliefs (doxastic or epistemic) from, the character of X. 'Mystical' perception of this type is basic, unanalysable, non-reducible: 'in fact, it just is what it is'. Alston, like James, resists the vivid, sensory content of other forms of what is claimed to be religious experience, such as visions of God, saints, the Virgin Mary and the heavenly city. They note that, when speaking of a direct awareness and presentation of God to their consciousness, true mystics do not refer to any other presented or perceived object associated (perhaps through the subject's religious tradition) with God.

   This portrayal of 'classical' spiritual experiences offers a marked difference, in my view, from the more florid and intense egocentric subjectivity of the feelings and sensations characterizing NDE narratives. The latter are rationalized, in retrospect by each subject, into their ultimate semantic constructions for presentation to the outside world. The experiences recorded are detailed descriptive accounts of God or Jesus, or of heaven, as opposed to the direct, but quietly focused, perception of a divine presence entering into the subject's consciousness. Furthermore, the oft-recorded sightings of deceased parents, grandparents and other dead relatives or friends, often appearing as they were last remembered on earth, or doing worldly things and, in particular, telling experients that they cannot stay and must return home, are, by comparison, foreign intrusions into the experience. Such events are emphatically lacking in the reports of James and Alston in what they regard as pure mystical encounters. Indeed, according to Alston, spiritually determined reports are invariably 'dim, meagre and obscure' and not overburdened by complex visual imagery. They are more full of affective ascriptions to God, Jesus or the Holy Spirit of tenderness, warmth, consummation, and articulated by linguistic similes appropriate to sensory perception, such as sweetness to the taste or gentleness of touch. Words, if communicated, are direct but gentle,

---

[20] Alston 1993, 9–67, 190, 228ff.

reassuring and directional, and hence of immediate relevance to the experient's future life. The communications are not about stern commands to go back, that the time is not right, or that staying around is no longer permissible or desired:

I heard his voice say, 'Go back!'. I said, 'Why me, Lord?' and whoever spoke said my work on earth wasn't over yet . . . All I heard was his voice: it was loud, thundering, just like a clap of thunder coming out of nowheres. (Sabom 1982, 54)

His [not identified] face was very serious. He returned to the discussion and then in a beautiful voice, very loud, he said. 'She must go back'. (Fenwick and Fenwick 1998, 103)

Neither do true mystics have to tumble and gyrate through the absurdity of a 'tunnel' so as to reach the so-called heavenly light. Nor are they frustrated by silly, garden-orientated physical barriers like gates, hedges, walls, trellis, fencing, or bridges over streams which invariably terminate ECE. Rather than having to go to some outer location to find the divine, the presence of the divine is directly instilled into the mystic's own body. For example:

God was present . . . my consciousness perceived him.

He appears to the soul by a knowledge brighter than the sun.

But as I turned . . . I received a mighty baptism of the Holy Ghost [who] descended through me . . . like a wave of electricity . . . in waves of liquid love . . . I could not express it in any other way.[21]

ECE, by comparison, are bright, technicolored vistas of trees, clouds, sky and flowers. Added to which are the very detailed, yet signally non-uniform, 'eyewitness' descriptions of Jesus which dominate these narratives.

11.2.b. Evaluating Narratives by the Criteria of Spiritual Encounter

William James defines the marks of myticism or spiritual encounter, or of a 'mystical state of consciousness',[22] as ineffable, noetic, transient and passive. James identifies ineffability as the 'handiest' of these defining criteria, by which I take it he means the most prominent or important. It is a characteristic that defies verbal capture and for which no adequate report on the pertinent experiential content can be effected in words. Likewise, in respect of ECE phenomenology, certain authors specifically draw attention to their

---

[21] Alston 1993, 14–15.
[22] James 1902, 371–372.

ineffabililty, especially Fenwick and Fenwick.[23] Ring, on the other hand, found that only 60% of his sample were lost for words,[24] while Moody[25] merely reiterates James's criteria without reference to his own collected data. Sabom (1982; 1998) and Grey (1985) appear not to be concerned with this aspect of the phenomenology. Clearly, these authors display no consistency on this point. But James and Alston are also not in agreement here. Alston[26] signally rejects inexpressibility as a criterion of mystical perception. While he admits that 'One cannot be struck in our examples and elsewhere, by the constantly re-iterated insistence that the experience is indescribable', Alston takes the widespread assumption of ineffability as blown out of all proportion.

Despite such varied observations, subjects do, indeed, manage to say 'quite a lot about their experiences and about what they take themselves to be explaining'. Alston interprets the emphasis on inexpressibility as a denial that the experience can be expressed *literally*, and affirms that recourse to simile, metaphor, analogy, symbolism and allied devices permit the offering of many useful and detailed accounts. That situation pertains not only to mystical presentations, but also to the sciences, religion and philosophy. Here I agree with Alston. I think it is generally accepted that the use of linguistic tropes permits articulation of the inexpressible, and without such measures, our culture, knowledge and understanding would be that much the poorer. If highly personal forms of experience that are (in the words of Alston) 'dim, meagre and obscure' are to be communicated as spiritual insights, then metaphor and symbol are required.

However, it is just here that ECE narratives seem to fail. I see little of metaphorical nuance in them, or little use of symbolic language to convey what might be termed the distinctive 'qualia-like feelings' as experienced by each subject. Descriptions have the everyday quality represented by terms such as 'brightly coloured', 'wonderful', 'beautiful'. In line with the previously articulated neurophysiological considerations, I suggest that NDE recollections are far more dream-like (hypnopompic) in their recalled content in comparison with the many mystical encounters recorded by James and Alston.

Second, if extra-corporeal experiences are not ineffable, are they noetic? James considers the meaning of 'noetic' to encapsulate 'far-reaching intellectual (cognitive) insights, illuminations and revelations into the depths of truth'.[27] Precisely how that interpretation of mystical noetics applies to NDE

---

23 Fenwick and Fenwick 1998, 22, 220.
24 Ring 1980, 84.
25 Moody 1977, 99.
26 Alston 1993, 39.
27 James 1902, 371.

is difficult to analyse. We derive from some NDE narratives the alleged acquisition of 'all knowledge', either absorbed from vast libraries or gained as answers to the imponderables concerning life and existence:

It seemed that all of a sudden all knowledge—of all that had been started from the very beginning, that would go on without end—that for a second I knew all the secrets of all ages, all the meaning of the universe, the stars, the moon—of everything . . . As the Bible says 'To you all things will be revealed'. For a minute, there was no question that did not have an answer. (Moody 1977, 10–11)

For a moment—it was like I knew all things. I thought whatever I wanted to know could be known. (Moody 1997, 14)

Neither the acquisition of such vast knowledge, nor the alleged insights and understandings derived during the encounter, seem to have any implications for the subsequent lives of these experients. Furthermore, the acquisition of 'all knowledge' is not the exclusive preserve of NDE (we saw a particularly striking example earlier from one of Dr Sacks's Parkinsonian patients over-dosed on L-dopa pills). It also typifies hypnagogic hallucinatory sleep-onset phenomenology, and like NDE, the data revealed are not remembered once the subject has emerged from that subliminal subconscious state and regained full conscious-awareness. In either case, since these revelations and insights cannot be remembered, they have unfortunately conveyed nothing of value to the possible benefit of the subject nor of civilization: we are none the wiser. On the other hand, it might be insisted that the noetic element involves encounters with divine persons. Yet these NDE-associated encounters seem to be fruitless episodes, on the grounds that the conversations only involve commands to subjects to return to earth forthwith, since it is 'not their time'. In terms of James's definition, that could hardly be taken to comprise a worthwhile noetic revelation. I am therefore led to the conclusion that ECE lack his specific noetic criterion.

These considerations bring us to James's third and fourth criteria of transience and passivity. I have drawn attention to the fact that some NDE subjects are passively told to return to earth. Indeed, the major proportion of all NDE phenomenology is passive. That includes, if undergone, the experi-encing of the tunnel, being propelled into some locus representing the afterlife, of bathing in the light, and undergoing the coercive command to return (to earth). Other subjects appear to make the decision themselves, but I regard that as the intrusion of conscious-awareness, and, in particular, of the reappearance of organized frontal lobe activity as the driving source of the moral dictate to return homewards. This is relevant to the transience of NDE, which occupies those brief moments, not when the brain is inopera-tive, but as it is regaining normal functioning while wakefulness and full conscious-awareness are being re-established. I have elucidated the ephemeral time-course of ECE in earlier chapters. While there are marks of passivity and transience in much ECE phenomenology, these seem to resemble the experiential dream-state.

11.2.c. Verdict: ECEs Are Not Convincing Examples of Spiritual Encounters

In the previous two sections, I have aimed to elucidate the distinctive contrasts between ECE regarded by some authors[28] as 'mystical' experiences, and the mountain-top examples given and analysed by Alston as evidential demonstrations of the presence of God. Mystical perceptions as defined by Alston represent divine influences on the percipient's mind and consciousness. The phenomenology of ECE, in comparison, is phenomenologically and experientially different. Here we see subjects seemingly travelling 'outwards' on a journey through a 'tunnel' into (the) 'light', describing vividly coloured panoramas, and having sight of God or Jesus—sightings which are totally lacking in uniformity of description, and then 'returning' because of moral doubts about going further. We would do well to consider the validity, even propriety, of the following overtly anthropomorphic accounts:

He was tall . . . he had a white robe on . . . his face was beautiful . . . his skin was glowing and absolutely flawless. (Sabom 1982, 49)

She [her mother] had a long sparkling silver gown on, and so did Christ . . . [he had] long hair . . . long beard . . . (Sabom 1982, 50)

I was walking across this wooden bridge over this running beautiful stream of water and opposite . . . there was Christ [with] a very white robe. He had jet-black hair . . . very black short beard. His teeth were extremely white and his eyes were blue, very blue. (Sabom 1982, 76)

[the form] had blond-gold hair and it had a beard, a very light beard and a moustache. It had a white garment on. And from this white garment there was all this shining gold . . . (Ring 1980, 60)

the light got brighter and I saw him. I saw Christ. He was incredibly beautiful . . . his feet were bare. He was wearing a bright garment. The bosom was open and you could see his chest. He had hair down to his shoulders and a beard. There was light coming out of his head like a star. (Fenwick and Fenwick 1998, 86)

---

[28] Fenwick and Fenwick 1998, 229; Sabom 1998, 214ff.

These major inconsistences, to my mind, devalue the general phenomenological claim that any NDE (or ECE) constitute veridical viewings of the afterlife, of God, or of Jesus. It is impossible to accept these multiple illusions as a credible realization of the hereafter. The images seem to be totally dependent on the usual precepts available from current forms of iconography of ecclesial or secular portrayals. A further paradox is uncovered by these considerations. While all authors I have considered variously try to make the NDE a venture into some outward metaphysical realm, the experients themselves bring back narrative accounts of their so-called other-worldly journeys which, by contrast, are extraordinarily geomorphic and anthropomorphic. These specific examples are tied to pre-existing visual memories of others' attempted solutions as to how Jesus, in particular, was thought to have looked or appeared.

Considerably fewer realized images or descriptions of God or the Holy Spirit are prevalent in ECE accounts. It is perhaps significant that images of the Spirit are very rarely expressed in visual art-forms, while there are relatively more images of God the Father, for example in the paintings of Michelangelo and Blake. Neither Father nor Spirit, however, have the widespread public appeal nor the same impact as do the varied depictions of Jesus typified either in religious iconography (stained-glass windows or Sunday school pictures), or in more recent times through popular dramatizations by press, cinema or television studios.

11.2.d. Allowing for the Neuropathological Brain-State

Not all spiritual perceptions, as they have been recorded through time, would necessarily satisfy Alston as to their authenticity. Conversely, from my own neurophysiological perspective, some of the examples he gives continue to illustrate the empirical uncertainty of knowing whether they could be veridical. Consider this report: 'Then it began to dawn on me that I was not alone in the room. Someone else was there, located precisely *about two yards to my right front*. Yet there was no sensory hallucination. I neither saw nor heard him, but he was there'[29] (my emphasis).

This account could be indicative of a 'unilaterally felt presence'[30] and this example suggests an (ipsilateral) right-sided temporal lobe focus. 'Felt presences' are commonly experienced phenomena within the community.[31] In >60% of 31 published case-reports, the invisible presence was sensed to the

---

[29] Alston 1993, 17.
[30] Brugger P, *Percept Motor Skills* 79: 1200–1202, 1994; Brugger et al 1996; Brugger et al 1997.
[31] Suedfeld P and Mocellin J, *Environ Behav* 19: 33–52, 1987.

right of the subject, arising from disruptions to the mechanisms controlling ego-/paracentric space, as explained throughout Chapter 6. There are varied types of lesional pathology which underlie the phenomenon, and which interfere with the integrative functioning of the temporal, temporo-parietal, and junctional temporo-parietal-occipital cortices of the right hemisphere. They include epilepsy, tumours, migraine, acute and chronic infections (viral, syphilitic) and cerebral trauma. The 'presence', invariably an illusory projection into the subject's paracentric forward space, is usually that of the subject, and towards which a feeling of closeness, empathy and familiarity ensues.

Other examples of divine presence quoted by Alston suggest that the perceptual disturbances could have arisen from severe depressive illness, despair and acute loneliness:

When I was middle-aged and the Second World War was upon us, there came a night when I was in *deepest distress of mind* [my emphases here and below]. I was *alone* in my bedroom, pacing the floor ... suddenly, I heard a voice firmly say, 'Be still and know that I am God!' It changed my life. I got into bed, calm and confident.[32]

At the time, I reached *utter despair and wept* and prayed to God for mercy instinctively and without faith in reply. That night I stood with other patients in the grounds waiting to be let into our ward ... Suddenly someone stood beside me in a dusty brown robe and a voice said 'Mad or sane, you are one of My sheep' ... this has been the pivot of my life.

Alston and James allow their considerations to apply only to subjects with presumptively normal brains. Neither author specifically refers to the formal possibility of neuropathological aetiologies as causes for divine per-/receptivity. In a later chapter Alston[33] offers a general dismissal of analogous causal aetiologies, since we can never be sure precisely how God might intend to reveal himself, even if through various brain-states. In fact, I have already suggested myself that God *might* use an aberrant pathology as a natural event through which to disclose himself. However, I believe that there is a cumulative case for regarding ECEs as caused solely by neuropathological conditions.

First, I have earlier brought forward sufficient reasons to make probable the belief that NDEs, in general, arise from brains involved in, and recovering from, major vascular and metabolic insults. The revelations claimed are not the function of normal but, on the contrary, temporarily abnormal brains. Second, they are thus directly analogous to the specifically 'God-centred' aberrations occasioned by cerebro-vascular ischaemic abnormalities, migraine, or temporal lobe pathology, as described in previous chapters.

[32] Alston 1993, 19.
[33] Alston 1993, 228ff.

Pathological perturbations of brain function elicit varied forms of 'religious experiences'. Compelling evidence is needed to overturn the probability that these experiences have solely internal causes. Third, then, we have to ask about the epistemic and moral value of claimed visionary experiences which arise in such a context, to see whether it makes any sense to talk about divine activity or influence in any specific instances. When analysed dispassionately, in comparison with the 'classical' spiritual tradition, we found that ECEs are not convincing as spiritual encounters, offering no greater significance or spiritual insight than those occasioned by any other event which it is reasonable to regard as hallucinatory. ECE narratives signally lack the experiential and quintessential loss of self in ecstatic union with the divine which is a key hallmark of the holy encounter between mystic and God. Nor do the markedly florid, anthropomorphic and geomorphic contours of these accounts reveal any new insights of what afterlife might entail.

In the light of this cumulative evidence, we must surely conclude that the weight of probability lies on the side of ECEs being caused by solely internal causes in a (temporarily) abnormal brain state. Nevertheless, phenomenologically, any such experience can be very real to the subjects undergoing them, irrespective of causal antecedent. For that reason it is important to consider the impact which NDE stamp on the further lives of those who have experienced NDE. That is the subject matter of the next chapter.

11.3. THE BRAIN AND THE 'MYSTICAL' EXPERIENCE

The fact that religious experience (or experiencing) is brain-based is a truism, and therefore 'should not be taken as an exceptional claim'.[34] For any divine disclosure the message must be comprehensible in order to exact some kind of response or action. From the neuropathological examples given earlier in this book, it is a further unexceptional fact that any part of the brain may be involved. There is no locus for a holy neural shrine, sheltered from the processed vulgarities of secular neurones. With the pathologies discussed above, the religious outcome is invariably heightened. But conversely, there may be blunting of the religious or spiritual temperament, in parallel with the progressive diminution of cognitive and affective competence: Alzheimer's dementia is a prime example. Professor Jeeves has summarized this whole situation with authority:

---

[34] Saver JL and Rabin J, *J Neuropsychiatr Clin Neurosci* 9: 498–510, 1997; Azari N, Nickel J, Wunderlich G, Niedeggen M, Hefter H, Tellmann L et al, *Europ J Neurosci* 13: 1649–1652, 2001.

Religious experience associated with brain [perturbations] has a number of weak-nesses as a general psychological model of religious conversion. Certainly the accounts of mystical/religious experiences in the clinical epilepsy literature are not characteris-tic of typical Christian or other forms of religious conversion. From a theological point of view, nothing is established by demonstrating that a particular conversion has been related to abnormal brain activity; the epistemological problem of the truth of the content of the experience is not solved. If St Paul [had a seizure] it would have little relevance to the theological question of the truth of what he subsequently preached, taught, and wrote.[35]

From another perspective, the need for a new terminology, such as the 'neurotheology' suggested recently by d'Aquili and Newberg,[36] seems unneces-sary. Their 'mystical mind', surely, is none other than the output of the same machinery which constructs and facilitates our daily mental commerce— thought, sensations, body-image and their integration. If we know one, we know the other.

D'Aquili and Newberg, however, have conducted some interesting studies with experienced Buddhist monks. Brain-scans were undertaken when the meditators achieved a blissful state of mind—which the authors describe as 'absolute unitary being' (AUB). Unfortunately, this work has only been pub-lished in preliminary form. Furthermore, there was frontal lobe 'noise' occa-sioned by the subjects' need to concentrate fixedly on their chosen object of meditation. Nevertheless, AUB seems to come about, in part, by disconnec-tion between frontal and parietal lobes. This is analogous to the neurophysi-ological processes involved in REM dream-state modalities providing the opportunity for other forms of subconscious mentation to be generated when frontal lobe executive brain function is altered, suppressed or deacti-vated. A similar neurological rearrangement may occur during NDE. In AUB, according to d'Aquili and Newberg, the language centres are bypassed, there-by (hypothetically) accounting for the ineffability experienced by subjects in attempting to recount what they had undergone.

The problem here is that ECE subjects, for example, can and do articulate their feelings and describe their ecstatic 'highs', albeit to varying degrees. Inarticulacy could thus result, not from the decoupling or bypassing of language centres, but because memory circuitry is inoperative (as brain-scans of dreaming subjects suggest). That is why it is so difficult to recall dreams other than with hypnopompic dream-awakenings when conscious memory function intrudes into the final moments of the dream sequence. In

---

[35] Jeeves Malcolm, Brain, Mind and Behaviour, in: Brown, Murphy and Malony 1998, 92–3 (my brackets and emphasis).
[36] d'Aquili E and Newberg A, *The Mystical Mind*, Minneapolis: Fortress Press 1999, 145ff.

connection with blissful episodes, a further point is that we need to dissect and compare the underlying neural circuitry of AUB, and that accompanying much ECE phenomenology. Hard data are difficult to come by: we should also be aware of the very limited neural repertoire through which such states could be generated.

Nevertheless, D'Aquili and Newberg seem to think that ECE (NDE) come about through the activation of two primitive 'archetypes'—one of transcendence and the other of dissolution.[37] NDEs are alleged to comprise an initial dissolution—the loss of self and allied symbolisms—for people perceiving themselves to be actually near death. We should note that there is a problem here of which they do not take account: that subjects[38] never actually know whether they are near death or not. Conversely,[39] the transcendent archetype assists in reintegration and restoration of the person, bringing light, peace, joy and wholeness. The implication from their account is that the brain is functioning normally: but they seem not to have recognized that this is clearly not the case, as I have shown. Another difficulty for these authors' use of 'archetypes' is their failure to explain why only 10–20% of actual near-death subjects have ECE. What, we may ask, is happening to these archetypes in those who do not undergo ECE? A more realistic account could be sought in the monoamine systems of the upper brainstem involving, for example, $5HT_{1A}$ (serotonin) and other polymorphic receptor densities which have been demonstrated to be inversely related to a spiritual temperament. This type of account might also, in part, offer a more extensive molecular-polymorphic, genetically based account of subjects' predisposition to undergo these experiences, or even to have variable experiences.[40]

In passing, I consider it curious that brain-scanning techniques should be employed to investigate the neurology of other-world typologies, while in explanation the authors have to regress to early twentieth-century (Jungian) modes of neurophysiological understanding. A further problem for d'Aquili and Newberg is why individual narratives are so obstinately idiosyncratic: there is, if one carefully analyses the reports, no expected pattern, or no guaranteed automatic sequence to these events which, therefore, renders

[37] d'Aquili and Newberg 1999, 134ff.

[38] Owens J, Cook E, Stevenson I, *Lancet* 336: 1990, 1175–1177; Gabbard G, Twemlow S, Jones F, *J Nerv Ment Dis* 169: 1981, 374–377.

[39] d'Aquili and Newberg 1999, 134; Newberg A, Alavi A, Baime M, Pourdehnad M, Santanna J, D'Aquili E, *Psychiatr Res: Neuroimag Sect* 106: 113–122, 2001.

[40] Borg J, Bengt A, Soderstrom H, Farde L, *Am J Psychiatr* 160: 1965–1969, 2003; Nilsson K, Damberg M,Ohrvik et al, *Neurosci Letts* 411: 233–237, 2007; Aghajanian G, Marek G, *Neuropsychopharmacol* 21: 16S–23S, 1999; Hoyer D, Hannon J, Martin G, *Pharmacol Biochem Behav* 71: 533–554, 2002.

them extremely difficult to categorize or explain by one or other functional category. That key fact calls into question the explanatory archetypal aetiology of these authors.

Finally, d'Aquili and Newberg suggest that ECE phenomenology has an advantage which is based in evolutionary development. If that is the case, the problem arises why so few near-death subjects undergo this phenomenology. And to suggest that it helps the aged enjoy a pleasant exit and thus be less of a worry on their carers seems to be illogical, if not absurd.[41] The argument is that it is to an evolutionary advantage for individuals in any life-threatening situation to 'remain calm, think clearly and rationally in slow-motion', and, use their brains 'efficiently or indeed, hyperefficiently'.[42] But we must ask whether there is a remote chance of that happening with the majority of ECE subjects, since that kind of phenomenology results from metabolically disturbed or temporarily hypoxic brains.

I am not convinced that this popularly acclaimed approach by d'Aquili and Newberg, at least in respect of ECE, offers any useful insights into the nature of the mechanisms underpinning ECE. Nor do we glean any new information about possible spiritual contours from these authors, since they explicate these events in terms of archetypes, and on the implicit assumption that the brain is functionally normal: at least, we do not hear any word from the authors to the contrary. That is patently not the situation, of course, as I have demonstrated in the earlier chapters of this book.

A more measured philosophical approach to spirituality is offered by Dr Caroline Franks Davis. For her, the criteria of true spiritual experience involve a unity with God, a sense of love with the Other, and a unity either in itself, or within a multiplicity. In addition, we could add a loss of self, and the ecstatic union of the 'I' with God.[43] Franks Davis[44] sees that even if narrated experiences are 'demythologized' from all contextual and cultural presupposition, and notwithstanding the 'word-perfectness' of the articulated accounts that are invariably offered to the world, there should still be a remnant—an indication of 'presence'. But even on these wider grounds, ECE narrative reporting would still not qualify. Subjects fail to couch their narratives in language which reflects the aspects of spirituality identified by Franks Davis, and notably omit language about 'union' with the divine.

---

[41] d'Aquili and Newberg 1999, 141.
[42] Ibid, 142.
[43] Franks Davis Caroline, *The Evidential Force of Religious Experience*, Oxford: Clarendon Press 1999, 177, 183, 214.
[44] Ibid, 9, 226–7.

In considering, therefore, whether ECE could be deemed to represent some form of deep, 'mystical' or spiritual experience, I conclude, in accord with the other scientific evidence offered in the first part of this book, that the most economic explanation is that ECEs are neurophysiologically grounded phenomena arising from brains metabolically recovering from various antecedent clinical crises. It is following this period of abnormal functioning, as the brain is recovering its full neurophysiological integrity, that the abnormal subconscious mentation experienced during these events is generated. The processes are therefore akin to the neuropathological auras of migraine, epilepsy and temporal lobe diseases, or schizophrenia, as well as to the physiological properties of hypnagogic and hypnopompic dream states.

One could hardly insist, viewed from objectively based perspectives, that anything of divine import concerning afterlife had been disclosed to ECE subjects, and from thence to society in general. Nor could we think with any confidence that ECE phenomenology represents a credible spiritual realm, when comprised of entry tunnels, barriers constructed with earth-bound props, and non-uniform anthropomorphic caricatures of Jesus, and when it culminates in forcible commands to the most recently arrived immigrants to reverse their journeys and return to their worldly responsibilities. These kinds of sequences do not ring true as belonging to a 'revelatory' typology. Nevertheless, the events themselves are clearly of profound significance to the subjects who undergo them, as may also be the case with other, non-spiritual or non-religious psychological crises which at certain unexpected times profoundly shatter the lives of many people. ECE may, therefore, *become* occasions of divine self-disclosure to the subjects involved in the process of reflection upon them, while offering no 'information' about spiritual realities and offering, in the way they happen, no evidence of divine presence.

12

Subjects' Interpretations of Their Experiences

For all that has been written about ECE, hardly anything has been systematically offered to indicate how subjects perceive their experiences and, more importantly, how they have dealt with the after-effects. Qualitative descriptions of the experienced phenomenology abound, often elicited through use of leading questions or other forms of suggestive interviewing, and based on what was, and was not, remembered. The oral narratives obtained from willing subjects are stylized, rehearsed accounts of retrospectively experienced phenomena, and then subsequently interpreted and incorporated by each of the authors into their respective texts. The opportunity to ask subjects individually not simply what they remembered, but what meaning they thought the NDE had offered them, appears to have been passed over without due concern by all authors. Indeed, we need to remain aware that authors' constructions deriving from the narratives they received would, excluding Sabom's, be hardly recognized by their respective subject base. For example, none of Ring's or Grey's subjects asserted, confirmed or even implied that they had ascended to the 'fourth dimension', been directly involved in 'holographic phenomenology', or almost become engrafted into a 'universal cosmic brotherhood or consciousness'.

We have statements from subjects who, in their judgement, did not consider themselves to have been dreaming or hallucinating. I have previously suggested that experients, in general, cannot be conversant with the variety of dream-state modes that have been identified and defined neurophysiologically. Even in retrospect, it is not clear how subjects can know or be possessed of such certainty, thus to assert categorically that they had not experienced one such oneiric mode of subconscious activity. Even people with a normal brain-state cannot make that distinction. On the other hand, hallucinatory hypnagogic and hypnopompic dream imagery is intensely vivid and memorable, rather like that induced by toxic-delirious states, or the dream sequences of aircrew regaining conscious-awareness from centrifuge-induced episodes of unconsciousness. There are obvious and distinctive neurophysiological parallels between hypnopompic dream-offset modes and the abrupt awakening from an NDE.

Certainly, dream-states and NDE are classes of mental activity quite different from the ordinary world of wakeful consciousness-awareness. But neurophysiologically there is another most important distinction. Dreaming, apart from certain pathological/genetic exceptions already encountered above, is a natural process and thus an ordered, neurophysiologically coordinated event. On the contrary, the NDE results from disordered cerebral physiology arising in 80% of subjects from a variable period of unconsciousness due to an antecedent cessation of cerebral blood-flow possibly lasting up to an hour during the resuscitative procedure, severe haemorrhage, drug overdosage, or the pain, stress and N_2O intoxication associated with childbirth.

The process of returning from that abnormal base to a continuation of full conscious-awareness could hardly be expected to occur via ordered neurophysiological processes. Recovery is dependent on the type and severity of insult, the speed with which appropriate resuscitative measures are instituted, the subject's age, and the degree of atheromatous arterial degeneration affecting the arteries, remembering that atheromatous vascular degeneration accounts for the greatest proportion of medical crises resulting in ECE. The particular amalgam of each of these factors ultimately determines, for each individual, the duration and the idiosyncratic mix of hallucinatory 'thought-forms' that will constitute the experience up to the return of full conscious-awareness. This is an area where further insight is needed. Since the neurophysiology and neurochemistry of the transition from dream-state to conscious-awareness is not, at present, fully understood, it is difficult to suggest immediately any useful ways forward for gaining further epistemic insights into the likely recovery process(es) from NDE. Since, as I have argued earlier, it is unlikely that there has been a veridical journey outside the body, it is admittedly intriguing why such a sense of reality and vividness pervades the remembered near-death event.

Although many experients are convinced of the reality of their visions of heaven or glimpses of the afterlife, few, if any, definitions of what 'afterlife' might mean are offered by either experients or authors. Such beliefs are, however, tenaciously held, despite the geomorphic contours descriptively applied to the 'location'. Subjects seem to be of the view, for instance, that they hurtled or twisted through a 'tunnel' in order to gain access to the other-world domain. On the face of it, such a construction seems to be absurd, since the tunnel would be idiosyncratically tied to each person's perception; it could not exist with any geographic coordinates, nor does it fit into a coherent metaphysic. The belief, though strongly held, only confirms that the perception is entirely dependent on hallucinatory brain activity.

From the above perspectives, I conclude that the content of ECE narratives, and the sparsely reported insights by subjects into these events, have together contributed little of interest theologically. I now examine the far more important consequences of NDE on the subsequent lives of these experients. While providing little about their subjects' personal interpretations and meanings of ECE, the tabulated data of Ring (1980; 1985) and Sabom (1982; 1998) does help to provide us with some generalized data about the spiritual changes in subjects' lives.

12.1. THE NDE AND THE SUBJECT: CONSEQUENTIAL OUTCOMES

12.1.a. External and Intrinsic Religiosity

One of the most striking consequences for near-death subjects, compared with non-NDE controls, is that they become far less afraid of dying or of facing the ultimate prospect of biological death.[1] In keeping with that perception, there is, comparatively, an enhanced conviction about the reality and tangibility of some continuity after death.[2] Although his methodology is not well clarified, Ring scored each of his subjects before and after the NDE to determine whether the event itself influenced beliefs in an afterlife (1980, pp. 168–169). Two groups of non-NDE subjects scored 2.73 and 3.03 respectively, while NDE subjects scored 2.10 before their experience, rising to 3.92 ($p < 0.1$) post-event. These data are important in indicating that it is the NDE and the opportunity to sample the properties of 'other-worldliness', and not the near-scrape with death itself, which are determinative. But these considerations pose further enquiries in regard to subjects' 'spirituality' and 'religiosity', pre- and post- the ND experience. Sabom[3] administered a 'spiritual beliefs' questionnaire to his group: unfortunately, pre-NDE data were only obtained once the NDE had occurred. Nevertheless >40% of subjects affirmed that their inherent religious beliefs had not been altered by the experience. The questionnaire is very fundamentalist, containing questions about the existence of hell, the nature of the Bible as God-inspired and inerrant, and about Satan as a real person and as the source of today's evils

---

[1] Ring 1980, 174–175, Tables 27, 28: $p < 0.005$; Sabom 1982, 212–213, Tables XIV, XV: $p < 0.005$.

[2] Ring 1980, 168–169, $p < 0.01$; Sabom 1982, 212, Table XIV, $p < 0.01$.

[3] Sabom 1998, 107ff, 229, Table 6.

in people and the world. These questions and the responses to them seem to confirm that, for the majority of subjects, ecclesial and doctrinal choices do not alter as a result of the NDE. In particular, there was no change of belief in God's existence, or in heaven, or hell.[4] Subjects manifested a greater motivation towards activity within their church communities[5] and professed an increase in their 'intrinsic faith'.

Now 'religion' and 'religiousness' are slippery terms, and David Hoge maintains that they are more effectively defined in terms of external and intrinsic orientation or religiosity: ER and IR.[6] He suggests that church attendance, when a manifestation of ER, is often related to high socio-economic status and educational achievement, resulting in a sense of self-justification, sociability and even security that involves connotations of revelation, election ('chosen people') and theo(auto)cracy. Conversely, IR embraces brotherhood, equality and compassion, and is closely allied to spirituality—that is, the non-profane and non-secular. In a secular environment, spirituality entails a willed effort to live a life devoted to one's chosen church, faith and doctrines, assisted by belief in divine grace imbued through prayer and by sacramental baptismal and eucharistic congress with the deity.

Following this analysis, while ER is not influenced by NDE, it is clear, as Sabom indicates, that IR is deepened following such experiences.[7] In order to substantiate that claim, Sabom uses Hoge's Intrinsic Religious Motivation Scale.[8] This is a 10-item questionnaire which elicits the kind of relationships denotative of a life lived according to its underlying credal values and motivations. Because it eschews doctrinal issues, Hoge's instrument is applicable to a variety of belief systems either within the Christian tradition, Judaism or Islam. For comparison, we note that in a later, independent study[9] of a mixed series of adults (n = 346), the mean IR (Hoge) score achieved was 26 ± 8 (m$\pm$sd). This latter study revealed that anxiety about death was inversely proportional to IR scores, a result likewise obtained, albeit by different means, by Groth-Marnat and Summers.[10]

Sabom, in presenting his data, seems to wander between Hoge's 10-point score and a 5-point cluster derivative from his Life Changes Questionnaire

[4] Ring 1980, 166.
[5] Sabom 1998, 226, Table 3.
[6] Allport G and Ross JM, *J Pers Soc Psychol* 5: 432–443, 1967; Bouchard T, McGue M, Lykken D, Tellegen A, *Twin Res* 2: 88–98, 1999.
[7] Sabom 1998, 96–97.
[8] Hoge D, *J Sci Stud Rel* 11: 369–376, 1972.
[9] Thorson J and Powell F, *J Clin Psychol* 46: 379–391, 1990.
[10] Groth-Marnat G and Summers R, *J Hum Psychol* 38: 110–125, 1998.

(LCQ).[11] For the NDE positive group of 47 subjects, their average Hoge (IR) score was 31.5 (Sabom 1998, p. 88), ranging for his three different subgroups from 25.1, 28.2 to 36.1 compared with two groups of non-NDE cardiac control patients, one group (n = 81) whose mean score was 27.8 (p < 0.05), and a second (n = 26), whose score was 26.2 (Sabom 1998, pp. 97, 234: p < 0.001). The 5-point LCQ cluster cites 42 ND experients compared with 32 control cardiac cases (p < 0.01). These data, therefore, seem to be consistent with Ring's, in that some increased sense of inner spirituality does ensue from the actuality of having an NDE, as opposed to the experiencing of a threat of death alone.

In addition, Sabom cites individual, post-NDE Hoge scores. He wondered, for example, whether the NDE affected the faith of subject 'GL' and whether the resultant increase in IR, in turn, influenced her survival and recovery (Sabom 1998, p. 182). Her post-ND score was 'an amazingly deep 38'! Thus, 'it appeared that GL's near-death experience had deepened her [IR] significantly' (pp. 83–84). For 'GR', 'his NDE strongly increased four [5-point cluster] and somewhat increased one of his intrinsic faith items' (p. 88). Then there was 'DA', whose 'near-death experience... strongly increased all [her] intrinsic faith items, scoring a near-perfect 39 on Hoge's scale' (p. 90), as did another subject ('RA') post-NDE. These anecdotal figures look impressive, but without pre-NDE data, their significance is considerably diluted if not possibly rendered entirely void.

Ring used his own devised Religiousness Index in evaluating the relationship between religiosity and NDE.[12] However, this score is really a measure of ER since it elicits views about beliefs in God, life after death, heaven and hell. There was no demonstrable relationship between the duration ('depth') and qualitative ('core') aspects of the NDE and pre-existing religious traits, but an increased religiosity as defined by this Index compared with non-NDE subjects.[13] This Index bears scant relationship to Hoge's inventory, which is much more aligned to IR. From more anecdotal material, Ring concluded that, in general, NDE subjects felt closer to God, prayed more, and became far less oriented toward organized religious activity, this latter conclusion being noticeably at variance both with Sabom, and with Groth-Marnat and Summers.

---

[11] Sabom 1998, 133–134.
[12] Ring 1980, 133–134.
[13] Ring 1980, 171, Table 26, p < 0.005.

12.1.b. A Universal Spirituality? Assessing Ring's Proposal

Ring's conclusions led him to assert that the spirituality, rather than religious-ness, of post-NDE subjects was intensified (Ring 1980, pp. 80, 171). He revisits this scene in his later book *Heading towards Omega* (1985) by means of a different Religious Beliefs Inventory.[14] In my view, this later research is grossly flawed on methodological and interpretative grounds. There is bias, in that his original core sample of 26 ND experients was expanded by the introduction of 146 members from the International Asso-ciation of Near-Death Studies or 'IANDS'. Of these, only 40 were NDE subjects, 30 had near-death crises but no NDE, and there were 66 other 'interested' members who had suffered neither an NDE nor a medical crisis. The entire group was divided into formal 'Christians' and 'All Others', the latter comprising a heterogeneous collection of Jews, non-institutional believ-ers, followers of other religions, believers with no specific religious affiliation, and others without any religious preferences. That, for statistical purposes is, by no means, what could sensibly be considered to comprise an unbiased, homologous, representative group. Although the analytical instrument looks at religious beliefs,[15] it poses a series of propositions biased towards a universal world religion for all, open to the possibility of reincarnation, and favouring a personalized, anti-church form of spirituality involving prayer and an internalized sense of God. The questionnaire begins with a religious beliefs approach, although results are expressed as a numerical 'Universality Index'. In my view, items 4, 5, 6, 10, 12 are not doctrinal beliefs which can be either directly assented to or not. Items 1, 2, 3, 8, 9, 11 are either ambiguous or meaningless, viewed from a wider Christian perspective. Item 7 asks whether the 'doctrine' of reincarnation is implausible: note the subtle negative here.[16]

The numerical Universality Index (U_s), is calculated by Ring from the formula

$$U_s = [\sum (U_a - U_d)] - [\sum (C_a - C_d)]$$

---

[14] Ring 1985, 144 and 282–283.

[15] Ring 1985, 282–283.

[16] 1: The essential core of all religions is the same; 2: I believe there is a heaven and a hell; 3: No matter what your religious belief, there is a life after death; 4: It is important to attend church regularly; 5: Private prayer is more important in the religious life of a person than is attendance at public church services; 6: More and more, I feel at home in any church; 7: I find the doctrine of reincarnation—very implausible; 8: Eternal life is a gift of God only to those who believe in Christ as savior and Lord; 9: God is within you; 10: In order to live a truly religious life, the church . . . is an essential; 11: The bible is the inspired word of God; 12: A universal religion embracing all humanity is an idea which strongly appeals to me.

where U refers to universality, C conventional religion, and subscript 's' a shift
to one or other. An increased (a) or decreased (d) 'agreement' with items 1–6
(U) or 7–12 (C) on the questionnaire is assessed as + or − respectively, while
zero indicates no change. Σ represents the sum of the differences between U_a
and U_d or C_a and C_d. The positive and negative scores for U and C are thus each
calculated with respect to the + or − sign, and then subtracted from each other.
Any 'shift' towards U requires a value >6 (Table 2, p. 316).

In criticism of this calculation, we should note that a zero score can never be
used in an algebraic (or logarithmic) series because of the impossibility of
assigning a value to it. We therefore cannot infer how many non-rated scores
resulted from this procedure; nor can we detect the degree of bias introduced
into each subject's final calculated U_s score. There are no prospective data for
U_s, pre- and post-event, for either NDE, or for non-NDE, subjects. Neither are
we given any indication of the degree of variance of U_s for each group, so that
the interpretation by Ring that '*shifts*' in beliefs occurred in all groups (that is,
giving the implication that subjects' opinions were, in fact, significantly altered)
is totally unwarranted and, indeed, is hardly likely. Thus the U_s values given for
mainline Christians, for either NDE subjects (4.45), non-NDE subjects (4.92)
or non-crisis controls (4.41), are by no means indicative of any deducible 'shift'
in view, given the very small numbers involved. Indeed, I suggest there are no
significant differences between this set of data for mainline Christians and the
other two groups. It is only possible to conclude that the heterogeneous 'All
Others' group did raise its score, but the level of statistical significance is not
given. A χ^2 test for all respondents with U_s scores >8 (ND+ 37; ND− 9; and nil
event, 10) gave a comparative significance level $p<0.0005$.

Many readers might therefore be taken aback by Ring's conclusion. He
asserts that his data reinforce the view that having an NDE 'shifts' a person's
viewpoint towards a 'universalistically-oriented spirituality' (Ring 1985,
p. 145). Ring's data certainly do not warrant that conclusion for the Christian
group: in fact, it is difficult to explain why those subjects collectively exhibited
such a low U_s score. Perhaps, like me, they found the propositions in the
inventory of little relevance to their individual spiritual leanings.

Moreover, there are other worrying trends about Ring's approach towards
ECE that emerge in his later book. In the first place, his approach indicates a
notable but also an extraordinarily careless drift away from good statistical
analysis: 'these words [of experients, he says] will convey what statistics can
never do'. That is, Ring puts an ever increasing reliance on the persuasiveness
of anecdotal material.[17] On a second point, belief in God (post-NDE) as far as

---

[17] Ring 1985, 6.

Ring is concerned means 'whatever adherence to a notion of God we may find in such people' (1985, p. 86). That is a non-definition of God or of (mono) theistic belief. Indeed, Ring now thinks 'that the NDE represents [one] means towards an awakening into a new evolutionary and higher mode of consciousness'—a 'planetary consciousness' based on the writings of Teilhard de Chardin (Ring 1985, p. 252)—and 'capable of bringing about this transformation in millions of people'. A generalized conviction of the authenticity of this view 'will ensue by data marshalled from this published [NDE] sample', although the sample is admittedly biased towards ~80% female respondents (p. 29) and it is 'not written solely to satisfy the empirical canons of scientific enquiry' (p. 307), but to provide the most cogent overall framework within which to understand the significance of NDE. The significance is to be found in the development of *Homo noeticus* (pp. 256ff) on his transcendent journey and to whose radiance, as a species, we are supposedly all being increasingly drawn.[18]

12.1.c. Imposing Interpretations

In 1980 Ring, as president of IANDS, cautioned against mingling the religious and spiritual implications of ECE research, noting the narrow line separating questions of religious import from religious doctrine. 'If NDE research ends up simply providing new swords with which to wage old religious wars, I will resent very bitterly my involvement with this work.'[19] Yet, based on his Religious Beliefs data,[20] Ring now claims that in assessing *doctrinal views*, ND experiencers are likely to 'shift' towards a universalistically spiritual orientation[21] transcending traditional Christian perspectives. He continues:[22] 'Indeed the strongest evidence of ND experiencers' universalistically spiritual orientation'... 'is their *belief* in the underlying unity of all religions and their *desire* for a universal religious faith that will transcend the historical divisions of the world's great religions. Thus the real significance of the NDE may not be simply that it promotes spiritual growth [that is IR] as much as the kind of spiritual growth [that is religious doctrine] it promotes'.[23] This indeed is a call for a new world religion extending beyond the limits of classical monotheism. But can such an unwarranted interpretation be

---

[18] In addition to my own criticisms of Ring, Sabom suggests there may be other, more subtle factors hovering in the background: Sabom 1998, 131ff and 143ff.

[19] Ring K, *J Near-Death Stud* 1: 14–16, 1980.

[20] Ring 1985, 312–315.

[21] Ibid, 145–147.

[22] Ibid, 162, my emphases.

[23] Ibid, 144.

drawn out of Ring's meagre findings, as I have critically presented them above? I certainly think not.

Sabom[24] expresses concern that the independence of the replicated NDE studies by many of Ring's associates might be compromised, and thus not wholly representative, because of their reliance on IANDS members (NDE subjects, near-death crisis individuals, and interested parties without any antecedent event). He is particularly concerned with Ring's assertion that NDEs often lead to a 'shift' in a person's religious worldview that embraces reincarnation. One of his Master's degree students, Amber Wells, has in fact shown that the evidence tends to support the opposite conclusion. Wells[25] questioned a group of NDE experients and a group of non-NDE crisis victims, both mainly recruited from local IANDS members. She also engaged a third casual group made up of shoppers emerging from a local grocery stall at her university town in Connecticut. Of the two former groups, 70% of NDE and 71% non-NDE IANDS members claimed to have a strong belief in reincarnation, while the figure was 30% for the group of shoppers. The national US rate for a belief in reincarnation is 23%.[26] Significantly, not one of Wells's subjects[27] was able to declare that 'any direct understanding of the nature or process of reincarnation' had arisen from the near-death event itself.

It is also significant that there was a high rate of belief in reincarnation in *both* the groups of Wells's subjects comprising IANDS associates, including the non-NDE group, when compared with the local shoppers and the national rate. This indicates clearly that other influences due to reading, promotions, or a heightened awareness and interest occasioned through personal or group contacts, were having a disproportionate effect on the subjects of Wells's studies. Ring's data[28] indicate changes in beliefs about reincarnation of ~60–65%: Sutherland[29] found an increase of 80%, while Atwater[30] declared that 'for most, it [reincarnation] becomes as a fact of life'. From the foregoing, it is evident that the progressively divergent variation in these results is indicative of other subtle influences, but occurring *post-NDE* in particular contexts. It seems unlikely, from the content of the claimed experience, that an NDE in itself would induce any subject to adopt, or become sympathetic to, the idea of reincarnation. Indeed, this would be inconsistent with the

[24] Sabom 1998, 136–137.
[25] Wells A, *J Near-Death Stud* 12: 17–34, 1993.
[26] Wells 1993, 25: Sabom 1998, 138; Gallup G and Newport F, *Skept Enquirer* 15: 137–146, 1991.
[27] Wells 1993, 25.
[28] Ring 1985, 317, Tables 3 and 4.
[29] Sutherland C, *J Near-Death Stud* 9: 21–31, 1990.
[30] Atwater Phyllis, *Coming Back to Life*. New York: Ballantine 1988, 151.

whole range of publications on the ECE phenomenon. For example, it is not a consequence of the independent experiences of Sabom's patients. Neither does it figure in the accounts of English subjects portrayed either by Grey (1985) or by Fenwick and Fenwick (1998).

In contrast to Ring's sets of data, Sabom's patients came from another area (a southern, 'Bible-belt' region of Atlanta); they were recruited clinically from consecutive, prospective admissions to his cardiac service, and were deficient in IANDS personnel. This group revealed a belief in reincarnation of ~22%, a figure well within the national US average. Moreover, those in his series, like the subjects carefully studied by Groth-Marnat and Summers, did not change their church affiliation, nor their doctrinal creed, and neither did they migrate from a church-based, to a non-ecclesial, form of 'spirituality' favouring a strong bias towards reincarnation. Usefully, the data of Groth-Marnat and Summers[31] are backed up by independent, statistically controlled responses to questionnaires from immediate, informed controls (usually comprising spouses or other intimate, within-family persons) who were able to substantiate the spiritual outcomes of their kin in the NDE group. Again, contrary to much American work, in both UK studies cited (Grey 1985; Fenwick and Fenwick 1998), reincarnation did not surface as a major post-NDE outcome. However, Grey's interpretations, not supported by the data she offers, are seemingly driven by her irresistible preference for anecdotal fragments and an overriding urge to engage in broader psychical and cosmic discussion. Contrary to other properly controlled analyses, Grey[32] erroneously sees a 'shift' (note how Ring's terminology creeps in again):

away from theological doctrines to a more spiritual ideology, a 'number' of respondents either becoming non-denominational or turning to theosophical or psychical associations, as former religious affiliations were unable to provide answers to the questions they were so ardently seeking to understand.

Not surprisingly, we are denied the crucial information deriving from those ardent questions, or some hint of how the subjects themselves interpreted their experiences.

The changes of attitude wrought by the NDE, according to Grey, included a more internally felt sense of God, a loss of interest in outward forms of religious practice and a newly sensed cosmic spirituality. It is highly unlikely that any impartial observer, presented only with the tabular data offered in her book (pp. 101, 107, 110), would be persuaded to come to the same conclusions, or be enabled to develop the same form of cosmic outlook

---

[31] Groth-Marnat and Summers 1998.
[32] Grey 1985, 108–110.

offered by Grey. Grey, and Ring, both appear to have been overly influenced by their own rhetoric and universalistic-spirituality manifesto. What is *read into* a study is quite different from what might legitimately be *read out of* a study.

12.2. NDE OUTCOMES: THE EXALTATION
OF PERSONHOOD

In this section, I wish to concern myself with theological perspectives on personhood. In pursuing that aim, I turn specifically to the influence of NDE on the subsequent changes wrought in subjects' lives, attitudes and behaviour. It is commonly agreed that post-NDE subjects are more likely to attribute to themselves a greater degree of self-respect, motivation and positive outlook towards life than was previously the case. They also exhibit an increased tendency to help, to show compassion, tolerance and acceptance towards others, to display a more focused ability to listen to different points of view and to understand other people's problems, and to empathize with them. Coupled with this tendency is a resurgence of respect, love and involvement with family groupings and in family affairs.[33]

In determining whether these changes in personality are due to being near death, or to having the NDE, Sabom compared responses to (Ring's) Life Changes Questionnaire[34] from ND experients and from 32 cardiac controls: the difference was significant.[35] Sabom refers to a study[36] of 28 German cardiac survivors, none of whom seemed to have undergone an NDE. Of this latter group, 68% considered their subsequent lives to have been unchanged, 25% thought that there was limited change, while only 7% indicated there had been a positive alteration in life attitudes. The combined data show that rather than the acute medical crisis playing a role, it is the NDE itself which engenders the subsequent modifications in the personality values of these subjects. These observations are important, deserving far greater attention than has been afforded them hitherto. That assertion is valid, irrespective of how the NDE is viewed—either as a veridical journey of 'free consciousness', or 'soul', into the realms of eternity, or (as I maintain) as a neurologically aberrant event arising as the brain is rapidly regaining conscious-awareness.

---

[33] Ring 1980 138ff; Grey 1985, 101; Sabom 1998, 79ff; Groth-Marnat and Summers 1998.
[34] Ring 1985, 122ff and 276–279.
[35] Sabom 1998, 96, and 227, Table IV.
[36] Roewer N, Kloss T, Puschel K, *Anasth Intensivther Notfallmed* 20: 244–250, 1985.

Nevertheless, from another perspective, the post-NDE influence on later behaviour cannot be regarded as unique. Changes in behaviour consequent upon many forms of crisis or deeply moving personal events are surprisingly common. Folk psychology which articulates these changes is emphatic of their foundational 'cultural consciousness'. 'My husband', laments the housewife, 'was never the same after coming out of hospital for his operation.' Or: 'We never knew he had it in him', opine neighbours when a local and somewhat reserved army recruit wins a prestigious medal for bravery during a fierce military engagement in which he suddenly displays enormous bravery and courage. Likewise, it is noticeable that many survivors of attempted suicide bids from the Golden Gate Bridge have emerged as wholly 'different' people. They no longer seek an end to their lives, but subsequently find renewed vigour, outlook, insights and hope in their futures, and new perspectives on society. The neurophysiological mechanisms corresponding to these abrupt changes in metamorphosed personhood, as well as the manner by which the brain comes to be 'reset' after varied forms of crisis-events, are currently poorly understood. These occurrences are, nevertheless, very common, disparate, but widely recognized.[37] To explore these personal changes further, especially in relation to NDE, we need to reflect on the wider meanings of what becoming a person entails, whether in life or in the face of extinction.

12.2.a. Humans as 'Becoming'

There is a tension between life and death. But life is also about possibilities, potentials, and their actualization. Clearly, that actualization begins in the womb, but may never come to have been fully realized or completed when death supervenes: hence there is a need for at least a modicum of continuity into the resurrectional life. From these early beginnings, we can trace the origin and development of each new person, a development beginning *in utero* and continuing throughout the earthly life (Chapter 10, section 4). Macquarrie's[38] approach in his book *In Search of Humanity* sees possibility and potential to lie at the very foundations of each person's existence and lifetime evolution. Of the many aspects evaluated in his quest for true humanity, Macquarrie considers human transcendence as a predominating feature in the realization of potentiality. This he sees as a striving, a continu-

---

[37] Wallace A, *Int Rec Med Gen Pract* 169: 761–774, 1956; Pahnke W, *Harvard Theol Rev* 62: 1–21, 1969; Gellhorn E and Kiely W, *J Nerv Ment Dis* 154: 399–405, 1972.

[38] Macquarrie 1983, 257ff.

ous process of development and creativity, deriving from the exercise of personal freedom (versus a deterministic universe). In these episodes of becoming,[39] we cross or 'transcend' apparent barriers into new realms and vistas, towards new goals, and into emergent opportunities and developments. It is a 'becoming more'. We see this illustrated in the reconstructed lives of NDE subjects, where living now exemplifies concerns for others, an ability to listen and weigh sympathetically other points of view, in the fostering of relationships within families and the neighbourhood, and in the promotion of love where there may have been previous breakdowns in respect, or personal relationships.[40]

These newly found characteristics influence NDE subjects whether of a religious leaning, or not; indeed, there is no reason to deny to either group these enriching and ennobling acquisitions in the further growth of their personalities.[41] These can be seen as important manifestations of God's grace permeating creation through various means, including the experiences of the NDE subject. As for those subjects with previous religious convictions, the NDE intensifies prevailing beliefs and aspirations. Here we see, in its partial realization, the biblical theme of mankind as fashioned in God's image and likeness. It is in this image, according to Irenaeus, that human life manifests a progression from creation, through moral growth to maturity, thence to recovery from sin and being glorified, and finally to 'seeing the Lord'.[42] That is, Irenaeus envisages a progressive unfolding of humanity towards deification, from potentiality ('image of God') to the realization of the glory in becoming closer to God ('likeness of God'). Similarly St Paul writes of a movement 'from glory to glory' (2 Cor 3: 18), and the author of the Second Letter of Peter describes becoming 'partakers of the divine nature' (2 Pet 1: 4).

12.2.b. Human Becoming and Divine Grace

Theologically, we cannot speak of human 'becoming' without the activity of the grace of God. The late William Vanstone begins his introductory chapter on grace in his final book with a quotation from Titus 2: 11: 'For the grace of God has appeared, bringing salvation to all people'.[43] The idea of a dawning,

---

[39] Macquarrie 1983, 26.
[40] Ring 1980 138ff, 159; Grey 1985, 95ff; Sabom 1982, 124ff; Sabom 1998, 79ff; Groth-Marnat and Summers 1998.
[41] Sabom 1998, 96–97, 226; Groth-Marnat and Summers 1998.
[42] Irenaeus, *Against Heresies* IV.38.1–3. Cf Macquarrie 1983, 33.
[43] Vanstone William H, *Fare Well in Christ*, London: Darton, Longman & Todd 1997, 1.

which can refer to the appearance of a new day, or of a new 'age', or of a new understanding or insight, is an apt image for the nativity of Jesus—as the epiphany of Grace enfleshed, the Word incarnate, a Saviour for all mankind. Vanstone is at pains to elucidate the degrees to which our lives are touched by the divine. True, those in the Hebrew frame of mind certainly recognized the mercy, justice, forgiveness and other moral virtues of Yahweh, and reckoned them as deserving of praise, respect, awe and rejoicing. But it is through Christ, as manifestation on earth of God's grace, that those virtues are disclosed, expressed and delivered most clearly. And, as is now evident in the story of Jesus, grace is nothing less than the gracious coming of God into the life of the world, a divine gift which is given freely and unconditionally in love, and a gift to be received with joy and gratitude. Divine grace, moreoever, might be experienced in the most unexpected places—in war, disasters, or at the death of a loved one. Grace abounds, there is no doubt. And it is this grace which supports us more than is realized throughout our moments of conscious-awareness. In that sense, we can conceive of an immanence of the divine in our lives, in the world and in the whole of nature, even though we may not always recognize it. But when it is recognized we know that there has been a revelation, a self-manifestation of God's presence within creation and within us.[44]

Earlier, I discussed the way in which any cognitive perception of divine presence in the world or in ourselves requires our brains for its realization, although its recognition or perception may not always be immediate or direct. Such cognition needs the same physical basis as any secular perceptions. The self-manifestation of God may even take place through aberrant forms of brain behaviour as grace takes hold of nature and transforms it. I took, as an example, the experience of Hildegard of Bingen, whose migrainous auras of light, at varying periods throughout her life, were instrumental in giving an enhanced meaning to her call throughout her monastic existence, although never providing the origin of her faith and beliefs. However, the neurophysiological world would see her 'light' as probable manifestations of cerebral visual regions subject to periodic decrements in regional blood flow.

In like manner for ECE, I have put forward arguments above that ECE phenomenology can be ascribed to disturbances in brains that are in process of recovering from life-threatening events occasioned by severely compromised cortical function. Thus, to the dispassionate observer, ECEs in themselves convey no information of any import relevant to the spiritual realm of the afterlife or of divine persons apparently confronted there. Neither do they

[44] See also Fiddes Paul, *Participating in God*, London: Darton, Longman & Todd 2000, for further insights on this theme.

hold out promise as evidential accounts of an ecape of mind or soul from corporeal shackles, or of the more nebulous concept of disembodied consciousness. Nevertheless the event, as a personal experience reflected upon afterwards, does have profound meaning for every subject, meanings that cannot be dismissed by observing non-experiencers. Thus, somewhat like Hildegard's lights, the experiential force of an ECE serves in modifying and amplifying the behaviour and attitudes of subjects during the remainder of their lives in a most substantial way. And those modifications and amplifications may justifiably be regarded as moments of divinely directed grace towards each individual.

Those reconfigurations stand in marked contrast to the egregious and strained interpretations forced on the narratives by authors like Ring and Grey. In their writings they have imposed on ECE a universalized spirituality that is foreign to the event, and which probably would not have been recognized by those giving the narratives. By contrast, I believe that, from their own accounts, the post-NDE transformation has far greater meaning for the relevant subjects than the NDE itself; it is certainly more significant than the speculative superstructures that have been attached to the event by subsequent authors. Furthermore, that greater, transcendental meaning has not been effectively drawn out of these experiences by the authorship considered in the present book. There has been an authorial failure, due to a lack of sensitivity towards the narratives offered, and to a predominance of preconceived ideas as to what authors perceived ECE to signify, working from their own agendas. We see that tendency grossly exemplified in the writings of Ring, and to a lesser extent in Grey.

If I were to make a suggestion for research, it would be to investigate critically the way that experients have been engaged by a kind of post-experiential transcendence. It would be to ask to what degree, and in what manner, this transcendent movement beyond the self has actually been translated into acts of mercy or good faith towards other persons, in the way that these subjects have testified. The current literature is, unfortunately, silent on such issues.

13

Overview and Recapitulation

13.1. CONSCIOUSNESS AND SOUL

The extra-corporeal experience (ECE) embodies notions of out-of-body, and near-death, phenomenology. Whether experiences are conflated, as is usual, or construed as separate neurophysiological and experiential events, ECEs have been regarded by the authors cited in this book, and by many others, as veridical manifestations of post-mortem survival experiences or evidence for the immortality of soul. Upon that premise, and the narratives received, it is postulated that when the brain is dead, either consciousness (Ring, Grey, Fenwick) or the soul (Sabom, Badham) vacates the brain or body, respectively, thus to gain access to a life beyond death and glimpse some of its features.

That is a view which I firmly reject. Here I think it is necessary to distinguish between conscious-awareness in itself and the projection of para-centric space beyond our immediate physical boundaries (as a sensed presence, or an ECE). The way that many of the authors favourable to ECEs use the notion of consciousness, or 'free consciousness', is often imprecise. On my definition, consciousness is a basic phenomenon enabling its subject to become aware of the prevailing environment, and which can be recognized in so immature a being as a 25-week-old foetus under hospitalized neonatal intensive care. That level of more-or-less-wakefulness, as opposed to frank unconsciousness, or some coexistent mode of subconsciousness, is incomparably different from those qualities of mind which any neonate will later acquire on reaching its twenty-fifth birthday. Throughout those formative years, the progressive aspects of mind and of personality will have evolved and been erected upon that initial basic state of primitive 'conscious' wakefulness. The mature evolved 'mind' will therefore be different from basic, raw consciousness; mind will be related to a consciousness that has been synthesized into personality which is inseparable from the body. There is no question then of detaching consciousness and sending it out 'somewhere'.

From another perspective, Sabom's account of soul is very much based on the traditional understanding of insubstantial essence encased in flesh, possibly acquired around the time of conception, and taken as agent of immortality. According to this account, at death the soul escapes, thereby ensuring the continuity of the personal being, memories, qualities and achievements of the deceased individual. I reject that ecclesial (and dogmatic) interpretation of soul. I remain uncertain as to what, in the Christian tradition and its liturgy, is precisely implied by the word 'soul', but it seems clear that 'soul' could not deliver all those attributes of living, earthbound personhood into the afterlife. There are now theologians who view the 'soul', according to their varying degrees and opinions, as equivalent to the ideas about personality that I have described above. Defined in this way, 'soul' depends on corporeal attributes (body + mind-brain) whose existence will largely cease at a death from which someone cannot be resuscitated.[1]

True death must be taken to represent a radical break, that is, a complete and irreducible break between the finitude of corporeal existence, and the promise of a new existence in the afterlife. In this study I have avoided use of the terms 'heaven' or 'eternity' because they imply egocentric concepts of location and temporality, neither of which can be properly thought, clearly, to characterize the hereafter. One is reminded of Mrs C. F. Alexander's hymn which is always popular at Christmas time: 'and He leads His children on/ to the *place* where He is gone/ . . . where like stars His children *crowned*/ all in *white* shall *wait around*'. That Jesus has gone to a 'place' where everyone is 'crowned and dressed in white' then having to hang 'around' (for ever and ever, perhaps?) creates imagery not too removed from the typical narrative adorning the pages of relevant ECE literature. 'That', as David Brown[2] has remarked in a similar vein, 'will not do'.

But what of that afterlife and its relationship to our previous earthly existence? Credal definitions call for our orientation towards 'resurrection of the dead and the life everlasting', not immortality vested in the receipt of eternal, immortal soul. That assent to resurrection, as I emphasized above in Chapter 10, is predicated firmly on the reality of Jesus' own resurrection. Nevertheless, the declaration προσδοκῶμεν ἀνάστασιν νεκρῶν καὶ ζωὴν τοῦ μέλλοντος αἰῶνος in the Niceno-Constantinopolitan promulgation of 381 CE[3] implies only the subsequent standing or rising up of the 'dead', but nothing more. The accounts in the gospels present Jesus' earthly body as being transformed and of a different quality in its appearances to the disciples, and yet it displayed, through certain signs, a continuity with the earthbound master whom the disciples had known. How our own personal transformations in 'resurrection-bodies' will come about, and what that renewed status

---

[1] Pannenberg 1994, 175ff.
[2] Brown D, *Tradition and Imagination*, Oxford: Oxford University Press 1999, 85.
[3] Kelly JND, *Early Christian Creeds*, London: Longman 1972, 297.

will entail, has not been revealed to us. We have to be content with metaphorical language and the historically rich and effulgent repertoire of poetic imagination[4] nuancing the ultimate reality of things about which we must confess, in humility and honesty, to have no direct knowledge: we really do not know. There is silence in the grave and beyond, a contrast that jars with NDE narrative accounts purporting to give descriptions of the life hereafter in glorious, vividly coloured, three-dimensional imagery so unacceptably anthropomorphic and geocentric. By contrast, as Paul Fiddes insists, 'we must take death seriously'.

Yet, as Fiddes also affirms, in taking death seriously, there must be some kind of continuity. My own argument has been to insist that what is taken over from the old creation to the new creation is very likely to be minimal. I see no need for inappropriate models like teletransportation or replicas which assume complete passage of one's entire self into the afterlife. That seems to me to be a completely wrong construal of what resurrection will be like, for 'we will be changed' (1 Cor 15: 52). Furthermore, I suggest that the New Creation will be about looking—and going—forward. It will be new in the sense of a re-creational and all-consuming act by God, and not about old reminiscences or regrets over lost causes: 'there will be no stoking of past embers'.

Given the widely varying biological circumstances under which each brain recovers, every descriptive narrative offered by NDE subjects is idiosyncratically fashioned, reflective of the memories and lifelong impressions unique to each professing individual. These aberrant mental images are not culled from any other-worldly journey but as a thorough-going, this-worldly event, occasioned by the reawakening to conscious-awareness of a brain subjected in ~80% of subjects to major antecedent circulatory/hypoxic insult. The return to conscious-awareness can only be envisioned as a chaotic process of re-perfusion and re-oxygenation, terminating abruptly as conscious-awareness fully re-emerges from the world of subconscious, dream-like mentation.

My strategy for demonstrating the validity of that claim has been to argue from a wide-ranging neurophysiological literature, exemplifying the varied brain-states capable of generating analogous, idiosyncratically determined, personal mental imagery. The ephemeral nature of these mental excursions, referable to minutes or seconds of real time, is secured by extrapolating retrogradely from the defined time-point of congruence—the NDE terminating with the re-establishment of conscious-awareness. Their short timescale, as evinced from word-counts derived from dream research methodologies,

---

[4] Hedley D, *Living Forms of the Imagination*, London: Clark (Continuum) 2008.

provides the evidential basis of that assertion. The NDE thus can be envisioned as an imagined trajectory into some sort of subconscious, mentally contrived other-worldly domain but one which, *of itself*, signifies very little.

13.2. ON TRUE RESURRECTION VERSUS A HALLUCINATORY METAPHYSIC

To the dispassionate observer outside the immediate circle of interest, ECE phenomenology occasions some curiosity or even fascination, but it has done little generally to inform the social mores, or to dissipate death-anxiety from those not directly involved with this movement. Theologically, there is scant basis for an ECE-type eschatology capable of meaningful interaction with Judaeo-Christian concepts of an afterlife, as thoroughly grounded in the raising of Christ from the dead, and as paradigm for faith and hope in a manner of being beyond the grave. The silence of revelatory disclosure and the need for quiet, persevered-for hope in faithfulness to scripture, creed, and ecclesial tradition contrasts sharply with the non-uniform provenance of NDE subjects' idealistic heavenly abode. Similarly in contrast is the earthbound portraiture of God or Jesus, whenever they are apparently encountered. Neither is NDE phenomenology recognizably apocalyptic, as reminiscent of the theophanies vouchsafed to Paul on the approaches to Damascus (Acts 9: 3–4) or to the exiled John on the island of Patmos (Rev 1: 12ff). It must at least be recognized that strong contrasts arise with the Judaeo-Christian tradition in relation to the way that ECE literature engages with the phenomenon. There we read of 'consciousness' ascending to higher levels of cosmic awareness and unity, of engagements with holographic frequency-analysis, and of support for the promise of future reincarnations.

Attempts to secure alignment of ND experience to the classical contours of eschatology, spiritual encounter or revelatory disclosure of the divine are thus hard to effect. From all this, my conclusion is that ECE cannot be construed in any theological sense as related to some other-worldly heavenly realm, or with a direct confrontation with Deity. When it is acknowledged that a wholly neurophysiological explanation is possible, the other-worldly edifice constructed by the authors of ECE literature is seen to be the more dependent on authorial presuppositions, weakening considerably any claims on truth. We can detect that their metaphysical conclusions are only loosely tied to the narrative accounts of their subject clientele. Moreover, the methodological criticisms reasonably applicable to certain parts of this literature further undermine the interpretational analysis which particular authors deploy on their experiential case-load.

In addition, I suggest that specific characteristics of NDE make it well-nigh impossible to construct a coherent and consistent account from the varied narratives published. For example, there are illogical antitheses between early-phase and late-phase subject behaviour, such as barriers which are initially crossed without difficulty but which subsequently offer insuperable resistance to subjects' further advances. Or there is an initial abandonment of concern for family or work, later to be sensed as urgent and morally compelling. Also, we note the banality and bizarreness of many published narratives, the absurd content of some of the reported conversations with either divine or deceased persons, their ephemeral nature, and the abruptness with which many experiences terminate. The phenomenology, viewed critically, is more akin to subconscious oneiric experience than to robust, credible accounts of an authentic, veridical glimpsing of the hereafter. That subjects recover surely must confirm the fact that they were never dead. Moreover, if they, or their brains, were dead the question arises as to how they were able to bring back memories of their supposed encounters, assuming these to be *true* and not completely fabulous, when such memory function depends on the cerebral organization of appropriate neural circuitry. That could only happen in viable brains in their recovery phase. Finally, one should at least be curious about why subjects undergoing multiple ECE never experience the same celestial parameters on successive occasions: this again points to neurological artefact rather than veridical extracorporeal travelling to where, in Augustine's words, we find ultimate rest.

It goes unnoticed by the authorship cited herein, that the data supposedly disclosed to subjects during their NDE, the global knowledge alleged to have been acquired, insights gained, answers to 'unanswerable' questions given, are *never* retained for subsequent use, or for the enlightenment of those never privileged with such experiences. These observations further corroborate my argument that the ECE is not some kind of outward-bound trip into the hereafter. It represents an inward-bound medley of pre-existing memories and presuppositions that come into the subconscious mental state as the brain, for most subjects, is recovering from an ischaemic/hypoxic insult.

Now the predominant affective-cognitive thought-mode prior to an ECE should be apparent. It is the fear of imminent death and human extinction. The resulting mental imagery represents the idiosyncratic perceptions of each of these subjects as to what the afterlife will entail for each of them. That a profound cognitive-affective issue can influence subsequent mental imagery, thence to spread and involve other parts of the brain, has been exemplified by the female epileptic after receiving information on her brother's war-grave, a case cited in Chapter 4 along with similar ones.

I therefore claim that the neurophysiological challenge put out by Ring, and reproduced in my Introduction, has been completely neutralized, if not eradicated, by my pursuit and deployment of in-depth neurophysiological explanation and possibility. But furthermore, I claim that the ECE literature, taken as a whole, completely fails to convince that its subjects have been witness to any location consistent with Christian concepts of a heaven. Neither should we allow ourselves to think that we have been offered revelational material pertinent to any other form of afterlife, however perspectivally construed.

13.3. THE FORGOTTEN POTENTIAL OF THE POST-EXPERIENTIAL SUBJECT

I come now to a second major point in conclusion. ECE phenomenology is not a one-sided event concerned with other-worldly matters. Janus-like, it looks in two directions, facing back on subjects' lives before the crisis overtook them, and forwards to their life afterwards. Indeed, it is my view that post-event phenomena for the subject, as a person continuing to live on earth, are of far greater importance than the disproportionate attention given to 'other-worldly' experiential concerns. This view, while emphatic of the dimorphic nature of ECE phenomenology and its other-worldly mythology, also lays particular stress on the reality of the changed lives of subjects, once recovered from the precipitating event. Those who do survive to tell the tale were clearly never dead, in the normal meaning of that word. So, in the absence of any non-neurophysiological explanation of the event itself, we are prompted to consider the influential outcomes of this type of phenomenology on subjects during their subsequent life histories. This aspect of the literature on ECE is particularly defective. Once again, then, we are here concerned with the subject of personhood.

We have already seen that human *becoming*[5]—or becoming that which *is*,[6] as the unique attribute of individual personhood—requires freedom and transcendence. Freedom of personal action derives from our cognitive and affective capacities, but also from not being part of a fixed, deterministic universe where control is effected either by a divine puppet-master, or by subconscious forces such as dream-state mode mentation. That capacity to

[5] Macquarrie 1982, 2ff.
[6] Zizioulas J, On Becoming a Person, in: Schwöbel C and Gunton C (eds), *Persons Divine and Human*, Edinburgh: Clark 1999, 34ff.

act and to reach outwards is what, in part, characterizes human transcendence. I regard the post-experiential change which is wrought in subjects' lives as the result of undergoing an ECE to be a significant manifestation of personal freedom and the will towards transcendence. A remarkable transition is seen in such aspects as a reduction in the fear of death, and a strengthened belief in the reality and tangibility of a continued existence in the hereafter.

Moreover, in the continuing earthly life of post-ECE subjects, there emerges an increased degree of personal motivation and self-respect. From that arises an urge to employ that changed perception of the self towards the well-being of other people, expressed as compassion, tolerance, empathy, and equanimity in respect of other points of view. Another emergent tendency embraces the promotion of family values, friendship and goodwill where these may have been lacking hitherto. For those subjects with a pre-existing religious belief, post-experiential belief in God, church attendance, or denominational affiliation was not altered. What did change was a heightened sense of internal religiosity in faith, strength of belief, increased spirituality and the meaning of the religious conviction in their lives. Such attitudes are at variance with the disputable conclusions of Ring and Grey[7] that post-experiential subjects are more likely to eschew their previous faith systems and ecclesial preferences in favouring individually tailored spiritualities, psychical expression or marked yearnings towards reincarnation. Other studies by Sabom, Amber Wells,[8] and British writers clearly argue against such tendentious conclusions.

It is regrettable that post-ECE personal behaviour has been ignored, with so little recognition paid to its importance, against a misplaced enthusiasm for esoterically based, speculative interpretations oriented towards other-worldly states. Clearly more studies are needed to evaluate more deeply the impact of changed attitudes on subjects' lives, and their knock-on influences where other people are concerned. There has been scarcely any appreciation of the implications or impact of the way in which subjects' lives are so radically turned about through ECEs, as a means for good or the promotion of inter-societal relationship. Yet we are informed[9] that possibly 8 million US citizens have undergone ECE. Ring rejoices in this number as potential recruits for his world religion of universal spirituality. Conversely, it is possible that the insights gained by some post-experiential subjects could be harnessed for the amelioration of society, for instance in engagement in the caring professions or personal counselling. Here is a worthwhile social task, but the

---

[7] Sabom 1998, 186–187.
[8] Wells 1993, 17.
[9] Ring 1985, 254.

suitability of ECE experients for particular vocations still awaits detailed study. It is an area where future research focus should be directed. Surely this would be of greater value than trying to determine whether ECE subjects out-of-body can 'see' marked cards deposited on top of operating theatre lights and cupboards. For these reasons, I regard this side of ECE coinage as of far greater import than its so-called 'other-worldly' obverse.

In a recent book, Marilyn McCord Adams[10] notes a transcendence in nature, from energetic physico-chemical processes, through plants and mobile animals in which life can interact with environment, be self-sustaining and self-replicating, and thence to the endowment of humankind with self-awareness, self-consciousness, and the capacity for self-reciprocating love and relationship. These characteristics, as integrated into personality in a contemporary view of soul, are a means through which transcendent outreach is manifested. It is noteworthy that we use the word apotheosis ($\dot{\alpha}\pi o\theta\acute{\epsilon}\omega\sigma\iota\varsigma$) to encapsulate the sublime heights of human striving and endeavour, the attempt to realize the divine. Within the Christian orbit, as Zizioulas[11] noted of patristic theology, *theosis* ($\theta\epsilon\hat{\omega}\sigma\iota\varsigma$), 'God-ness' or 'divinization' of humankind, represents the projection of a person's newly born 'baptismal being' into a eucharistic communion with the divine life of the Godhead. The (apo) theosis of being concerns *who*, not *what*, is. Apotheosis is a transcendent state capturing the essence of *imago Dei*, which is less a physically conceived, even statuary resemblance (בצלמו), than an incorporation of the human into the Divine, of hypostasis into Hypostasis, or as St Paul expressed it, of being 'in Christ' ($\dot{\epsilon}\nu$ $\chi\rho\iota\sigma\tau\hat{\omega}$).

But that projected view of personhood, however resurgent, courageous, glorious, is lop-sided. Death, in its abrupt excision of life, reduces human transcendent striving to nothing, forcing relinquishment of work uncompleted, business yet to be conducted, personal affairs unconsummated. That is the 'tragedy' of corporeal existence upon which death brings radical disruption.[12] Not only in death is life in its fullness cut down like the grass of the field, to wither. At its other extreme there are victims of early brain damage, acquired defects of cerebral and mental function, starvation, disease and malnutrition, or of the brutality of civil war, whose lives are robbed of that capacity for freedom of action and transcendent over-reach. In parenthesis, these reasons surely give hope, against all reductionism and nihilism, that life is not all. For

---

[10] Adams Marilyn McCord, *Horrendous Evils and the Goodness of God*, Ithaca: Cornell University Press 2000, 165.

[11] Zizioulas 1995, 55–56; idem, *Sobornost* 5: 644–652, 1969; and see Barr's non-committal views on 'image' in Barr J, *Bull J Rylands University Library Manchester* 51: 11–26, 1968.

[12] Zizioulas 1993, 51–52.

while there may be some kind of relief in another world as 'recompense' for annihilation, for loss of potential, for the scourge of non-entity, and for mankind's inhumanity to mankind, there must also be the opportunity in the New Creation to fulfil that which remains incomplete, or even to achieve what was unstarted in the old creation. Even in 'normal' development McCord Adams, rightly, has recently reminded us of 'inefficient adaptation strategies', the entrenched aberrant viewpoint enforced on the developing child, the later 'distortions of perception and behaviour', a state of 'impaired adult freedom', and the ever-present death-anxiety overshadowing all that is yearned for, accomplished, but, come the end, never achieved.[13]

In developing the pursuit of becoming what *is*, it should become clear why I posit the post-experiential ND alteration in the subject as so vital, clearly extending beyond anything usefully salvageable from the NDE phenomenon itself, manifesting as it does a brain-recovering chaotic mentation. Even some neurophysiologists seem to regard ECE as 'normal' events rather than narrow escapes from threatened hypoxic brain-death, but I maintain that the tangible outcome of ND phenomenology is the measurable qualitative alteration in subjects' behavioural profiles towards themselves and, importantly, to others. In this situation there lies the nascent claim that ECEs are occasions of divine grace and hence of revelation, not in the experience itself but in the after-effect.

That God's grace has dawned upon us in a new day, and lived among us as incarnate Word, is the burden of an essay by William Vanstone.[14] He alerts us here to the echo of transcendence derivative from the successive parables of the virgins, the talents, and the sheep and goats (Matthew 25). From these stories keywords emerge—preparedness, resourcefulness, watchfulness—which are calls for outward personal motivation and action. Transcendence is conceivable as a movement outwards from the bodily confines of introspection, the latter maintaining separation and distance. Such an experiential transcendence gives shape to the idea of what *is*, in other words, an 'ec-static' (= 'standing out') being, reaching beyond self through and into relationship. Being, that which *is*, is constituted in relationship with and towards others, human and divine.[15] Mankind's relationship-through-person reflects the perfection of relationship, or the absolute, divine love of the triune God.

Given this human context, when persons who have experienced ECE have discovered new qualities, talents and capabilities, there will be benefit in deploying them in the further development of personhood, in the making

---

[13] Adams 2000, 37.
[14] Vanstone William H, *Fare Well in Christ*, London: Darton, Longman & Todd 1997.
[15] Zizioulas, 1993, 88.

of further relationship in ec-stasy, and in improving the well-being of society. Incapacity, to use the term employed by Zizioulas, can be turned into capacity,[16] and thus used to help those for whom life means continued stress, poverty, indignity, abuse, and lack of opportunity.

It is here that seams of untapped treasure lie hidden, awaiting some future mobilization and application. Here is the potential for a practical outcome of ECE, one outweighing any virtues that others find in a free-consciousness ascending to a fourth dimension, of promises of holographic wizardry, of the prospect of reincarnation in the hopelessness of endless biological recycling, or of finding unity in some ill-defined 'cosmic brotherhood'. I am not attempting to promulgate a research programme, but only to urge recognition of a potential which at present lies dormant, and which awaits thought and action.

13.4. THE ESCHATOLOGICAL MEANING OF SALVATION

Final salvation comes with the development of relationships which are truly revealed, not in any ECE brain-based hallucinatory commerce with an illusory 'heaven' or so-called 'beings of light'. These neurally conjured beings, ill-defined in ontological status, epistemologically bereft of credible meaning, lack the credentials of the triune Persons revealed through prophet, scripture, tradition, and personal encounter. Salvation comes through ec-static freedom of willed conscious and not subconscious choice, of action effected through love.[17] Love is the ultimate basis of all authentic relational-otherness, with humans ('love your neighbour ... enemy') and, perfectly, within the triune Godhead. Love is gained in the knowledge of the divine, enhanced through transcendent yearning for 'Otherness', and resident in the dynamic of personal being which has individual transcendence.

But as a phenomenon which engages the will, spiritual transcendence ceases, like faith and hope, on death of the mind-brain. Mind-brain, and its emergent personality, offer no inbuilt guarantee of post-mortem resurgence. This is proper for created beings, since resurrectional life is not for our own personal taking, assumption, or choosing. Neither is it merely a question of a 'soul' slipping through the gates of death, unnoticed, accompanied by the cherished reassurance that alone, it can sufficiently and capably represent the entire personality in the afterlife. Real death is a death rooted firmly in the inexorable decay of all fleshly existence; it is not a pseudo-death, accompanied

---

[16] Zizioulas J, *Scot J Theol* 28: 401–448, 1975.
[17] Zizioulas 1993, 49.

by aspects of a dream-world, from which one can be recalled or resuscitated later on. Our renewed resurrectional life is only a divine gift, bestowed through Christ's death on the cross and His glorious resurrection and ascension to God, as Father of all.

The renewal of the personhood of human beings, expressed within the Christian church by what Zizioulas calls the 'baptismal hypostasis', always remains incomplete in this life. Since this is so, the Christian tradition looks for an eschaton or fulfilled ending (ἔσχατον), assuring us of existence beyond natural life. Here and now in the Eucharist, history, the apostolic past and the eschatological future are drawn with the many into the One[18] (1 Cor 10: 17), each baptized personality sharing in the eucharistic elements to become 'one in Christ'. This is the pledge or down-payment of the 'not yet' of salvation which Paul describes—the promise of eternal being within the triune Godhead. It is a coming together into an ecclesial communion which is the location of earthbound, but still spiritual, relations-in-otherness, reflecting the triune divine life of three Persons bound by perfect love into the One.

The symbolism of baptism nevertheless promises that the hypostasis of transformed personality, incomplete as it is through its contingent biological ontology, will—through a newly creative act of God—become the basis of the new resurrection body with, and in, Christ. While the baptismal symbol points to a genuine continuity with our present existence, precisely what shape the new resurrection body will take we cannot know, since the achievement of resurrection may entail the loss of many of our worldly ties, mental and physical, as we assume the New Creation, our unique resurrection 'self'. Only in steadfast faith borne up by our increasing transcendent outreach to the divine hope and promise, granted to us in prophecy, true revelation and grace sacramentally received and experientially encountered, can we be assured that eventually we shall arrive at our destination. This may well mean, however, lacking much of our long-accumulated, cherished earthbound props and luggage.

The least we might expect is that we shall come face-to-face with the reality of the triune Unity of our former desires, hope and faith, as anticipated most simply, yet in quiet confidence, by the Psalmist:

[19]אני בצדק אחזה פניך אשבעה בהקיץ תמונתך

---

[18] Zizioulas 1993, 49–65, 143–149, 158–161.
[19] Ps 17: 15: 'For in righteousness myself shall I gaze upon your face: then, in my awakening shall I be replete with your image' (my translation).

Glossary

ACHROMATOPSIA. Inability to see in colour during wakefulness or in dreams. Due to lesions of V4 in the fusiform gyrus of the occipital cortex (see Figure 4).

AFFERENT/AFFERENCE. Pertaining to neural impulses travelling towards the brain and subserving major peripheral sensations—visual, auditory, somaesthetic (touch, hot and cold, pain and joint position), olfactory (smell) and gustatory (taste).

AGNOSIA (S). Lack of knowing or knowledge (from Greek *gnosis* = knowledge). Neurophysiologically, a reference to a specific functional defect, such as finger agnosia, left—right agnosia, or inability to recognize faces (prosopagnosia).

AMYGDALA. (From Greek *amugdalon* = almond-shaped) ovoid collections of nerve cells situated in the medial-frontal region of the temporal lobe and concerned with affect, including fear. Each conglomeration lies at the tip of the hippocampus.

ANTERIOR. To the front (of the body or organism): same as rostral.

APLASIA. Lack of organ or tissue development.

APOPHATIC. The way of negation as the basis for perceiving God: that is, his attributes are beyond any human comprehension—we can say only what God is not.

ARE = The Association for Research and Enlightenment. An American organization with an interest in psychic and allied phenomena, such as the paranormal, dreams, meditation, holistic approaches to health, and psi occurrences. The latter include OBE, apparitions, communications with the dead, hauntings, memories of past lives, and the déjà vu phenomenology. It comprises at least 30,000 members nationwide. (See Kohr, R, *Theta* 10: 50–53, 1982.)

AURA. The period before an epileptic seizure when a variety of symptoms may be experienced. These may be entirely bodily (abnormal sensations of smell, nausea, pain, movement) or transcendent (visions, divine calls). Auras may occur without the ensuing epileptic discharge. Similar phenomenology may precede migraine attacks. Note that I define aura clinically, and not from a psychical or 'mystical' perspective.

BILATERAL. On both sides of an animal, organ or tissue.

BISPECTRAL ANALYSIS. A computerized system for analysing the EEG. The process creates a numerical score useful in determining levels of consciousness. A value of 100 equates with full conscious-awareness: a score around 60 is consistent with good anaesthesia: lower values indicate deeper levels of unconsciousness. Its methodology is simple and thus lends itself to the study of OBE, in that it could be used to compute the fluctuating levels of consciousness manifested during these events. It would therefore give a clearer picture as to the competence of subjects to be aware of their surroundings throughout their experience. Such studies have yet to be done. (See Figure 7.)

BRAINSTEM. Region of brain comprising: (anteriorly) the diencephalon (thalamus and hypothalamus), (centrally) the midbrain (tectum and tegmentum) and pons, and (posteriorly) the medulla (see Figure 4).

BRODMANN AREAS. Referring to the German neuroanatomist Korbinian Brodmann (1868–1918), who classified brain regions according to the detailed microscopic structure of the cortex in relation to specific functional patterns which he detected had emerged throughout evolutionary history.

CATECHOLAMINE. Class of amine neurotransmitter substances including dopamine, epinephrine (adrenaline) and nor-epinephrine and all synthesized from the primary amino acid tyrosine (tyrosine → dopamine → nor-epinephrine → epinephrine). The general term 'aminergic' refers to the neural activities of one or other amine transmitter. Amine implies possession of an -NH$_2$ group.

CORTEX (CEREBRAL). The thin layer of nerve cell bodies (neurones) covering each cerebral hemisphere. Also known as grey matter.

DEPERSONALIZATION. Applied to persons who appear to be detached and separated from their bodies and from their mental activities.

DEREALIZATION. A failure to know, or relate to, one's environment or location.

DISSOCIATION. A combination of depersonalization and derealization.

EEG (ELECTROENCEPHALOGRAM). A tracing obtained by measuring brain electrical activity through the application of multiple surface scalp electrodes. During waking moments the mean rhythm (α: 8–14Hz) is fast and of low amplitude. In stages I and II of sleep onset, the rhythm slows (θ: 4–7Hz), while in stages III/IV the rhythm is very slow and of very high voltage amplitude (δ: <4Hz). Periods of REM sleep are characterized by a faster rhythm known as β (>14Hz) during which the brain is in an alert or 'awake' phase.

EFFERENT. Pertaining to outcomes, brought about by neural axons travelling towards the periphery, or end-responses, such as motor or affective consequences.

ENDORPHIN. An endogenously produced peptide (small protein molecule) within the brain with opium-like actions, thus simulating the calming and pain-relieving effects of morphine.

EPISTEMOLOGY. (From Greek *episteme* = understanding or knowledge), thus meaning the nature of perceptions or a system of beliefs regarding the significance of a series of facts or observations.

ESCHATOLOGY. (From Greek *eschaton* = end or last) referring to the theology of the end-times, in terms of prophetic rule of God, or the apocalyptic realization of the Kingdom of God and the coming of Jesus on the clouds to judge the nations.

FRONTAL LOBE. That part of the cerebral cortex lying in front of the central sulcus of each hemisphere (see Figure 4). It comprises the motor and pre-motor cortex together with the pre-frontal cortex (q.v.).

GABA (gamma-aminobutyric acid). The major inhibitory amino acid transmitter within the central nervous system, derived from glutamate (glutamic acid).

GENICULATE BODY. A neural (synaptic) relay station between retinae (eyeballs) and the visual tracts (IInd cranial nerve), and from which second-order neurones originate to sweep down to the primary visual cortex (V1/V2) located at the pole of the occipital cortex.

GYRUS. An irregular bulging fold on the surface of the cerebral cortex. Many are descriptively named, such as pre-central gyrus, angular gyrus, or fusiform gyrus.

HAPTIC. Referring to touch sensation.

HIPPOCAMPUS. (From Greek *hippos* = horse; *kampos* = sea-monster.) These are comma-shaped structures located in the antero-medial aspect of either hemisphere, and whose lower tips are in contact with the amygdalar nuclei. The hippocampus is concerned with declarative memory—of events that have occurred (as opposed to procedural learning or the how-to-do-type remembered abilities). Damage to the hippocampus causes 'amnesia' or loss of memory, that is, failure to know that such-and-such happened, or is.

HYDROCEPHALUS ('water on the brain'). Due to blockage within the ventricular system of the brain, leading to an accumulation of cerebro-spinal fluid (CSF). Usually amenable to neurosurgical procedures for relieving, or bypassing, the obstruction. The latter may be achieved inserting a mechanical shunt in order to permit flow of CSF into some other body cavity or vessel.

HYPERVENTILATION. Deep overbreathing brought on by deliberate conscious effort or by underlying disease, such as advanced renal acidosis or diabetic keto-acidosis.

HYPNAGOGIC. Pertaining to the period during which sleep is entered, or sleep-onset.

HYPNOPOMPIC. Pertaining to the period of awakening from sleep, or sleep-offset.

IANDS = International Association for Near-Death Studies.

ICTAL. Referring to an epileptic discharge.

IDIOPATHIC. Cause or origin of a clinical syndrome or pathological process unknown or uncertain.

IPSILATERAL/IPSILESIONAL. Effect caused by (brain) disturbance on *same* side (as opposed to contralateral, as with a stroke: that is, the paralysis is apparent on the side opposite to the side of the brain lesion: see also unilateral).

ISCHAEMIA/ISCHAEMIC. Referring to the effects on tissues of a lack of, or reduction in, blood flow to that specific region.

LATERAL. Away from the mid-line axis towards the side.

LIMBUS/LIMBIC. Pertaining to structures involved in emotion, memory and learning. The limbus or limbic system, located on the inner surfaces of each hemisphere, comprises amygdala, hippocampal and parahippocampal gyri, the cingulate gyrus, and connections with the PFC and other cortical association areas.

LOCUS COERULEUS. A group of bilaterally disposed neurones throughout the pontine brainstem which secretes nor-epinephrine (nor-adrenaline) and whose axons project widely within the cerebral cortex (see Figure 8).

MEDIAL. Pertaining to the mid-line axis.

MEDIAL (PARACENTRAL) PARIETAL CORTEX. Pertaining to that part of the parietal cortex disposed along the inner (or medial) aspect of each hemisphere.

MICROSOMIA/MACROSOMIA. The illusion that one or other body parts are diminishing, or enlarging, in size.

MIDBRAIN. Located between diencephalon and pons, comprising the upper tectum and lower tegmentum (see Figure 4).

MRI (Magnetic Resonance Imaging). A technique dependent on the behaviour of hydrogen ions in a strong magnetic field. The signals emitted by the atoms are collected by sensors on the head and computerized, thus providing an internal image of the brain. fMRI, or functional magnetic resonance imaging, employs the difference in properties between oxygenated haemoglobin (oxyhaemoglobin) and deoxygenated haemoglobin (deoxyhaemoglobin) in a magnetic field. More deoxyhaemoglobin occurs in areas where blood flow is increased due to an elevated neural metabolic activity, and hence oxygen utilization. These scans can be performed quickly, have good resolution, and are non-invasive.

MYSTICAL. Not an easy term to define, hence my use of quotes in referring to others' use of this word. Could mean personal experience of God and reflection upon it. Or a heightened sense of God given to those pursuing a devout life of prayer. Its usage in the ECE literature suggests a vaguer understanding loosely associated with other-worldly events and activities.

N_2O. Nitrous oxide or 'laughing gas'. Used for short-term anaesthesia, as in childbirth or the reduction of simple fractures or dislocated joints.

NEURONE. This is the basic cellular unit of the nervous system (in addition to other supportive cells including oligodendrocytes, astrocytes, and microglia). Each neurone has many projections (= dendrites) through which contact with other neurones is effected by means of special terminals (= synapses). Neurones also put out longer processes, termed axons, which make contact with distant effector cells such as muscles and tendons. The functional efficiency of the neuronal corpus is amplified several thousand-fold through synaptic connectivity.

NMDA (n-methyl-D-aspartate). A subtype of the glutamate receptor. A gated ion channel permeable to the ions of sodium (Na^+), potassium (K^+), or calcium (Ca^{2+}). Its permeability is dependent on magnesium (Mg^{2+}) ions which are expelled by marked depolarizations of the cell membrane before inward transfer of K^+ and Ca^{2+} can occur.

NEOPLASIA. The medical term given to malignant, cancerous transformation of a tissue.

NREM (non-REM sleep). Sleep occurring during sleep-onset phases III and IV and characterized by slow waves in the EEG, muscular relaxation, very reduced bodily metabolism, and few dreams.

NUCLEUS. Neurophysiologically refers to a collection of neurones concerned with a specific function. Some may have eponymous names, such as Meynert's nucleus (see Figure 8) or a more romantic name deriving from earlier anatomical studies, such as locus coeruleus (the 'blue place'). This usage differs from that referring to the compartment within each cell which contains the chromosomes.

OCCIPITAL LOBE. Rear part of cerebral cortex behind parietal lobe and concerned with visual perception (see Figure 4).

ONEIRIC. Relating to dreams and dreaming.

ONTOLOGY. The basis of, and theories pertaining to, being and existence (from Greek participles *on* and *ontos*, meaning being or that which is, derived from verb 'to be').

OTOLITH. Hair-like processes within the utricle and saccule of the inner ear which bend with different forms of motion. These signals are transduced by the brain and interpreted as changes in body position, movement in space, rotation, and the influence of gravitational force.

PARIETAL LOBE. Situated between the frontal and occipital lobes (see Figure 4). Its anterior part is concerned with somaesthetic afferent receptivity. The posterior parietal cortex is concerned in the coordination of body-image and comprises the upper or superior parietal lobule (Brodmann areas 5 and 7), and the inferior or lower lobule (Brodmann 39, 40).

PET (Positron Emission Tomography). This requires injection of a radioactive compound which emits positively charged particles. In practice, a fluorinated isotope of 2-deoxyglucose is used, which is taken up at sites of neuronal activity. The substance is retained within those active neurones as a result of phosphorylation, thus allowing a picture of brain activity to be assembled. Disadvantages are the use of an isotopic marker, poor resolution, and long timespan for image generation.

POSTERIOR. To the rear.

PRE-FRONTAL CORTEX. The area of cortex at the anterior end of the frontal lobe, comprising the dorso-lateral PFC (Brodmann areas 9, 10, 44, 45, 46) and the medial orbito-frontal PFC (Brodmann areas 11, 13, 25, 32, 47) (see Figure 4). It receives major inputs from all areas of the brain and is concerned in their integration, hence contributing to the emergence of personality, personal drive and demeanour, appropriate affective and physiological responses to environmental events and challenges, and to moral sensibility. Deactivation of the PFC during REM sleep-mode may account for the bizarre, illogical content of dreams; similar effects may be operative as the brain recovers form insults giving rise to ECE phenomenology and the equally bizarre, illogical mentation which characterizes those experiences.

PROPRIOCEPTION/PROPRIOCEPTIVE. The sense of joint movement and position.

RAPHE NUCLEI. Consists of clusters of nerve cell bodies distributed along the medial aspect of the midbrain which synthesize the amine neurotransmitter serotonin (or 5-hydroxytryptamine). These neurones project widely to the cortical regions. (See Figures 8 and 10.)

REM SLEEP. Follows deep Stage III/IV slow-wave sleep of the sleep-onset period. During the next 30–45 minutes, the brain seems to awaken with very fast, low amplitude β rhythms demonstrable in the EEG and associated with vivid, bizarre, illogical dream sequences. There is widespread paralysis of anti-gravity musculature thereby preventing the enactment of actions arising during these episodes of dreaming. The exceptions are the eye musculature giving rise to rapid eye oscillations and the thoracic musculature permitting continued respiratory effort.

SEROTONIN (5-hydroxy-tryptamine, or 5-HT). Neurotransmitter derived through oxidation of the amino acid tryptophan. Serotonin-producing neurones play important roles in the regulation of sleep, affective behaviour and mood (see Figure 8).

SLOW-WAVE SLEEP (SWS). The deepest level of sleep occurring during stages III/IV of the sleep-onset period, and characterized by a very slow waveform (theta) in the EEG.

SOMAESTHETIC. Pertaining to sensory signals coming in from the peripheral parts of the body, subserving touch, pain, temperature (warmth and coldness).

SYNAPSE. A structural connection between adjacent, or groups of, neurones, serving to increase the functional capacities of the nervous system. Given there are $\sim 10^{11}$ neurones in the brain, synaptic density is estimated at $\sim 10^{15}$, that is on average, approximately 10,000 synapses per neurone.

TEMPORAL LOBE. The lateral part of the hemisphere projecting away from the parietal lobe (see Figure 4).

THALAMUS. Major relay station between incoming afferent nerve fibres from all regions of the periphery and the association centres in the cortical hemispheres. It occupies the dorsal region of the diencephalon.

THEOPHANY. An appearance of God to, or before, mankind (from Greek *theos* = God; *phanero* = to reveal or show forth). In the Christian tradition, the greatest theophany would be the Incarnation, God as man.

TRANSMITTER-GATED ION CHANNEL. A pore-forming membrane protein permeable to ions and 'gated' (that is, opened or closed) by a neurotransmitter. The latter acts on the membrane protein thereby changing its configuration so as to allow passage of a charged ion (such as potassium (K^+) or calcium (Ca^{2+})) through the membrane into the interior of the cell.

UNILATERAL. Restricted to one or other side of an animal.

VENTRICULAR SYSTEM. Pertains to the circulation of cerebro-spinal fluid (CSF) through the cerebral cortices and brainstem. Anatomically, the system comprises two lateral ventricles in the R and L cerebral hemispheres (see Figure 9), connected to the third ventricle in the diencephalon. Circulation is continued through the midbrain and pons by a narrow channel which opens out into the fourth ventricle on the surface of the lowermost part of the brainstem (medulla). Blockages in the flow of fluid, due to various causes, may lead to a build-up of fluid and hydrocephalus.

VESTIBULAR SYSTEM. Deriving from the inner ear and comprising semicircular canals, saccule and utricle. Changes in body posture are transduced, through fluid movements in the semicircular canals and of the otolith hairs within the saccule and utricle, via the VIIIth cranial nerve (vestibular division) through the brainstem and onwards to the cortex. Vestibular information is integrated in multi-sensory 'association areas' with ocular information and messages arriving via somaesthetic nerve pathways (from skin and joints). This system contributes to the body-image and the person's sense of body-in-space, and relationship to immediate environment (paracentric space), and to gravitational force. (See Figure 5.)

WEBER-VALSALVA MANOEUVRE. Occasion when forced expiration is attempted against a closed larynx.

WHITE MATTER. This refers to the long processes of nerve cells, or axons, which connect one with the other in the subcortical regions of the brain. Many axons are covered with a whitish waxy substance known as myelin. Thus myelinated, or non-myelinated, nerve fibres.

Bibliography

Reference Texts

A Hebrew and English Lexicon of the Old Testament. Brown F, Driver SR, Briggs CA. Oxford: Clarendon Press 1906 (Rev GR Driver 1951).

A New Dictionary of Christian Theology. Richardson Alan and Bowden John (eds). London: SCM Press 1983.

Catechism of the Catholic Church. London: Chapman/Libreria Editrice Vaticana 1994

Exegetical Dictionary of the New Testament (vols 1–3). Balz Horst and Scheider Gerhard (eds). Grand Rapids (MI): Eerdmans 1994.

Greek—English Lexicon. Liddell HG and Scott R (rev HS Jones) with a Revised Supplement. Oxford: Clarendon Press 1996.

New Dictionary of Theology. Ferguson Sinclair, Wright David, Packer James (eds). Leicester: InterVarsity Press 1988.

Septuaginta. Stuttgart: Deutsche Bibelgesellschaft 1979.

The Greek New Testament. Aland K, Black M, Martini C, Metzger BM, Wikgren A (eds). Stuttgart: Deutsche Bibelgesellschaft 1994.

The Holy Bible (RSV). London: Collins 1973.

The Holy Scriptures [תורה נביאים כתובים]. Jerusalem: Koren Publishers.

The Old Testament Pseudepigrapha (vol 1). Charlesworth James H (ed). New York (NY): Doubleday 1985.

The SCM Dictionary of Christian Spirituality. Wakefield Gordon (ed). London: SCM Press 1983.

Neuroscience: Exploring the Brain. Bear Mark, Connors Barry and Paradiso Michael (eds). Baltimore (MD): Lippincott Williams & Wilkins 2001, 2nd edn.

Neuroscience. Stein, John F with Stoodley CJ. Chichester: Wiley 2006.

The Oxford Companion to the Mind. Gregory Richard L (ed). Oxford: Oxford University Press 2004, 2nd edn.

Books and Articles

Adams Marilyn McCord. *Horrendous Evils and the Goodness of God.* Ithaca (NY): Cornell University Press 2000.

Adler Alexandra. Disintegration and restoration of optic recognition in visual agnosia. *Arch Neurol Psychiatr* 51: 1944, 243–259.

Adler Alexandra. Course and outcome of visual agnosia. *J Nerv Ment Dis* 111: 1950, 41–51.

Adler Caleb, Goldberg Terry, Malhotra Anil, Pickar David, Breier Alan. Effects of ketamine on thought disorder, working memory, and semantic memory in healthy volunteers. *Biol Psychiatr* 43: 1998, 811–816.

Aghajanian G, Marek G. Serotonin and hallucinogens. *Neuropyschopharmacol* 21: 1999, 16S–23S.

Aizenberg D and Modai I. Autoscopic and drug-induced perceptual disturbances. *Psychopathol* 18: 1985, 237–240.

Albala A Ariav, Weinberg Naimah, Allen Stephen. Maprotiline-induced hypno-pompic hallucinations. *J Clin Psychiatr* 44: 1983, 149–150.

Aldrich, Michael. The clinical spectrum of narcolepsy and idiopathic hypersomnia. *Neurology* 46: 1996, 393–401.

Alkire MT. Quantitative EEG correlations with brain glucose metabolic rate during anesthesia in volunteers. *Anesthesiology* 89: 1998, 323–333.

Allen Thomas and Agus Bertrand. Hyperventilation leading to hallucinations. *Am J Psychiatr* 125: 1968, 632–637.

Allport Gordon and Ross J Michael. Personal religious orientation and prejudice. *J Pers Soc Psychol* 5: 1967, 432–443.

Alston William P. *Perceiving God: The Epistemology of Religious Experience.* Ithaca (NY): Cornell University Press 1993.

Andersen R. Multimodal integration for the representation of space in the posterior parietal cortex. *Phil Trans R Soc Lond* B 352: 1997, 1421–1428.

Andersen R, Snyder L, Bradley D, Xing J. Multimodal representation of space in the posterior parietal cortex and its use in planning movements. *Ann Rev Neurosci* 20: 1997, 303–330.

Andersen R, Shenoy K, Snyder L, Bradley D, Crowell J. The contributions of vestibular signals to the representations of space in the posterior parietal cortex. *Ann NY Acad Sci* 871: 1999, 282–292.

Antrobus John. REM and NREM sleep reports: comparison of word frequencies by cognitive classes. *Psychophysiol* 20: 1983, 562–568.

Ardilo Alfredo and Gomez Jaime. Paroxysmal 'feeling of somebody being nearby'. *Epilepsia* 29: 1988, 188–189.

Ardis J Amor and McKellar Peter. Hypnagogic imagery and mescaline. *J Ment Sci* 102: 1956, 22–29.

Arena R, Murri L, Piccini P, Muratorio A. Dream recall and memory in brain lesioned patients. *Res Commun Psychol Psychiatr Behav* 9: 1984, 31–42.

Arnow B, Desmond J, Banner L, Glover G, Solomon A, Polan M, Lue T, Atlas S. Brain activation and sexual arousal in healthy, heterosexual males. *Brain* 125: 2002, 1014–1023.

Aserinsky E and Kleitman N. Regularly recurring periods of eye mobility, and concomitant phenomena, during sleep. *Science* 118: 1953, 273–274.

Aston-Jones G, Bloom F. Activity of norepinephrine-containing locus coeruleus neurons in behaving rats anticipates fluctuations in the sleep-waking cycle. *J Neurosci* 1: 1981, 876–886.

Aston-Jones Gary, Rajowski Janusz, Cohen Jonathan. Locus coeruleus and regulation of behavioral flexibility and attention. *Progr Brain Res* 126: 2000, 165–182.

Atwater Phyllis. *Coming Back to Life.* New York (NY): Ballantine 1988.

Avis Paul (ed). *The Resurrection of Jesus Christ.* London: Darton, Longman & Todd 1993.

Ayer AJ. What I saw when I was dead. In: Miethe Terry and Flew Antony (eds), *Does God Exist?* San Francisco (CA): HarperCollins 1991, 223–228.

Ayer AJ. What I saw when I was dead. In: Edwards Paul (ed), *Immortality*. New York (NY): Prometheus Books 1997, 269–275.

Azari Nina, Nickel Janpeter, Wunderlich Gilbert, Niedeggen Michael, Hefter Harald, Lutz Tellmann, Herzog Hans, Stoerig P, Birnbacher Dieter, Seitz Rudiger. Neural correlates of religious experience. *Eur J Neurosci* 13: 2001, 1649–1652.

Badham Paul. The Significance of Jesus' Resurrection. In: *Christian Beliefs About Life After Death*. London: Macmillan 1976, 18–43.

Badham Paul. The Meaning of the Resurrection of Jesus. In: Avis P (ed), *The Resurrection of Jesus Christ*. London: Darton, Longman & Todd 1993, 23.

Badham Paul. *The Contemporary Challenge of Modernist Theology*. Cardiff: University of Cardiff Press 1998.

Badham Paul and Badham Linda. *Immortality or Extinction?* London: Macmillan 1982.

Baker John Austin. *The Foolishness of God*. London: Darton, Longman & Todd 1970.

Barr James. The image of God in the book of Genesis: a study of terminology. *Bull J Rylands Univ Library (Manchester)* 51: 1968, 11–26.

Barrett CK. *The First Epistle to the Corinthians*. London: Black 1992.

Bartels Andreas and Zeki Semir. The neural basis of romantic love. *NeuroReport* 11: 2000, 3829–3834.

Barton John. Why does the resurrection of Jesus matter? In: Barton S and Stanton G (eds), *Resurrection*. London: SPCK 1994, 108–115.

Barton Stephen and Stanton Graham. *Resurrection*. London: SPCK 1994.

Bechara Antoine, Damasio Antonio, Damasio Hanna, Anderson Steven. Insensitivity to future consequences following damage to human prefrontal cortex. *Cogn* 50: 1994, 7–15.

Becker Karl. The centrality of near-death experiences in Chinese Pure Land Buddhism. *J Near-Death Stud* 1: 1981, 154–171.

Becker Karl. The Pure Land revisited: Sino-Japanese meditations and near-death experiences of the Next World. *J Near-Death Stud* 4: 1984, 51–68.

Bede. *A History of the English Church and People*. London: Penguin Classics (trans Leo Sherley-Price: rev RE Latham) 1968.

Benson D and Greenberg J. Visual form agnosia: a specific defect in visual discrimination. *Arch Neurol* 20: 1969, 82–92.

Benviste H, Drejer J, Schousboe A, Diemer N. Elevation of the extracellular concentrations of glutamate and aspartate in rat hippocampus during cerebral ischemia monitored by microdialysis. *J Neurochem* 43: 1984, 1369–1374.

Berkels Reinhard, Taubert Dirk, Grundemann Dirk, Schomig Edgar. Agmatine signalling: odds and threads. *Cardiovasc Drug Rev* 22: 2004, 7–16.

Blackmore Susan. *Dying To Live*. Buffalo (NY): Prometheus Books 1993a.

Blackmore Susan. Near-death experiences in India: they have tunnels too. *J Near-Death Stud* 11: 1993b, 205–217.

Blackmore Susan and Troscianko Tom. The physiology of the tunnel. *J Near-Death Stud* 8: 1989, 15–28.

Blanke O, Perrig S, Thut G, Landis Th, Seeck M. Simple and complex vestibular responses induced by electrical cortical stimulation of the parietal cortex in humans. *J Neurol Neurosurg Psychiatr* 69: 2000, 553–556.

Blanke Olaf, Ortigue Stephanie, Landis Theodor, Seeck Margitta. Stimulating illusory own-body perceptions. *Nature* 419: 2002, 269–270.

Blanke Olaf, Landis Theodor, Spinelli Laurent, Seeck Margitta. Out-of-body experience and autoscopy of neurological origin. *Brain* 127: 2004, 243–258.

Blanke Olaf, Mohr Christine, Christoph M, Pascual-Leone A, Brugger P, Seeck M et al. Linking out-of-body experience and self processing to mental own body imagery at the temporo-parietal junction. *J Neurosci* 25: 2005, 550–557.

Blanke Olaf and Arzy Shahar. The out-of-body experience: disturbed self-processing at the temporo-parietal junction. *The Neuroscientist* 11: 2005, 16–24.

Blanke Olaf and Mohr Christine. Out-of-body experience, heautoscopy, and autoscopic hallucination of neurological origin: implications for neurocognitive mechanisms of corporeal awareness and self-consciousness. *Brain Res Rev* 50: 2005, 184–199.

Blood Anne and Zatorre Robert. Intensely pleasurable responses to music correlate with activity in brain regions implicated in reward and emotion. *Proc Nat Acad Sci (USA)* 98: 2001, 11818–11823.

Bocher M, Chisin R, Parag Y, Freedman N, Weil Y, Lester H, Mishani E, Bonne O. Cerebral activation associated with sexual arousal in response to a pornographic clip: a ^{15}O-H$_2$O PET study in heterosexual men. *NeuroImage* 14: 2001, 105–117.

Bockmuehl Markus (ed). *The Cambridge Companion to Jesus*. Cambridge: Cambridge University Press 2001.

Bockmuehl Markus. Resurrection. In: Bockmuehl (ed) 2001, 102.

Bodineau L, Larnicol N. Brainstem and hypothalamic areas activated by tissue hypoxia: Fos-like immunoreactivity induced by carbon monoxide inhalation in the rat. *Neuroscience* 108: 2001, 643–653.

Boller Francois, Wright David, Cavalieri Ralph, Mitsumoto Hitoshi. Paroxysmal 'nightmares': sequel of a stroke responsive to diphenylhydantoin. *Neurology* 25: 1975, 1026–1028.

Borg J, Bengt A, Soderstrom H, Farde L. The serotonin system and spiritual experiences. *Am J Psychiatr* 160: 2003, 1965–1969.

Borg MJ and Wright NT (eds). *The Meaning of Jesus*. San Francisco: Harper 1999.

Bors Ernest. Phantom limbs of patients with spinal cord injury. *Arch Neurol Psychiatr* 66: 1951, 610–631.

Bossi L, Nobili M, Benedetto P. Peduncular hallucinosis in a young woman with vertebrobasilar insufficiency. *Arch Sci Med (Torino)* 137: 1980, 347–350.

Bottini Gabriella, Sterzi Roberto, Paulesu Eraldo, Vallare Giuseppe, Cappa Stefano, Erminio Francesco et al. Identification of the central vestibular projections in man: a positron emission tomography activation study. *Exp Brain Res* 99: 1994, 164–169.

Bouchard Thomas, M McGue, D Lykken, A Tellegen. Intrinsic and extrinsic religiousness: genetic and environmental influences and personality correlates. *Twin Research* 2: 1999, 88–98.

Boudouresque J, Gosset A, Sayag J. Maladie d'Urbach-Whiethe: crises temporales avec phénomènes extatiques et calcification des deux lobes temporaux. *Bull Acad Med* (*Paris*) 156: 1972, 416–421.

Braaten Carl and Jenson Robert J. *The Last Things*. Grand Rapids (MI): Eerdmans 2002.

Bradshaw John. *Developmental Disorders of the Frontostriatal System: Neuropsychological, Neuropsychiatric, and Evolutionary Perspectives*. Hove (East Sussex): Psychology Press 2001.

Brain Russell. Loss of visualisation. *Proc R Soc Med* 47: 1954, 288–290.

Brandt Thomas and Dieterich Marianne. The vestibular cortex: its locations, functions, and disorders. *Ann NY Acad Sci* 871: 1999, 293–312.

Brandt Thomas, Dieterich Marianne, Danek A. Vestibular cortex lesions affect the perception of verticality. *Ann Neurol* 35: 1994, 403–412.

Braun A, Balkin T, Wesensten N, Carson R, Varga M, Baldwin P, Selbie S, Belenky G, Herscovitch P. Regional cerebral blood flow throughout the sleep—wake cycle. *Brain* 120: 1997, 1173–1197.

Breier Alan, Malhotra Anil, Pinals Debra, Weisenfeld Neil, Pickar David. Association of ketamine-induced psychosis with focal activation of the prefrontal cortex in healthy volunteers. *Am J Psychiatr* 154: 1997, 805–811.

Breiter H, Gollub R, Weisskoff R, Kennedy D, Makris N, Berke J Goodman J, Kantor H, Gastfriend D, Riorden J, Mathew R, Rosen B, Hyman S. Acute effects of cocaine on human brain activity and emotion. *Neuron* 19: 1997, 591–611.

Britton Willoughby and Bootzin Richard. Near-death experiences and the temporal lobe. *Psychol Sci* 15: 2004, 254–258.

Broughton R, Valley V, Aguirre M, Roberts J, Suwalski W, Dunham W. Excessive daytime sleepiness and the pathophysiology of narcolepsy-cataplexy: a laboratory perspective. *Sleep* 9: 1986, 205–215.

Brown David. *Tradition and Imagination: Revelation and Change*. Oxford: Oxford University Press 1999.

Brown Warren. Cognitive Contributions to the Soul. In: Brown, Murphy and Malony (eds) 1998, 99.

Brown Warren S, Murphy Nancey, Malony H Newton. *Whatever Happened to the Soul? Scientific and Theological Portraits of Human Nature*. Minneapolis (MN): Fortress Press 1998.

Brueggemann Walter. *Texts under Negotiation*. Minneapolis (MN): Fortress Press 1993.

Brugger Peter. Are 'presences' preferentially felt along the left side of one's body? *Percept Motor Skills* 79: 1994, 1200–1202.

Brugger Peter. Reflective mirrors: perspective-taking in autoscopic phenomena. *Cogn Neuropsychiatr* 7: 2002, 179–194.

Brugger Peter, Regard M, Landis Th. Unilaterally felt 'presences': the neuropsychiatry of one's invisible doppelganger. *Neuropsychiatr Neuropsychol Behav Neurol* 9: 1996, 114–122.

Brugger Peter and Regard Marianne. Illusory reduplication of one's own body: phenomenology and classification of autoscopic phenomena. *Cogn Neuropsychiatr* 2: 1997, 19–38.

Brugger Peter, Kollias Spyros, Muri Rene, Crelier Gerard, Hepp-Reymond Marie-Claude, Regard Marianne. Beyond re-membering: phantom sensations of congenitally absent limbs. *Proc Nat Acad Sci (USA)* 97: 2000, 6167–6172.

Burns NT. *Christian Mortalism from Tyndale to Milton*. Cambridge (MA): Harvard University Press 1972.

Burton Russell R. G-induced loss of consciousness: definition, history, current status. *Aviat Space Environ Med* 59: 1988, 2–5.

Butler Stephen and Watson Robert. Individual differences in memory for dreams: the role of cognitive skills. *Percept Motor Skills* 61: 1985, 823–828.

Buzzi Giorgio. Near-death experiences. *Lancet* 359: 2002, 2116–2117.

Buzzi Giorgio and Cirignotta Fabio. Isolated sleep paralysis: a web survey. *Sleep Res Online* 3: 2000, 61–66 (http://www.sro.org/2000/Buzzi/61/).

Bynum Caroline and Freedman Paul (eds). *Last Things: Death and the Apocalypse in the Middle Ages*. Philadelphia (PA): University of Pennsylvania Press 1999.

Calvert Gemma, Campbell Ruth, Brammer Michael. Evidence from functional magnetic resonance imaging of crossmodal binding in the human heteromodal cortex. *Curr Biol* 10: 2000, 649–657.

Caplan L. 'Top of the basilar' syndrome. *Neurology* 30: 1980, 72–79.

Carlen P, Wall P, Nadvorna H, Steinbach T. Phantom limbs and related phenomena in recent traumatic amputations. *Neurology* 28: 1978, 211–217.

Carlson E and Putnam F. An update on the dissociative experiences scale. *Dissociation* 1: 1993, 16–27.

Carmichael M, Warburton V, Dixen J, Davidson J. Relationships among cardiovascular, muscular, and oxytocin responses during human sexual activity. *Arch Sex Behav* 23: 1994, 59–79.

Carnley Peter. *The Structure of Resurrection Belief*. Oxford: Clarendon Press 1993.

Carr Daniel B. Endorphins at the approach of death. *Lancet* 1: 1981, 390.

Carr Daniel B. Pathophysiology of stress-induced limbic lobe dysfunction: a hypothesis for NDEs. *J Near-Death Stud* 2: 1982, 75–89.

Cash William. Did atheist philosopher see God when he 'died'? *National Post (Washington, DC)*, 3 March 2001.

Catafu J, Rubio F, Serra J. Peduncular hallucinosis associated with posterior thalamic infarction. *J Neurol* 239: 1992, 89–90.

Chalmers David. *The Conscious Mind: In Search of a Fundamental Theory*. Oxford: Oxford University Press 1997.

Charles N, Froment C, Rode G, Vighetto A, Turjman F, Trillet M et al. Vertigo and upside down vision due to an infarct in the territory of the medial branch of the posterior inferior cerebellar artery caused by dissection of a vertebral artery. *J Neurol Neurosurg Psychiatr* 55: 1992, 188–189.

Cherkin Arthur and Harroun Phyllis. Anesthesia and memory processes. *Anesthesiology* 34: 1971, 469–474.

Chetrit M, Besset A, Damci D. Lelarge C, Billiard M. Hypnagogic hallucinations asociated with sleep onset REM period in narcolepsy-cataplexy. *J Sleep Res* 3: 1994, 43.

Cheyne J Allan, Newby-Clark Ian, Rueffer Steve. Relations among hypnagogic and hypnopompic experiences associated with sleep paralysis. *J Sleep Res* 8: 1999a, 313–317.

Cheyne J Allan, Rueffer Steve, Newby-Clark Ian. Hypnagogic and hypnopompic hallucinations during sleep paralysis: neurological and cultural construction of the night-mare. *Consc Cogn* 8: 1999b, 319–337.

Cheyne JA, Girard TA. Spatial characteristics of hallucinations associated with sleep paralysis. *Cogn Neuropsychiatr* 9: 2004, 281–300.

Chugani H and Phelps M. Maturational changes in cerebral function in infants determined by [18]FDG positron emission tomography. *Science* 231: 1986, 840–843.

Cirignotta F, Todesco C, Lugaresi E. Temporal lobe epilepsy with ecstatic seizures. *Epilepsia* 21: 1980, 705–710.

Cogan David. Visual hallucinations as release phenomena. *Albrecht v Graefes Arch Klin Exp Ophthalmol* 188: 1973, 139–150.

Cohn Robert. Phantom vision. *Arch Neurol* 25: 1971, 468–471.

Colby Carol L and Goldberg Michael E. Space and attention in parietal cortex. *Ann Rev Neurosci* 22: 1999, 319–349.

Collier Barbara. Ketamine and the conscious mind. *Anaesthesia* 27: 1972, 120–134.

Comings David, Gonzales N, Saucier Gerard, Johnson J Patrick, MacMurray James. The DRD4 gene and the spiritual transcendence scale of the character temperament index. *Psychiatr Genet* 10: 2000, 185–189.

Cooper John W. *Body, Soul and Everlasting Life: Biblical Anthropology and the Monism—Dualism Debate.* Grand Rapids (MI): Eerdmans 2000.

Cottingham John. *The Spiritual Dimension.* Cambridge: Cambridge University Press 2005.

Counts Dorothy Ayers. Near-death and out-of-body experiences in a Melanesian society. *J Near-Death Stud* 3: 1983, 115–135.

Crevenna R, Homann N, Feichtinger M, Ott E, Korner E. Spontaneous orgasms: an epileptic case without structural correlate. *Br J Psychiatr* 176: 2000, 300–303.

Crick Francis. *The Astonishing Hypothesis: The Scientific Search for the Soul.* London: Simon & Schuster 1994.

Cullmann Oscar. *Immortality of the Soul or Resurrection of the Dead?* In: Stendahl Krister (ed) 1965, 9.

Currier R, Jackson M, Little S, Suess J, Andy O. Sexual seizures. *Arch Neurol* 25: 1971, 260–264.

D'Aquili Eugene and Newberg Andrew. *The Mystical Mind: Probing the Biology of Religious Experience.* Minneapolis (MN): Fortress Press 1999.

D'Costa Gavin (ed). *Resurrection Reconsidered*. Oxford: Oneworld 1996.

D'Onofrio B, Eaves L, Murrelle L, Maes H, Spilka B. Understanding biological and social influences on religious affiliation, attitudes and behaviors: a behavior genetic perspective. *J Personality* 67: 1999, 953–984.

de Silva Lynn A. *The Problem of the Self in Buddhism and Christianity*. London: Macmillan 1979.

Dahl Murdoch E. *The Resurrection of the Body*. London: SCM Press 1962.

Daly David. Ictal clinical manifestations of complex partial seizures. *Arch Neurol* 11: 1975, 57–83.

Damas Mora JMR, Jenner FA, Eacott SE. On heautoscopy or the phenomenon of the double: case presentation and review of the literature. *Br J Med Psychol* 53: 1980, 75–83.

Datta Subimal. Neuronal activity in the peribrachial area: relationship to behavioral state control. *Neurosci Biobehav Rev* 19: 1995, 67–84.

Datta Subimal. Cellular basis of pontine ponto-geniculo-occipital wave generation and modulation. *Cell Molec Neurobiol* 17: 1997, 341–365.

Davis Stephen T (ed). *Death and Afterlife*. London: Macmillan 1989.

Davy Humphry. *Researches Chemical And Philosophical, Chiefly Concerning Nitrous Oxide And Its Respiration*. London: 1799–1800.

Decety Jean and Sommerville Jessica. Shared representations between self and other: a social cognitive view. *Trends Cogn Sci* 7: 2003, 527–533.

Dement W and Kleitman N. The relation of eye movements during sleep to dream activity: an objective method for the study of dreaming. *J Exp Psychol* 53: 1957, 339–346.

Devinsky Orrin, Edward Feldmann, Kelly Burrowes, Edward Bromfield. Autoscopic phenomena with seizures. *Arch Neurol* 46: 1989, 1080–1088.

Devinsky O, Feldmann E, Bromfield E, Emoto S, Raubertas R. Structured interview for partial seizures: clinical phenomenology and diagnosis. *J Epilepsy* 4: 1991, 107–116.

Dewhurst Kenneth and Beard AW. Sudden religious conversions in temporal lobe epilepsy. *Br J Psychiatr* 117: 1970, 497–507.

Dieterich M and Brandt Th. Thalamic infarctions: differential effects on vestibular function in the roll plane (35 patients). *Neurology* 43: 1993, 1732–1740.

Dorpat TL. Phantom sensations of internal organs. *Comprehens Psychiatr* 12: 1971, 27–35.

Dossey Larry. *Recovering the Soul: A Scientific and Spiritual Search*. New York (NY): Bantam Books 1989.

Drab Kevin. The tunnel experience: reality or hallucination? *J Near-Death Stud* 1: 1981, 126–152.

Dunbar Ernest. The light thrown on psychological processes by the action of drugs. *Proc Soc Psychic Res* 19: 1905, 62–77.

Dunn D, Weisberg L, Nadell J. Peduncular hallucinosis caused by brainstem compression. *Neurology* 33: 1983, 1360–1361.

Dunn James DG. *A Theology of Paul the Apostle*. Edinburgh: Clark 1998.

Duvoisin Roger. Convulsive syncope induced by the Weber maneuver. *Arch Neurol* 7: 1962, 219–226.

Dybowski-Poznan Mieczyslaw. Conditions for the appearance of hypnagogic visions. *Kwart Psychol* 11: 1939, 68–94.

Edwards Paul. *Immortality*. New York (NY): Prometheus Books 1997.

Ehrsson H Henrik. The experimental induction of out-of-body experiences. *Science* 317: 2007, 1048.

Epstein Arthur. Recurrent dreams: their relationship to temporal lobe seizures. *Arch Gen Psychiatr* 10: 1964, 49–54.

Epstein Arthur. Body image alterations during seizures and dreams of epileptics. *Arch Neurol* 16: 1967, 613–619.

Epstein Arthur. Observations on the brain and dreaming. *Biol Psychiatr* 17: 1982, 1207–1215.

Epstein Arthur and Freeman Norman. The uncinate focus and dreaming. *Epilepsia* 22: 1981, 603–605.

Fadul C, Stommel E, Dragnev K, Eskey C, Dalmau J. Focal paraneoplastic limbic encephalitis presenting as orgasmic epilepsy. *J Neuro-Oncol* 72: 2005, 195–198.

Farrell Martin and Robertson Ian. The automatic updating of egocentric spatial relationships and its impairment due to right posterior cortical lesions. *Neuropsychologia* 38: 2000, 585–595.

Feinberg W and Rapcsack S. Peduncular hallucinosis following paramedian thalamic infarction. *Neurology* 39: 1989, 1535–1536.

Fenwick Peter. *Dying: A Spiritual Experience as Shown by Near Death Experience and Deathbed Vision*. http://www.rcpsych.ac.uk/college/sig/spirit/publications/NL_15/PFenwickNearDeath.pdf 2004a.

Fenwick Peter. *The Possible Significance of the Near-Death and Approaching Near-Death Experiences*. http://eureka.ya.com/cadernostci/congresotci/peterl.htm 2004b.

Fenwick Peter. *Science and Spirituality: A Challenge for the 21st Century*. http://iands.org/research/fenwick4.php 2004c.

Fenwick Peter, Galliano Stephen, Coate Mary, Rippere Vicky, Brown Diana. 'Psychic sensitivity', mystical experience, head injury and brain pathology. *Br J Med Psychol* 58: 1985, 35–44.

Fenwick Peter and Fenwick Elizabeth. *The Truth in the Light*. New York (NY): Berkeley Books 1998.

ffytche D, Howard R, Brammer M, David A, Woodruff P, Williams S. The anatomy of conscious vision: an fMRI study of visual hallucinations. *Nature Neuroscience* 1: 1998, 738–742.

Fiddes Paul. *Participating in God: A Pastoral Doctrine of the Trinity*. London: Darton, Longman & Todd 1999.

Fiddes Paul. *The Promised End: Eschatology in Theology and Literature*. Oxford: Blackwell 2000.

Flower Michael. Neuromaturation of the human fetus. *J Med Philos* 19: 1985, 237–251.

Foldvary N, Lee N, Thwaites G, Mascha E, Hammel J, Kim H et al. Clinical and electrographic manifestations of lesional neocortical temporal lobe epilepsy. *Neurology* 49: 1997, 757–763.

Forster Estrella and Whinnery James. Recovery from G_z-induced loss of consciousness: psychophysiologic considerations. *Aviat Space Environ Med* 59: 1988, 517–522.

Foulkes David. Dreaming and REM sleep. *J Sleep Res* 2: 1993, 199–202.

Foulkes David and Vogel Gerald. Mental activity at sleep onset. *J Abn Psychol* 70: 1965, 231–243.

Foulkes David, Spear Paul, Symonds John. Individual differences in mental activity at sleep onset. *J Abn Psychol* 71: 1966, 280–286.

Foulkes David, Hollifield M, Sullivan B, Bradley Laura, Terry Rebecca. REM dreaming and cognitive skills at ages 5–8: a cross-sectional study. *Int J Behav Devel* 13: 1990, 447–465.

Fox Mark. *Religion, Spirituality and the Near-Death Experience*. London: Routledge 2003.

Frank Jan. Clinical survey and results of 200 cases of prefrontal leucotomy. *J Ment Sci* 92: 1946, 497–508.

Frank Jan. Some aspects of lobotomy (prefrontal leucotomy) under psychoanalytic scrutiny. *Psychiatry* 13: 1950, 35–42.

Frankl Viktor E. *Man's Search for Meaning*. New York (NY): Pocket Books 1985.

Franks Davis Caroline. *The Evidential Force of Religious Experience*. Oxford: Clarendon Press 1999.

Freemon Frank and Nevis Arnold. Temporal lobe sexual seizures. *Neurology* 19: 1969, 87–90.

Friberg L, Olsen T, Roland P, Paulson O, Lassen N. Focal increase of blood flow in the cerebral cortex of man during vestibular stimulation. *Brain* 108: 1985, 609–623.

Furst Peter (ed). *Flesh of the Gods*. London: Allen & Unwin 1972.

Gabbard Glen, Twemlow Stuart, Jones Fowler. Do 'Near Death Experiences' occur only near death? *J Nerv Ment Dis* 169: 1981, 374–377.

Gallassi Roberto, Morreale Agela, Montagna Pasquale, Gambetti Pierluigi, Lugaresi Elio. Fatal familial insomnia: neuropsychopathological study of a disease with thalamic degeneration. *Cortex* 28: 1992, 175–187.

Gallup George and Newport Frank. Belief in the paranormal among adult Americans. *Skeptical Enquirer* 15: 1991, 137–146.

Gautier-Smith P. Cerebral dysfunction and disorders of sexual behaviour. *Rev Neurol (Paris)* 136: 1980, 311–319.

Gellhorn Ernst and Kiely William. Mystical states of consciousness: neuro-physiological and clinical aspects. *J Nerv Ment Dis* 154: 1972, 399–405.

Gibson JCL. *Language and Imagery in the Old Testament*. London: SPCK 1998.

Gloor Pierre. Experiential phenomena of temporal lobe epilepsy. *Brain* 113: 1990, 1673–1694.

Gloor Pierre, Olivier Andre, Quesney Luis, Andermann Frederick, Horowitz Sandra. The role of the limbic system in experiential phenomena of temporal lobe epilepsy. *Ann Neurol* 12: 1982, 129–144.

Goadsby Peter. Recent advances in understanding migraine mechanisms, molecules and therapeutics. *Trends Molec Med* 13: 2007, 39–44.

Goodwin Guy, McCloskey Ian, Matthews Peter. Proprioceptive illusions induced by muscle vibration: contribution by muscle spindles to perception? *Science* 175: 1972, 1382–1384.

Gorji Ali. Spreading depression: a review of the clinical relevance. *Brain Res Rev* 38: 2001, 33–60.

Gotoh Fumio, Meyer John, Takagi Yasuyuki. Cerebral effects of hyperventilation in man. *Arch Neurol* 12: 1965, 410–423.

Green Celia E. Spontaneous 'paranormal' experiences in relation to sex and academic background. *J Soc Psychic Res* 43: 1966, 357–366.

Green Celia E. Ecsomatic experiences and related phenomena. *J Psychic Res* 44: 1967, 111–131.

Green E, Green A, Walters D. Voluntary control of internal states: psychological and physiological. *J Transpers Psychol* 1: 1970, 1–26.

Gresty Michael, Bronstein Adolfo, Brandt Thomas, Dieterich Marianne. Neurology of otolith function: peripheral and central disorders. *Brain* 115: 1992, 647–673.

Grey Margot. *Return from Death.* Boston (MA): Arkana 1985.

Greyson Bruce. The near-death experience scale: construction, reliability, and validity. *J Nerv Ment Dis* 171: 1983a, 369–375.

Greyson Bruce. Increase in psychic phenomena following near-death experiences. *Theta* 11: 1983b, 26–29.

Greyson Bruce. Dissociation in people who have near-death experiences: out of their bodies or out of their minds? *Lancet* 355: 2000, 460–463.

Greyson Bruce. Incidence and correlates of near-death experiences in a cardiac care unit. *Gen Hosp Psychiatr* 25: 2003, 269–276.

Groth-Marnat Gary and Summers Roger. Altered beliefs, attitudes, and behaviors following near-death experiences. *J Hum Psychol* 38: 1998, 110–125.

Grush Rick. Self, world and space: the meaning and mechanisms of ego- and allocentric spatial representation. *Brain Mind* 1: 2000, 59–92.

Guidice Mary Ann and Berchou Richard. Post-traumatic epilepsy following head injury. *Brain Injury* 1: 1987, 61–64.

Gunton, Colin. *The Christian Faith.* Oxford: Blackwell 2002.

Haberny Kathleen, Paule Merle, Scallet A, Sistare F, Lester David, Hanig J et al. Ontogeny of the N-methyl-D-Aspartate (NMDA) receptor system and susceptibility to neurotoxicity. *Toxicol Sci* 68: 2002, 9–17.

Halligan, Peter. Phantom limbs: the body in the mind. *Cogn Neuropsychiatr* 7: 2002, 251–268.

Halligan Peter, Marshall John, Wade Derick. Three arms: a case study of supernumerary phantom limb after right hemisphere stroke. *J Neurol Neurosurg Psychiatr* 56: 1993, 159–166.

Halligan Peter, Marshall John, Ramachandran Vilayanur. Ghosts in the machine: a case description of visual and haptic hallucinations after right hemisphere stroke. *Cogn Neuropsychol* 11: 1994, 459–477.

Hansen Gustav, Jensen Svend, Chandresh Lars, Hilden Tonnes. The psychotropic effect of ketamine. *J Psychoact Drugs* 20: 1988, 419–425.

Hanson Anthony and Hanson Richard. *Reasonable Belief.* Oxford: Oxford University Press 1981.

Haraldsson Erlendur, Asa Gudmundsdottir, Asthor Ragnarsson, Johann Loftsson, Sigtryggur Jonsson. National survey of psychical experiences and attitudes towards the paranormal in Iceland. In: Roll WG, Morris RL, Morris JD (eds) 1977, 182–186.

Hay David. *Exploring Inner Space.* London: Pelican 1982.

Hay David. *Something There: The Biology of the Human Spir*it. London: Darton, Longman & Todd 2006.

Hay David and Nye Rebecca. *The Spirit of the Child.* London: Fount 1999.

Hays Richard B. *The Moral Vision of the New Testament.* Edinburgh: Clark 1997.

Heath Robert. Pleasure and brain activity in man. *J Nerv Ment Dis* 154: 1972, 3–18.

Hebblethwaite Brian. *The Essence of Christianity.* London: SPCK 1996.

Hedley Douglas. *Living Forms of the Imagination.* London: Clark (Continuum) 2008.

Hemmingsen R and Rafaelsen O. Hypnagogic and hypnopompic hallucinations during treatment with amitryptyline. *Acta Psychiatr Scand* 62: 1980, 364–368.

Henderson Yandall and Haggard Howard. *Noxious Gases and the Principles of Respiration Influencing their Action.* New York (NY): Reinhold 1943.

Hengel Martin. *Studies in Early Christology.* Edinburgh: Clark 1995.

Hengel Martin. The Son of God. In: *The Cross of the Son of God.* London: SCM Press, Xpress Reprints 1997.

Henriksen Steven, Bloom Floyd, McCoy Frank, Ling Nicholas, Guillemin Roger. β-endorphin induces nonconvulsive limbic seizures. *Proc Nat Acad Sci (USA)* 75: 1978, 5221–5225.

Hobson J Allan. *Dreaming: An Introduction to the Science of Sleep.* Oxford: Oxford University Press 2003.

Hobson J Allan and McCarley Robert. The brain as a dream state generator: an activation-synthesis hypothesis of the dream process. *Am J Psychiatr* 134: 1997, 1335–1348.

Hobson J Allan, Stickgold Robert, Pace-Schott Edward. The neuropsychology of REM sleep dreaming. *NeuroReport* 9: 1998, R1–R14.

Hobson J Allan, Pace-Schott Edward, Stickgold Robert. Dreaming and the brain: toward a cognitive neuroscience of conscious states. *Behav Brain Sci* 23: 2000, 793–842.

Hoenig J and Hamilton Christina. Epilepsy and sexual orgasm. *Acta Psychiatr Scand* 35: 1960, 448–456.

Hoge David. A validated intrinsic religious motivation scale. *J Sci Stud Relig* 11: 1972, 369–376.

Holstege G, Georgiadis J, Paans A, Meiners L, van der Graaf F, Reinders A. Brain activation during human male ejaculation. *J Neurosci* 23: 2003, 9185–9193.

Hori T, Hayashi M, Morikawa T. Topographic EEG changes and the hypnagogic experience. In: Ogilvie RD and Harsh JR (eds), *Sleep Onset: Normal and Abnormal Processes*. Washington (DC): American Psychological Association 1994.

Horne J. Human slow wave sleep: a review and appraisal of recent findings, with implications for sleep functions, and psychiatric illness. *Experientia* 48: 1992, 941–953.

Horne J. *Sleepfaring: A Journey through the Science of Sleep*. Oxford: Oxford University Press 2006.

Horowitz Mardi. Flashbacks: recurrent intrusive images after the use of LSD. *Am J Psychiatr* 126: 1969, 565–569.

Howard Julius. Incidents of auditory perception during anesthesia with traumatic sequelae. *Med J Austral* 146: 1987, 44–46.

Howard P, Leathart G, Dornhorst A, Sharpey-Schafer E. The 'mess trick' and the 'fainting lark'. *Br Med J* 3: 1951, 382–384.

Hoyer D, Hannon J, Martin G. Molecular, pharmacological and functional diversity of 5-HT receptors. *Pharmacol, Biochem and Behav* 71: 2002, 533–554.

Hudson Benjamin. *Time is Short: The Eschatology of the Early Church*. In: Bynum Caroline and Freedman Paul (eds) 1999, 101–123.

'I.B.' Experience under the influence of ether. *Psychol Rev* 6: 1899, 104–106.

Insel Thomas. Oxytocin—a neuropeptide for affiliation: evidence from behavioural, receptor autoradiographic, and comparative studies. *Psychoneuroendocrinol* 17: 1992, 3–35.

Ionasescu J. Paroxysmal disorders of the body image in temporal lobe epilepsy. *Acta Psychiatr Neurol (Scand)* 35: 1960, 171–181.

James William. Subjective effects of nitrous oxide. *Mind* 7: 1882, 186–208.

James William. *The Varieties of Religious Experience*. London: Longmans, Green & Company 1902.

Jansen Karl. Near death experience and the NMDA receptor. *Br Med J* 298: 1989, 1708.

Jansen Karl. Neuroscience and the near-death experience: roles for the NMDA-PCP receptor, the sigma receptor and the endopsychosins. *Med Hypotheses* 31: 1990, 25–29.

Jansen Karl. Using ketamine to induce the near-death experience. http://www.members.tripod.com/ketotal/ket6.html 2000.

Janszky J, Szucs A, Halasz P, Borbely C, Hollo A, Barsi P, Mirnics Z. Orgasmic aura originates from the right hemisphere. *Neurology* 58: 2002, 302–304.

Janszky J, Ebner A, Szupera Z, Schulz R, Hollo A, Szucs A, Clemens B. Orgasmic aura—a report of seven cases. *Seizure* 13: 2004, 441–444.

Jasper H and Rasmussen T. Studies of clinical and electrical responses to deep temporal stimulation in man with some considerations of functional anatomy. *Res Publ Assoc Res Nerv Ment Dis* 36: 1958, 316–334.

Jeeves Malcolm. *Mind Fields: Reflections on the Science of Mind and Brain.* Leicester: Apollos 1994.

Jeeves Malcolm. *Brain, Mind, and Behavior.* In: Brown, Murphy and Malony (eds) 1998, 9S3.

Jenson Robert W. *The Great Transformation.* In: Braaten and Jenson (eds) 2002, 33.

Jevtovic-Todorovic V, Todorovic S, Mennerick S, Powell S, Dirkanian K, Benshoff N et al. Nitrous oxide (laughing gas) is an NMDA antagonist, neuroprotectant and neurotoxin. *Nature Med* 4: 1998, 460–463.

Johnson Aubrey. *The One and the Many in the Israelite Conception of God.* Cardiff: University of Cardiff Press 1961.

Johnson Aubrey. *The Vitality of the Individual in the Thought of Ancient Israel.* Cardiff: University of Wales Press 1964.

Johnson Brian. Psychosis and ketamine. *Br Med J* 4: 1971, 428–429.

Jones E. Some aspects of the organisation of the thalamic reticular complex. *J Comp Neurol* 162: 1975, 285–308.

Joseph Rhawn. *Neuropsychology, Neuropsychiatry, and Behavioural Neurology.* New York (NY): Plenum Press 1990.

Judson I and Wiltshaw E. A near-death experience. *Lancet* 2: 1983, 561–562.

Jus A, Jus K, Villeneuve A, Pires A, Lachance R, Fortier J, Villeneuve R. Studies on dream recall in chronic schizophrenic patients after prefrontal lobotomy. *Biol Psychiatr* 6: 1973, 275–293.

Kahan Tracey, LaBerge Stephen, Levitan Lynne, Zimbardo P. Similarities and differences between dreaming and waking cognition: an exploratory study. *Consciousn Cogn* 6: 1997, 132–147.

Kaplan Dora. Nitrous Oxide and the Surreal Condition. In: Sheldin M, Wallechinsky D, Salyer S (eds) 1973, 36–38.

Karagulla Shafica and Robertson Elizabeth. Psychical phenomena in temporal lobe epilepsy and the psychoses. *Br Med J* 1: 1955, 748–752.

Karama S, Lecours A, Leroux J, Bourgouin P, Beaudoin G, Joubert S, Beauregard M Areas of brain activation in males and females during viewing of erotic film excerpts. *Hum Brain Mapp* 16: 2002, 1–13.

Kellehear Allan. Culture, biology and the near-death experience. *J Nerv Ment Dis* 181: 1993, 148–156.

Kellehear Allan, Stevenson Ian, Pasricha Satwant, Cook Emily. The absence of tunnel sensations in near-death experiences from India. *J Near-Death Stud* 13: 1994, 109–113.

Kelly JND. *Early Christian Creeds.* London: Longman 1972.

Kennedy Raymond. Self-induced depersonalisation syndrome. *Am J Psychiatr* 133: 1976, 1326–1328.

Kerr N and Foulkes D. Reported absence of visual dream imagery in a normally-sighted subject with Turner's syndrome. *J Ment Imagery* 2: 1978, 247–264.

Kirk Katherine, Eaves Lindon, Martin Nicholas. Self-transcendence as a measure of spirituality in a sample of older Australian twins. *Twin Research* 2: 1999, 81–87.

Klein L, Saltzman H, Heyman A, Sieker H. Syncope induced by the Valsalva maneuver. *Am J Med* 37: 1964, 263–268.

Knox John. Can the self survive the death of its mind? *Relig Stud* 5: 1969, 85–97.

Kohr Richard. A survey of Psi experiences among members of a special population. *J Am Soc Psychic Res* 74: 1980, 395–411.

Kohr Richard. Near-death experience and its relationship to Psi and various altered states. *Theta* 10: 1982, 50–53.

Kroll Jerome and Bachrach Bernard. Visions and psychopathology in the Middle Ages. *J Nerv Ment Dis* 170: 1982, 41–49.

Krystal J, Karper L, Seibyl J, Freeman G, Delaney R, Bremner J et al. Subanesthetic effects of the non-competitive NMDA antagonist, ketamine in humans: psychomimetic, perceptual, cognitive, and neurendocrine responses. *Arch Gen Psychiatr* 51: 1994, 199–214.

Kumar R, Behari S, Wahi J, Banerji D, Sharma K. Peduncular hallucinosis: an unusual sequel to surgical intervention in the suprasellar region. *Br J Neurosurg* 13: 1999, 500–503.

Laberge Stephen, Levitan Lynne, Brylowski Andrew, Dement William. 'Out-of-body' experiences occurring in REM sleep. *Sleep Res* 17: 1988, 115.

La Barre Weston. Hallucinogens and the shamanic origins of religion. In: Furst Peter (ed), *Flesh of the Gods: The Ritual Use of Hallucinogens*. London: Allen & Unwin 1972, 261–278.

Lackner James. Some proprioceptive influences on the perceptual representation of body shape and orientation. *Brain* 111: 1988, 281–297.

Lackner James. Sense of body position in parabolic flight. *Ann NY Acad Sci* 656: 1992, 329–339.

Ladd George Eldon. *A Theology of the New Testament*. Grand Rapids (MI): Eerdmans 1975.

Lambert Edward and Wood Earl. The problem of blackout and unconsciousness in aviators. *Med Clin N Am* 30: 1946, 833–844.

Lammers G, Arends J, Declerck A, Ferrari M, Schouwink G, Troost J. Ritanserin, a 5-HT2 receptor blocker, as add-on treatment in narcolepsy. *Sleep* 16: 1993, 216–220.

Lampe GWH and MacKinnon DM. *The Resurrection*. London: Mowbray 1967.

Lamuso S, Ruottinen H, Knuuti J, Harkonen R, Ruotsalainen U, Bergman J et al. Comparison of [^{18}F]FDG-PET, [^{99}Tc]-HMPAO-SPECT, and [^{123}I]-iomazenil-SPECT in localising the epileptogenic cortex. *J Neurol Neurosurg Psychiatr* 63: 1997, 743–748.

Lance James W. Simple formed hallucinations confined to the area of a specific visual field defect. *Brain* 99: 1976, 719–734.

Lance James, Cooper Bryan, Misbach Jusuf. Visual hallucinations as a symptom of right parieto-occipital lesions. *Proc Austral Assoc Neurol* 11: 1974, 209–217.

Laughlin Charles, McManus John, d'Aquili Eugene. *Brain, Symbol and Experience: Toward a Neurophenomenology of Human Consciousness*. New York (NY): Columbia University Press 1992.

Laureys Steven. Eyes open, brain shut. *Scientific American* 296: 2007, 66–71.

Leaning FE. An introductory study of hypnagogic phenomena. *Proc Soc Psychic Res* 35: 1926, 289–409.

Leker R, Karni A, River Y. Microsomatoagnosia: whole body schema illusion as part of an epileptic aura. *Acta Neurol Scand* 94: 1996, 383–385.

Lempert T, Bauer M, Schmidt D. Syncope: a videometric analysis of 56 episodes of transient cerebral hypoxia. *Ann Neurol* 36: 1994, 233–237.

Lempert T, Bauer M, Schmidt D. Syncope and near-death experience. *Lancet* 344: 1994, 829–830.

Lenggenhager Bigna, Tadi Tej, Metzinger Thomas, Blanke Olaf. Video ergo sum: manipulating bodily self-consciousness. *Science* 317: 2007, 1096–1099.

Lesser R, Luders H, Klem G, Dinner D, Morris H, Hahn Wyllie E. Extraoperative cortical functional localization in patients with epilepsy. *J Clin Neurophysiol* 4: 1987, 27–53.

L'Hermitte J. Syndrome de la callote du pedoncle cerebral: les troubles psycho-sensoriels dans les lesions du mesocephale. *Rev Neurol (Paris)* 38: 1922, 1359–1365.

Liberson W and Liberson C. EEG records, reaction times, eye movements, respiration, and mental content during drowsiness. *Rec Adv Biol Psychiatr* 8: 1965, 295–302.

Lindley James, Bryan Sethyn, Conley Bob. Near-Death experiences in a Pacific Northwest American population. *J Near-Death Stud* 1: 1981, 104–124.

Lippman Caro. Hallucinations in migraine. *Am J Psychiatr* 107: 1951, 856–858.

Lippman Caro. Certain hallucinations peculiar to migraine. *J Nerv Ment Dis* 116: 1952, 346–351.

Lippman Caro. Hallucinations of physical duality in migraine. *J Nerv Ment Dis* 117: 1953, 345–350.

Lippman Caro. Recurrent dreams in migraine: an aid to diagnosis. *J Nerv Ment Dis* 120: 1954, 273–276.

Llinas R and Pare D. Of dreaming and wakefulness. *Neuroscience* 44: 1991, 521–535.

Lopez William. The effects of nitrous oxide. In: Sheldin M, Wallechinsky D, Salyer S (eds) 1973, 20–22.

Louria Donald B. Sexual use of amyl nitrate. *Med Asp Hum Sex* 4: 1970, 89.

Lu Jun, Sherman David, Devor Marshall, Saper Clifford. A putative flip-flop switch for control of REM sleep. *Nature* 441: 2006, 589–594.

Lugaresi Elio, Medori Rossella, Montagna Pasquale, Baruzzi Agostino, Cortelli Pietro, Lugaresi Alessandra, Tuniper Paolo, Zucconi Marco, Gambetti Pierluigi. Fatal familial insomnia and dysautonomia with selective degeneration of thalamic nuclei. *N Engl J Med* 315: 1986, 997–1003.

Lunn Villars. Autoscopic phenomena. *Acta Psychiatr (Scand)* 46 (Suppl 219): 1970, 118–125.

Mabille H. Hallucinations religieuses et délire religieux transitoire dans l'épilepsie. *Ann Med-Psychol* 9–10: 1899, 76–81.

Mackinnon Donald. 'Substance' in Christology—A Cross-Bench View. In: Sykes Stephen and Clayton John (eds), *Christ, Faith and History: Cambridge Studies in Christology.* Cambridge: Cambridge University Press 1972, 279–300.

Macquarrie John. *Principles of Christian Theology.* London: SCM Press 1966.

Macquarrie John. *In Search of Humanity: A Theological and Philosophical Approach.* New York (NY): Crossroad 1983.

Maddocks Fiona. *Hildegard of Bingen.* London: Headline 2001.

Mahowald Mark, Woods Sharon, Schenck Carlos. Sleeping dreams, waking hallucinations, and the central nervous system. *Dreaming* 8: 1998, 89–102.

Makarec Katherine and Persinger Michael. Temporal lobe signs: electroencephalographic validity and enhanced scores in special populations. *Percept Motor Skills* 60: 1985, 831–842.

Makarec Katherine and Persinger Michael. Electroencephalographic validation of a temporal lobe signs inventory in a normal population. *J Res Personal* 24: 1990, 323–337.

Malhotra Anil, Pinals Debra, Weingartner Herbert, Sirocco Karen, Missar David, Pickar David. NMDA receptor function and human cognition: the effects of ketamine in healthy volunteers. *Neuropsychopharmacol* 14: 1996, 301–307.

Malow B, Lin X, Kushwaha R, Aldrich M. Interictal spiking increases with sleep depth in temporal lobe epilepsy. *Epilepsia* 39: 1998, 1309–1316.

Manford M and Andermann F. Complex visual hallucinations: clinical and neurobiological insights. *Brain* 121: 1998, 1819–1840.

Maquet Pierre. Sleep function(s) and cerebral metabolism. *Behav Brain Res* 69: 1995, 75–83.

Maquet Pierre. Functional neuroimaging of normal human sleep by positron emission tomography. *J Sleep Res* 9: 2000, 207–231.

Maquet Pierre, Peters Jean-Marie, Aerts Joel, Delfiore Georges, Degueldre Christian, Luxen Andre, Franck Georges. Functional neuroanatomy of human rapid eye movement sleep and dreaming. *Nature* 383: 1996, 163–166.

Maquet Pierre, Degueldre Christian, Delfiore Guy, Aerts Joel, Peters Jean-Marie, Luxen Andre, Franck Georges. Functional neuroanatomy of human slow wave sleep. *J Neurosci* 17: 1997, 2807–2812.

Markowitsch HJ and Kessler J. Massive impairment in executive functions with partial preservation of other cognitive functions: the case of a young patient with severe degeneration of the prefrontal cortex. *Exp Brain Res* 133: 2000, 94–102.

Martin-Achard Robert. *From Life to Death: A Study of the Development of the Doctrine of the Resurrection in the Old Testament.* London: Oliver & Boyd 1960.

Martinez-Conde Susana. Fixational eye movements in normal and pathological vision. *Progr Brain Res* 154: 2006, 151–176.

Marxsen Willi. The resurrection of Jesus as a historical and theological problem. In: Moule CFD (ed) 1968, 15–50.

Matsuhashi Masao, Ikeda Akio, Ohara Shinji, Matsumoto Riki, Yamamoto Junichi, Takayama Motohiro et al. Multisensory convergence at human temporo-parietal junction—epicortical recording of evoked responses. *Clin Neurophysiol* 115: 2004, 1145–1160.

Mazzoni Giuliana and Loftus Elizabeth. When dreams become reality. *Consc Cogn* 5: 1996, 442–462.

McBride William, Murphy James, Ikemoto Satoshi. Localisation of brain re-inforcement mechanisms: intracranial self-administration and intracranial place-conditioning studies. *Behav Brain Res* 101: 1999, 129–152.

McFadyen Alistair I. *The Call to Personhood: A Christian Theory of the Individual in Social Relationships.* Cambridge: Cambridge University Press 1990.

McIntosh Alastair. Beliefs about out-of-the-body experiences among the Elema, Gulf Kamea and Rigo peoples of Papua New Guinea. *J Soc Psych Res* 50: 1980, 460–478.

Meduna LJ. CO_2 *Therapy: A Neurophysiological Treatment of Nervous Disorders.* Springfield (IL): Thomas 1950.

Mehler Mark. Complete visual inversion in vertebrobasilar ischaemic disease. *J Neurol Neurosurg Psychiatr* 51: 1988, 1236–1237.

Melzack Ronald. Phantom limbs, the self and the brain (The DO Hebb Memorial Lecture). *Canad Psychol* 30: 1989, 1–16.

Melzack R and Bromage P. Experimental phantom limbs. *Exp Neurol* 39: 1973, 261–269.

Melzack Ronald and Loeser John. Phantom body pain in paraplegics: evidence for a central 'pattern generating mechanism' for pain. *Pain* 4: 1978, 195–210.

Merikle Philip, Smilek Daniel, Eastwood John. Perception without awareness: perspectives from cognitive psychology. *Cognition* 79: 2001, 115–134.

Mesulam M-Marsel. Dissociative states with abnormal temporal lobe EEG: multiple personality and the illusion of possession. *Arch Neurol* 38: 1981, 176–181.

Miethe Terry and Flew Antony. *Does God Exist?* New York (NY): Harper Collins 1991, 414–417.

Mishkin Mortimer, Ungerleider Leslie, Macko Kathleen. Object vision and spatial vision: two cortical pathways. *Trends in Neuroscience* October 1983, 414–417.

Mittelstaedt Horst. The role of the otoliths in the perception of the orientation of self and world to the vertical. *Zool Jhrb Physiol* 95: 1991, 419–425.

Mittelstaedt Horst and Glasauer S. Illusions of verticality in weightlessness. *Clin Invest* 71: 1993, 732–739.

Moerman N, Bonke B, Oostling J. Awareness and recall during general anesthesia. *Anesthesiol* 79: 1993, 454–464.

Moersch Frederick. Psychic manifestations in migraine. *Am J Psychiatr* 3: 1924, 697–716.

Moghaddam Bita, Adams Barbara, Verma Anita, Daly Darron. Activation of gluta-minergic neurotransmission by ketamine: a novel step in the pathway from NMDA receptor blockade to dopaminergic and cognitive disruptions associated with the prefrontal cortex. *J Neurosci* 17: 1997, 2921–2927.

Mohr Christine and Blanke Olaf. The demystification of autoscopic phenomena: experimental propositions. *Curr Psychiatr Reports* 7: 2005, 189–195.

Montplaisir J, Godbout R. Nocturnal sleep of narcoleptic patients: revisited. *Sleep* 9: 1986, 159–161.

Montplaisir J, Godbout R. Serotininergic reuptake mechanisms in the control of cataplexy. *Sleep* 9: 1986, 280–284.

Moody Raymond. *Life after Life.* New York (NY): Bantam Books 1976.

Moody Raymond. *Reflections on Life after Life.* New York (NY): Bantam Books 1997.

Morris M, Bowers D, Chatterjee A, Heilman K. Amnesia following a discrete basal forebrain lesion. *Brain* 115: 1992, 1827–1847.

Morse Melvin, Castillo Paul, Venecia David, Milstein Jerrold, Tyler Donald. Childhood near-death experiences. *Am J Dis Child* 140: 1986, 1110–1114.

Morse Melvin, Perry Paul. *Closer to the Light: Learning from the Near-Death Experiences of Children.* New York (NY): Villard Books 1990.

Moses John. *One Equall Light: An Anthology of the Writings of John Donne.* Grand Rapids (MI): Eerdmans 2004.

Mott R, Small I, Anderson J. Comparative study of hallucinations. *Arch Gen Psychiatr* 12: 1965, 595–601.

Moule Charles FD. *The Birth of the New Testament.* London: Black 1966.

Moule Charles FD. *The Significance of the Message of the Resurrection for Faith in Jesus Christ.* London: SCM Press 1968.

Muddiman John. 'I believe in the resurrection of the body'. In: Barton S and Stanton G (eds), *Resurrection.* London: SPCK 1994, 128–138.

Murphy M, Checkley S, Seckl J, Lightman S. Naloxone inhibits oxytocin release at orgasm in man. *J Clin Endocrinol Metab* 71: 1990, 1056–1058.

Murphy Nancey. *Bodies and Souls, or Spirited Bodies?* Cambridge: Cambridge University Press 2006.

Murphy-O'Connor Jerome. *Paul: A Critical Life.* Oxford: Oxford University Press 1997.

Murray Craig D. Toward a phenomenology of the body in virtual reality. *Metaphys Epistemol Tech* 19: 2000, 149–173.

Murray Craig and Fox Jezz. The out-of-body experience and body image: differences between experients and nonexperients. *J Nerv Ment Dis* 193: 2005, 70–72.

Murri Luigi, Arena Roberto, Siciliano Gabriele, Mazzotta Raffaele, Muratorio Alberto. Dream recall in patients with focal cerebral lesions. *Arch Neurol* 41: 1984, 183–185.

Myles P, Leslie K, McNeil J, Forbes A, Chan M et al. Bispectral index monitoring to prevent awareness during anesthesia: the B-aware randomised controlled trial. *Lancet* 363: 2004, 1757–1763.

Nausieda P, Weiner W, Kaplan L, Weber S, Klawans H. Sleep disruption in the course of chronic levodopa therapy: an early feature of the levodopa psychosis. *Clin Neuropharmacol* 5: 1982, 183–194.

Nelson Kevin, Mattingly Michelle, Lee Sherman, Schmitt Frederick. Does the arousal system contribute to near death experience? *Neurology* 66: 2006, 1003–1009.

Nelson Kevin, Mattingly Michelle, Schmitt Frederick. Out-of-body and arousal. *Neurology* 68: 2007, 794–795.

Neppe Vernon and Kaplan Charles. Short-term treatment of atypical spells with carbamazepine. *Clin Neuropharmacol* 11: 1988, 287–289.

Newberg Andrew, Abass Alavi, Baime Michael, Pourdehnad Michael, Santanna Jill, D'Aquili Eugene. The measurement of regional cerebral blood flow during the complex cognitive task of meditation: a preliminary SPECT study. *Psychiatr Research: Neuroimaging Section* 106: 2001, 113–122.

Nielsen Kai. The Faces of Immortality. In: Davis ST (ed) 1989, 1–30.

Nilsson K, Damberg M, Ohrvik J, et al. Genes encoding for AP–2β and the serotonin transporter are associated with the Personality Character Spiritual Acceptance. *Neurosci Letts* 411: 2007, 233–237.

Nofzinger Eric, Mintun Mark, Wiseman MaryBeth, Kupfer David, Moore Robert. Forebrain activation in REM sleep: an FDG PET study. *Brain Res* 770: 1997, 192–201.

Ogilvie Robert. The process of falling asleep. *Physiol Rev* 5: 2001, 247–270.

Ohayon Maurice. Prevalence of hallucinations and their pathological associations in the general population. *Psychiatr Res* 97: 2000, 153–164.

Ohayon Maurice, Zulley J, Guilleminault C, Smirne S. Prevalence and pathologic associations of sleep paralysis in the general population. *Neurology* 52: 1999, 1194–1200.

Ohayon M, Priest R, Zulley J, Smirne S, Paiva T. Prevalence of narcolepsy symptomatology and diagnoisis in the European general population. *Neurology* 58: 2002, 1826–1833.

Olesen Jes. Cerebral and extracranial circulatory disturbances in migraine: pathophysiological implications. *Cerebrovasc Brain Metab Rev* 3: 1991, 1–28.

Osis Karlis and Haraldsson Erlendur. *At the Hour of Death.* New York (NY): Avon Books 1977.

Osis Karlis and Mitchell Janet Lee. Physiological correlates of reported out-of-body experiences. *J Soc Psychic Res* 49: 1977, 525–536.

Otto, Rudolf. *The Idea of the Holy.* Oxford: Oxford University Press 1936.

Overeem Sebastian, Mignot Emmanuel, van Dijk J, Lammers G. Narcolepsy: clinical features, new pathological insights, and future perspectives. *J Clin Neurophysiol* 18: 2001, 78–105.

Owens J, Cook E, Stevenson I. Features of 'near-death experience' in relation to whether or not patients were near death. *Lancet* 336: 1990, 1175–1177.

Oyama Tsutomu, Jin Toshiro, Yamaya Ryuji. Profound analgesic effects of β-endorphin in man. *Lancet* 1: 1980, 122–124.

Pacia Steven, Devinsky Orrin, Perrine Kenneth, Ravdin Lisa, Luciano Daniel, Vazquez Blanca, Doyle Werner. Clinical features of neocortical temporal lobe epilepsy. *Ann Neurol* 40: 1996, 724–730.

Pahnke Walter. The psychedelic mystical experience in the human encounter with death. *Harvard Theol Rev* 62: 1969, 1–21.

Palmer John. A community mail survey of psychic experiences. *J Am Soc Psychic Res* 73: 1979, 221–251.

Pang Elizabeth and Fowler Barry. Dissociation of the mismatch negativity and processing negativity attentional waveforms with nitrous oxide. *Psychophysiol* 36: 1999, 552–558.

Pannenberg Wolfhart. *Systematic Theology,* vol 2 (trans GW Bromiley). Edinburgh: Clark 1994.

Pannenberg Wolfhart. The task of Christian eschatology. In: Braaten and Jenson (eds) 2002, 1.

Pannenberg Wolfhart. *Anthropology in Theological Perspective.* London: Clark 2004.

Parnia S, Waller D, Yeates R, Fenwick P. A qualitative and quantitative study of the incidence, features and aetiology of near-death experiences in cardiac arrest survivors. *Resuscitation* 48: 2001, 149–156.

Parnia Sam and Fenwick Peter. Near-death experiences in cardiac arrest: visions of a dying brain or visions of a new science of consciousness. *Resuscitation* 52: 2002, 5–11.

Pasricha Satwant. Near-death experiences in South India: a systematic survey in Channapatna. *Nat Inst Ment Health Neurosci* 10: 1992, 111–118.

Pasricha Satwant. A systematic survey of near-death experiences in South India. *J Sci Explor* 7: 1993, 161–171.

Pasricha Satwant and Stevenson Ian. Near-death experiences in India. *J Nerv Ment Dis* 174: 1986, 165–170.

Pavani Francesco, Spence Charles, Driver Jon. Visual capture of touch: out-of-body experiences with rubber gloves. *Psychol Sci* 11: 2000, 353–359.

Penfield Wilder. Some mechanisms of consciousness discovered during electrical stimulation of the brain. *Proc Nat Acad Sci* (USA) 44: 1958, 51–66.

Penfield Wilder. A surgeon's chance encounters with mechanisms related to consciousness. *J R Coll Surg Edin* 5: 1960, 173–190.

Penfield W and Perot Phanor. The brain's record of auditory and visual experiences. *Brain* 86: 1963, 595–696.

Perel A and Davidson J. Recurrent hallucinations following ketamine. *Anaesthesia* 31: 1976, 1081–1083.

Perry Michael. *Psychical and Spiritual.* Louth (Lincolnshire): Churches' Fellowship for Psychical and Spiritual Studies 2003.

Persinger Michael. Propensity to report paranormal experiences is correlated with temporal lobe signs. *Percept Motor Skills* 59: 1984, 583–586.

Persinger Michael. MMPI profiles of people who report temporal lobe signs. *Percept Motor Skills* 64: 1987, 1112–1114.

Persinger Michael. Sense of a presence and suicidal ideation following traumatic brain injury: indications of right-hemispheric intrusions from neuropsychological profiles. *Psychol Reports* 75: 1994, 1059–1070.

Persinger Michael and Makarec Katharine. Complex partial epileptic signs as a continuum from normals to epileptics: normative data and clinical populations. *J Clin Psychol* 49: 1993, 33–45.

Podoll K and Robinson D. Out-of-body experiences and related phenomena in migraine art. *Cephalalgia* 19: 1999, 886–896.

Poeck K. Phantoms following amputation in early childhood and in congenital absence of limbs. *Cortex* 1: 1964, 269–275.

Polkinghorne John. *The God of Hope and the End of the World.* London: SPCK 2002.

Polkinghorne John. *Is there Life beyond Death?* Lecture 10. Perth: St George's Cathedral 2003.

Posner M, Petersen S, Fox P, Raiche M. Localization of cognitive operations in the human brain. *Science* 240: 1988, 1627–1631.

Powell TJ. Episodic unconsciousness in pilots during flight: report of nine cases. *Aviat Med* 8: 1956, 301–316.

Previc Fred. The role of the extrapersonal brain systems in religious activity. *Consciousn Cogn* 15: 2006, 500–539.

Price HH. Survival and the idea of 'another world'. In: Smythies JR (ed) 1965, 1.

Price J, Whitlock F, Hall R. The psychiatry of vertebro-basilar insufficiency with the report of a case. *Psychiatria Clinica* 16: 1983, 26–44.

Puizillout J, Foutz A. Vago-aortic nerves stimulation and sleep: evidence of a REM-triggering and a REM-maintenance factor. *Brain Res* 111: 1976, 181–184.

Puizillout J, Foutz A. Characteristics of the experimental reflex sleep induced by vago-aortic stimulation. *Electroencephalogr Clin Neurophysiol* 42: 1977, 552–563.

Purcell Sheila, Mullington Janet, Moffit Alan, Hoffmann Robert, Pigeau Ross. Dream self-reflectiveness as a learned cognitive skill. *Sleep* 9: 1986, 423–437.

Ramachandran VS and Rogers-Ramachandran D. Synaesthesia in phantom limbs induced with mirrors. *Proc R Soc London* B 263: 1996, 377–386.

Ramachandran VS and Hirstein William. The perception of phantom limbs. *Brain* 121: 1998, 1603–1630.

Rampil I. A primer for EEG signal processing in anesthesia. *Anesthesiology* 89: 1998, 980–1002.

Rauch S, Shin L, Wright C. Neuroimaging studies of amygdala function in anxiety disorders. *Ann New York Acad Sci* 985: 2003, 389–410.

Rawlings Maurice. *Beyond Death's Doors.* New York (NY): Nelson 1978.

Redoute J, Stoleru S, Gregoire M-C, Costes N, Cinotti Luc, Lavenne F, Le Bars D, Forest M, Pujol J-F. Brain processing of visual sexual stimuli in human males. *Hum Brain Mapp* 11: 2000, 162–177.

Reed Catherine and Farah Martha. The psychological reality of the body schema: a test with normal participants. *J Exp Psychol Hum Percept Perf* 21: 1995, 334–343.

Resnik H. Erotized repetitive hangings: a form of self-destructive behavior. *Am J Psychother* 26: 1972, 4–21.

Revonsuo Annti. Consciousness, dreams and virutal realities. *Philosoph Psychol* 8: 1995, 35–58.

Riddoch George. Phantom limbs and body shape. *Brain* 64: 1941, 197–222.

Ring Kenneth. *Life at Death.* New York (NY): Coward, McCann & Geoghegan 1980.

Ring Kenneth. Psychologist comments on the need to keep religious bias out of near-death research. *J Near-Death Stud* 1: 1980, 14–16.

Ring Kenneth. *Heading Towards Omega.* New York (NY): Morrow 1985.

Ring Kenneth and Cooper Sharon. Near-death and out-of-body experiences in the blind: a study of apparent eyeless vision. *J Near-Death Stud* 16: 1997, 101–147.

Roberts L. Activation and interference of cortical functions. In: Sheer DE (ed), *Electrical Stimulation of the Brain*. Austin (TX): University of Texas Press 1961, 547.

Roberts Richard, Varney Nils, Hulbert James, Paulsen Jane, Richardson Emily, Springer Jane et al. The neuropathology of everyday life: the frequency of partial seizure symptoms among normals. *Neuropsychology* 4: 1990, 65–85.

Robinson John AT. *The Body: A Study in Pauline Theology*. London: SCM Press 1957.

Rocca W, Sharbrough F, Hauser W, Annegers J, Schoenberg B. Risk factors for complex partial seizures: a population-based case-control study. *Ann Neurol* 21: 1987, 22–31.

Rodd Cyril S. Introduction. In: Wheeler-Robinson H, *Corporate Personality in Ancient Israel*. Edinburgh: Clark 1981, 1–14.

Roewer N, Kloss T, Puschel K. Long-term result and quality of life following preclinical cardiopulmonary resuscitation. *Anasth Intensivther Notfallmed* 20: 1985, 244–250.

Rogers A, Meehan J, Guilleminault C, Grumet F, Mignot E. HLA DR15 (DR2) and DQB1*0602 typing studies in 188 narcoleptic pateints with cataplexy. *Neurology* 48: 1997, 1550–1556.

Rogers Ben. *A.J. Ayer—A Life*. London: Chatto & Windus 1999.

Rogerson JW. The Hebrew conception of corporate personality. *J Theol Stud* NS 21: 1970, 1–16.

Rogo D Scott. Ketamine and the near-death experience. *J Near-Death Stud* 4: 1984, 87–96.

Roll W, Morris R, Morris J (eds), *Research in Parapsychology*. New York: Harper Collins 1977, 182–186.

Rosanski J. Peduncular hallucinosis following vertebral angiography. *Neurology* 2: 1952, 341–349.

Rosen David. Suicide survivors: a follow-up study of persons who survived jumping from the Golden Gate and San Francisco-Oakland Bay bridges. *West J Med* 122: 1975, 289–294.

Rosow Carl and Manberg Paul. Bispectral monitoring. *Anesthesiology Clinics N Am* 19: 2001, 947–966.

Ross Colin and Joshi Shaun. Paranormal experiences in the general population. *J Nerv Ment Dis* 180: 1992, 357–361.

Rossen Ralph, Kabat Herman, Anderson John. Acute arrest of cerebral circulation in man. *Arch Neurol Psychiatr* 50: 1943, 510–528.

Rowland Christopher. Interpreting the resurrection. In: Avis P (ed), *The Resurrection of Jesus Christ*. London: Darton, Longman & Todd 1993, 68.

Rowland Christopher. *Christian Origins: The Setting and Character of the Most Important Messianic Sect of Judaism*. London: SPCK 2002.

Saavedra-Aguilar Juan and Gomez-Jeria Juan. A neurobiological model for near-death experiences. *J Near-Death Stud* 7: 1989, 205–222.

Sabom Michael. *Recollections of Death.* New York (NY): Harper & Row 1982.

Sabom Michael. *Light and Death.* Grand Rapids (MI): Zondervan 1998.

Sabom Michael and Kreutziger Sarah. The experience of near-death. *Death Educ* 1: 1977, 195–203.

Sabom Michael and Kreutziger Sarah. Physicians evaluate the near-death experience. *Theta* 6: 1978, 1–6.

Sacks Oliver. *The Man who Mistook his Wife for a Hat.* London: Picador 1986.

Sacks Oliver. *Migraine.* London: Picador 1995.

Sacks Oliver. *An Anthropologist on Mars.* London: Picador 1995.

Salanova V, Andermann F, Rasmussen T, Olivier A, Quesney L. Parietal lobe epilepsy: clinical manifestations and outcome in 82 patients treated surgically between 1929 and 1988. *Brain* 118: 1995, 607–627.

Salzarulo P, Lairy G, Bancaud J, Munari C. Direct depth recording of the striate cortex during REM sleep in man: are there PGO potentials? *Electroencephalogr Clin Neurophysiol* 38: 1975, 199–202.

Sanders EP. *The Historical Figure of Jesus.* London: Penguin 1995.

Saver Jeffrey and Rabin John. The neural substrate of religious experience. *J Neuropsychiatr Clin Neurosci* 9: 1997, 498–510.

Schacter Daniel. The hypnagogic state: a critical review of the literature *Psychol Bull* 83: 1976, 452–481.

Schanfald Darlene, Pearlman Chester, Greenberg Ramon. The capacity of stroke patients to report dreams. *Cortex* 21: 1985, 237–247.

Schlauch Robert. Hypnopompic hallucinations and treatment with imipramine. *Am J Psychiatr* 136: 1979, 219–220.

Schultz Geoffrey and Melzack Ronald. The Charles Bonnet syndrome: 'phantom visual images'. *Perception* 20: 1991, 809–825.

Sedman G. Being an epileptic: a phenomenological study of epileptic experiences. *Psychiatr Neurol (Basel)* 152: 1966, 1–16.

Sedman G and Hopkinson G. The psychopathology of mystical and religious conversion experiences in psychiatric patients. *Confin Psychiatr* 9: 1966, 65–77.

Seiden Richard. Where are they now? A follow-up study of suicide attempters from the Golden Gate bridge. *Suicide Life-Threat Behav* 8: 1968, 203–216.

Sell L, Morris J, Bearn J, Frackowiak R, Friston K, Dolan R. Activation of reward circuitry in human opiate addicts. *Eur J Neurosci* 11: 1999, 1042–1048.

Serdahely William. Variations from the prototypic near-death experience: the 'individually tailored' hypothesis. *J Near-Death Stud* 13: 1995, 185–196.

Sharf B, Moskovitz Ch, Lupton M, Klawans H. Dream phenomena induced by chronic levodopa therapy. *J Neural Transm* 43: 1978, 143–151.

Sheer DE (ed). *Electrical Stimulation of the Brain.* Austin (TX): University of Texas Press 1961.

Sheils Dean. A cross-cultural study of beliefs in out-of-the-body experiences, waking and sleeping. *J Soc Psychic Res* 49: 1978, 697–741.

Sheldin Michael, Wallechinsky David, Salyer Saunia. *Laughing Gas (Nitrous Oxide).* Berkeley (CA): And/Or Press 1973.

Shintani S, Tsuruka S, Shiigai T. Prevalence of genuine epilepsy among adult emergency room patients with an episode of unconsciousness. *J Neurol Sci* 182: 2001, 129–135.

Sigl Jeffrey and Chamoun Nassib. An introduction to bispectral analysis for the electroencephalogram. *J Clin Monit* 10: 1994, 392–404.

Singer Charles. *From Magic to Science: Essays on the Scientific Twilight.* New York (NY): Dover 1958.

Sitaram N, Wyatt R, Dawson S, Gillin J. REM sleep induction by physostigmine infusion during sleep. *Science* 191: 1976, 1281–1283.

Sitaram N, Moore Angela, Gillin Christian. Experimental acceleration and slowing of REM sleep ultradian rhythm by cholinergic agonist and antagonist. *Nature* 274: 1978, 490–492.

Slavin M and LoPinto R. Isolated environmental tilt in association with lateral medullary compression by dolichoectasia of the vertebral artery: is there a cause and effect relationship? *J Clin Neuro-Ophthalmol* 7: 1987, 729–733.

Smith Bernard. Vestibular disturbances in epilepsy. *Neurology* 10: 1960, 465–469.

Smith PB. *Chemical Glimpses of Heaven.* Springfield (IL): Thomas 1972.

Smythies JR (ed). *Brain and Mind.* London: Routledge & Kegan Paul 1965.

Snow John. *On the Inhalation of Ether in Surgical Operations.* London: Churchill 1847.

Snyder Richard and Snow Clyde. Fatal injuries resulting from extreme water impact. *Aerosp Med* 38: 1967, 779–783.

Solms Mark. *The Neuropsychology of Dreams: A Clinico-Anatomical Study.* Mahwah (NJ): Erlbaum & Associates 1997.

Solms Mark. Dreaming and REM sleep are controlled by different brain mechanisms. *Behav Brain Sci* 23: 2000, 843–850.

Solms Mark, Kaplan-Solms Karen, Saling Michael, Miller Percy. Inverted vision after frontal lobe disease. *Cortex* 24: 1988, 499–509.

Sonders M, Keana J, Weber E. Phencyclidine and psychomimetic sigma opiates: recent insights into their biochemical and physiological sites of action. *Trends Neurosci* 11: 1988, 37–38.

Spetzler Robert, Hadley Mark, Rigamonti Daniele, Carter Philip, Raudznes Peter, Shedd Steven, et al. Aneurysms of the basilar artery treated with circulatory arrest, hypothermia, and barbiturate cerebral protection. *J Neurosurg* 68: 1988, 868–879.

Stacey W. David. *The Pauline View of Man in Relation to its Judaic and Hellenistic Background.* London: Macmillan 1956.

Stein John F. The representation of egocentric space in the posterior parietal cortex. *Behav Brain Sci* 15: 1992, 691–700.

Stein John with Stoodley C. *Neuroscience: An Introducton.* Chichester: Wiley 2006.

Steiner Israel, Shain Radi, Melamed Eldad. Acute 'upside down' reversal of vision in transient vertebrobasilar ischemia. *Neurology* 37: 1987, 1685–1686.

Stendahl Krister. *Immortality and Resurrection.* New York (NY): Macmillan 1965.

Stevens Janice and Livermore Arthur. Kindling of the mesolimbic dopamine system: animal model of psychosis. *Neurology* 28: 1978, 36–46.

Stevenson Ian and Greyson Bruce. Near-death experiences: relevance to the question of survival after death. *J Am Med Assoc* 242: 1979, 265–267.

Stevenson I, Cook Emily, Clean-Rice Nicholas. Are persons reporting 'near-death experiences' really near death? A study of medical records. *Omega* 20: 1989–1990, 45–54.

Stewart J and Bartucci R. Postraumatic stress disorder and partial complex seizures. *Am J Psychiatr* 143: 1986, 113–114.

Stickgold Robert, Malia April, Maguire Denise, Roddenbury David, O'Connor Margaret. Replaying the game: hypnagogic images in normals and amnesics. *Science* 290: 2000, 350–353.

Stracciari Andrea, Guarino Maria, Ciucci Gabriele, Pazzaglia Paolo. Acute upside down reversal of vision in vertebrobasilar ischaemia. *J Neurol, Neurosurg Psychiatr* 56: 1993, 423–429.

Suedfeld P and Mocellin JS. The 'sensed presence' in unusual environments. *Environ Behav* 19: 1987, 33–52.

Sutherland Cherie. Changes in religious beliefs, attitudes, and practices following near-death experiences: an Australian study. *J Near-Death Stud* 9: 1990, 21–31.

Sveinbjornsdottir S and Duncan J. Parietal and occipital lobe epilepsy: a review. *Epilepsia* 34: 1993, 493–521.

Swinburne Richard. *The Evolution of the Soul*. Oxford: Oxford University Press 1997.

Sykes S and Clayton J (eds). *Christ, Faith and History*. Cambridge: Cambridge University Press 1972.

Tart Charles. A second psychophysiological study of out-of-the-body experiences in a gifted subject. *Int J Parapsychol* 9: 1967, 251–258.

Tart Charles. A psychophysiological study of out-of-the-body experiences in a selected subject. *J Am Soc Psychic Res* 62: 1968, 3–27.

Tart Charles. Six studies of out-of-the-body experiences. *J Near-Death Studies* 17: 1998, 73–99.

Taylor K, Brugger P, Schwarz U. Audiovisual peduncular hallucinations: a release of cross-modal integration sites? *Cogn Behav Neurol* 18: 2005, 135–136.

Teuber Hans-Lukas and Mishkin Mortimer. Judgement of visual and postural vertical after brain-injury. *J Psychol* 38: 1954, 161–175.

Thorson James and Powell F. Meanings of death and intrinsic religiosity. *J Clin Psychol* 46: 1990, 379–391.

Tiihonen J, Kuikka J, Kupila J, Partanen K, Vainio P, Airaksinen J, Eronen M, Hallikainen T, Paanila J, Kinnunen I, Huttunen J. Increase in cerebral blood flow of right prefrontal cortex in man during orgasm. *Neurosci Lett* 170: 1994, 241–243.

Tiliket Caroline, Ventre-Dominey Jocelyne, Vighetto Alain, Grochowicki Michele. Room tilt illusion: a central otolith dysfunction. *Arch Neurol* 53: 1996, 1259–1264.

Tillich Paul. *Systematic Theology*, vol 1. London: SCM Xpress Reprints 1997.

Todd J. The syndrome of Alice in Wonderland. *Canad Med Assoc J* 73: 1955, 701–704.

Trelles J and Lagache D. Intoxication barbiturique recidivante s'accompagnant d'hallucinose pedonculaire. *Arch Med Psychol* 90: 1932, 565.

Tsukamoto H, Matsushima T, Fujiwara S, Fukui M. Peduncular hallucinosis following microvascular decompression for trigeminal neuralgia: Case report. *Surg Neurol* 40: 1993, 31–34.

Tucker Gary, Price Trevor, Johnson Virginia, McAllister Thomas. Phenomenology of temporal lobe dysfunction: a link to atypical psychosis—a series of cases. *J Nerv Ment Dis* 174: 1986, 348–356.

Twemlow Stuart, Gabbard Glen, Jones Fowler. The out-of-body experience: a phenomenological typology based on questionnaire responses. *Am J Psychiatr* 139: 1982, 450–455.

Valentino Rita, Page Michelle, Curtis Andre. Activation of noradrenergic locus coeruleus neurons by hemodynamic stress is due to local release of corticotrophin-releasing factor. *Brain Res* 555: 1991, 25–34.

Van Bogaert, L. Syndrome inférieur du noyau rouge: troubles psycho-sensoriels d'origine mesocephalique. *Rev Neurol (Paris)* 40: 1924, 417–423.

Van Lommel Pim, van Wees Ruud, Meyers Vincent, Elfferich Ingrid. Near-death experience in survivors of cardiac arrest: a prospective study in the Netherlands. *Lancet* 358: 2001, 2039–2045.

Van Lommel Pim. About the continuity of our consciousness. *Adv Exp Med Biol* 550: 2004, 115–132.

Van Reeth P, Dierkens J, Luminet D. L'hypersexualité dans l'épilepsie et les tumeurs du lobe temporal. *Acta Neurol Belg* 58: 1958, 194–218.

Vanstone William H. *Fare Well in Christ.* London: Darton, Longman & Todd 1997.

de Vesme C. The sensation of flying during sleep. *Ann Psychic Sci* 4: 1906, 325–331.

Vidal Fernando. Brains, Bodies, Selves, and Science: Anthropologies of Identity and the Resurrection of the Body. *Critical Inquiry* 28: 2002, 930–974.

Vihvelin H. On the differentiation of some typical forms of hypnagogic hallucinations. *Acta Psychiatr Neurol* 23: 1948, 359–389.

Vogel G, Buffenstein A, Minter K, Hennessey A. Drug effects on REM sleep and on endogenous depression. *Neurosci Biobehav Rev* 14: 1990, 49–63.

Vollenweider F, Leenders K, Oye I, Hell D, Angst J. Differential psychopathology and patterns of cerebral glucose utilisation produced by (S)- and (R)-ketamine in healthy volunteers using positron emission tomography (PET). *Eur Neuropsychopharmacol* 7: 1997a, 25–38.

Vollenweider F, Leenders K, Scharfetter C, Antonini A, Maguire P, Missimer J et al. Metabolic hyperfrontality and psychopathology in the ketamine model of psychosis using positron emission tomography (PET) and [^{18}F]Fluoro-deoxyglucose (FDG). *Eur Neuropsychopharmacol* 7: 1997b, 9–24.

Vuilleumier P, Despland P, Assai G, Regli F. Heautoscopie, extase et hallucinations expérientielles d'origine épileptique. *Rev Neurol (Paris)* 153: 1997, 115–119.

Wakefield Gordon S. *The SCM Dictionary of Christian Spirituality.* London: SCM Press 1983.

Walker Francis O. A nowhere near-death experience: heavenly choirs interrupt myelography. *J Am Med Assoc* 261: 1989, 3245–3246.

Wallace Anthony. Stress and rapid personality changes. *Int Rec Med Gen Pract* 169: 1956, 761–774.

Wallace Brian, Wagner Amy, Wagner Eugene, McDeavitt James. A history and review of quantitative electroencephalography in traumatic brain injury. *J Head Trauma Rehabil* 16: 2001, 165–190.

Waller N, Kojetin B, Bouchard T, Lykken D, Tellegen A. Genetic and environmental influences on religious interests, attitudes, and values: a study of twins reared apart. *Psychol Res* 1: 1990, 138–142.

Ward Keith. *In Defence of the Soul.* Oxford: Oneworld 2004.

Warnek Lorne B. A case of temporal lobe epilepsy with an orgasmic component. *Canad Psychiatr Assoc* 21: 1976, 319–324.

Waxman Stephen and Geschwind Norman. The interictal behaviour syndrome of temporal lobe epilepsy. *Arch Gen Psychiatr* 32: 1975, 1580–1586.

Wegner DM and Wheatley T. Apparent mental causation: sources of the experience of the will. *Am Psychol* 54: 1999, 480–492.

Weinstein Sidney and Sersen Eugene. Phantoms in cases of congenital absence of limbs. *Neurology* 11: 1961, 905–911.

Weinstein Sidney, Sersen Eugene, Vetter Robert. Phantoms and somatic sensation in cases of congenital aplasia. *Cortex* 1: 1964, 276–290.

Weinstein Sidney, Vetter Robert, Sersen Eugene. Phantoms following breast surgery. *Neuropsychologia* 8: 1970, 185–197.

Welch K, Levine S, D'Andrea G, Helpern J. Brain pH in migraine: an in vivo phosphorus–31 magnetic resonance spectroscopy study. *Cephalalgia* 8: 1988, 273–277.

Wells Amber D. Reincarnation beliefs among near-death experiencers. *J Near-Death Studies* 12: 1993, 17–34.

Wheeler-Robinson H. *Corporate Personality in Ancient Israel.* Edinburgh: Clark 1981.

Whinnery James. Psychophysiologic correlates of unconsciousness and near-death experiences. *J Near-Death Stud* 15: 1997, 231–258.

Whinnery James and Jones David. Recurrent +G_z-induced loss of consciousness. *Aviat Space Environ Med* 58: 1987, 943–947.

Whinnery James and Whinnery Angela. Acceleration-induced loss of consciousness: a review of 500 episodes. *Arch Neurol* 47: 1990, 764–776.

White Paul, Way Walter, Trevor Anthony. Ketamine—its pharmacology and therapeutic uses. *Anesthesiology* 56: 1982, 119–136.

White Vernon. *Life beyond Death.* London: Darton, Longman & Todd, 2006.

Whitty Charles and Lewin Walpole. Vivid day-dreaming: an unusual form of confusion following anterior cingulectomy. *Brain* 80: 1957, 72–76.

Wieser HG. Depth recorded limbic seizures and psychopathology. *Neurosci Biobehav Rev* 7: 1983, 427–440.

Williams Denis. The structure of emotions reflected in epileptic experiences. *Brain* 79: 1956, 28–67.

Williams D and Wilson T. The diagnosis of the major and minor syndromes of basilar insufficiency. *Brain* 85: 1962, 741–774.

Williams Mark, Rainer Gerald, Fieger Henry, Murray Ives, Sanchez Mary. Cardiopulmonary bypass, profound hypothermia, and circulatory arrest for neurosurgery. *Ann Thoracic Surg* 52: 1991, 1069–1075.

Williams Rowan. *Resurrection: Interpreting the Easter Gospel.* London: Darton, Longman & Todd 1982.

Williams Rowan. Between the cherubim: the empty tomb and the empty throne. In: D'Costa G (ed) 1996, 87.

Williams Rowan. *On Christian Theology.* Oxford: Blackwell 2000.

Wilson Ian. *Life After Death: The Evidence.* London: Pan Books 1997.

Wilson Susan, Vaughan Robert, Stephen Ronald. Awareness, dreams, and hallucinations associated with general anesthesia. *Anesthesia Analgesia* 54: 1975, 609–617.

Woerlee GM. Darkness, tunnels, and light. *Skeptical Enquirer* 28: 2004, 28–33.

Wolfson Harry A. Immortality and resurrection in the philosophy of the church fathers. In: Stendahl Krister (ed), *Immortality and Resurrection.* New York (NY): Macmillan 1965.

Wright NT. *The Resurrection of the Son of God* (Christian Origins and the Question of God, 3). London: SPCK 2003.

Wynn-Parry CB. Pain in avulsion lesions of the brachial plexus. *Pain* 9: 1980, 41–53.

Zacks Jeff, Rypma Bart, Gabrieli J, Tversky Barbara, Glover Gary. Imagined transformations of bodies: an fMRI investigation. *Neuropsychologia* 37: 1999, 1029–1040.

Zaleski Carol. *Otherworld Journeys: Accounts of Near-Death Experience in Medieval and Modern Times.* Oxford: Oxford University Press 1998.

Zizioulas John D. Some reflections on baptism, confirmation and eucharist. *Sobornost* 5: 1969, 644–652.

Zizioulas John D. Human capacity and incapacity: a theological exploration of personhood. *Scot J Theol* 28: 1975, 401–448.

Zizioulas John D. *Being as Communion.* Crestwood (NY): St Vladimir's Seminary Press 1993.

Zizioulas John D. The doctrine of the Holy Trinity: the significance of the Cappodocian contribution. In: Schwöbel Christoph (ed), *Trinitarian Theology Today.* Edinburgh: Clark 1995, 44–60.

Zizioulas John D. On being a person: towards an ontology of personhood. In: Schwöbel Christoph and Gunton Colin (eds), *Persons Divine and Human.* Edinburgh: Clark 1999, 33–46.

Index